A HISTORY OF HOPE

A
HISTORY
OF
HOPE

When Americans Have Dared
to Dream of a Better Future

James W. Fraser

First published 2002 by PALGRAVE™
First published by PALGRAVE MACMILLAN™ in 2004
175 Fifth Avenue, New York, N.Y. 10010 and
Houndmills, Basingstoke, Hampshire, England RG21 6XS.
Companies and representatives throughout the world.

PALGRAVE MACMILLAN is the global academic imprint of the Palgrave Macmillan division of St. Martin's Press, LLC and of Palgrave Macmillan Ltd. Macmillan® is a registered trademark in the United States, United Kingdom and other countries. Palgrave is a registered trademark in the European Union and other countries.

ISBN 1-4039-6600-1 paperback

The hardcover edition has been cataloged by the Library of Congress as follows:

Library of Congress Cataloging-in-Publication Data

Fraser, James W., 1944-
A history of hope : when Americans have dared to dream of a better future / by James W. Fraser.
    p. cm.
  Includes bibliographical references and index
  ISBN 0-312-23904-1
    1. United States—History—Anecdotes. 2. Hope—Anecdotes. 3. Unites States—Biography—Anecdotes. 4. Poltical activists—United States—Biography—Anecdotes. 5. Social reformers—United States—Biography—Anecdotes. 6. National characteristics, American—Anecdotes. 7. Social movements—United States–Histroy—Anecdotes. I. Title

E179.F83 2002
973—dc22   2002025257

A catalogue record for this book is available from the British Library.

Design by Letra Libre, Inc.

First paperback edition: March 2004
10 9 8 7 6 5 4 3 2 1

Printed in the United States of America.

For

Julia
Lily
Madison
Kaitlin
Rebecca
Megan

My daughters and granddaughters who give me hope.

CONTENTS

Fourteen pages of photographs and artwork
appear between pages 120 and 121.

ACKNOWLEDGMENTS

My ACKNOWLEDGMENTS MUST START with my extraordinary research assistant at Northeastern University, Gina Sartori, who tracked down obscure quotations, found basic materials, and reviewed, edited, and critiqued the entire volume in detail. She also collected the illustrations and organized the bibliography. I am deeply in her debt.

Once again, my editors at Palgrave Macmillan, Michael Flamini and Amanda Johnson, along with Alan Bradshaw and Erin Chan, have been unfailingly encouraging, patient, and helpful. It is a pleasure to work with such publishers. Thanks also to Lisa Rivero for speed and care in the preparation of the index.

In addition, I wish to thank several other people who helped find some of the stories reported in these pages. Gerald Horton, Russell Irvine, Diane Moore, and Peter Murrell offered valuable critiques of the manuscript. Melissa T. Salazar, senior archivist at the State of New Mexico Records Center and Archives in Santa Fe, New Mexico, was very helpful to me in my effort to find more firsthand accounts of *las Gorras Blancas*. Michelle Kazeminejad of the California State Department of Parks and Recreation aided my understanding of Mariano Vallejo. Jennifer Dawson's expertise as a typist and editor is much appreciated. As with my previous efforts, William Fowler and the staff of the Massachusetts Historical Society, especially Kate DuBose, have been unfailingly helpful. James Stellar, dean of the College of Arts & Sciences at Northeastern University, has kept his half of our bargain that neither of us would let the other stop our scholarship because of our administrative duties. And the faculty and staff at the School of Education at Northeastern have been exceedingly supportive in this effort.

My family, as always, has been wonderful, especially my son-in-law Robert who kept asking, "Are you ever going to finish?" and my wife, Katherine, who is my best friend, protector, and encourager. The dedication to our granddaughters and daughters speaks to the hope they give us.

FOREWORD

WHEN JESSE JACKSON ENGAGES CROWDS of high school students or senior citizens with his plea "keep hope alive," he is tapping into a theme deeply rooted in the American dream: the belief that this land and people can be a *novus ordo seclorum*, a new order of the ages, and a land of hope for a better future for its own and for all people. Few serious people really have that hope in the twenty-first century. The terror of September 11, 2001, robbed many Americans of their hope. The cockeyed optimism for which the country had once been famous did not match the staggering tragedy that continues to unfold. But hope was in retreat long before that tragic fall day. The failings of the United States, from the sinister racism that included a genocidal policy toward Native Americans and slavery for Africans, to imperialism around the world from Mexico to Vietnam, to the continuing economic and cultural injustice suffered by too many citizens, to the absurdity of the most recent counting of the votes for president, have left hope as little more than a rhetorical flourish or an empty husk. The failings are true. Indeed, the more we learn of the nation's history, the longer the list gets. But the failings are not the whole story. And when failure and cynicism become the whole story, then, as Jackson understands better than most contemporary leaders, something terribly important is lost.

This book is written in the belief that keeping hope alive is a rational choice and an essential element in building a better future. When people lose hope, they also lose the will and the courage to act for change for a better future. When people lose hope, they may also lash out in hatred and fear, and ultimately in repression. Hopelessness is a powerful force in favor of the status quo or the descent into tyranny. This book is not meant as a simple chronicle of the good things and people in our history, as opposed to the bad. It is not a story of saints and heroes. It is rather the story of individuals and movements that dared to dream of a better future and then took action to make that dream a reality. It is about people who refused to be paralyzed by the tragedies of their times. All of the individuals whose stories are told in *A*

History of Hope had their faults. Many of their dreams were flawed in some
ways and partial in others. Yet taken together, the people and movements discussed in these pages, like many more that could have stood equally well in
their place, represent a powerful reminder that over the past centuries Americans have at times joined together in the very real hope that the country
could be better, and in doing so they have made important progress toward
justice and humanity in this land. They have built a history of hope that can
serve us well if we remember it.

If we look at the current state of American politics and American culture,
hope seems to be in short supply. Cynicism is safer and more fashionable. But
this decline of hope is more than a swing of the pendulum. It is a political action with political consequences. As Peter Gabel has written recently, "over
the course of the last twenty years, beginning with the collapse of the social
movements of the 1960s and the election of Ronald Reagan, the Right has successfully and gradually capitalized on the doubt pervading the forces of social
transformation in such a way as to make people lose faith in the existence of a
hopeful and idealistic universal public sphere in which there is a 'We'—an activist and more-or-less united public community struggling for a better world
against the fearful forces of the status quo." If this is true, if, as Gabel argues,
many people and social movements have been consumed by a "loss of faith or
confidence in their capacity to fundamentally transform the world," then we
can be fairly certain that the world will not be transformed, at least not in any
positive and hopeful ways.[1] That international voice of hope, the Dalai Lama,
is right when he says, "Under no circumstances should you lose hope. Hopelessness is a real cause of failure."[2]

I have chosen to focus on hope and not on virtue or goodness for a very
specific reason. Virtue can be the attribute of a good person. But hope, by its
nature, is more collective. A person can withdraw from society, or live in an
evil society, and still seek to maintain a life of personal goodness. But hope requires more. Hope as I have described it here requires envisioning a better future not only for oneself and one's family, but also for the larger society in
which one lives and then acting with others to make that hope a reality. In this
sense, I have departed significantly from William J. Bennett's indomitable effort in chronicling stories of virtue.[3] I do not quarrel with his virtues, but I find
his goal is too modest. Living virtuously is important but insufficient. Hope, as
the stories in this volume show so clearly, demands a larger vision and an effort
to mobilize one's comrades to make that hope a reality in the lives of others.

There are, in fact, powerful sources in the American tradition that support the choice for hope. A few of those sources—people and movements that
were founded on hope for the future and that provide models for what can yet

be done—are recounted in these pages. The story reported here is far from complete. This is not meant as an exhaustive history, merely an illustrative one. The examples in these pages are but that—examples of something much larger. But the vision of hope for new beginnings should be clear. In all of these cases it is a vision based on the active agency of the women, children, and men. It is a part of the history of the nation every bit as much as the tarnished and tawdry reality of other chapters in our history. It deserves to be told. And in the telling, the story can generate yet more hope, which is so badly needed if the nation is to flourish.

My goal in writing this book is not for one minute to excuse the inexcusable, the genocide, war, and hate that has been part of the American story. It is not to recast the American story as more lovely than it has been. It is most certainly not to glorify the role of great white men. There are precious few military, political, or business leaders in *A History of Hope*. Hope has been the enterprise of the agitator and the poet, the organizer and the unorganized more often than it has been the work of official leaders. But hope is part of our history, a part that must not be forgotten if the full story is to be told.

Some of the hopeful visions reported in this volume are alive and well today; others are currently limited to the margins of society. Certainly the civil rights movement continues to fuel political engagement especially—but far from exclusively—in African American communities across the nation. Feminist, antiwar, and other similar movements are alive and well and having a dramatic impact on the public discourse and political life of the nation. There is a growing concern for global economic justice, an energized labor movement, and indications of a revived student movement on many college campuses. Civil libertarians and peace activists are again marching in our nation's capital. Indeed, these movements form the core of the resistance to more selfish and oppressive agendas. After decades of slumber organized labor seems to be on the move again as one of the nation's most important efforts to build a better future. At the same time small utopian communities are continuing their own hopeful efforts far from the mainstream of society. On the other hand, many of the communal efforts that fascinated and frightened so many nineteenth- or mid-twentieth-century Americans have virtually disappeared. And the nineteenth-century brand of liberalism or the radical anarchism or socialism of the first half of the twentieth century cannot easily be found in early twenty-first century political discourse. Nevertheless, this book is not intended merely to be a history of success. Some hopeful streams continue for decades, even centuries. Others go underground for long periods of time. But historians must not allow them to be forgotten. As the historian E. P. Thompson reminded us, there is reason to remember many who have had hope in the past. So he wrote of his own now-classic examination of the emergence of the English working class between 1780 and 1832:

> I am seeking to rescue the poor stockinger, the Luddite cropper, the "obsolete" hand-loom weaver, the "utopian" artisan . . . from the enormous condescension of posterity. . . . Our only criterion of judgment should not be whether or not a man's actions are justified in the light of subsequent evolution. After all, we are not at the end of social evolution ourselves. In some of the lost causes of the people of the Industrial Revolution we may discover insights into social evils which we have yet to cure.[4]

There may indeed be much to be learned from Mother Jones, Nicola Sacco and Bartolomeo Vanzetti, Mariano Vallejo, or the women and men of the nineteenth-century Oneida Community—just as there is much to learn from the more familiar histories reported here—that may help make the twenty-first century a more hopeful time in the nation's history. The past is full of stories of people who dared to dream of a more just world and who in their dreams gave hope to many of their own generation. These hopes have made a difference in the past, and learning their stories can give contemporary citizens a renewed faith in what can be done in the twenty-first century.

Hopefulness is essential if we as a people are to recapture the energy and enthusiasm that will allow us to build a better world for our successors in this new century and millennium rather than to be caught in a long cycle of cynicism and despair. Ultimately I have written this book because I believe that the choice between hopefulness and cynicism is one of the essential personal and political choices facing individuals and communities in every moment of their history. Much rests on the outcome of that choice. And I believe that the choice can be an informed one . . . that there are powerful and good precedents for choosing hope. I have written this history in the service of that larger goal.

HISTORICAL MEMORY AND HOPE AS A POLITICAL CHOICE

Hope is not an easy choice. At the beginning of the twenty-first century America is a profoundly unhopeful and unethical place. Any informed person can name many of the problems. Racism, sexism, classism, and homophobia mar the land. The rich are getting rapidly richer and those left behind are falling further and further. Former labor secretary Robert Reich has said in light of his analysis of the different economic subsets of today's workforce, "No longer are Americans rising or falling together, as if in one large national boat. We are increasingly in different boats . . . one sinking rapidly, one sinking more slowly, and the third rising steadily."[5] We hear a great deal of talk about compassionate conservatism and education for economic competitiveness, but Reich is right in reminding us that we need to talk about who is winning and who is losing.

Greed has also fostered a culture of nihilism among too many youth; believing in no particular future, they have little investment in any particular present. We see this nihilism on city streets in a sometimes reckless flirtation with jail and death; we see it on college campuses as the children of the affluent spend weekends getting drunk literally out of their minds; and we see it in schools as students and teachers reach the compromises described by Theodore Sizer in which teachers ask little of their students and in return students keep the hassle to a minimum.[6] We live in a world accurately described by Maxine Greene as one "with little historical memory. . . . On the side streets of our great cities, in the crevices, in the burnt-out neighborhoods, there are the rootless, the dependent, the sick, the permanently unemployed. There is little sense of agency, even among the brightly successful; there is little capacity to look at things as if they could be otherwise."[7]

This last point—this inability to look at things "as if they could be otherwise"—is perhaps the greatest problem of our society. We need to find ways to change this culture if it is to be one worth living in for us and for future generations. Just as Maxine Greene does, I too believe it is essential that we find new ways to "look at things as if they could be otherwise." I also believe the best way to do that is to rekindle our historical memory. American history gives us many examples of greed and injustice, and badly written history can foster an unthinking patriotism. But in the history of the United States there are also examples of courage and hope on which a new and different future can be built. There have been, in every generation, people who stood with courage for a different kind of community and a different kind of country in which hope could be a rational choice and not merely the hiding place of the uninformed. There are traditions that we have never lived up to, but traditions that are important nonetheless.

When Thomas Jefferson wrote in the Declaration of Independence, "We hold these truths to be self-evident that all . . . are created equal," he was giving voice to these traditions. Although Jefferson himself had some problems living by these words, he set a vision. And just as we misjudge Jefferson if we forget his failings, we also misjudge Jefferson and impoverish our contemporary culture if we forget the vision of hope that he held up.

Too much of contemporary politics is about "I want what is good for me . . . and I don't much care about the rest." Jefferson had a vision that was bigger than he was. And others have built on it in ways he could not have imagined. The poet Langston Hughes imagined American slaves hearing the words about equality and the inalienable rights to life, liberty, and the pursuit of happiness, and making them their own. And so, while Jefferson's words were adopted by the Continental Congress for white males, Hughes wrote,

> But in their hearts the slaves believed him, too,
> And silently took for granted
> That what he said was also meant for them.[8]

Hughes is not excusing Jefferson for his failings. Indeed, Hughes the poet seems to understand, as too few historians have, that the study of the past is more than an exercise in journalistic exposure, or the work of an impartial jury sifting the evidence for saints and sinners, or a search for cardboard heroes who will reinforce European cultural dominance. For Hughes, at some point, it does not matter what Jefferson did or failed to do; what he truly believed in his heart of hearts. Jefferson's words and his vision have come to belong to others, whether that reality would have appealed to the author of the vision or not. So in his poetry Hughes seems to ask, Who owns these words? For him the answer is clear: the slaves and many of their American successors indeed, "silently took for granted that these words were meant for them." They have taken it for granted so deeply that almost two hundred years later, when the great twentieth-century preacher of civil rights, Martin Luther King Jr., lifted Jefferson's words, there was a resonance that few of King's fellow citizens across the racial spectrum could ignore.

At the first inauguration of William Jefferson Clinton as president of the United States, Maya Angelou warned us to move beyond our fears and our divisions. She said:

> Do not be wedded forever
> To fear, yoked eternally
> To brutishness. . . .

And she asked us, as a nation, "on the pulse of this new day," to look in each other's eyes and say:

> Very simply
> With hope—
> Good morning.[9]

If we can have grace to look into our sister's eyes and our brother's face and say, "Good morning," then we will have the grace to break down all the walls of hate and fear that divide us as a people. We will have the courage to hope again.

HOPE AND DESPAIR AMONG CONTEMPORARY HISTORIANS AND SOCIAL CRITICS

The study of American history has changed dramatically in the last half century. In the aftermath of this nation's crusade against fascism and in the midst of the cold war, many historians saw their role as leading the celebration of America's uniqueness and the nation's role in the defense of freedom. Historians in the 1960s challenged this sort of historical scholarship as activists in that decade challenged so much else in the United States. My friend and former colleague Jim Green, writing about the start of his graduate studies in 1966 says, "I was committed to traditional political history, intrigued by the outcomes of 'critical elections,' but soon I joined others of my generation in a search for America's radical past."[10] The result was a new kind of historical scholarship that included attention to marginalized peoples, to a mostly forgotten dissenting tradition, to mass movements, and often to stories that were recorded only orally. At the same time, many historians of the 1960s and later began to look more and more carefully at the underside of the American tradition, the centuries-long genocidal war on Native Americans, the racism and sexism that has been central to the nation's politics and culture, the tendency of "great men" to build their greatness on what they have taken from others. History is a much more sophisticated discipline, a more questioning discipline, and sometimes a more depressing discipline than it was a generation or two ago. But without historical truth no progress can be made. Historical amnesia is a very fragile foundation for a meaningful hope.

Historians have properly told the stories of the failures of the American dream, the many times when Americans have projected great visions while excluding large numbers of their fellows from the vision. Whether it is John Winthrop preaching of a new and shining City on a Hill while also thanking his God for the smallpox that had rid the land of its former inhabitants, or Thomas Jefferson writing that all are created equal while owning slaves (some of whom appear to have been his own children), or nineteenth-century champions of the liberation of women who urged Congress to give women the vote as a way to offset the rising power of Irish immigrants and newly freed African Americans, or some in the twentieth-century preaching racial justice while defending rape and other forms of misogyny, our leaders have been humans, with feet—and sometimes brains—of clay. All of the historical work that has gone into unveiling the faults of the past is right and good. The cardboard heroes of the high school history textbooks are of little value to us. Talk of recovering a golden age that never was deflects us from the difficult work of living well in the present and building well for the future. Bad history creates cartoons, entertaining at best but cut off from any reality to which we can connect.

In the course of the last decade, a new school of historical scholarship has emerged. A group of neoconservative historians, of whom Arthur M. Schlesinger Jr. is the best known, are challenging many of the critiques of the historians of the 1970s and 1980s. *A History of Hope* is written from a very different perspective than that of Schlesinger and his colleagues, however. For Schlesinger, the current goal of historians must be a recovery of appreciation for the centrality of European political and cultural ideals in our national discourse. Concomitantly, Schlesinger and his colleagues focus on the contribution of a limited number of "great white men" to the shaping of the nation's identity. Schlesinger and others like him reject a multicultural perspective as one that undermines the importance of European leaders and European ideas in both shaping and continuing the public culture of the United States.[11]

A History of Hope, on the contrary, is explicitly written from a multicultural perspective. Slaves and former slaves, including Sojourner Truth, Nat Turner, and Frederick Douglass; immigrants and labor organizers such as Mother Jones, Margaret Haley, and Walter Reuther; Native Americans, from the inhabitants of the Taos Pueblo in the 1600s to those at the Wounded Knee sit-in in the 1970s; and dissidents like Myles Horton, Margaret Sanger, and *las Gorras Blancas*—they are every bit as important in this story as the European males from the dominant culture. The immigrant, the union member, the slave, and the civil rights worker whose names are not known at all are also as important as those whose names are household words. All of them have helped shape the vision of hope contained here.

As a new century dawns, I find myself more and more fatigued with the cynicism of our politics, the cynicism of much current discourse, and yes, the cynicism of history. Exposing the sins of the past is important. But only exposing the sins of the past creates fatigue, not the energy needed for change. On the other hand, the neoconservative response does not work either. Our predecessors had very real weaknesses that need to be remembered honestly. They also left a powerful heritage. And some of them dared to dream great dreams, to transcend their own cynicism, to create a vision of a better society, a better America, and a better world that inspired many of their fellow citizens in their own time and many who followed in later generations. None of the dreamers were without faults, but some of them managed to dream dreams that transcended those faults.

One of the most difficult issues that I have faced in writing this book is the issue of violence. In the aftermath of the terrible suffering of September 11, 2001,

I find myself more appalled than ever by any form of violence. Some of those whose stories are told here, from Mother Ann Lee who founded the Shakers in the eighteenth century, to Martin Luther King Jr. who made a Gandhian plea for nonviolence the core of his twentieth century civil rights strategy, were pacifists. There have certainly been those who stood for peace throughout this nation's history. Many others whose stories are told here were not so peaceful. When the Pueblo Indians drove the Spanish colonizers out of New Mexico in the 1600s they were not afraid to use violence. When newly freed slaves joined the Union army during the Civil War they were not afraid of violence. And there were many among the twentieth century anarchists, socialists, and civil rights activists who believed that violence would be necessary before the greater violence of their oppressors could be ended. Of course, the American revolutionaries of 1776 and the U.S. Presidents whose stories are recounted here—John Adams, Thomas Jefferson, Abraham Lincoln, and Franklin Delano Roosevelt—were hardly pacifists.

All violence cannot be equated with terrorism. All of the violence that is reported in this volume was in response to greater violence from others. Violence, terror, and oppression, from sixteenth-century European conquistadors to their twenty-first-century counterparts who would stamp out all hope among oppressed peoples, naturally breeds violence in response. Sometimes violence is the only way of stopping greater violence. My telling of the stories of those who bravely—and sometimes violently—resisted is in no way an endorsement of violence. Personally I find myself coming closer and closer to pacifism. But a rejection of the hopes of those who violently resisted the far greater violence of European colonialism or American slavery and the crushing misery of economic imperialism is a mistake. A limitation of the narrative of hope to absolute pacifists impoverishes the story. All of the heroes in this book had their faults as well as their virtues. All of their hopes were partial, and sometimes flawed. But those who struggled for a better future, including those who struggled violently, did have hopes and dreams that should not be forgotten. And in our day, as never before, hope demands courage and increasing levels of creativity if violence is to be prevented, or at least limited, and if hope is to be made a part of the continuing history of this nation.

When I talk of historical precedents for optimism about building community or the development of what Martin Luther King Jr. called "the beloved community," I am also not talking about describing a past golden age. I am not interested in finding a few heroes and heroines whose ideals we can simply adopt. No one whose story is told in this volume had all of the answers for the twenty-first century. Indeed, none had all of the answers for their own day. But I am interested in exploring the experiences of women and men who, at certain moments in this nation's history, were willing to dream and sacrifice and work to build a better future for themselves and their children and successors. We have much to learn from them.

It would be a tragedy for Americans to return to the historical amnesia of the past. The celebratory history of the 1950s and early 1960s and the more recent neoconservative approach both represent bad history and bad politics. It is bad history because many of the claims of the conservatives about their European-American heroes are simply not true. And it is bad politics because their version of American history excludes both the prior contribution and the current role of the majority of the nation's diverse citizens—including women, people of color, poor people, many of whose individual stories will never be told. Nevertheless we are also not served by the historical cynicism of the present. We need a new synthesis in which the faults, but also the dreams and hopes, of our predecessors—the wonderfully diverse range of our predecessors—are truly understood and owned by all of us. *A History of Hope* seeks to make its own modest contribution to that new synthesis which is so badly needed for a fair reading of the past and, more important, for a healthy approach to the future.

THE FIRST REVOLUTION: TAOS, 1680

AUGUST 1680

EARLY ON A SATURDAY MORNING, August 10, 1680, a revolutionary uprising of the normally peace-loving Pueblo Indians of northern New Mexico led to the greatest defeat of European imperialism in the history of the Americas. It was a revolution of both hope and despair. And it was highly effective. By the end of August 1680 the entire Spanish community that had ruled the region for eighty years, including all of the government and religious leaders and their followers, had been forced out of New Mexico. For the next twelve years, the Pueblo Indians again governed themselves, the revolt's leader lived in the Governor's Palace in Santa Fe, and the various villages resumed their community life and their ancient religion completely free of outside political or cultural interference.

The Taos revolt permanently changed the culture of what would become the southwestern part of the United States. And it is now virtually forgotten. A book focused on occasions where the hope of the people has changed history in the lands that are now the United States can have no better starting point than this Pueblo Indian revolt centered in Taos, New Mexico.[1]

In a carefully coordinated attack, the native residents of pueblos across the region made their move on the same August morning. In the region's northernmost corner, in the area of Taos, nearly all of the seventy Spanish residents—priests, magistrates, and their staff and families—were killed by noon. Only two messengers sent at the beginning of the attack escaped to Santa Fe with the news of what was happening. Similar news poured into Santa Fe throughout the day. The Pueblo Indians, whom the Spanish conquerors were sure both feared and loved them, had attacked with a precision and a devastating result never expected by the haughty conquerors.[2]

In the heart of the Hopi tribe's community, the Oraibi pueblo, far from the center of the main action, the schedule was the same. The leaders of the uprising donned their kachina masks and, as elsewhere, attacked the church at dawn, killing the soldier on guard and the rest of the Spanish garrison. One of the Hopi leaders, a man named Haneeya, wearing the kachina mask of the Warrior, broke through the roof of the building where the Franciscan priests—José de Espeleta and Agustín de Santa Maria—were living and killed them both. In short order all of the Spaniards in the Oraibi pueblo were dead. The church was demolished. The bell and sacramental vessels were buried. The soldiers' spears were given to one of the Hopi secret societies, the One Horn Society. Tradition says that the spears are still kept safely at Oraibi. The same thing took place in village after village. In isolated haciendas where extended Spanish families lived and in the pueblos of San Ildefonso and Nambe, in San Juan, in Pecos, Santa Clara, San Cristobál, Santa Cruz, Picuris, San Marcos, and, of course, Taos itself, the priests and everyone else were dead. The first phase of the long-planned revolution of the Pueblo peoples was won in half a day.[3]

The capital of Santa Fe was not attacked on the first day although there was plenty of terror there too. The few survivors from the outlying communities, such as the messengers from Taos, along with the residents of the nearby settlements poured into the capital with the possessions they could carry and the animals they could lead. By evening over a thousand people, only around seventy-five of them trained soldiers, were in the walled town. The siege of Santa Fe began on Monday, August 12, as Indians from the various pueblos, traditionally separated by different languages and the fierce independence of each community, joined together in their attack on the city. For the Spanish residents, the sight of these Indians, many in traditional but forbidden costumes, others in Spanish armor and carrying Spanish swords and guns, and all full of defiance, was terrifying indeed.

One of the revolt's leaders, a man the Spanish knew as Juan and whom they considered a trusted Christian convert, came to the city to parley with Governor Antonio de Otermín. Reports of the conversation tell of Otermín's incredulity that someone he trusted could be participating in the revolt and of the governor's fury at being treated as a military equal by someone whom he considered a servant. But the reports also make it clear that Juan ignored all of that. He had a choice to offer Governor Otermín. He had two crosses, one white and one red. He told the governor to choose. "If you choose the white," Juan said, "there will be no war, but you must all leave the country. If you choose the red, you must all die, for we are many and you are few. Having killed so many Spaniards and priests, we will kill all the rest."[4] Otermín in return offered Juan only the unacceptable option of an Indian surrender and a potential Spanish pardon. He was not nearly ready to choose between exile and death, although he would be soon enough. The siege of Santa Fe began.

For the following days, a battle raged around Santa Fe with the circle around the Spanish garrison getting smaller and smaller. On August 16 the Indians cut the city's water supply, and in the days that followed they burned more and more of the outlying buildings while continuing to taunt the besieged garrison with word of other dead Spaniards and of new Indian allies, including the feared Apache. On August 21 Otermín and his lieutenants and the clergy made a collective decision to give up. They took the terrible risk of a retreat to the south out of Santa Fe with the likelihood of an attack on their convoy at any time rather than stay any longer. As Otermín recalled, they retreated, "without a crust of bread or a grain of wheat or maize, and with no other provision for a convoy of so many people except four hundred animals and two carts belonging to private persons, and, for food, a few sheep, goats, and cows."[5]

It was a terrible march to the south. In spite of the fears of the beleaguered group of Spaniards, the Indians did not attack. No one knows quite why. The fleeing Spaniards were in no position to mount a strong defense. But then, for the Indians, the Spanish exodus was in itself the victory that they had hoped for. For the Spanish community, the retreat meant coming face to face with what had happened, as they discovered their dead countrymen in the wreckage of the haciendas and desecrated churches along the way south toward Mexico. Eventually they met up with other refugees who had moved south from Isleta in a separate group and with a Spanish relief party stalled by the high waters of the Rio Grande at what would become El Paso, Texas. And there they stopped. Settlements around El Paso on the north side of the river and Juárez, Mexico, on the south still reflect the marks of the exiled community of Spanish conquerors and those Pueblo Indians who had chosen to stay with them. In the north, throughout all of New Mexico, the Pueblo peoples ruled themselves. Their hope for freedom had been won beyond their wildest dreams.[6]

THE INSPIRATION

Like the history of many popular movements, far too little has been recorded of the voices of those leaders and their supporters whose vision and whose hope led to the events of the revolution of 1680. As Alfonso Ortiz, Princeton University professor and a Tewa from the same Pueblo as the revolt's leader, Popé, warns, far too much of this history is exclusively from a Spanish perspective or, at best, from Indians interviewed by the Spanish who recorded their words through the prism of their own deep prejudices. Nevertheless, in those voices, and in a few cases in continuing Pueblo traditions, a picture of what the revolutionaries hoped for and why they acted as they did can be pieced together.[7]

During their retreat south from Santa Fe, Otermín and his refugees were joined by groups of Indians who had stayed loyal to them. One told him that the revolt happened because the people were "tired of the work they had to do for the Spaniards and the clergy [who] did not allow them to plant, to do other things for their own needs; and that being weary they had rebelled." Another old man told the governor that it was because "the Spaniards had tried to take away . . . the ways of their ancestors, the faith by which they have lived and thrived." As with another revolution a century later, freedom from oppression and freedom to live and worship as they pleased were certainly central to what happened in the Taos revolt.[8]

Alfonso Ortiz lists three reasons for the revolt. First there was the *encomienda* system that the Spanish authorities had instituted in New Mexico, which "provided for the involuntary seizure of a percentage of each Pueblo farmer's crop every year to support Spanish missionary, military, and civil institutions." Then there was the *repartimiento*, a system by which the Pueblo Indians were forced to work in the Spanish-held fields while "Other Indians were confined to sweatshops in the Governor's Palace in Santa Fe, weaving cloth, often without pay, for the Spaniards." And finally there was the European import, the *Inquisition*, the religious persecution that characterized Spain and all of the Spanish territories in the seventeenth century. It was often used to bring "charges of heresy and witchcraft" that justified the enslavement of the victims. But as Ortiz concludes, "during the terrible decades of the *Inquisition*, the Pueblo people were persecuted for practicing their own religion, one which they clung to tenaciously because it had evolved through untold centuries of living in partnership with the land; and it sustained them well throughout all this time."[9] The taxes, the slavery—potential and real—and the religious persecution of the Pueblos make the complaint of "taxation without representation" of a century later seem a meager one, indeed.

Every successful revolution needs much more than a series of grievances against the standing order no matter how severe the grievances may be. It also requires articulate leadership and a sense of hope that things actually can change. As far as the incomplete historical record shows, the leadership and the voice for hope came primarily from a spiritual leader of the kachina faith from the San Juan pueblo, a medicine man named Popé who had refused to convert to

Christianity. Popé was the essential person in the revolt for two reasons. First, for all of his commitment to the traditional religion, Popé led his people in a significant departure from the old ways. He was able to convince the various pueblos that, in spite of their differences in language and their customary absolute independence from each other, it was more important to unite in the effort to drive the hated Spanish from the land than to maintain their separation. Without this unity, the revolt could never have happened. No one pueblo or cluster of pueblos could have accomplished what was won. Secondly—although virtually none of his speeches or conversations have been preserved—Popé was somehow able to convince the people of his own pueblo and the entire community of pueblos that there was reason for hope, reason to take the risk, reason that victory was possible.[10]

Popé first gained broader attention five years before the revolt when he was already well into middle age, probably between fifty and sixty years old. In 1675 the then-governor Juan Francisco de Treviño sought to heal the division between the secular and religious authorities of New Mexico by bringing the full power of the state to the effort to stamp out what he and the other Spanish authorities saw as paganism: the kachina religion of the Pueblo people. Kivas, the underground places of gathering and worship, were wrecked. Masks and other materials were confiscated and burned. Forty-seven of the heads of the secret religious societies who organized the kachina dances and the healing rites were arrested and brought to Santa Fe for trial. All were found guilty. Four were hung and the other forty-three, including the medicine man from San Juan, Popé, were whipped in the plaza and jailed.[11]

The attack on their religion and their religious leaders resulted in the first signs of interpueblo unity as all of the pueblos mourned for their leaders and feared for their traditions. In time a delegation of seventy Pueblo Indians who were well known as Christians were sent to Santa Fe. They met with Governor Treviño and, in the traditional way, simply described the future possibilities. As summarized by Robert Silverberg from his reading of the original Spanish records, the delegates told Treviño:

> If they were not freed soon, . . . it might come to pass that every Indian in New Mexico would abandon his home and flee into Apache country, leaving the Spaniards masters of an empty realm. How would the Spaniards enjoy having to till their own fields and build their own houses and weave their own cloth? On the other hand, the delegates remarked, it was also possible that the continued imprisonment of the 43 would inspire the Indians of the province to rise in armed revolt and, striking with sudden ferocity, slaughter every Spaniard in New Mexico in a single day.[12]

It was a preview of the choices that would be offered to Treviño's successor five years later.

In 1675 the governor did not want to test the Pueblo people's resolve, so he released the 43 prisoners. All of them returned to their pueblos and their traditional practices. Sometime soon thereafter (although others have said he began as early as 1668), Popé, now wearing the scars of the Spanish beating as well as his lifelong allegiance to the traditional ways, began to tell others in San Juan that it was time to drive the Spaniards out. He probably found little disagreement but also little enthusiasm for such a seemingly hopeless cause. In time, however, he began to win allies both for his hopes for freedom and in his hopes for interpueblo unity in action. In the Santo Domingo pueblo a local leader named Catiti joined with Popé. Farther north at Picuris, Tupatú, a chieftain, joined with him, as did a man named Jaca from Taos. Ironically, the names of these successful rebels have been preserved only in the records of their enemies. But at least we do know who they were. At the time, of course, this was a dangerous conspiracy and those involved consciously kept their numbers small and the information about what they were planning quiet. After the success of the revolt, the Pueblo Indians returned to their old ways, which did not include keeping written records, although they did tell powerful stories, some of which have also continued down through the generations.

Some time in the late 1670s Popé took the highly unusual step for a religious leader of leaving his own pueblo. He relocated in the much larger pueblo of Taos where he continued to preach and organize for revolt. He assured those around him that the spirit world from which the Pueblo peoples had emerged so long ago was with them. He spoke of Caudi, Tilini, and Tleume, spirits from the underworld who visited him in his kiva in Taos and who advised him on the ways to victory. He told of a black giant—who may have been a former African slave living in Taos or may have been another spirit—who was a spokesman of the Pueblo war god and who counseled Popé on the next steps. And by 1680 nearly all of the leaders of the Pueblo Indians had agreed to join with Popé and with each other in the revolt. Knowing that a supply train with new munitions from Mexico was due in the early fall, knowing that the harvest would soon begin but that food supplies were still low, the leaders picked August for the revolt. Runners were sent out with symbols telling everyone that the date would be August 13. Either as a pre-arranged trick or because they realized that word was leaking out, the date was moved back to August 10. Runners carried the new date, and with military precision never expected of native peoples, the dawn of that morning changed the history of New Mexico forever.[13]

THE RESULT

In time, of course, the Spanish reconquered the territory. The forces of history, the technology of their arms, and the sheer brutality of their military made that inevitable. But it took twelve years. Nowhere else in the Americas, not even among the powerful Aztecs and Incas, was a revolt against European dominance so successful or long lasting. For a dozen years those Spaniards who remembered the revolt saw no reason to put themselves in harm's way again. A few military campaigns were tried, but they were generally half-hearted and quite unsuccessful.[14]

Popé and his successors lived in the governor's mansion in Santa Fe. They cleared their lands of nearly all of the remnants of the Spanish ways. Churches were leveled and statues were destroyed. Kivas were rebuilt and kachina masks brought out of hiding or made afresh. Pueblo life returned more or less to what it had been before 1598 when the first Spanish governor, Don Juan de Oñate, had crossed the Rio Grande to begin governing New Mexico. The distant and defeated Spanish were mocked. A story was passed down of one parody of a Spanish feast in which Popé, seated at one end of a Spanish dining table, saluted a friend with a looted chalice, "To your paternal reverence's health." His friend, playing the role of the father-president of the Franciscans, responded, "Here is to your lordship's health, my lord governor." The audience joined in laughter and in the sense of the victory of their hopes.[15]

Popé seems to have been better at inspiring revolt than at governing afterward. Like many successful revolutionary leaders, he seems to have had a lust for power, something quite unusual among Pueblo people. In any case, the unity that he inspired would probably have been impossible to maintain in the absence of the immediate Spanish threat. Popé himself died in 1688, and while the various pueblos continued to enjoy their freedom and to practice the old ways in religion and in their domestic life, they certainly drifted further and further apart.

In spite of the succeeding events, it is important for historians to do a better job of recording the heroic hopes and actions of these revolutionaries. As Alfonso Ortiz wrote, "Our continued failure to recognize the Pueblo revolution is to ignore an important chapter in our common history." And he is also right that for Indian peoples and all who care about their fate, it is important to record hopes and victories as well as the terrible tragedies of defeat.

It will be good for them to know as well that the Indian history of this land consists of much more than the terrible tragedies at Fallen Timbers, Sand Creek, and Wounded Knee. These tragedies, real as they were, have already drawn too much emphasis in history and in the popular media. Besides, they are not the stuff from which dignity and confidence in self can be engendered.[16]

Hope, and the actions and victories that it has spawned, on the other hand, can be a powerful source of dignity and confidence.

In 1690 the Spanish viceroy in Mexico City appointed a new governor for New Mexico, Don Diego de Vargas. De Vargas had not experienced the terror of the revolt and he seems to have been a man of considerable personal courage as well as military skill. He also had an ability to compromise lacking in many of his predecessors. De Vargas left El Paso with his army in the spring of 1692. Slowly moving north, he offered each pueblo he encountered the possibility of a full pardon in exchange for their renunciation of the revolt and their reconversion to Christianity. During their decade of freedom the pueblos had drifted apart from each other and in the process they had lost their power and their potential for a united defense. Initially all of the individual pueblos looked at the force of arms that de Vargas had, considered his willingness to grant them greater freedom, especially in maintaining their own religious traditions, than any of his predecessors had offered, and agreed to his terms. On September 14, 1692, de Vargas reentered Santa Fe. He had parleyed with its residents for the previous twenty-four hours, and he took the calculated risk of acquiescing to their demand that he enter the town with only one priest and six soldiers. He could easily have been killed but the good-faith effort and the show of personal courage seems to have turned the tide. The new Spanish governor proclaimed a general pardon, children who had been born during the intervening twelve years were baptized, and Santa Fe was returned peacefully to Spanish hands. The peace of 1692 did not hold and in the subsequent years a number of pueblos revolted against the rule of de Vargas and his successors. But the Spanish and Mexican population of the area grew and the Indian population declined. Unity was hard to achieve. Never again was there the kind of long-lasting and successful revolt that had shaken not only New Mexico but the entire Spanish empire in 1680.[17]

The reconquest, although complete, was neither the end of the story nor the end of the Pueblo hopes. While many terrors still lay ahead for the Pueblo Indians under the rule of Spain, Mexico, and then the United States, some of what they experienced during the first eighty years of Spanish rule never returned. In an unspoken compromise de Vargas and his successors never engaged in the wholesale effort to stamp out the old religious ways as the Inquisition had done in the 1600s. Franklin Folsom has stated the new compromise well, "The Indians once again attended Mass in the churches of the Spaniards, but now they also openly entered their kivas and held dances in public. The revolution of 1680 had won much for the Indians."[18] In spite of many future challenges the Inquisition never returned to New Mexico.

When the United States conquered the northern half of Mexico and annexed New Mexico along with Texas and California in 1846, the Pueblo people feared for the compromise they had won over 150 years before. Most history books report the fact that U.S. General Stephen Watts Kearny entered Santa Fe without a shot in 1846—just as de Vargas had in 1692—but the following year, in January 1847, Pueblo Indians in Taos attacked the house of the new American governor, Charles Bent, and killed him and several others. At times in the nineteenth century, the Pueblo religion again went underground, attacked now by boarding schools and the culture of the new masters of the land. At other times, it survived as a cultural artifact, studied by anthropologists who had no idea of how deeply the Pueblo peoples held their faith. But the traditions and the independence that had fueled the events of that remote summer continued.

Marc Simmons, historian of the southwest, has well summarized the power of the hopes of the revolutionaries of 1680: "As a result of that long-ago event, the Pueblo people are to this day still easily identifiable as Indians, speaking their several original languages, performing ceremonies the Spaniards failed to stamp out, and producing traditional crafts that in some cases have evolved to rank as fine arts. Clearly the effects of what happened in 1680 are with us even yet."[19] One only needs to visit one of the many Indian ceremonies in the Santa Fe and Taos area today to see the truth of that statement. The continuity of these traditions is a powerful tribute to the courage and daring of a few brave Pueblo souls who dared to hope in the face of the greatest military and political power on earth in their day. It is a legacy not to be forgotten.

CHAPTER ONE

THE REVOLUTIONARIES
OF 1776

DECLARING INDEPENDENCE, 1776

ON A BEAUTIFUL FRIDAY MORNING in Philadelphia, June 7, 1776, Richard Henry Lee, a delegate to the Continental Congress from Virginia, concluded his speech to the assembly with a motion:

> Resolved . . . that these United Colonies are, and of a right ought to be, free and independent states, that they are absolved from all allegiance to the British Crown, and that all political connection between them and the state of Great Britain is, and ought to be, totally dissolved.

John Adams, one of the Massachusetts delegates, immediately seconded the motion. The debate on the question of independence of the United States—a question whose fate was far from assured at that point—had begun in earnest.[1]

In the debate that took place the following day, a number of delegates led by the respected John Dickinson from Pennsylvania vigorously opposed the resolution. While they had come to Philadelphia in 1774 to join together in resistance to what they described as British tyranny, most of the delegates to this Congress of representatives of thirteen British North American colonies had come with the hope of reconciliation and a new spirit of cooperation with their homeland, not with any plan for a permanent separation.

The debate on the Lee-Adams resolution raged throughout the day and into the evening. When the Congress reconvened on Monday, June 10, no unanimity was in sight and so two compromise resolutions were adopted. First, the Congress agreed to delay a final vote on the question of independence until July 1. At the same time, a Committee of Five was appointed to draft a fuller declaration in case the Congress moved in the direction of independence. Thomas Jefferson, John Adams, Roger Sherman, Robert Livingston, and Benjamin Franklin were appointed to the select committee to draft an appropriate statement.[2]

For some time Adams had been the most prominent spokesperson for severing all ties with Great Britain. In a private letter to Patrick Henry, Adams had voiced his own hope that the time was right for moving forward. "The decree is gone forth, and it cannot be recalled, that a more equal liberty than had prevailed in other parts of the earth must be established in America."[3] That hope, for a "more equal liberty than had prevailed" before was a powerful motivator for a group who clearly understood that in voting for independence they were committing treason, and if they failed in their effort they would surely hang.

When the committee to draft the declaration convened, Jefferson was a junior member in terms of both the Congress (he had arrived as an alternate delegate from Virginia the year before) and in terms of age and recognition. Adams and Franklin were clearly the senior members. But Jefferson already had a reputation for his skill with words, the others were all busy with other matters, and so, as Joseph Ellis stated it, "Jefferson was asked to draft the Declaration of Independence, then, in great part because the other eligible authors had more important things to do."[4] Whatever the case, Jefferson was the lead author with Adams and Franklin and ultimately the full Congress making adjustments along the way; all of which frustrated and hurt the sensitive Jefferson. The most important of the changes included removing Jefferson's hypocritical but also passionate attack on the slave trade and his nostalgic note that if Britain had behaved differently, "We might have been a free and great people together." Far too many in the Congress had investments in the slave trade to accept the former and the tide against Britain had moved too far for the latter sentiment. Nevertheless, for all of the fears, hypocrisy, and calculations that went into it, the committee and eventually the Congress produced a document that was greater than they were.[5]

The twenty-day waiting period paid off. Though a number of delegates still had reservations, by July 1776 no one was willing to go on record as opposed to independence. So a unanimous Congress voted on July 2 for independence, and on July 4 for an explanation of their decision that has become a beacon of hope for many who were never given consideration in Philadelphia that morning:

When, in the course of human events, it becomes necessary for one people to dissolve the political bands which have connected them with another, and to assume among the powers of the earth, the separate and equal station to which the laws of nature and of nature's God entitle them, a decent respect to the opinions of mankind requires that they should declare the causes which impel them to the separation.

We hold these truths to be self-evident, that all men are created equal; that they are endowed by their Creator with certain unalienable rights; that among these are life, liberty, and the pursuit of happiness. That, to secure these rights, governments are instituted among men, deriving their just powers from the consent of the governed; that, whenever any form of government becomes destructive of these ends, it is the right of the people to alter or to abolish it, and to institute new government, laying its foundation on such principles, and organizing its powers in such form, as to them shall seem most likely to effect their safety and happiness.[6]

The hope of these words has transcended the immediate context and the very real limitations of the authors themselves almost from the moment of their publication. The right of revolution, the right of the people to "alter or to abolish" destructive governments, and the right of all people to "life, liberty, and the pursuit of happiness" have become a powerful set of hopes around the world in the more than two centuries since the vote in Philadelphia.[7]

Citizens in Philadelphia celebrated with "bonfires and ringing bells, with other great demonstrations of joy," according to one observer, when the vote for independence was finally announced on July 8. A crowd in New York tore down the statue of George III on July 9 and the celebrations continued up and down the coast in the weeks that followed. Though there would be many setbacks in the coming years of war, the summer of 1776 was a season of hope for many.[8]

"THE BIRTHDAY OF A
NEW WORLD IS AT HAND"

Looking back on those days in the summer of 1776 and on the revolutionary war that had begun the year before and that lasted for six more difficult and bloody years after that hopeful summer, John Adams asked the critical question: "But what do we mean by the American Revolution? Do we mean the American war? The Revolution was effected before the war commenced. The Revolution was in the minds and hearts of the people."[9]

Any real revolution, any action in history that is to offer hope to those participating and to those who come after must begin and remain first of all, as Adams said, "in the minds and hearts of the people." And no single thing did more to confirm the American revolution in the people's hearts and minds than the words of one revolutionary whom John Adams would later come to despise, Thomas Paine.[10]

Where Adams and most of the leaders of the revolutionary effort were third or fourth generation residents of the North American colonies, Thomas Paine had arrived from England only the year before he wrote his famous pamphlet. While Adams and most of his revolutionary colleagues were reasonably well off, if not as wealthy as the Virginians such as Jefferson and Washington, and among the colonial elite, Paine had come with no resources and never acquired many. While Adams and his colleagues were scholarly and careful, Paine was impatient and ready for immediate action. It may have been true, as Adams complained, that Paine "has a better hand at pulling down than building," but in North America in the early months of 1776 there was some serious pulling down needed, and Paine was the person who was more prepared than any others to be clear about the nature of the job.[11]

In publication as in other actions, timing can be everything. Paine wrote and published *Common Sense* at exactly the right moment when many people were ready and willing to hear his question, "Why is it that we hesitate? . . . for God's sake, let us come to a final separation. . . . The birthday of a new world is at hand." Paine's pamphlet was first published—after several other printers had rejected it for fear of its treasonous sentiments—by Robert Bell's print shop in Philadelphia in January 1776. Within a few months over 100,000 copies were in circulation, and *Common Sense* had received more printings than any other publication in the history of North America up to that time.[12]

In a relatively short pamphlet filled with both detailed analysis and soaring rhetoric, Paine made two basic points. First, he argued that monarchy was always a bad way for people to be governed. And then, getting very specific, he argued that no time was better for Britain's North American colonies to separate than the present moment, and that no outcome other than separation would work in the midst of the current crisis.[13]

While Paine's focus in his attack on monarchy was a particular monarch, George III of England, and on "the remains of monarchial tyranny in the person of the king" and "the remains of aristocratical tyranny in the persons of the peers," he cast his net much more broadly.[14] Beginning with the Old Testament—a document far more familiar to Paine's American readers than many of the Enlightenment philosophers of revolution—Paine reminded his readers of Gideon's refusal to be king of ancient Israel: "Gideon doth not decline the honor, but denieth their right to give it." No one, Paine was saying, had a right to give or accept a crown.

Continuing his argument, Paine cast himself in the role of the Old Testament prophet Samuel in warning Americans of the harms that kings could do. A King, Samuel had said, "will take your sons and appoint them for himself . . . to reap his harvest, and to make his instruments of war, and instruments of his chariots; and he will take your daughters to be confectionaries, and to be his cooks and to be bakers . . . and he will take your fields and your olive yards, even the best of them." In other words, as Samuel asked ancient Israel, so Paine asked colonial America and England itself, "why in the world would you want to have a king at all?"[15]

As for George III and the divine rights of the British monarchy, Paine was even more scornful. Who could defend the monarchy in England, Paine asked? After all, there was not much that was legitimate about George III's rule:

> England, since the conquest [of 1066], hath known some few good monarchs, but groaned beneath a much larger number of bad ones; yet no man in his senses can say that their claim under William the Conqueror is a very honorable one. A French bastard landing with an armed banditti, and establishing himself king of England against the consent of the natives, is in plain terms a very paltry rascally original.—It certainly hath no divinity in it.[16]

And that, dear friends, Paine said to the Americans, is the royal family with whom you must now break the connection if you are to be free.

Paine's second argument was much more specific: now was the time for North America to separate from Britain. Postponing action or arguing for reconciliation was courting disaster. The only hope for the future was in independence. Referring again and again to the sacrifices of those who had fought at Lexington and Concord in 1775 and those who suffered in the British siege of Boston the following winter, Paine insisted, "Every thing that is right or natural pleads for separation. The blood of the slain, the weeping voice of nature cries, 'tis time to part.'"[17]

Paine heaped ridicule on those who sought reconciliation. They were, "Interested men, who are not to be trusted; weak men who cannot see; prejudiced men, who will not see; and a certain set of moderate men, who think better of the European world than it deserves." Whichever category they fit, in Paine's mind, the moderates and the cowards were willing to pay for the repeal of the most recent British outrages such as the stamp act with the blood of those who had died for something much greater.[18] It no longer made sense to argue if the time was right to declare independence, Paine insisted. Six months before Adams had the votes or Jefferson had written the words, Paine argued, "the time hath found us."[19] It was time for action.

O! ye that love mankind! Ye that dare oppose, not only the tyranny, but the tyrant, stand forth! Every spot of the old world is overrun with oppression. Freedom hath been haunted round the globe. Asia, and Africa, have long expelled her. Europe regards her like a stranger, and England hath given her warning to depart. O! receive the fugitive, and prepare in time an asylum for mankind.[20]

With this appeal to hope for the future, Paine rallied the inhabitants of his new home.

In one of those moments of rich historical irony, *Common Sense* appeared on the same day as the publication of George III's speech to Parliament declaring the North American colonies to be in a state of rebellion. The two could not have contrasted more clearly. The king was calling on the colonists to lay down their arms and become loyal subjects once again. Paine was calling on the same people to raise an army and navy and to declare both independence for themselves and an end to monarchy around the globe. Paine knew how to seize the moment. He immediately added to *Common Sense* an appendix which appeared with all but the earliest editions of his pamphlet responding to the King's speech. "The Rubicon is passed," Paine insisted. "We ought not now to be debating whether we shall be independent or not, but anxious to accomplish it on a firm, secure, and honorable basis, and uneasy rather, that it is not yet began upon."[21] The King's speech was the last straw for Paine if one had been needed.

> However, it matters very little now, what the king of England either says or does; he hath wickedly broken through every moral and human obligation, trampled nature and conscience beneath his feet; and by a steady and constitutional spirit of insolence and cruelty, procured for himself an universal hatred.[22]

There was but one response. It was time for unity and for freedom.

> Wherefore, instead of gazing at each other, with suspicious or doubtful curiosity, let each of us hold out to his neighbor the hearty hand of friendship, and unite in drawing a line, which, like an act of oblivion, shall bury in forgetfulness every former dissention. Let the names of whig and tory be extinct; and let none other be heard among us, than those of a good citizen; an open and resolute friend; and a virtuous supporter of the RIGHTS OF MANKIND, and of the FREE AND INDEPENDENT STATES OF AMERICA.[23]

With his passionate words, his exquisite timing, and his willingness to risk all, Paine in this short pamphlet became a prophet of a more hopeful future for his adopted country and for those far from it. Although John Adams was no admirer of Paine or his pamphlet, he wrote to Abigail saying that he expected *Common Sense* to become the "common faith" of the new nation.[24] In fact, it has been virtually forgotten, but in its day *Common Sense* stirred the hopes of many residents of the colonies with a powerful new vision of freedom. It did much to win the revolution in the hearts of many colonists.

GENERAL GEORGE WASHINGTON

Of course, the American revolution was not won on the battlefield of pamphleteers or congressional debaters. It was, in fact, a long and bloody war between rebel militias in all of the colonies and well-trained and organized British troops, loyalist colonists, and imported mercenaries like the hated Hessian troops from Germany. Ultimately three factors led to the success of the ragtag rebels.

Howard Zinn has argued, correctly, that the white population was used to carrying arms for protection and for hunting. They did not have to be trained and they did not have to be equipped. They only had to be recruited to the effort and kept at it. So, Zinn says, "The American victory over the British army was made possible by the existence of an already-armed people. Just about every white male had a gun, and could shoot."[25] As with subsequent revolutionary struggles, the British found it far more difficult than they had originally thought to either awe or conquer indigenous resistance. As many other historians have noted, the American revolution was the prototype of a revolutionary war for liberation. And that made it possible for ill-trained and restless troops to continue in spite of seeing, as one soldier remembered, the "horrors of battle . . . in all their hideousness." Much has been made of the lack of discipline in the revolutionary army, but it was this undisciplined army that won the war and independence against the mightiest empire in the world.[26]

George Washington is remembered as many things—the father of his country, the marble face on the dollar bill, the first president, the man with wooden false teeth. The list can go on and on. But seldom is Washington remembered for one of his great claims to fame, as one of the world's first great guerrilla leaders. Washington understood all too well that though his army could fight and shoot, they could not withstand a direct battle with the well-trained and disciplined British regulars. Yet it was the very training and discipline that narrowed the conception of war for the British and that gave Washington the edge.

In early 1776 the revolution almost seemed lost before it had begun. The British control of Boston was complete. They held the city and controlled the harbor, and they had guns ready to destroy any attack from the only direction they imagined it could come—from the sea. Washington, however, had imagination and supporters willing to make unbelievable sacrifices. Henry Knox, a young Boston bookseller, and his troops had taken the guns captured by Ethan Allen and his troops at Fort Ticonderoga, New York, and moved them on sleds and in pieces over the mountains of western Massachusetts back to Boston. The terrible winter that made life so difficult kept the ground snow-covered and frozen solid under the sleds. On the night of March 1 more than a thousand of Washington's troops working silently with their ox teams had assembled the guns on Dorchester Heights (now South Boston), and on the morning of March 2 they began a bombardment of the city from a direction the British never expected. The attack lasted until March 17, a day now celebrated in Boston as both St. Patrick's Day and Evacuation Day because the British evacuated the city that morning. In London, the Duke of Manchester summed up the significance of the event for the House of Lords, "the fact remains, that the army which was sent to reduce the province of Massachusetts Bay has been driven from the capital, and the standard of the provincial army now waves in triumph over the walls of Boston."[27] Two hundred years before the Ho Chi Minh Trail, backbreaking labor, a new kind of thinking, and hope triumphed over the greatest military power in the world.

Finally, of course, the revolution was won because France and Spain were willing to help and they had major interests in reducing British power. In arguing for a declaration of independence at the same time Washington was bombarding the British in Boston, Adams had told the Congress: "Foreign powers can not be expected to acknowledge us, till we have acknowledged ourselves and taken our station among them as a sovereign power, an independent nation."[28] The Congress accepted Adams' logic. It later called on him to be one of its representatives in gaining the needed foreign acknowledgment and foreign aid. Even before Adams departed for France, however, an American delegation led by Benjamin Franklin had secured important supplies and, on February 6, 1778, a full French alliance with the United States of America, the first diplomatic recognition for the new nation and the beginning of essential diplomatic and military support that ultimately turned the tide of war for the Americans.[29] But important as the French aid was—and it was very important—it would not have turned the tide without both the military imagination of Washington and the bravery and hope of the unnamed and unrecognized soldiers who fought, and in many cases, died in the hope of a better liberty than they or the world had known.

A WALL OF SEPARATION
BETWEEN CHURCH AND STATE

At the time of the American Revolution, every European nation had a state church. The new United States offered a degree of religious freedom unknown anywhere else in the world at the time. In arguing for the special destiny of his adopted land, Thomas Paine saw it as a sign of divine favor for the cause of independence that North America was developing as a place for religious freedom and refuge for peoples from all parts of Europe. He said, "The reformation was preceded by the discovery of America, as if the Almighty graciously meant to open a sanctuary to the persecuted in future years, when home should afford neither friendship nor safety." If the winners were always going to persecute the losers in Europe's long-running religious wars, America could offer something different—freedom for all. "This new world hath been the asylum for the persecuted lovers of civil and religious liberty from every part of Europe," he wrote. "Hither have they fled, not from the tender embraces of the mother, but from the cruelty of the monster."[30] The English might celebrate their liberties, but in matters of faith, England maintained an established church and dissenters experienced a range of disabilities that grew with their distance from the reigning Anglicanism.

On the eve of the revolution all was not as rosy in the American colonies as Paine painted it. In Massachusetts, Baptists who refused to pay taxes to support the ministers and buildings of the Congregational establishment were still being arrested for their contempt of authority. "While our country are pleading so high for liberty," Isaac Backus complained, "yet they are denying of it to their neighbors."[31] As in other arenas, however, the revolution launched currents that would eventually overwhelm the established churches in all of the colonies, but it took a long time for this to happen. Massachusetts only ended its support for the established Congregational-Unitarian churches in 1833. But with the revolution and independence, the separation of church and state was inevitable in the new nation. In fact, there were many different forces that in spite of their wide differences worked together to create the revolutionary hopefulness anticipated by Jefferson when as president he spoke of the American constitutional protection that was "thus building a wall of separation between Church and State."[32]

Jefferson was one of the most ardent and consistent, if not the most effective, defenders of religious freedom for all throughout his career.[33] He showed the importance he placed on the issue when he listed his authorship of the Virginia Statute for Religious Freedom along with the Declaration of Independence and his role in founding the University of Virginia on his epitaph. In 1779, while the outcome of the revolution was still very much in doubt, Jefferson introduced a bill to the Virginia Assembly that was ultimately passed seven years later in 1786. In that statue, which ended the tax support and other privileges of the Anglican church in Virginia and placed all religious groups on an equal footing quite separate from the state, Jefferson described his vision of religious freedom:

> Well aware that the opinions and belief of men depend not on their own will, but follow involuntarily the evidence proposed to their minds; that Almighty God hath created the mind free, and manifested his supreme will that free it shall remain by making it altogether insusceptible of restraining; that all attempts to influence it by temporal punishments, or burthens, or by civil incapacitations, tend only to beget habits of hypocrisy and meanness, and are a departure from the plan of the holy author of our religion, who being lord both of body and mind, yet chose not to propagate it by coercions on either, as was in his Almighty power to do, but to extend it by its influence on reason alone.[34]

While individual reason alone has hardly been a major source of faith for many, Jefferson's clear belief that God had created the human mind as free and that any attempt to support religion by "temporal punishments, or burthens, or by civil incapacitations" tended to create the opposite of deep faith has survived the test of time.

As president, Jefferson continued to voice similar views. Thus in 1802, after one year in the White House, he wrote what is probably his most often quoted statement on the issue in a letter to the Danbury Baptist Association of Connecticut:

> Believing with you that religion is a matter which lies solely between man and his God, that he owes account to none other for his faith or his worship, that the legislative powers of government reach actions only, and not opinions, I contemplate with sovereign reverence that act of the whole American people which declared that their legislature should "make no law respecting an establishment of religion, or prohibiting the free exercise thereof," thus building a wall of separation between Church and State.[35]

Few lines of presidential correspondence have entered the nation's language as firmly as Jefferson's "wall of separation between Church and State."

However much the careful logic of deists like Jefferson provided the ideology for the separation of church and state, it was actually an accidental accomplishment, a compromise when all else failed. Most of the colonists, whom generations of school children have learned came to North America for religious freedom, actually came for a very narrow kind of freedom. With rare exceptions, such as the Baptist followers of Roger Williams in Rhode Island and some of the Quakers who came to William Penn's colony of Pennsylvania, the colonists came seeking religious freedom for themselves and the right to persecute, or at least banish, anyone who did not share the colony's faith. In their early years, most colonies enforced a uniformity at least as strict as had their homelands, whether it was in the form of Puritan intolerance in Massachusetts and Connecticut, or of the Royalists who settled in Virginia and insisted that everyone follow their Anglican/Episcopal traditions.

There were, however, important exceptions. Lord Baltimore established religious tolerance in his Maryland colony as a means of protecting his own beleaguered fellow English Catholics. William Penn and his Quakers were far more tolerant than the Presbyterians who shared the land of Pennsylvania with them. And Roger Williams and the Baptists who founded Rhode Island actually practiced and believed in religious freedom for all, although for this they were widely distrusted by most of the other colonists who shared with them what fast became British North America.[36] Yet, within little more than a century and a half of Rhode Island's founding, the polity of this small colony became the national model. The historian Sydney Mead has offered the most accurate analysis of the move to religious freedom. For all of the power of Roger Williams's traditions or Jefferson's arguments, religious freedom actually arrived in the new nation because it was everyone's second choice. If the Congregationalists of New England, the Presbyterians of the Middle Colonies, or the Anglicans of Virginia could not get enough votes in Congress to establish themselves as the state church of the new nation, Mead argued, then they preferred toleration to someone else winning, even if the toleration also included Baptists, deists, Catholics, Jews, and unbelievers.[37] And as a result the United States, in spite of failures and exceptions, has offered more freedom to those who have wanted to practice a wide variety of religions, or none, than any other nation. It is part of the hope that the revolutionary generation gave its successors, however accidentally they gave it.[38]

THE GREAT CONTRADICTION: SLAVERY IN THE MIDST OF LIBERTY

Early in the revolutionary struggle another Bostonian, Phillis Wheatley, wrote her own petition to the King's Secretary of State for North America. Like many other patriots, Wheatley petitioned for a day of freedom in which:

No more, America, in mournful strain
Of wrongs, and grievance unredress'd complain,

> No longer shalt thou dread the iron chain,
> Which wanton Tyranny with lawless hand
> Had made, and with it meant t' enslave the land.

Except for the shift from the rhetoric of sermon and speech to poetry, Wheatley's poem at that point echoed the same sentiments as the majority of Bostonians, from the cousins Samuel and John Adams to the crowds that had gathered at the time of the Boston massacre or the tea party.

Wheatley's next line was radically different, however, because Wheatley's experience in life had been radically different from most residents of the Bay State. She was, after all, an African slave, and she explained that her own commitment to the cause of freedom was different and far deeper than most.

> Should you, my lord, while you peruse my song,
> Wonder from whence my love of Freedom sprung,
> Whence flow these wishes for the common good,
> By feeling hearts alone best understood,
> I, young in life, by seeming cruel fate
> Was snatch'd from Afric's fancy'd happy seat:
> What pangs excruciating must molest,
> What sorrows labour in my parent's breast?
> Steel'd was that soul and by no misery mov'd
> That from a father seiz'd his babe belov'd;
> Such, such my case. And can I then but pray
> Others may never feel tyrannic sway?[39]

Wheatley addressed her poem to the King's minister. But her audience was closer to home. How could her countrymen, she asked, argue and fight for an end to tyranny's sway when they continued to sustain the most terrible kind of tyranny for those "snatch'd from Afric's fancy'd happy seat"? She was not alone in asking the question.

In 1775 Lemuel Haynes, a member of the Massachusetts militia, wrote his own poem commemorating the battle of Lexington and Concord, "the inhuman tragedy perpetrated on the 19th of April 1775 by a Number of British Troops." Like Wheatley, Haynes focused his poem on the courage and righteousness of those who fought in the patriotic cause and the battle for liberty against "Tyrants fill'd with horrid Rage." Like Wheatley, he also did not end there. Consigning the patriots who died that day to the arms of death and honor, Haynes then reflected on what the battle meant for Africans and their descendents like himself:

Thrice happy they who thus resign
Into the peaceful Grave
Much better there, in Death Confin'd
Than a Surviving Slave
This Motto may adorn their Tombs,
(Let tyrants come and view)
"We rather seek these silent Rooms
"Than live as Slaves to You."[40]

To die for the cause of freedom, Haynes made clear, was not a laurel to be offered only to free whites in North America. It was a note to both inspire and
terrify many of the patriots who led the revolutionary effort.

A year later Haynes, who went on from his militia career to be a highly regarded minister, argued that Americans needed to "extend" the definition of
freedom as "an innate principle." After all, Haynes continued, "even an
African [had] as equally good a right to his liberty in common with English-
men." The logic of liberty's hope, Haynes and a good many others argued,
could admit no divisions by race or any other form.[41]

A good number of whites shared the view of Wheatley, Haynes, and their
many contemporaries of African descent. Philadelphia's most famous physician,
Benjamin Rush, called for "advocates for American liberty" to "espouse the cause
of ... general liberty," by avoiding "national crimes" that would inevitably bring
"national punishments."[42] Abigail Adams reflected, "It always seemed a most in-
iquitous scheme to me—[to] fight ourselves for what we are daily robbing and
plundering from those who have as good a right to freedom as we have." She also
worried about her husband's colleagues from Virginia since, "I have sometimes
been ready to think that the passion for liberty cannot be equally strong in the
breasts of those who have been accustomed to deprive their fellow creatures of
theirs."[43] John Allen, a Massachusetts clergyman, warned that Americans were
making a mockery of their cause "by trampling on the sacred natural rights and
privileges of the Africans." And Jefferson himself, the ever-contradictory Virgin-
ian who owned slaves and depended on slavery for every aspect of his daily life yet
declared that all were created equal, also condemned slavery and understood that
it was an institution "one hour of which is fraught with more misery than ages of
that which [the colonies] rose in rebellion to oppose."[44]

Perhaps more than anyone, Jefferson in his own person represented all of
the contradictions that allowing slavery in a new nation conceived in liberty
represented. Jefferson could be one of slavery's most eloquent attackers. At the
same time, it is true, as David McCullough has observed, that "It was not just
that slaves worked his fields; they cut his firewood, cooked and served his

meals, washed and ironed his linen, brushed his suits, nursed his children, cleaned, scrubbed, polished, opened and closed doors for him, saddled his horse, turned down his bed, waited on him hand and foot from dawn to dusk."[45] And, as recent scholarship has confirmed, bore his children.[46]

The politics of a new nation, however, allowed something quite different than the logical untangling of the contradictions in Jefferson's mind and life or the proper answer to the arguments of slaves and former slaves who saw in slavery the ultimate betrayal of liberty. On the issue of slavery, the revolutionary generation failed the test of their own hopes more deeply than on any other. Partly it was a problem of their own ideology. As Eric Foner has noted, if "nothing was more essential to liberal freedom than the rights of self-government and protection of private property," then all private property, including property consisting of other human beings, was sacrosanct from state interference.[47] More basically, the problem was simply that those whose fortunes depended on slavery were not about to give up their fortunes no matter what other contradictions were involved. While slavery was fast disappearing in the North, it was gaining ground in the South and southern leaders would not be part of any union that threatened the peculiar institution. The Constitutional Convention of 1787, which included a large number of slaveholders and a small number of abolitionists of various stripes, developed a governing document for the new nation in which the compromises around slavery actually strengthened slavery. Although the original Constitution does not mention slavery as such, one contemporary, Luther Martin, a Maryland attorney who opposed the Constitution, noted the framers were "willing to admit into their system those *things* which the *expressions signified*."[48] The result was a document that a half century later the great abolitionist William Lloyd Garrison would condemn as "the source and parent of the other atrocities." At a Fourth of July picnic in 1854, Garrison burned a copy of the Constitution proclaiming, "So perish all compromises with tyranny."[49]

In the constitutional convention itself, James Madison, who played such a crucial role in the development of the governing document, recalled, "the institution of slavery and its implications formed the line of discrimination" on many of the issues and dominated some of the most contentious debates. Madison, like his fellow Virginians Jefferson and Washington, embodied all of the contradictions of slavery. He owned slaves yet he despised the institution of slavery. He told the convention itself that the "distinction of color" represented the basis for "the most oppressive domination ever exercised by man over man." Yet he also assured the Virginia ratification convention that the new Constitution offered slavery "better security than any that now exists."[50] And so it did for the next seventy-five years. The hopes of Wheatley and

Haynes and so many others were a dream long deferred, but they were a dream that would not die.

HOPE FOR THE FUTURE

More than any other group of people in American history, the revolutionary generation, and especially leaders such as Washington, Adams, and Jefferson, have become cardboard characters. Their words have been invoked too often, their deeds sanitized too much. They are hard to see as real people. Recently historians such as David McCullough and Joseph J. Ellis have sought with considerable success to bring the "founding brothers" back to us as real humans who lived real lives full of flaws, ambitions, and great hopes.[51]

The real revolutionaries of 1776, however, were not the ones whose names and faces dot the history books. For a subset of the population of British North America, but a fairly large subset, the revolution changed everything. Historian Eric Foner has noted that "Inequality had been fundamental to the colonial social order; the Revolution in many ways made it illegitimate."[52] Inequality's illegitimacy did not mean its immediate end. In spite of Abigail Adams's plea to "remember the ladies" or Jefferson's assertions about slavery in his original drafts of the Declaration of Independence, sexism, slavery, and many other forms of inequality survived the revolution quite thoroughly intact, and in the case of slavery, with renewed power. Nevertheless something had changed. No form of inequality survived the war and the separation from England intact. All forms of suppression of liberty were now at least suspect. Forces had been unleashed that would give hope to those who sought to undermine every form of oppression whether the revolutionaries meant to do so or not. Thomas Paine, ever the most optimistic recorder of events, wrote, "We see with other eyes; we hear with other ears, and think with other thoughts, than those we formerly used." "Whenever I use the words freedom or rights," Paine continued, "I desire to be understood to mean a perfect equality of them. . . . The floor of Freedom is as level as water."[53]

Not all of Paine's contemporaries, indeed probably not the majority, were willing to take the revolution as far as he was. But in 1774 when one unknown Bostonian wrote, "We are also, from the cobbler up to the senator, become politicians," he announced a *novus ordo seclorum* that could not be stopped. That belief and that hope, far more than the immediate political impact of the establishment of a new government for the thirteen colonies, was a heritage of hope that the generation of the revolution bequeathed to their successors.[54] The bequest flourished far beyond the imaginations of even the bravest.

CHAPTER TWO

UTOPIAN COMMUNITIES

RELIGION, DEMOCRACY, AND SOCIALISM

THE FIRST HALF-CENTURY OF THE LIFE of the new nation witnessed an extraordinary development of hopeful experiments and ideas. Idealists like Thomas Owen founded utopian socialist communities while religious enthusiasts like Mother Ann Lee came to the United States seeking a place to start experiments like her Shaker communities. The combination of space that allowed people to develop their own communities relatively undisturbed and a philosophy that emphasized liberty, even the liberty to be eccentric, made the United States fertile ground for many radical experiments. Throughout the nineteenth century, various communitarian experiments were tried. Some were very short lived while others lasted for several generations, and a few continued into the twenty-first century. While there was a brief upsurge of interest in these early communal experiments by the participants in latter-day communes of the 1960s and 1970s, for the most part this story is a forgotten chapter in the nation's history.[1]

MOTHER ANN LEE AND THE SHAKERS

Shakers may be one of the most romanticized of American religious communitarian movements, although at times it is hard to know the focus of the romanticism. Today the communitarian impulse is not the only thing that Shakers are known for. Indeed, at the beginning of the twenty-first century, it is probably far from the top of the list. Mildred Barker, leader of the Shaker Community at

Sabbath Day Lake, Maine, who died in 1990, reflected, "I almost expect to be remembered as a chair or a table."[2] While Shaker furniture has grown in popularity, the kind of beloved community created by the Shakers that produced both the physical beauty of their furniture and the spiritual beauty of their worship and community life recedes farther and farther from view.

The United Society of Believers in Christ's Second Appearing, called Shakers, dates back to the spiritual ferment that took place in France in the century before the French Revolution. A group of spiritualists attacked the Catholic Church as a false religion. Like other Protestants of the time, they called for reformation. And like other Protestants in France, they were not welcomed by the authorities. Some were silenced, others fled to England where they linked up with some dissident Quakers, especially in the emerging industrial center of Manchester.[3]

The Shakers—sometimes called the Shaking Quakers in the early days because of the enthusiasm and ecstasy in their worship—were one of the products of this merger of reform-minded French spiritualists and English Quakers. From these Shaking Quakers Ann Lee—known among the Shakers as Mother Ann Lee—gathered a small group of supporters in England, immigrated with them to the United States, and founded the first Shaker communities here.

As with many charismatic religious leaders and founders, much of Lee's life and early teaching remains a mystery. She was born in Manchester, England, in 1736 and was influenced by "inspirationists" from France and the English Quakers. She was married and had four children all of whom died in infancy. By her mid-thirties her spiritualism had led her and her fellow believers to disrupt the worship services of the Established Church of England, which she saw as a dead ritual that diverted people from true spirituality. As a result she was arrested several times for disrupting the worship of other denominations.[4] In 1770, while in jail on these charges, she had a powerful mystical experience. It convinced her of two things: that she was receiving a very special revelation from God that she was to share and that made her a special prophetic leader; and that human sexuality was the key to all sin—from Adam and Eve to the present—and celibacy was the only way to live a godly life. (Psychologists have had a field day wondering if the loss of four infants had played a role in her new rejection of sex, but there is really no way to know.)

Lee was jailed several more times in England because of her continued preaching and practice of her beliefs. Indeed, she did much more than just preach. Like many a prophetic voice, she condemned the established churches to their faces, entering worship where, as one report noted, she "willfully and contemptuously in the time of divine service, disturb[ed] the congregation then assembled at morning prayer." For that particular offense she was jailed for two days.[5]

Lee came to America in 1774 and eventually inspired the creation of celibate colonies that shared the pacifism and communitarianism of which she spoke. Ann Lee's pacifism led to her being jailed by New York in 1780 on charges of undermining the American Revolution. In the first years after their arrival, the small Shaker community was content to live their own lives and did not seem much interested in seeking converts. However, after her release from jail in December 1780, Lee and two of her followers crisscrossed New York and New England founding "families" of Shakers. This famous missionary journey, which lasted from May 1781 to September 1783, established Lee's mythic leadership. She suffered abuse from the unconvinced in many towns, but she also made many converts to her own version of the Christian faith. Lee died the following year, in September 1784, but the authority of her teachings was well established by that time.[6]

As Stephen Stein has noted in his carefully researched study of the Shakers, it is hard to know exactly what Lee did teach. One source that Stein uses is a 1780 publication from Valentine Rathbun, a Baptist minister who was deeply hostile to the Shakers. According to Rathbun, who viewed the movement as a "new scheme . . . the spirit of witchcraft," Shakers had several key characteristics. They believed that marriage was sinful, they viewed Ann Lee as "the mother," and some seemed to believe that she had "the fullness of the God Head" and was "the queen of heaven, Christ's wife." Many of the earliest Shakers also shared their meals and lodging and were clearly an intimate, although celibate, community. Perhaps most interesting, their worship was ecstatic. "Their actions in worship is according to the dictates of the spirit that governs them," Rathbun reported. Shaker worship did not involve the traditional prayer or preaching. Instead their worship reflected their understanding of the new "spiritual dispensation," including, as Stein notes, "shaking and singing, hopping and turning . . . and running, groaning and laughing. The believers viewed all these actions as manifestations of divine power and union with God."[7] That one of the Shakers' harshest critics should describe their early lives in ways so similar to the actual practice of their later communities leads one to conclude that these characteristics were all established quite early in Shaker life.

While Lee and her closest followers had lived together in a small community just outside of Albany, New York, at the time of her death Shakers were scattered in many homes and villages across New England. Almost immediately after her death in 1784, however, Shakers began the process of selling their homes and moving into a small number of tightly organized Shaker communities. In part this was a response to the hostility of neighbors who took a dim view of their approach to marriage, their unique form of worship, and their harsh critique of established churches. Lee's successors urged the Shakers to share all of their possessions and "have all things in common," as had the earliest Christian communities. The core of the first Shaker community in New Lebanon, New York, was established when they built their first meeting house in 1785. Soon thereafter, a lively Shaker village sprung up around it.[8]

The Shaker community at New Lebanon thrived, as did the whole movement, and within a decade after Lee's death there were ten communities with over 2,000 members. The revivals of the early nineteenth century added to the Shakers' membership and they became one of the largest and most successful of the nineteenth-century communitarian movements.

Early in the nineteenth century, the Shaker Community began the difficult process of writing their own history and defining their basic beliefs. At its core, Shakerism is a faith based on ecstatic worship and ordered community life, with both open to the continued leading of the Holy Spirit. As a result, Shakers have always been distrustful of written statements of their theological beliefs. Nevertheless, the growth of the Shaker community, the geographical dispersion of their communities, and the hostility of their neighbors led Shakers to feel the need to clarify some of their most basic beliefs.

In 1814 members of the church family signed an amended covenant designed not only to clarify some of their beliefs but also to assure continuity in the leadership, as the generations after Lee sought a clear basis for their own authority. After some initial reluctance because of their fears of being misunderstood by others, they publicly asserted that "our Lord and Saviour Jesus Christ did make his second appearance, by his Spirit, first in Ann Lee, whom we acknowledge to be the first Mother of all souls in the work of regeneration, and the first spiritual head of the Church of Christ then in the body." They then continued their statement tracing the authority of the current leadership to Lee and her successors. They agreed "that the spiritual lead of the Church descended from her to James Whittaker. . . . That since the decease of the said Joseph Meacham, the ministration of the gifts of God, and the spiritual protection of souls, have rested with the said Lucy Wright, whom we still acknowledge, love and respect, as our spiritual Mother in the Church." For close to two centuries following the 1814 statement, Shaker theology and the centralized leadership of the Shaker movement was clearly established.[9]

While the early Shaker correspondence shows that there were quarrels about the topic, it is clear that by 1814, one of the most powerful and unique aspects of Shaker theology was the placement of Ann Lee on a par with Jesus and the parallel commitment within the society to the equal leadership of women with men. The Shakers were quite clear about this. There could be no "spiritual union and relation" until a woman was appointed to "complete the order in the foundation of the new creation." And Shaker community life as well as the community's leadership reflected these theological beliefs.[10]

While they felt the need for these basic statements of their creed to clarify their views to an often hostile world, Shakers were in fact willing to give their members wide latitude regarding their theological beliefs. Where they were not flexible was the practice of community life. What united all Shakers, indeed what was absolutely required in order to be a Shaker, was celibacy and commitment to community. The celibacy always limited the community's appeal and meant that all new members had to come from the outside as converts. The commitment to community—to sharing all things in common—also led to a series of complaints by those who sought to leave and take their share of the communal property with them. These complaints and lawsuits produced many of the most widely available Shaker writings, explaining their unique communities and defending themselves from a wide range of public complaints.

For those who wanted to join the Shaker community, there were a series of stages. The Declaration of Junior Membership—the first stage of apprenticeship for full acceptance—stated the rules, expectations, and hopes of the community very clearly. Junior members were not asked for any long-term commitment to the community; only the promise that by their free act and will they would live fully by the community's norms for as long as they chose to be part of the community. So they sang:

Whereas with the Shakers, at present I live,
This plain Declaration I honestly give.
To show the condition on which we agree—
How I'm to treat them, and how they're to treat me.
To be a good member, my honor's at stake,
That all my old sins I confess and forsake;
And then, as a brother, it is understood
That I be employed in doing some good.
In uniform clothing we're equally dress'd.
And to the same table I go with the rest.
In health and in sickness, as long as I'm here,
In all their enjoyments I equally share.
I am in my senses, I'm candid and free;
There is no imposition practiced on me:
The terms of the gospel I well understand;
I'm bound to observe them, as witness my hand.[11]

By making this pledge, junior members could try out living in a community where all were celibate, where all shared all things together in equality, and where not only the worship but every aspect of community life seemed infused with the ecstatic presence of God.

It is in their many hymns, some of which have become well known, that Shaker theology is best preserved. One less well-known hymn expresses the joy and hopefulness of Shaker life:

> Come old and young, come great and small,
> There's love and union free for all,
> And everyone that will obey
> Has now a right to dance and play.
> For dancing is a sweet employ.
> It fills the soul with heav'nly joy,
> It makes our love and union flow
> While round and round and round we go.[12]

One can conceive of many reasons that nineteenth century Americans might reject the Shaker way, the demand of celibacy being high on the list. But one can also imagine that in spite of the celibacy, many Shakers experienced life with a far more heightened consciousness, a far greater sense of joy, and a far more profound sense of passion and love than many of their contemporaries.

Shaker life thrived throughout the nineteenth century and well into the twentieth. By the time of the Great Depression and World War II, however, the Shakers were a fast-shrinking community. Their orphanages, which had long been a source of recruits, were taken over by state agencies or more modern foster care arrangements. Few people seemed interested in joining the group and the membership was aging quickly. By 1960 the society had shrunk to two communities—Canterbury, New Hampshire, and Sabbath Day Lake, Maine. The members of these two communities were old and growing feeble. They also faced several new threats. Though their numbers were small, their real estate had become very valuable. They also had archives and were determined to be remembered. And with the coming of the 1960s, a new generation seemed much more interested—too interested in the minds of some of the elders—in joining the Shaker community.

In 1965 the leadership at Canterbury, the acknowledged head of the United Society, decided to close the society and give their attention to preserving their historical memory as a witness on which future generations might build in different ways. That was not, however, the end of the Shakers. The community at Sabbath Day Lake, Maine, under the leadership of Mildred

Barker, rejected the ban on new members. As a result, the two communities split and Sabbath Day Lake continues into the twenty-first century as a small but young and hopeful Shaker community giving witness to the joyful spirituality of the over two centuries-old movement.[13]

At the same time, the simplicity and joyfulness of the Shakers has infiltrated American culture in a wide variety of ways. Certainly they have been romanticized beyond recognition at times, but that is also not the whole story. Shaker furniture, now so popular, was not just a product for them. As the Catholic monk and mystic Thomas Merton said in 1966, "The peculiar grace of a Shaker chair is due to the fact that it was made by someone capable of believing that an angel might come and sit on it." Or as the Shaker Mildred Barker said, behind all of the physical artifacts, "There's the religion."[14] And while many of their hymns and their more complex theological ideas have largely been forgotten, the basic joy, humility, and playfulness of the Shakers continues to be remembered in this familiar hymn that dates to the 1830s:

'Tis the gift to be simple, 'tis the gift to be free;
'Tis the gift to come down where we ought to be;
And when we find ourselves in the place just right,
'Twill be in the valley of love and delight.
When true simplicity is gain'd,
To bow and to bend we shan't be asham'd
To turn, turn will be our delight,
'Till by turning, turning we come round right.[15]

In the gift of music, freedom, and delight, the Shakers represent hope for many.

JOHN HUMPHREY NOYES AND THE ONEIDA COMMUNITY

If the Shakers sought perfection in their own community life and in the relationship of their members to God through celibacy, John Humphrey Noyes and his followers at the Oneida Community, who lived not far from some of the Shakers in upstate New York, took a very different route to the same goals.

The Oneida Community that flourished in Oneida, New York, between 1848 and 1879 was one of the most successful of the many nineteenth-century efforts to build a perfect society on a small scale that might, its members hoped, be a model of the good life for the larger society. For three decades, hundreds of middle-class European Americans participated in the life of this extended family. Where the Shakers sought to build up their communal life and to support the equality of women and men through celibacy, members of the Oneida family sought similar goals in a very different way. At Oneida, as with the Shakers, the members owned all property in common. But where the Shakers were celibate, at Oneida they practiced what they called complex marriage in which all members of the community were considered to be married to all other members. Monogamy and jealousy were seen as barriers to the kind of loving community that they wanted to create at Oneida. Under the leadership of the charismatic John Humphrey Noyes, members of the community worked, played, made love, nurtured children, and lived together in relative harmony for most of their years together. They shared their ideas and their way of practicing the good life with any who would pay attention, recording every aspect of their life, issuing a steady stream of publications, and entertaining visitors on a grand scale.

The founder and spiritual guide for Oneida throughout its existence was John Humphrey Noyes. Noyes, born in Brattleboro, Vermont, in 1811, was the child of a storekeeper and future Vermont congressman and a strong-willed and devoted mother who wanted her son to be a minister. After considering a number of options, Noyes began studying for the ministry first at Andover Theological Seminary in 1831 and then at Yale Divinity School beginning in 1832.[16]

It was at Yale that Noyes began to develop the theological basis that eventually became the Oneida way, although neither he nor those with whom he was studying had any idea of where Noyes's ideas would ultimately take him. While studying with the leading theologian of the day, Nathaniel William Taylor, Noyes began to question not only the focus on sin and predestination in the reigning Calvinist theology but also Taylor's more liberal belief that people could earn redemption through their own effort and the confession of their sins.

Noyes became convinced that repentance from sin was not enough. People, he believed, should simply stop sinning. Though the notion that any human could stop sinning was anathema to Calvinists, Noyes was not the first to believe that perfection was possible for some Christians in this life. Indeed, John Wesley founded Methodism on a similar belief that Christians should try—and some might succeed—in "going on to perfection."[17] But Noyes defined perfectionism quite differently from Wesley. He became convinced that a second conversion was available to all Christians in which they not only repented but also moved to a state "in which all the affections of the heart are given to God, and in which there is no sin."[18]

During the course of the next decade, Noyes developed his perfectionist beliefs in more and more detail. He was far from alone. There were many who embraced the doctrine of perfectionism during the revivals that were sweeping the

United States in the 1830s. As Noyes defined it, perfectionism did not mean that one would never make mistakes. It did mean for those who were fully converted that their hearts and souls belonged fully to God and that sin could no longer have any power over them. For such people the old moral law was no longer the guide. A person who had experienced true conversion could, Noyes believed, follow the rule in which God said, "Do as you please; for I promise that your pleasure shall be mine. I will write my law upon your heart."[19]

It was over a decade after his initial embrace of perfectionism that Noyes proceeded to apply the concept to the realm of sexuality. For several years after his break with Taylor and the Calvinism of Yale, he was an itinerant preacher and publisher of his perfectionist theology. Eventually he gathered a small community, mostly members of his own family, at a farm in Putney, Vermont. There, in part it seems because of a growing attraction that Noyes felt for one of his converts, Mary Cragin, and in part because of his changing theological views, he expanded his definition of Christian perfectionism to include what he called complex marriage or, at times, communist marriage. Noyes explained his growing belief that "In a holy community, there is no more reason why sexual intercourse should be restrained by law, than why eating and drinking should be—and there is as little reason for shame in the one case as in the other." As part of the celebration of the new Christian community that Noyes and his followers saw as fast approaching, they came to believe that just as in heaven people "neither marry nor are given in marriage," so in the community of the already perfect there could be no "jealousy of exclusiveness." "I call a certain woman my wife—she is yours, she is Christ's, and in him she is the bride of all saints . . . she is dear in the hand of a stranger, and . . . I rejoice."[20]

As news of the Putney Perfectionist community's beliefs and practices became known, the Vermont clergy and the Vermont legal authorities began to take a very dim view of their affairs. In the fall of 1847 Noyes was arrested for breaking the state's laws against adultery. Rather than face trial, and possible jail, Noyes and his followers moved to a farm near Syracuse, New York, and founded their lasting home at Oneida. Within a year the Oneida Association, as it became known, had eighty-seven members drawn from Perfectionist converts across New England and New York. After some difficult early days—romanticized in later years as in many communities—Oneida grew and prospered financially and socially.[21]

At Oneida, Noyes's understanding of complex marriage was at the heart of the community and all who joined had to do so on Noyes's terms, accepting many different sexual partners for themselves and forgoing any jealous hold on a specific partner. The Oneida community made no effort to hide its sexual beliefs and practices. In 1848 Noyes published *Bible Argument: Defining the Relations of the Sexes in the Kingdom of Heaven.* It that book he argued that monogamy was clearly incompatible with the Bible's emphasis on universal love and with human nature which led many to see marriage as a prison that "gives to sexual appetite only a scanty and monotonous allowance." Sexual pleasure was a gift from God to be enjoyed by God's children, Noyes insisted. And the perfect communism of the early Christian community demanded the sharing of that love without any exclusive or jealous reservations.[22]

There was much more to Oneida than its sexual practices, however. Communist marriage was part of a much larger effort at building a utopian Christian communal society on a small scale. As Noyes wrote and said repeatedly, absolute communism in property—in which nothing was jealously held back or "owned"—was a way of recreating what the early Christians experienced after the day of Pentecost when "all that believed were together and had all things in common; and sold their possessions and goods and parted them to all, as every man had need." In fairly short order they consolidated their community by moving from a number of small buildings into one large Mansion House that provided housing for most members and a communal meeting space for up to several hundred.[23]

From most of the accounts, Oneida was a happy but complicated place for people to live. Noyes and his inner circle dominated every aspect of the community's life. One needed permission from the leaders to select a new sexual partner. And Noyes's theological views were not to be challenged. On the other hand, there was a strong bond among the community members; there was unusual equality among individuals and between the sexes. Work was shared, and after the first few years the burdens were relatively light compared to the work life of most other nineteenth-century Americans. The inventiveness of the community members ensured economic prosperity.

Writing after the dissolution of the community in 1879, Jessie Catherine Kinsley tried to describe for her own daughter what life had been like at Oneida. It must have been a daunting task, in late Victorian America, to try to explain to a child of those times what her mother's life had been like one generation but a cultural millennium earlier. Kinsley reflected on her initiation into complex marriage as a young teenager.

> There came a time when we entered the social life of the Community [at Oneida social was a euphemism for sexual]. I will not speak too intimately of that. Looking back upon it, I do not wholly understand it, nor do I unreservedly approve of all that experience. I see faults of a grave nature. Perhaps there was "self seeking" in the conduct of some; nevertheless, the thought to forestall stolen loves and to make desire legitimate was, I believe, the purpose

of those in authority—those who managed our lives—while in our hearts was innocence and struggle for unselfishness, and toward Mr. Noyes, loyalty as to one almost divine. I was sixteen when I loved G. A. (George Allen). The love began in a romantic way and was a part of my happy life for years. At length I saw him become interested in a woman greatly my superior in looks and in mentality, and because I would not then strive for what I thought would be selfishly sought, we drifted apart. . . . I loved G. (George Allen) and C. (Charles Cragin) and O. (Orrin Wright).

Kinsley continued with a plea to her daughter to try to understand what must have seemed exceedingly strange to her. Remember, she seems to be saying, that there was a larger purpose to it all, that we were trying to achieve something great in our own faith and for the world.

Dear Edith, if imagination carries you back into the unusual past that I cannot describe you must think that religious devotion was a part of it all. In its religion you will find the key to this Community life. We applied religious phraseology to everyday life curiously and, if I mistake not, without hypocrisy (truly without hypocrisy to those of us who knew no other existence, no other explanation). The fulfillment of Complex Marriage was an "Ordinance"—a loving "ordinance of fellowship"—more earnest than the kiss or the everyday handclasp, no doubt, but simple, sacred, without guile or unrestrained passion; "a communion of spirit and body."[24]

The fact that Oneida with its ordinance of complex marriage and its commitment to Bible Communism flourished for three decades is a tribute to the degree that this communion of spirit and body worked for many of its members.

Oneida was not equal in its treatment of women. But it did offer women far more equality than was available almost anywhere else in the United States in the nineteenth century. Noyes had developed a method of male contraception that seems to have worked very well and dramatically freed Oneida women from unwanted pregnancy. He and the community also insisted that both partners had a duty to attend to the sexual pleasure of the other and a man who failed at this duty could be severely criticized. A woman who chose to become pregnant received support from her sisters and brothers. For the first year after the child's birth, she was freed from work to care for the child. After that the child was turned over to the Children's House to be reared collectively while the mother returned to the general life of the community. Oneida memoirs provide a mixed picture of collective child rearing, some finding in it a great freedom and others a wrenching separation from the children they had born and loved.[25]

Members of the Oneida community not only shared their worldly goods and their sexual loves. They also sought to make Oneida a beautiful place and to add to their comfort and prosperity through an amazing number of inventions. They studied the major landscapers of the mid-nineteenth century, including Frederick Law Olmsted, and designed gardens and buildings at Oneida that are still beautiful one hundred years later.[26]

The Oneida community embraced technology, celebrating the introduction of steam heat to their buildings in 1869. Technology was also the key to the community's prosperity. In the mid-1850s, at a low point in their financial fortunes, Sewall Newhouse, a member of the community, began building a new form of hunting trap that was widely sought. Other members of the community quickly developed methods for the mass production of the traps, and by the Civil War the community was producing 275,000 steel traps a year and its fortune was assured. Well before the demand for the traps began to decline, another venture that started with the making of tin spoons would assure Oneida's legacy. The Oneida silverware empire emerged only after the dissolution of the community, but that company's fortune assured employment for the community's descendants and the financial resources to preserve the Oneida story and the Oneida buildings into the twenty-first century.[27]

In the end Oneida fell victim to the prudishness of the Victorian era. It also fell victim to its dependence on a single charismatic leader and to internal debates by a generation that came to chafe at his dictates. Between 1875 and 1879 Oneida was torn by debates between loyalists who insisted on the old ways and dissidents who believed that members of the community should be given much more freedom in the selection of sexual partners—without needing the permission of the inner circle. Jessie Kinsley described the change: "There were scenes in the Evening Meetings. The disaffected began to sit in the gallery and from there hurl words upon the loyalists. Open scorn, hatred and rebellion were shown in many places. You will understand the misery of this if you contrast it with the almost complete harmony of the past extending backward beyond the limits of my life."[28]

Pre-1875 Oneida may never have been as harmonious as Kinsley thought, but something significant had changed. Noyes's efforts to get the community to elect his son, Theodore Noyes, as his successor only made matters worse. And after a decade of quiet, the outside world was again intruding with threats of arrests for Oneida's clear and public flouting of the marriage laws of the state of New York.

In 1879 Noyes himself suddenly fled to Canada, partly to avoid arrest but probably also to escape the tensions growing up around his leadership. In the year that followed, the community, with Noyes' blessing from Canada, abandoned its system of complex marriage, and couples who wanted to joined in conventional marriages. As its publications had prophesied for thirty years, economic communism could not be sustained in the face of monogamy, and communal ownership was exchanged for shares in the communal enterprises, the Oneida Community, Ltd. The silverware part of the business insured that the descendants lived well and the historical record was preserved. But the community itself had ended.[29]

Nevertheless, the Oneida Community was a beacon of hope to many for the thirty years of its existence. At one time Noyes had hoped that the community would be recreated over and over again, but that did not happen. Still, Oneida remains a symbol of the hopeful exuberance, the willingness to break out from ancient constraints, and the embrace of a better—even a potentially perfect—future that is part of the American heritage.

ROBERT OWEN AND THE NEW HARMONY COMMUNITY

John Humphrey Noyes clearly saw Oneida as part of a larger communitarian movement. In 1870 he published *History of American Socialisms*. While Oneida emerges from Noyes's history as perhaps the best example of a utopian socialist community, it is far from the only example. Indeed, Noyes acknowledges his debt to the work of Robert Owen and the members of the community Owen founded at New Harmony, Indiana.[30]

Owen himself was a product of the dislocation of the Industrial Revolution in England. Born in a working class family in Wales in 1771, he began work in a drapery shop in London at the age of ten. His early interest in religion ended by the time he was fourteen when, he wrote, "my religious feelings, were immediately replaced by the spirit of universal charity—not for a sect or a party, or for a country or a colour—but for the human race, and with a real and ardent desire to do them good."[31] In time Owen was one of the winners in industrializing England, but he did not forget his early commitments. After making a considerable fortune for himself, he founded a utopian model factory town at New Lanark, Scotland, in which he sought to put the spirit of universal charity into practice. Owen championed child labor legislation, and supported factory inspection and unemployment legislation at a time when few of the industrial leaders of Britain were prepared to even consider such socialistic ideas. But the heart of his effort was in the creation of a utopian socialist community where a new and different model of human economy could emerge.[32]

After what he considered success at New Lanark in the early 1820s, Owen decided to seek a wider stage for his version of utopian socialism in the United

States. He purchased land in New Harmony, Indiana, and published his plans in *Discourses on a New System of Society*. In that announcement he said: "By a hard struggle you have attained a political liberty, but you have yet to acquire real mental liberty, and if you cannot possess yourselves of it, your political liberty will be precarious and of much less value."[33] At New Harmony, Owen meant to show the way to "real mental liberty."

Owen's vision for establishing his utopia in the New World seemed to be an immediate success. He was welcomed in Indiana and also in Washington, D.C. where he spoke twice before Congress. In the early months of 1825 some nine hundred people arrived at New Harmony including, as Owen's son, Robert Dale Owen, wrote, "a heterogeneous collection of radicals, enthusiastic devotees to principle, honest latudinarians, and lazy theorists, with a sprinkling of unprincipled sharpers thrown in."[34]

There are differing accounts of life at New Harmony, but all of them reflect the high level of energy and commitment of many of the community's members. There was music and dancing, a Female Social Society, and a range of other gatherings. Visiting preachers were welcome, but the community espoused no religious creed.

In launching New Harmony, Owen set it up with a temporary government vested solely in himself, but with a plan for a relatively quick transition toward a radical communitarianism. Within months, Owen announced that it was time for the transition and a Community of Equality with power vested equally in all of the adult residents was declared. At about the same time, in 1826, Owen personally condemned the institutions of private property, organized religion, and marriage, a move that strengthened the loyalty of some and alienated others.

In reality, New Harmony failed within a year. The transition from Owen's benevolent but centralized rule to totally shared government was probably far too quick. The community was never able to attract enough skilled workers to make it economically successful. The socializing was controlled by an elite and not necessarily welcomed by all of the community's residents. As one disaffected resident recalled, the "aristocrats" quarreled and the cabbage fields went to ruin. Owen himself lost the great bulk of his fortune, which he had invested in New Harmony, but returned to England to continue to advocate his version of social reform.[35]

Nevertheless, New Harmony was a powerful example in the early years of the nineteenth century. Many later reformers—whether deeply religious as the Shakers or the Oneida community or secular as New Harmony—tried to copy its successes and avoid its failures. The nineteenth-century history of the United States is far from complete unless the wonderful and diverse range of utopian, communal, and communistic ventures, from the relatively tame New England Transcendentalists at Brook Farm to the wildly controversial and successful Mormons who ultimately gathered in Utah, are included as major players in the story. In later generations, the stories of these communities would inspire some, horrify others, and give hopes to many that human society could be organized along more loving and humane lines than had yet been invented.

CHAPTER THREE

MEXICO IN THE UNITED STATES

WAR WITH MEXICO, 1846–1848

THE ATTACK ON MEXICO and the subsequent conquest by the United States of the northern half of its southern neighbor's territory represents one of the least hopeful stories in this nation's history. A decade before the war began in earnest, former President John Quincy Adams warned the Congress of what was to come: "Sirs, the banners of freedom will be the banners of Mexico . . . and your banners, I blush to speak the word, will be the banners of slavery. . . . Again I ask, what will be the cause of such a war? Aggression, conquest and the establishment of slavery where it has been abolished!" A decade later much to his regret, Adams was proved right on all points.[1]

The war with Mexico from 1846 to 1848 represents, at best, a footnote in most studies of the history of the United States. Nevertheless, the war was a terribly important event in the history of both nations. It shaped the geography as well as the culture and world view of the citizens of both lands, and most of all it impacted the many citizens of Mexico who virtually overnight found themselves to be citizens—but second-class citizens—of the United States.

The Mexican War, as it was known in the United States, was significant in several ways. It was the first clearly imperialistic war in the nation's history. Although both the Revolution and the War of 1812 had some imperialistic connotations—one of the causes of the Revolution was the British refusal to let whites settle beyond the fall line of the Alleghenies, and the War of 1812 was sparked by U.S. interest in conquering Canada—the Mexican War was specifically waged in the name of a "manifest destiny" to conquer the land of another nation and expand this one.

The War with Mexico was also a precursor of the American Civil War in many ways; it was waged to expand the slaveholding portions of the United States and to support legalized slavery in Texas. The Republic of Mexico had outlawed slavery in 1830. The Americans who already lived in Texas had no intention of giving up slaves, and the existing slave states not only had sympathy for the slaveholding Texans, they wanted more slave states represented in the U.S. Senate. With Texas in the Union, the slave states would have a two-vote margin over the free states in any controversial measure that might come before the national Congress.[2]

The War with Mexico was an unusually brutal war. While there have probably never been any nonbrutal wars, in this war the thirst for land and the racism of the American forces led to a terrorism with few restraints. Ulysses S. Grant, then just beginning his army career, wrote, "Some of the volunteers and about all the Texans seem to think it perfectly right to impose on the people of a conquered city to any extent, and even to murder them where the act can be covered by dark. And how much they seem to enjoy acts of violence too!"[3]

At the war's end in 1848, the Treaty of Guadalupe Hidalgo officially added Texas and California and most of what would be the states of New Mexico, Arizona, Utah, and Colorado to the United States. The thirst for land, for fulfilling a manifest destiny to be a continental nation had fueled the war spirit long before hostilities began. But the war can only be understood by examining events that were taking place in the two largest states—California and Texas—that would be added to the Union by it.

European settlements in California had begun in the mid-1700s. Unlike Spain's elite conquerors who had explored the lands north of Mexico in earlier times, the California settlers were for the most part from Mexico's, and occasionally Spain's, poorest classes. The majority were mestizos of mixed European, African, and Indian families. In 1781 the settler population stood at around six hundred and as late as 1821 California's total Mexican population was around three thousand. The majority lived on large ranches spread along the coast. A few immigrants from the United States had also moved to California in the early 1800s; most of them converted to Catholicism, took on Mexican citizenship, and became part of the local culture of the region known as Alta California.[4]

Beginning in the 1840s a different group of immigrants from the United States, people specifically interested in California as part of the United States, came to the region. They were supported by the U.S. government, specifically by President James K. Polk (1845–1849) who told Congress that California's harbors "would afford shelter for our navy, for our numerous whale ships, and other merchant vessels employed in the Pacific ocean, and would in a short period become the marts of an extensive and profitable commerce with China, and other countries of the East."[5]

Emboldened by this show of support, a group of armed Americans awakened the symbol of Mexican authority in Sonoma, General Mariano Vallejo, on the morning of June 6, 1846, and jailed him at Fort Sutter near Sacramento, even though Vallejo had previously retired from active duty. With no other Mexican leaders in sight, the Bear Flag rebels declared California to be an independent Republic. To the Mexicans like Vallejo, these new immigrants were *los Osos*, the bears who came as thieves to take their cattle and their land. And the bears were winning. Soon after Vallejo's arrest, the U.S. Navy sailed into Monterey Bay and California was declared a possession of the United States. The independent republic had been a short lived convenience.[6]

At the same time, events in Texas had taken a dramatic turn. As in California, small groups of immigrants who had come north from the heartland of Mexico mixed with other small groups of immigrants who had come west from the United States. Coexistence in Texas was never as smooth as it had been in the early days of California. American imperial designs appeared much earlier. The first large-scale insurrection against Mexican authority had taken place in 1836 when a group of American sympathizing rebels seized an old mission, the Alamo, in San Antonio. They achieved immortality by getting themselves killed by the much larger Mexican army. Sam Houston had then organized the counterattack and forced the Mexican general Santa Anna to cede Texas from Mexico to a newly independent Texas Republic. Although Mexican authorities quickly repudiated the terms of Santa Anna's surrender, Texas functioned as a separate nation for almost a decade until, under the newly inaugurated President James K. Polk, it was annexed by the United States in 1845.

As a result of the U.S. annexation of Texas, land that Mexico still claimed as its own, Mexico broke off diplomatic relations with the United States. In 1846, President Polk sent the U.S. Army to enforce its claimed border at the Rio Grande River. A skirmish with Mexican troops on May 11, 1846, led Polk to declare war with Mexico and launch the U.S. forces on a brutal march into Mexico. Also in 1846, U.S. Army general Stephen Watts Kearny led his troops to the Governor's Palace in Santa Fe, New Mexico, and won that region's surrender without firing a shot.[7] Kearny then went on to Los Angeles where his arrival, linked to the navy's landing under Commodores John D. Sloat and Robert F. Stockton, completed the annexation of California.

In September 1847, the U.S. Army occupied Mexico City, and early in 1848 the government of Mexico signed the Treaty of Guadalupe Hidalgo under which the United States paid Mexico $15 million and Mexico ceded

Texas, California, New Mexico, Nevada, and parts of Colorado, Arizona, and Utah, to its northern neighbor. The Mexican Republic lost half of its land area and the United States became a continental nation. Of course, the Mexican citizens who lived in this northern half of their country suddenly became what the historian Ronald Takaki called "foreigners in their native land." In spite of treaty guarantees, they lost both land and voting rights, and were reduced to the cultural margins in a land in which they had lived for generations.[8]

In its largest outlines, there is little that is hopeful in this early adventure in American imperialism. And yet, at the same time, the very horror of this virtually forgotten war and its aftermath led to many hopeful developments: notably, the protests of the antiwar movement, especially as expressed in the work of Henry David Thoreau, remain a part of this nation's memory to the present. Other parts of the story, including the liberal democratic hopes of California's old aristocracy as illustrated in figures such as Mariano Vallejo, and the active and sometimes violent resistance of the conquered poorest Mexicans of the southwest, *las masas de los hombres pobres* (the masses of poor men), need to be rediscovered.[9] They are as much a part of the history of the United States, a prouder and more hopeful part, than the too-often-told tales of wars and presidents, conquers and oppressors.

THE FIRST AMERICAN ANTIWAR MOVEMENT

While individual Americans have always opposed war, be they pacifist Quakers and Shakers, loyalist opponents of the American Revolution, or the New England resisters to the War of 1812, the war with Mexico created a larger, better organized, and far more articulate peace movement than the nation had seen up to that time. President Polk's call for war, though popular, did not pass Congress unanimously. Fourteen congressmen and two senators led by the old John Quincy Adams campaigned and voted against the president's call for war. As an aspiring Whig politician from Illinois, Abraham Lincoln was elected to Congress in the middle of the war. In spite of the urging of the majority of his friends and political supporters that he not get caught up in the opposition to a popular war, Lincoln quickly joined the Adams camp. Only weeks into his term, Lincoln went on record, first with a series of questions to President Polk and then with his own response. If Polk did not provide a satisfactory answer to his questions about the origins of the war, Lincoln said,

> . . . then I shall be fully convinced, of what I am more than suspect already, that he is deeply conscious of being in the wrong; that he feels the blood of

this war, like the blood of Abel, is crying to Heaven against him; that he or-dered General Taylor into the midst of a peaceful Mexican settlement, pur-posely to bring on a war; that originally having some strong motive—what I will not stop now to give my opinion concerning—to involve the two coun-tries in a war, and trusting to escape scrutiny by fixing the public gaze upon the exceeding brightness of military glory—that attractive rainbow that rises in showers of blood—that serpent's eye that charms to destroy—he plunged into it and has swept on and on, till, disappointed in his calculation of the ease with which Mexico might be subdued, he now finds himself he knows not where. How like the half-insane mumblings of a fever dream is the whole war part of the late message![10]

Lincoln was a minor player in these events compared to many in Con-gress and elsewhere, however. But perhaps the most influential response came from a poet rather than a politician. While he is remembered today mostly for his reflective stay at Walden Pond, Henry David Thoreau was a much more complex figure. His Transcendental theology made him a kind of anarchist. He believed in the all-sufficient individual and had little use for social obliga-tions of any kind—good or bad. Indeed, for all of its beautiful stories of nature, *Walden* is more than a reflection on the beauty of the created world. It is really, as its author said in conclusion, a theological brief for a certain form of belief. "I learned this, at least, by my experiment: that if one advances confidently in the direction of his dreams, and endeavors to live the life which he has imag-ined, he will meet with a success unexpected in common hours. He will put some things behind, will pass an invisible boundary; new, universal, and more liberal laws will begin to establish themselves around and within him." [11] Live simply, live well, and first the individual, and then the society in which that in-dividual lives, will start to change, Thoreau was saying.

In *Civil Disobedience*, Thoreau moved further. His basic anarchism was quite clear. Accepting the motto "that government is best which governs least," Thoreau expanded it to voice his hope that the day would come when the watchword would be, "that government is best which governs not at all."[12] While the nation's war policy and the taxes levied on him personally to support that policy were the focus of his essay, the heart of Thoreau's message was a more far-reaching attack on all government as inherently oppressive. "The ob-jections which have been brought against a standing army, and they are many and weighty, and deserve to prevail," he argued, "may also at last be brought against a standing government." For it was the standing government, in the present case, that had sent the standing army to its terrible war against Mexico.[13]

Short of the abolition of government, Thoreau asked "at once" for a "bet-ter government." But what, he then asked, was a better government? It was one in which the right of conscience was supreme; in which no one would "resign his conscience to the legislator." He clearly asserted "The only obligation which I have a right to assume is to do at any time what I think right."[14] It would be a difficult philosophy around which to organize a society, but it clearly gave a much needed voice of passionate protest to the evils of a federal government that was expanding slavery and waging a vicious war against another nation.

In the case of the war with Mexico, Thoreau's civil disobedience focused where he could act most immediately. He had little patience with petitions or voting, which was not in any case likely to make much of a difference as far as he could see. But "I meet this American government, or its representative the State government, directly, and face to face, once a year, no more, in the person of its tax-gatherer." And this was the clear opportunity to resist the government's injustice.[15] He was not willing to be like "the thousands who are in opinion opposed to slavery and to the war, who yet in effect do nothing. . . . They hesitate, and they regret, and sometimes they petition; but they do nothing in earnest and with effect."[16] For Thoreau there was a clear and obvious way to do something in earnest, to publicly wash his hands of the twin evils of slavery and the war on Mexico. He would refuse to pay taxes and accept the consequences.

He did not mind being sent to jail for his crime of conscience. Indeed, he saw jail as the only place to assert the kind of society he most deeply longed for:

> Under a government which imprisons any unjustly, the true place for a just man is also a prison. The proper place today, the only place which Massachusetts has provided for her freer and less despondent spirits, is in her prisons. . . . It is there that the fugitive slave, and the Mexican prisoner on parole, and the Indian come to plead the wrongs of his race, should find them; on that separate but more free and honorable ground, where the State places those who are not *with* her but *against* her,—the only house in a slave-state in which a free man can abide with honor.[17]

And so Thoreau meant to abide, in freedom and honor.

Civil Disobedience was an essay that made little difference in the war. Thoreau was too easy to dismiss as an amiable crank. But in the longer run of history, Thoreau's essay and his action in refusing to pay taxes in support of what he considered an unjust war became a model of a different kind of society—of a beloved community—that influenced Mohandas Gandhi, resistance fighters in Nazi-occupied Europe, and, of course, Martin Luther King Jr., and protesters against a later U.S. imperialistic venture in Vietnam.

MEXICAN LIBERALISM
IN CALIFORNIA

The American conquest of California was much less protracted and much less bloody than the war along the Rio Grande in Texas. Indeed it seems as if they were different wars. The Mexican government was much less interested in California than in Texas, a reality that had allowed a unique Californian culture to develop in the early decades of the nineteenth century. And Mexican citizens of California, the products of this culture, had a decidedly ambivalent attitude toward annexation by the United States.

In a total of eight battles and skirmishes between July of 1846 and the end of hostilities on the west coast in January 1847, approximately thirty-five of those fighting on the American side died in battle while an estimated eight Californians (those fighting with more or less commitment for the Mexican cause) were killed. The Californians also suffered much greater losses in property and eventually they lost their whole way of life.[18] While tragic, this was a tiny toll in death and suffering compared to the horrors of Texas and the American army's march to Mexico City.

There were many reasons for the limited nature of the warfare in California. The total population of California was very small and most of the regular Mexican forces had abandoned the region before hostilities even began. Probably even more significant, most of the Mexican leaders in California, men such as Mariano Vallejo and Juan Bandini, were really hoping for an American takeover to replace the distant and inept Mexican administration and the lawlessness of the American frontiersmen of the independence movement, who were seeking to create their own Bear Flag Republic. Indeed, many historians have concluded that if it had not been for the grandiose bungling of U.S. military leader John C. Fremont—bungling for which he was later court-marshaled—California might have become part of the United States with no shots having been fired.[19]

The historian Robert J. Rosenbaum has captured the worldview of the Californios, the elite of the Mexican community that controlled California, virtually free from any meaningful influence from the government in Mexico City in the decades leading up to American annexation. In Rosenbaum's account, three characteristics of these leaders—their secularism, their liberalism, and their romantic attitude toward American democracy—made them ready to welcome a takeover by the United States even if the actual result left them disillusioned and embittered.

To begin with, the Californios were secularists. Although he remained a lifelong Roman Catholic, Vallejo's relationship with the church reflected the same tension experienced by other liberals around the world. Indeed, early in his life a Catholic priest with whom Vallejo was feuding excommunicated him—temporarily it seems—for smuggling forbidden copies of the works of Voltaire and Rousseau into California from an American ship. As Vallejo recalled the incident in his *Memoirs*, he noted that for the church, "books were the most to be feared emissaries of the goddess whom we call Liberty. . . ." And given these choices, liberty was the higher good for Vallejo.[20]

While most of them maintained nominal ties to the Roman Catholic Church, the Californios were deeply at odds with the church and the priests on both economic and intellectual matters. In 1824 the Mexican Constitution authorized the secularization of church lands. Beginning in 1831, the California missions were transferred from the padres to ranchers like Vallejo. As a result, the ranchers moved from being moderately well-off to being very rich while their major political competitors—the religious orders—were removed from contention.

As with many things in his life, Vallejo's deep commitment to secularism and freedom served him well. When the government of Mexico secularized the California missions, Vallejo managed to have himself appointed as the administrator of the Mission San Francisco de Solano. Half of the mission's considerable resources were to be used to support the Sonoma pueblo and the other half for the support of the Native American tribes who had created most of the mission's wealth, but Vallejo did not suffer financially for his administrative duties.[21]

Although control of the land was at the heart of their secularism, there was more. As Rosenbaum has noted, "The liberal spirit that spurred Mexican independence and shook all of Latin America influenced many young Californios. Scions of prominent families like Mariano Vallejo and the brothers Andres and Pio Pico yearned for education, freedom of expression, and self-government. They reacted against religious institutions first." They saw traditional Catholic orthodoxy as mere superstition at odds with their Enlightenment worldview. So, Rosenbaum says, "Men refused to participate in devotions until by the end of the Mexican regime only women, children, and neophytes attended mass, and many of the gentry refused to pay their tithe."[22]

Yet even while they were deeply immersed in the liberal spirit of the original Mexican Revolution, Vallejo and his counterparts became more and more alienated from the prevailing Mexican governments. Indeed, their words started to sound more and more anti-Mexican. They saw the government as a faraway institution that viewed California as too distant to be interesting but a good place to send convicts who undermined the genteel lifestyle they were trying to build. Their loyalty was to their families, their land, and their way of life. Patriotism to the Mexican nation was a very weak attribute.

As military coup followed military coup in Mexico City, the needs of the distant Californios received less and less attention. Coups and countercoups among California's Mexican governors, some of them involving Vallejo himself, added to his cynicism. He wanted a government that would work. And increasingly the government of the United States seemed the right one. In 1845 the president of Mexico, José Joaquin de Herrera, had organized an army of six hundred troops ready to sail from Acapulco to the defense of California. But in December a military coup led by General José Paredes ended that campaign. It was the last straw for Vallejo. While a few of the old California leaders clung loyally to Mexico, the majority were debating the various merits of independence, annexation to the United States, or some form of protectorate by England or France.

Between the mid-1820s and the crucial 1840s, the Californios became more and more aware of and enamored with the American Revolution and the American form of government. They read the works of Thomas Jefferson and others. They knew the United States better in theory than in reality. As Rosenbaum notes, "Those fired by the spirit of *liberalismo* found the theory of American government attractive. The maritime trade strengthened this attraction. Trade turned the products of the rancheros' land into wealth and provided the luxury goods essential to a grand style of living." American republicanism and American capitalism appealed to them more than what they saw as Mexican corruption and feudalism.[23]

Now virtually forgotten but for the fact that a town and a submarine are named after him, Mariano Vallejo is a fascinating and enigmatic voice for hope in the midst of a painful era of change. Mariano Guadalupe Vallejo was born in Monterey, California, in 1807, when California was still a part of the Spanish empire. His father had been among the soldiers sent with the Franciscan missionaries led by Junipero Serra to establish missions and conquer California for the Catholic Church and the Spanish monarchy. Though living at the farthest end of Spain's new world empire, Vallejo was positioned to receive a very cosmopolitan education.

Living in the presidio at Monterey, the capital of Alta California, the young Vallejo was taken under the wing of the Spanish governor Pablo Vicente de Sola, who taught him the nineteenth-century liberalism of Spain and Mexico. It was a liberalism of individualism, tolerance, and secularism. Throughout his life, Vallejo maintained all of these characteristics. His individualism could be seen in both his careful attention to his own interests and those of his family and his unwillingness, even in the face of extreme provocation, to respond to all Californians or all Americans as a group. His tolerance was reflected in both his intellectual ideas and his approach to the fast-changing issues of his homeland.

And his secularism allowed him to remain a nominal Catholic while, when the time was right, quickly taking over the land and resources of the secularized California missions. Institutional loyalty to the Catholic Church or patriotism to Spain, Mexico, or later the United States rested far more lightly on him. In his basic approach to life, this Californian was not very different from many of the liberals who dominated European politics in the Victorian era.[24]

When Vallejo wrote his memoirs late in his life, he remembered the welcome he extended to the first Americans. It was a welcome based on his inherent Spanish and Mexican notion of required hospitality. But it was also a welcome extended out of his newly defined idea of the form that enlightened self-interest should take for a liberal and ambitious California leader:

> The arrival of so many people from the outside world was highly satisfying to us "arribenos" [northern Californians] who were . . . gratified to see numerous parties of industrious individuals come and settle among us permanently. Although they were not possessed of wealth, due to their goodly share of enlightenment, they could give a powerful stimulus to our agriculture which, unfortunately, was still in a state of inactivity, owing to the lack of strong and intelligent workers. . . . [25]

Like other liberals in the old world and the new, Vallejo was rejecting the feudalism of the past. Three decades before the birth of the Republican party, Vallejo had developed his own vision of "free soil and free men" for the California situation.

During the crucial year of 1846 Vallejo traveled through much of the region indicating his clear determination of the course to follow. Vallejo's stump speech was first published a few years later. Vallejo was still an official of the Mexican government at the time and it would have been unwise to have a formal copy available in 1846. Nevertheless, the version of the speech that was eventually recorded seems to represent a good summary of Vallejo's political views in the mid-1840s at the time of the greatest conflict between the United States and Mexico.[26]

> It is most true, that to rely any longer upon Mexico to govern and defend us, would be idle and absurd. . . . We are republicans—badly governed and badly situated as we are—still we are, in sentiment republicans. . . . Why then should we hesitate still to assert our independence? We have indeed taken the first step, by electing our own governor, but another remains to be taken . . . annexation to the United States.

There was no ambiguity in the future Vallejo wanted for California.

As he continued his speech, Vallejo also made it clear that he had given considerable thought to what American citizenship meant for the residents of California.

> Why should we go abroad for protection when this great nation is our adjoining neighbor? When we join our fortunes to hers, we shall not become subjects, but fellow citizens, possessing all the rights of the people of the United States and choosing our own federal and local rulers. We shall have a stable government and just laws. California will grow strong and flourish, and her people will be prosperous, happy, and free.[27]

With resistance of this sort, it is no wonder that the American cause triumphed so easily in Mexican California. Vallejo knew the ideals of the United States far better than he knew the reality. And so he dreamed of a union of equals that would serve both well. It was not to be.

Not all of the Californios shared Vallejo's and the Pico brothers' optimism about the United States. Antonio Maria Osio, less well known than Vallejo or the Picos but still an important merchant and land holder in the Mexican era, described himself as "a Californio who loves his country and a Mexican on all four sides and in my heart." He wanted little to do with the conquering Americans for he was convinced that "experience has always shown that conquerors never have been able to maintain a brotherhood with those they have conquered."[28] His words were more prophetic than Vallejo's. And Osio did not try to make the adjustments that Vallejo later did. Instead, remaining a loyal citizen of Mexico, he left Alta California in 1852 for San Jose del Cabo in Baja California, Republic of Mexico, where he lived until his death in 1878.[29]

The war, such as it was, and the transfer of authority in California took place in two stages. In June 1846, a group of frontiersmen declared California to be an independent Republic. They raised their own Bear Flag—still the state flag of California—on the plaza in Sonoma and arrested Vallejo in his own home. He was held until ordered released by the American forces that finally took control of the area at the end of the summer.[30] At the time of his release he wrote to the American counsel, "The political change has cost a great deal to my person and mind, and likewise to my property." The worst was yet to come.[31]

In 1847 the final skirmishes between California defenders under Andres Pico and the American troops took place in southern California. For all of their ambivalence about Mexican authority, these Mexican citizens were reluctant to allow themselves to be conquered. Antonio Osio recorded their guerrilla warfare. "Let it be known for all time that even though they were unable to do more for their native land and for the country of their birth, these men should serve as an example for other places invaded by forces from the United States."[32] As it became increasingly clear that no support could be expected from Mexico, Pico negotiated the terms of what he saw as an honorable surrender. In January 1847, Pico's troops marched into Los Angeles on their own and disbanded. The American control of the region was complete.[33]

Vallejo played a modest role in the transition to American statehood. He served in the 1849 constitutional convention that wrote the state's charter. It incorporated Mexico's prohibition of slavery and granted Native Americans the right to vote. Vallejo played a leading role in the successful effort to ensure the right of wives to own property, not an easy victory in 1849 but consistent with his own longstanding liberalism.[34]

Ultimately the greed of those newly arrived from the United States, supported by the corruption of the American legal institutions, virtually destroyed the economic base for the new culture that Vallejo hoped to build and with it his dreams of a new society of equals. Looking back, Vallejo described the impact of American statehood and the concurrent gold rush on California. He described the havoc wrought by representatives of many parts of the globe, including escapees from the British penal colony of Australia, and continued:

> But all these evils became negligible in comparison with the swollen torrent of shysters who came from Missouri and other states of the Union. No sooner had they arrived than they assumed the title of attorney and began to seek means of depriving the Californians of their farms and other properties. The escaped bandits from Australia stole our cattle and our horses; but these legal thieves, clothed in the robes of the law, took from us our lands and our houses, and without the least scruple, enthroned themselves in our homes like so many powerful kings. For them existed no law but their own will and their caprice.[35]

In fact Vallejo's angry characterization was quite accurate. His dreams of being an equal citizen of the United States never materialized.[36]

The vehicle by which the "legal thieves" stole the land of the Californians was an institution established even before statehood was granted: The United States Land Commission was set up by the constitutional convention specifically to challenge the Mexican land grants on which Vallejo's and his compatriots' fortunes rested. Although the Treaty of Guadalupe Hidalgo had specifically promised that all residents of these lands "shall be maintained and protected in the free enjoyment of their liberty and property," the Land Commission treated every grant as invalid until documented and proven. The result for many of the old families was that they lost their land, either to the lawyers who defended their claims or to the process itself. In 1862 the United States Supreme Court ruled against Vallejo. The vast majority of the lands on which his fortune and his way of life had been based were lost and he was deeply in debt. Thanks to the good will of others, especially his American son-in-law, Vallejo lived out his life in a kind of genteel poverty. Others were not nearly so lucky. For at least the next century and a half, being of Mexican descent in California meant second-class citizenship.[37]

Vallejo's dream of a liberal, American future for California was deeply flawed, most of all by his own romanticism about the racist reality of the United States in the 1840s. Other historians have debated the merits of Vallejo's life and work and the impact of the old Californians on the subsequent experience of Mexicans in California, both the descendants of the old residents and the far more numerous later immigrants.[38] While there were many flaws in Vallejo's worldview, in his speeches and his actions both before and after the annexation, he also represented a vision of a better future that should not be forgotten.

It is reported that when the American frontiersmen of the Bear Flag revolt entered Vallejo's home to arrest him, they could not have been more surprised to find a "parlor . . . furnished with handsome chairs, sofas, mirrors, and tables of mahogany framework, and a fine piano. . . . Several paintings and some superior engravings ornamented the walls."[39] Further, they could not have comprehended the fact that the symbolic leader of Mexican authority was, in fact, a liberal republican, much more deeply committed to the best notions of democracy in the American republic than they were. Vallejo's type of nineteenth-century liberalism has virtually disappeared from public discourse, not only in California and the United States but elsewhere. It was naïve. It was too individualistic to deal with the complex reality of industrialized society. It did not account for the power of racism to shape human affairs. But it also contained the hope for a humane, tolerant, prosperous, and democratic future well worth remembering.

LAS GORRAS BLANCAS

In 1936 a historian employed by the Works Progress Administration interviewed Mary A. Fulgenzi, one of the long-time residents of San Miguel County, New Mexico. Fulgenzi recalled a time earlier in her life when hope and resistance came together within the Mexican community of the northeastern corner of New Mexico. She described the situation that led to the growth of a powerful resistance movement nearly half a century after the war that had removed the New Mexico region from Mexico's control:

In the early days of Las Vegas [New Mexico] the wealthier people wanted to
take possession of most of the lands. They fenced in any land they fancied,
whether it belonged to them or not. The poor people also needed land to
graze their stock and felt that they should have their share, for, according to
the land grant, lands not allocated to individuals were to be used by the community in general.[40]

Throughout much of the west, the battle between those who wanted to
fence and control the land and those who wanted free and common grazing
land for their herds was one of the great divides of the late nineteenth century. Many historians have noted that the emergence of cheap barbed wire
probably did more than any sophisticated technology to change the face of
the land and people of the west.[41] In New Mexico it was the newly arrived
Anglo ranchers and speculators who wanted to fence the land. The poor
peasant-class Mexicans who had been on the land for more than a century
knew that fencing the land meant an end to their livelihood and their
lifestyle. Fulgenzi continued: "In 1889 the Herrera family from Ojitos Frios
organized a group of men into an order, Los Caballeros de Labor, the gentlemen of labor, whose purpose it was to destroy all fences so that the poor
man's stock could be pastured. They worked at night, wearing white robes
and tall pointed caps. Hence they were termed Gorras Blancas, white
caps."[42] Looking back from her vantage point to events over forty years before, Fulgenzi captured the essence of this powerful but now generally forgotten movement of resistance and hope.

Not all of the Mexicans who suddenly found themselves in a different
nation accepted the changes with the equanimity of Mariano Vallejo. Many
in California and across the southwest had traditionally lived on the margins of the society that the Vallejos dominated. For Vallejo, hope lay with a
liberal and secular republican government—Vallejo just wanted it to be fair
and respectful—for those on the margins, hope rested with being left undisturbed in their families and communities and with their land rights intact.
For the Mexicans of the southwest, hope needed to be reevaluated and
recreated in a new and different cultural and political setting once they became part of the United States. And while Vallejo made his peace as best he
could, others saw open revolt against American authority as the only hopeful road.

There were many examples of Mexican resistance in the southwest after
the official end of the war. They began with the Taos Revolt in 1847 and
continued well into the twentieth century, more than a half century after
American annexation. Flamboyant bandits, community peasant revolts,

armed bands—some organized with military precision—all fought against the oppression they were experiencing in the new American context.[43] And while the established regional authorities and the United States government viewed these revolts as simple acts of lawlessness, they were, in fact, representative of a response by one of the major groups of involuntary American citizens to Anglo-American aggression. The revolts, in their own way, also represented a hope for a different future for the Mexican communities of the American southwest.

Robert J. Rosenbaum describes the beginning of what came to be known as the White Cap uprising:

> On the night of April 26, 1889, masked and armed horsemen rode toward a ranch near the village of San Geronimo in San Miguel County, New Mexico Territory. Two Englishmen named William Rawlins and Frank Quarrell claimed the ranch, which boasted four miles of new wire fence erected at a cost of over $750. The masked band leveled the entire fence, leaving only kindling and glittering fragments. Neither posts nor wire would ever fence anything again.

Thus began a revolt that would undermine the political and legal institutions of New Mexico, that would ultimately involve the nation's then strongest labor union, the Knights of Labor, and that would have an impact on the presidential election of 1892. It also ultimately involved people as far away as the leaders of the U.S. Department of the Interior and investors on Wall Street and in other countries.

The revolt undermined the assumption that Mexican resistance to the annexation of the region by the United States was a thing of the distant past. The story of the fence-cutting rebellion in San Miguel County, New Mexico, is a fascinating and forgotten chapter. It represents a clear example not only of organized discontent but also of an alternative vision of community and of the nature of land ownership from that of individualistic capitalism, an alternative vision that encompassed "an egalitarian and anticapitalistic ideology."[44] At the heart of the battle in San Miguel County were two different views of the nature of citizenship and land ownership. Indeed, the views were so different that the two sides could never begin to understand each other and therefore, inevitably perhaps, came to see their opponents as evil.

For the vast majority of Mexicanos, especially those who saw themselves as *las masas de los hombres pobres* (the masses of the poor) the change in nationality meant very little. Their loyalty had not been to the distant government of the Republic of Mexico but to a culture and community much closer to home.

And at the very foundation of their culture and community was a view of land ownership in which most of what was not specifically part of the home or the irrigated farmland of one family was held in common. Unlike many places where Mexicano traditions were overturned immediately after the war, in San Miguel County this common ownership of the land had actually been recognized quite explicitly when the U.S. Congress in 1860 confirmed the common ownership of a huge tract of 496,446 acres of the former Spanish and Mexican government's Las Vegas Grant by the almost exclusively Mexicano town of Las Vegas, New Mexico. In this town, the older tradition in which individuals owned a small portion of land but the community collectively owned the uninhabited grazing lands would continue far longer than in most other parts of the United States.[45]

By the 1880s, however, Anglo-Americans with very different views of their nation, of land ownership, and of private property were arriving in San Miguel County. The arrival of the Atchison, Topeka, and Santa Fe Railroad in Las Vegas on New Year's Day of 1879 began a series of major changes for northeast New Mexico that would accelerate rapidly. Representing investors from the east coast of the United States and from Britain, land speculators who could not imagine any alternative to private ownership of all lands began buying up the land that was available. When they purchased specific lands from the heirs of original grant holders, they also claimed the right to an appropriate fractional interest in the communal areas. For them such an approach only made sense. For the older residents, ownership of the individual homesteads might change hands, but the communal nature of the larger areas remained inviolate.

The two viewpoints did not meet as equals in the New Mexico of the 1880s, however. A specific court case, *Millhiser v. Padilla*, was tried in San Miguel County from 1887 to 1889. When it became clear that the court was going to rule in favor of the collective land holdings, the Anglo plaintiffs withdrew and paid all court costs to avoid creating a precedent. At the same time, however, the plaintiffs continued building fences. By 1889 large areas of the land grant in sections from 1,000 to 10,000 acres were being fenced off and the Mexicanos of San Miguel County saw not only their ancient rights being trampled but also their immediate opportunities to make a living raising cattle and sheep being drastically reduced. Faced with economic disaster, they began taking matters into their own hands.[46]

If the fences were threatening their way of life, the remedy for at least a few of *las masas de los hombres pobres* was simple: get rid of the fences. The official papers of New Mexico's governor of the time, L. Bradford Prince, contain many letters like the following dated July 25, 1890:

Dear Sir,

 In reply to your favor of the 22th inst would say in regard to white caps, last year in June they cut first my pasture fence then I bought wire and repaired the fence again. In a month after they cut the same fence again and set fire in a large wood house that I had for the use of threshing wheat and the shearing machine was burned the same night. In two weeks after that they cut my farming fence and also they set fire in my sawmill and barn besides about 100,000 feet of lumber. So I am quit now on account that we have no protection in the law. This is what I can inform you of my own.

I am yours truly,
J. Y. Lujan[47]

Another correspondent sent the governor a copy of a notice that had been posted on a ranch belonging to a Mr. Waddingham on the evening of July 18, 1890:

This notice is with the object of requesting you to coil up your wire as soon as possible from the North and South sites. These wire fences which are harming the unhappy people and we request you further to coil up your wire as soon as you can to the agricultural land, and if you do not do it, you will suffer the consequences from us.

Your servants,
The White Caps.[48]

Although he initially did not take the fence cutting terribly seriously, in time the governor requested federal troops for San Miguel County to bring the crisis to an end.

 The Anglos might have American understandings of private property, American lawyers, and American troops on their side, but as the crisis continued it became clear that the majority of the residents of San Miguel County had far more sympathy for the fence cutters than for those who wanted to enclose the land. By the end of the 1880s some 3,500 Anglos had joined a Mexicano population of approximately 20,000. While the new arrivals had money and power, and could purchase strategic alliances, they were always outnumbered.[49] And in the face of large distances, the cover of darkness, and popular support from the majority of San Miguel County residents, there was surprisingly little the authorities could do.

 There has been some debate among the few historians who have attended to the White Cap story as to the role of individual leaders. Clearly the movement was mass based and had widespread popular support. Like most movements, it also probably had strong leadership. Because it was illegal and because its supporters were so marginalized in the larger society, the story must at best be pieced together.

The men seen by many as the leaders of the movement were Juan Jose Herrera and his brothers Pablo Herrera and Nicanor Herrera. Certainly this was true for Mary Fulgenzi when she recalled the movement for her 1936 interview.

Miguel Salazar, district attorney of San Miguel County throughout the fence-cutting era and an ardent opponent of Las Gorras Blancas, saw it as a highly centralized operation:

> It appears that about two years ago a certain person came from Utah or Colorado, who since his arrival in the Territory has been organizing such societies under the name first, of White Caps, but now under the name of Knights of Labor. He has about seven Lieutenants who control the horde of members, and those who are put under oath and penalty of being killed in the event they disobey or divulge any thing that they hear, or transpires in their reunions, blindly obey the orders of those officers.[50]

Like many public officials in the next century who could not believe in mass-based protest, Salazar was convinced that the whole movement was the work of a few fanatics and a large number of unenlightened followers.

Salazar had part of his story right however. In 1887 or 1888 Juan Jose Herrera had returned to San Miguel County where he had previously lived and was well known, having spent the last several years in both Utah and Colorado during the height of labor unrest there. Although there is no direct report of his involvement in the 1880s labor struggle in the Rockies, there is good reason to assume that he might have been involved or, at least, that he was deeply influenced by the labor solidarity he saw there. Herrera did not leave an account of his own intellectual development, but his later actions exhibit clear influences from the radical wing of the emerging labor movement.

In 1888, soon after his return to San Miguel County, Herrera received a commission from the Knights of Labor to serve as a district organizer for northeast New Mexico, where he organized more than twenty local assemblies of the Knights. There was a direct and almost immediate correlation between the emergence of these new assemblies of the Knights and the outbreak of fence cutting in the area. A person far less suspicious than Salazar might at least wonder about the connections.[51]

Isolated as it was, San Miguel County was not cut off from the radical developments that were taking place in many other parts of the United States in the 1890s. The *Las Vegas Daily Optic*—the newspaper that provided the best, if not the most favorable, coverage of Los Gorras Blancas—reported in May of 1890 that, "According to Bradstreet's Review, there were recently 90,000 men engaged in strikes throughout the country."[52] News of labor's struggles in the coal regions of the Alleghenies and in the western mines in Colorado and Utah certainly reached the residents of this area of the country.[53]

Joseph R. Buchanan of Denver, the western leader of the Knights of Labor, also helped organized a branch of the Red International in Colorado in 1883. Through the newspaper *Labor Enquirer*, through his own speeches, and through his leadership of a successful strike against the Union Pacific Railroad, Buchanan's more radical unionism may well have influenced Herrera.[54]

Terence V. Powderly, the national leader of the Knights, was not nearly as conservative as he has been portrayed or, indeed, as he later became. Although focused on the right to organize and on the eight-hour day, Powderly once observed that "the main all-absorbing question of the hour" was land reform. In 1889, with Powderly's strong support, the Knights adopted a resolution that said, "the land, including all the natural sources of wealth, is the heritage of all the people and should not be subject to speculative traffic. Occupancy and use should be the only title to the possession of the land." An industrial union and a rural land reform campaign had more in common than might initially be thought.[55]

Local Anglo leaders of the Knights were less enthusiastic about Herrera's efforts. They worried that the illegal activity could undermine their own reputation and their other reform efforts. Eventually they wrote to the national leadership asking for a break with Herrera:

> Just how many Assemblies he has organized, we are not prepared to say, but fence cutting and other depredations are by far too frequent occurrences. . . . But the Mexican people who are being organized as K of L are of the poorer class and consequently they are more ignorant, as they have had no advantages of education, there being very few schools in the Territory.
>
> Now we, as members of the K of L would request that no more assemblies be organized or Charters granted to those already organized until the present condition of affairs changes for the better.[56]

Break as they might with Herrera, the local Anglo leaders of the Knights were not a powerful force. For those who liked to call themselves Los Caballeros de Labor, far more important than official sanction from the national union was their ideological connection to the movements for the rights of workers and for the rights of peasants to the common land that were emerging in several places in the United States in the last decades of the nineteenth century. And for the residents of San Miguel County, their deepest beliefs were rooted far more in their Mexican heritage than in any distant Anglo labor organization.

Important as Juan Jose Herrera and his brothers were as leaders in Las Gorras Blancas, they were leaders with very wide-based support. The changes they demanded were seen as essential to the survival of the vast majority of the people who lived in San Miguel Country and who tried to gain a meager living from the unforgiving country while also maintaining a culture and a way of life that was now foreign in the land where they had lived for generations. Without this broad-based support, the Herreras would have been ineffective. With it, they were able to do a great deal in a very short amount of time.

What is clear is that while the violent actions of actually cutting fences, fence posts, and railroad ties and threatening their defenders were carried out by a relatively small group of individuals, the support of the wider public in San Miguel County was strong. For District Attorney Salazar, this was just a matter of the strong leading the weak and the sophisticated tricking the simple minded. So he wrote to the territorial governor:

> Most of the members of said organization are ignorant people, easily deceived and swayed by such wicked and evil designing persons as this leader and his lieutenants are; and I must confess that the majority of our ignorant Mexican population, are just as easy prey to such monsters of society as those who already belong to it; and I am afraid that unless an effective and strong remedy is used against the said leader and his lieutenants, the organization will increase throughout the Territory to monster proportions. This organization is getting stronger and bolder every day, and it behooves every good citizen, the Executive of the Territory, aye the U.S. Government to [take[immediate and effective and strong measures against such growing evil; or our fair Territory is doomed; as no life or property will be secure within its limits.[57]

In fact, although the organization was getting stronger and bolder, the story was considerably more complex than Salazar imagined.

As Robert Rosenbaum has argued, "Herrera and his lieutenants coordinated; they did not create. They did not make the issues. Fences went up on common land before assemblies of Los Caballeros de Labor spread across the county . . . the dislocation was severe in a marginal land where the loss of grazing privileges brought starvation near." And in such a situation, common action, direct and forceful action, was a natural next step.[58]

Early in the fence-cutting episode, when Bernabel Gallegos was tried for the crime of fence cutting in November 1889, the jury found him not guilty in spite of some fairly convincing evidence. The *Las Vegas Daily Optic*, in spite of its strong distaste for the movement, warned: "It will be a very difficult matter to obtain a jury who can be persuaded into punishing their fellow citizens and neighbors for the commission of acts, though illegal, that they, in their own hearts, feel to be right and about the only adequate and speedy remedy at their command."[59] The warning was wise and also prophetic.

A month later when forty-seven individuals were indicted for White Cap activities, including Juan Jose Herrera and his brother Nicanor, the sheriff telegraphed the governor for fifty rifles for fear of a mob attack on the jail. By the middle of December all forty-seven were in jail but the judge, having no desire to test the dangers of mob attack or to hold the accused for a spring trial, released them on bond.[60]

A crowd of some three hundred citizens of the county greeted the alleged fence cutters. A celebration of women with American flags, recent prisoners, and children paraded down the main streets of Las Vegas. For the Mexicano community, it was a day of triumph. For the unhappy editors of the *Daily Optic* it was odd that "These people in some ways, regard themselves as martyrs." Martyrs perhaps; but much more, victorious defenders of their world.[61]

By the summer of 1890 events in San Miguel County had come to something of a standstill. Los Caballeros de Labor was still small with less-than-clear connections to the larger labor movement. But it had made its point in the county. Local juries would not convict its members; fences were not being rebuilt, and new Anglo settlers were avoiding the county.

At this point another national movement—the rising Populist Party—came to be the focus of effort. The Populists are remembered as an example of agrarian radicalism emerging out of Kansas and Nebraska that reached national proportions. Their presidential candidate in 1892, James B. Weaver of Iowa, received over one million votes and twenty-two electoral votes in the presidential election of that year, making this one of the largest third-party movements in the nation's history. The Populists have been seen as a crucial element in paving the way for the populist takeover of the Democratic Party by William Jennings Bryan in 1896 and the growing progressive movement in both major parties at the beginning of the twentieth century.[62] They also impacted, and were impacted by, developments in San Miguel County, New Mexico.

In August 1890 thirty-four citizens, including leaders of Los Caballeros de Labor, issued a call for an organizing convention for El Partido del Pueblo Unido. The Populist Party of San Miguel County included more than the White Cap leaders. The Anglo leaders of the Knights of Labor who had sought to block them, new young leaders of the Mexicano community, older politicians looking for a fresh start—all came together in this movement. Like many successful political parties, it was an odd coalition with mixed goals. But it clearly owed much of its existence in San Miguel County to the work of Los

Gorras Blancas. In the election of 1890 the party captured the leadership of the county on an "anticapitalistic, antimonopolistic" anti-Santa Fe Railroad platform. For a brief period of time the party's representatives held the balance of power between traditional Republicans and Democrats in the New Mexico territorial legislature. The turn to electoral politics also brought an end to the movement's clandestine fence cutting. By the time of the Panic of 1893, one of the many economic depressions of the late nineteenth century, however, the uneasy alliance of Hispanic and Anglo, poor and middle class within the party became too difficult to maintain and the movement, like the national Populist Party, splintered in several different directions.[63]

For a brief period of time between 1889 and 1891, however, Los Caballeros de Labor, as the antifencing movement came to be called, represented an alternative cultural and economic vision for the United States. Grounded much more in Mexican than in American values and in peasant rather than aspiring middle-class attitudes toward the land, they sought to honor the community over the individual and the needs of the larger group over the rights of the smaller.

At the height of the movement's activity in March, 1890, members of Los Gorras Blancas—the nameless militia of the larger movement—rode through Las Vegas posting *Nuestra Platforma*. The brief document summed up their beliefs and goals:

> Not wishing to be misunderstood, we hereby make this our declaration.
>
> Our purpose is to protect the rights and interests of the people in general; especially those of the helpless classes.
>
> We want the Las Vegas Grant settled to the benefit of all concerned, and this we hold is the entire community within the grant.
>
> We want no "land grabbers" or obstructionists of any sort to interfere. We will watch them.

They went on to insist that they would support the authority of the territorial courts "only when 'Justice' is its watchword." And they noted, in words that later civil rights leaders of the following century might echo, "There is a wide difference between New Mexico's 'law' and 'justice.' And justice is God's law, and that we must have at all hazards." Finally they warned "Be fair and just and we are with you, do otherwise and take the consequences." The document was signed, "The White Caps, 1,500 Strong and Growing Daily."[64]

Nuestra Platforma, the most extended piece of writing to emerge directly from the anonymous militants, is an excellent summary of what they represented. They meant to be the voice of those who were being victimized daily by the land grabbers. They were not willing to be victims. They had another vision of justice for which they were willing to fight at great risk. And they were asserting a sacred right to survival to do all that needed doing, within the law or outside of it, to protect their basic rights to their survival, their community, and their vision of the good society.

Communal ownership of the land was hardly a successful movement in the United States, in New Mexico or elsewhere. Individualistic and industrial capitalism had far too much power behind it to be stopped for long. But the now generally forgotten movement of a few hundred desperately poor *las masas de los hombres pobres* along with a few thousand of their supporters does represent an alternative vision of a nation's life. It is as important a part of our heritage of hope from the nineteenth century as are Lincoln's words to Congress in opposition to the War with Mexico and Thoreau's essay on civil disobedience. And all of these diverse voices—the rural poor of New Mexico, the Mexican liberals of California, the congressmen such as Adams and Lincoln, and the poets such as Thoreau—offered the nation a hopeful vision that President Polk and his generals could not imagine.

CHAPTER FOUR

REBELLIOUS SLAVES, FREE BLACKS, AND ABOLITIONISTS

PLANTATION REBELS AND RUNAWAY SLAVES

IN 1837 JOSEPH TAPER AND HIS FAMILY who were slaves on a Frederick County, Virginia, plantation had enough of the "bad usage" they were receiving from their owners. Following a pattern of protest more common than has sometimes been reported, the Taper family took the ultimate risk. They ran away. The first steps in leaving a large plantation could be fairly easy—one simply walked away—but further movement was extremely difficult and dangerous in the days that followed. Throughout the nineteenth century, chasing and catching runaway slaves was a growth industry in the South. The chances of being caught were great and the punishments—from flogging, to having the family separated and sold into the deeper South, farther from the opportunity for a second escape, to being killed—were harsh. Nevertheless, many slaves like the Tapers ran away in the course of the over two hundred year history of the "peculiar institution" in North America.

Like most runaways, the Tapers did not go far at first. They made their way from the plantation, across Virginia's northern border, arriving in Somerset County, Pennsylvania. Joseph Taper, who was literate, found work enough there to support himself and his family. He also read the notice of his escape and the offer of a reward for his return. Fearing for their freedom, the family moved farther west to Pittsburgh, which seemed safer. But while there, they learned that an infamous slave hunter, George Cremer, was in the vicinity. Rather than take any further risks in a state that did not allow slavery but in which the authorities still regularly returned slaves to their owners in the South, the family turned much farther north, leaving the United States and settling in St. Catherines, Ontario, in the fall of 1839.[1]

In November 1840, a year after their arrival in Canada, Joseph Taper wrote to an acquaintance back in Virginia to inform him "that I am in a land of liberty, in good health." He continued, "My wife and self are sitting by a good comfortable fire happy, knowing that there are none to molest or make afraid." Taper described with some glee his success at earning a living in Pennsylvania and eluding those who were looking to capture him. He was prospering in Canada, having raised "316 bushels potato, 120 bushels corn, 41 bushels buckwheat, a small crop of oats, 17 Hogs, 70 chickens." But most of all, Taper was happy with the freedom that he had gained. "Since I have been in the Queen's dominions I have been well contented, Yes well contented for Sure, man is as God intended he should be. That is, all are born free & equal. This is a wholesome law, not like the Southern laws which puts man made in the image of God, on the level with brutes." For Taper and for thousands like him who were less able to put their feelings on paper, the belief was the same. In spite of all of the slave masters' efforts to teach them otherwise, they knew in their hearts that they were born free and equal and they meant, one way or another, to end their days that way.[2]

As happy as the ending is for the Taper story, the trip for any who made the long and dangerous journey north—to the free states or to Canada—was harrowing. Harriet Jacobs, another successful runaway, described her 1843 voyage by boat. Her paid passage on a vessel bound for freedom had been arranged by courageous friends in Virginia. But getting to the boat did not end her fears. She remembered, "we were filled with constant apprehensions that the constables would come on board. Neither could I feel quite at ease with the captain . . . might he not be tempted to make more money by giving us up to those who claimed us as property?" Jacobs felt guilty that the captain knew of her distrust but also said, "Ah, if he had ever been a slave he would have known how difficult it was to trust a white man." But all proceeded smoothly and "the next morning I was on deck as soon as the day dawned . . . for the first time in our lives, on free soil." Yet her troubles were far from over. She said, "We had escaped from slavery, and we supposed ourselves to be safe from the hunters. But we were alone in the world, and we had left dear ties behind us; ties cruelly sundered by the demon Slavery."[3] The price of freedom for many was continued fear and loneliness. And yet in spite of the danger and the loss, generations of runaway slaves made it clear that the freedom they hoped for was worth the cost.

The Taper and Jacobs stories are unusual in two ways. Most slaves who ran away were caught in a short period of time and even those who managed to escape for a longer period usually stayed relatively close to home. The Underground Railroad to Canada was a powerful symbol for many but a reality for few. And both Taper and Jacobs were among the small minority of slaves who were literate, which no doubt helped Taper to elude the authorities and enabled him to prosper in Pennsylvania and Canada and to write his extraordinary letter. But Jacobs and Taper and his family were not nearly so unusual in terms of their basic steps. Throughout the history of slavery in the United States, thousands of slaves risked everything for freedom. Some simply walked. Others made careful plans. They used a moment of opportunity when they were asked to travel or were hired out to another plantation. They were supported, at great risk, by other slaves or by free people, blacks and whites. They were caught, punished, and ran away again. In what is by far the best and most thorough study of runaway slaves, John Hope Franklin and Loren Schweninger conclude: "Perhaps the greatest impact runaways had on the peculiar institution—among whites and blacks alike—was in their defiance of the system. Masters and slaves knew that there were blacks who were willing to do almost anything to extricate themselves from bondage."[4]

Slavery, at its core, depended on hopelessness. Slaves who could imagine no other fate than the one they had been assigned could be counted on to be relatively docile. But a careful reading of history shows that most slaves did not accept their fates. They lashed out and rebelled when they could, escaped when there was an opportunity, and when all else failed, followed the course of oppressed peoples everywhere with small acts of day-to-day resistance, from feigned illness to staged laziness to acts of sabotage against owners' property. In all of these ways, slaves kept hope alive in the midst of the most hopeless institution to exist in the history of the United States.[5]

Perhaps more typical of runaway slaves than those who made it to Canada was a slave named Joe, also known as Forest, who ran away from a South Carolina plantation around 1820. Like the vast majority of runaway slaves, Joe sought freedom close to home. Some hid in remote areas, while others were taken in and hidden by other slaves or, in some cases, nearby Indian tribes. Joe followed this pattern and hid in a nearby swamp.

In Joe's case, however, according to a petition by a group of white planters, he did not merely run away. He killed George Ford, "a highly worthy and respectable Citizen of our State," and then disappeared into the impenetrable Santee River Swamp. There he was joined by other runaways from neighboring plantations. Joe's camp became a source of fear to white planters from a wide area of South Carolina. They feared the robberies committed by the runaways. Much more, however, they feared that the success of Joe and his followers planted dangerous ideas in the minds of other slaves. They feared that a camp of free and freedom-loving blacks could ultimately inspire the idea of a larger revolt among South Carolina slaves.[6]

As a petition from a large group of planters to the South Carolina legislature in 1824 stated the planter's case:

> Most of the runaways flew to his Camp and he soon became their head and their life. He had the art and the address to inspire his followers with the most Wild and dangerous enthusiasm. Such was his Cunning that but few of the enterprises for mischief planned by himself fail'd of success. We believe that nearly four years have now elapsed since the murder of Mr. Ford, the whole of which time until [Joe's] merited death was marked by Crimes, by mischiefs and by the dissemination of notions the most dangerous among the blacks in our Sections of the Country. (Such as were calculated in the end to produce insubordination and insurrection with all the hideous train of evils that usually follow.)[7]

Staying free, living where other slaves could join him, and preaching freedom was clearly a crime of the most dangerous sort.

The South Carolina authorities offered a reward of $1,000, an unheard of sum, for Joe's capture, but he remained free for years and more slaves joined him. Eventually the planter community from several counties around took matters into their own hands, organized a militia to march through the Santee swamp, and finally induced another slave to betray Joe and his followers. Joe and a number of his supporters were killed in the clash, others were executed, and still others disappeared, either returning to their plantations or moving on to new hiding places.

Joe's situation is unusual because of the size of the community he drew around him, and the size of the reward offered. In other ways, however, Joe's story is more common than has sometimes been recognized. Part of Franklin and Schweninger's contribution to recent scholarship is their use of petitions, such as the one submitted to the South Carolina legislature in Joe's case, and the many advertisements placed by slave owners offering rewards and seeking the return of runaway slaves. As Franklin and Schweninger argue, "Masters who advertised for a return of their property had little reason to misinform their readers and every reason to be as precise as possible."[8] And these advertisements yield another important piece of information—there were a lot of them. A single issue of the *New Orleans Daily Picayune* in the 1850s offered rewards for Jack, Sam, Zip or Harry, Edward, Daniel, Henrietta, Mary Mackendish, William, and Tom. Based on their careful tabulation, Franklin and

Schweninger estimate that by 1860 50,000 slaves ran away every year. Given the relatively low success rate of runaways and the harsh punishments, this number represents an extraordinary level of hope within a community that was not supposed to hope at all.[9]

Some of the greatest abolitionist and reconstruction leaders were themselves runaway slaves. Henry Highland Garnet, who became a respected and sometimes feared radical abolitionist in New York, was born a slave in Maryland. While he was a child, his family set out for the funeral of a slave on a nearby plantation. They went instead to the home of a Quaker Underground Railroad conductor in Delaware who hid them and moved them on to freedom in New York City where each member of the family took a new name in a "baptism to Liberty" ceremony.[10]

Probably the most widely recognized African American in the nineteenth century, Frederick Douglass began his life as a slave on a plantation on the Eastern Shore of Maryland around 1817. As with many slaves, no one kept an exact record of his birth and Douglass was separated from his family early in his life. He did remember late night visits from his mother who lived on another plantation twelve miles away and who made the journey on foot at night before returning for the next day's work. "She was a field hand, and a whipping is the penalty for not being in the field at sunrise . . . I do not recollect of ever seeing my mother by the light of day" he recalled.[11]

Douglass made his first attempt to run away in 1835. He recalled the fear that he and the four comrades who shared the plan felt when they thought about their escape. Douglass had secretly learned to read and write, and he used these skills to forge statements from their owners giving the five young men permission to go to Baltimore, which was to be their first stop on the way north. Nevertheless, in their minds the fears persisted:

> Whenever we suggested any plan, there was shrinking—the odds were fearful. Our path was beset with the greatest obstacles; and if we succeeded in gaining the end of it, our right to be free was yet questionable—we were yet liable to be returned to bondage. . . . In coming to a fixed determination to run away, we did more than Patrick Henry, when he resolved upon liberty or death. With us it was a doubtful liberty at most, and almost certain death if we failed.[12]

In spite of the fears, the five remained committed to their hopes more than their fears. Douglass found himself reminding the others, "we had talked long enough; we were now ready to move; if not now, we never should be; and if we did not intend to move now, we had as well fold our arms, sit down, and acknowledge ourselves fit only to be slaves. This, none of us were pre-pared to acknowledge."[13] For all the fears, the hope was greater.

The day before they were to begin their trip, however, the five were be-trayed and arrested. Douglass was separated from the other four and sent to a former master in Baltimore. Ironically, from there escape was easier. He finally succeeded in running away to freedom in New York in 1838. Again he faced the fear that "if I failed in this attempt, my case would be a hopeless one—it would seal my fate as a slave forever." He knew that this time he would be sold much farther south. But still he ran—he would not tell the path when he wrote in 1845 for fear of closing it to others—and arrived in New York City. "It was a moment of the highest excitement I ever experienced," Douglass said of his first day of freedom. However, like others, he also experienced the terrible fears of being caught and the terrible loneliness of being cut off from friends and family:

> I was yet liable to be taken back, and subject to all the tortures of slavery. This in itself was enough to damp the ardor of my enthusiasm. But the loneliness overcame me. There I was in the midst of thousands, and yet a perfect stranger; without home and without friends, in the midst of thousands of my own brethren—children of a common Father, and yet I dared not to unfold to any one of them my sad condition.

At the beginning Douglass adopted as his motto "Trust no man!" Fortunately, in time, Douglass did allow himself to be befriended and was helped to move to a new home in New Bedford and to launch his spectacular career.[14]

Three years later he was asked to speak at an abolitionist meeting in Nan-tucket, Massachusetts, and from that time on he was a nationally known leader, first in the antislavery movement and then for the rights of free African Americans. His *Narrative of the Life of Frederick Douglass: An American Slave*, published in 1845, is an extraordinary account of his slave years, his learning—illicitly and in spite of his master's vigorous opposition—to read and write, and his escape. It helped educate many nineteenth-century Americans about the reality of slavery, the hopes that so many slaves had for freedom, and it re-mains today a powerful record of the victory of hope over despair.

Another one of the most famous runaway slaves was Harriet Tubman who not only ran away but also conducted between 200 and 300 other former slaves on the Underground Railroad's track to freedom. By most reckonings she was responsible for freeing more slaves than any other person in the insti-tution's long history.

Tubman was born about 1820 and grew up in a strong and supportive slave family. In spite of her strong family, however, Tubman experienced the full terrors of slavery. At one point her family suffered one of the ultimate traumas of the institution when two of her older sisters were sold away from the rest of the family to a plantation farther south. Tubman never shook her own fears of a similar fate.

When she was a young adolescent of about fourteen, she received a severe head injury when she tried to protect another slave from a beating. As a fellow field hand ran away, the overseer threw a two-pound weight at him. It hit Tubman instead and she almost died from the severity of the injury. For the rest of her life she had bouts of suddenly falling asleep because of the injury to her head. In the short run, however, the experience changed her life. She spent months recovering, months that also gave her time to think about the institution and the world in which she lived, and to develop a rich spiritual life that would continue to give her strength for the rest of her days.[15]

After the Civil War, Tubman recalled the prayers she had spoken during the time of her convalescence:

> I was always praying for poor old master. 'Pears like I didn't do nothing but pray for old master. "Oh, Lord, convert old master; Oh, dear Lord, change that man's heart and make him a Christian." And all the time he was bringing men [buyers] to look at me and they stood there saying what they would give and what they would take, and all I could say was, "Oh Lord, convert old master."
>
> Then I heard that as soon as I was able to move I was to be sent with my brothers, in the chain gang to the far South. Then I changed my prayer, and I said, "Lord, if you ain't never going to change that man's heart, kill him."[16]

Tubman's spirituality was never sentimental!

Tubman recovered enough to return to work for her master. In 1844 she married John Tubman who was himself a free black. The free husband appears to have been more content with life in Maryland than his slave wife. It was said that he thought his wife worried too much about her condition as a slave. Worry she did, but she also took action. In 1849 alone and unaided Tubman ran away and made her way north to Philadelphia. It was a harrowing trip. Tubman had no way of knowing where she was going—other than north—and no one to rely on. When she got to Philadelphia and succeeded in getting work as a domestic, she recalled with emotions very similar to those of Harriet Jacobs, "I had crossed the line of which I had so long been dreaming. I was free; but there was no one to welcome me to the land of freedom." Everyone she knew and cared for was "down in the old cabin quarters, with the old folks and my brothers and sisters." A weaker person might have given in to despair at the loneliness. For Tubman, the solution was a much more hopeful approach to the issue—most would have said an absurdly optimistic one. She decided to return to the South and lead her family to freedom.[17]

After working in Philadelphia for a year, Tubman made her first foray south. She brought her slave sister and her sister's children from Baltimore to freedom in Philadelphia. She developed a pattern that she would continue until the outbreak of the Civil War. She worked for a while, raised some money, and then made a trip south to free a group of slaves. By 1857 she had freed her entire family, including her aging parents. She did not stop there. Between 1850 and 1861, Tubman made trip after trip helping more and more slaves escape farther and farther north. As the full impact of the 1850 fugitive slave law took effect, she did not stop with the trip to Pennsylvania but accompanied each group to St. Catherines, Ontario, where they would be fully free of American slavery since Britain had abolished slavery throughout its empire in 1838.

Tubman's leadership, her songs of freedom, and her toughness became legendary. There are numerous accounts of the time when one member of a group that she was conducting north wanted to turn back out of fear and exhaustion. Tubman, who also properly feared an informer, put a gun to his head and said, "Dead niggers don't tell no tales. Move on or die." Asked later if she would really have shot the man, she said, "Yes. If he was weak enough to give out, he'd be weak enough to betray us all, and all who had helped us; and do you think I'd let so many die just for one coward man?"[18] In dealing with the utter hopelessness of slavery, hope required extraordinary courage and toughness.

As her work continued, Tubman's fame grew. This fame brought support from northern abolitionists and hatred from slaveholders and their allies. The reward for her capture grew steadily in the South to which she kept returning. At the same time, northern abolitionists including the African American Quaker William Still and the white Unitarian Thomas Wentworth Higginson became her supporters. In 1859 Higginson took up a collection at the Massachusetts Anti-Slavery Society so that Tubman could "resume the practice of her profession!"[19]

Tubman also became a strong supporter of John Brown as he prepared for his raid on Harpers Ferry and of Susan B. Anthony's crusade for the vote for women. During the Civil War Tubman aided the Union Army both in work with newly freed slaves on the coast of South Carolina and as a spy for raiding parties of Union soldiers. She continued a wide range of activities long after the Civil War until her death at the Harriet Tubman Home for Aged and Indigent Colored People in Auburn, New York, in 1913. But her greatest fame and her greatest contribution were as the woman known as Moses, the leader and the symbol of freedom for so many.[20]

Tubman and Douglass were unusual in their leadership ability and in the fame that their experiences brought. The Taper family and the slave Joe were unusual in the detailed records of their escape that were left behind. But the Underground Railroad and the many other routes to freedom for slaves have often been underestimated. While the vast majority of slaves lived and died in bondage, more ran away for shorter or longer periods of time than has sometimes been recorded by historians. Franklin and Schweninger's conservative estimate of 50,000 runaway slaves each year by 1860 suggests a significant economic and social impact on the nation's 385,000 slave owners. If one in seven slaveholders could expect someone to run away each year, none could ignore the problem. Most runaways returned or were recaptured within a short period of time and the cost to the owner was that of lost labor and search parties. For those whose slaves found freedom, who never returned, the cost was much greater. But the greatest cost was to the image that slaveholding society tried to paint of itself. If slavery was beneficial to all, why did so many seek to escape it? If most slaves were happy, why did so many run?

A range of theories abounded in the slaveholding society. A new disease, "drapetomania" (a combination of the Greek words for runaway slave and mad), was invented. Outsiders were easy to blame. Sometimes the outsiders were slaves brought to the United States from Haiti, who told of the ideas of revolution and revolt on that island where freedom and independence had been won in the 1790s under the leadership of Toussaint L'Ouverture. Sometimes they were northern abolitionists whose "meddlesome ways" were a constant source of anger to slave owners. One way or another, slave owners felt that they had to find an explanation for the large number of runaway slaves. If hope on the part of the slaves themselves, a belief that action on their part could actually bring about a better future for themselves and their children, was the cause of so much difficult and dangerous human movement, then the institution of slavery was doomed.[21]

REVOLTS AND REVOLUTIONS

Most frightening to slaveholders and their society were large-scale slave revolts. Compared to running away or other forms of resistance, full-fledged slave revolts were relatively rare. Yet the historian Herbert Aptheker documented over two hundred slave revolts in the United States in the sixty years leading up to the Civil War. A violent revolt against slavery could be seen as either an act of utter despair or of great hope. There was probably a measure of each, but in those relatively rare cases when the participants in revolts had their voices recorded, the power of hope seemed great indeed.[22]

On August 30, 1800, over 1,000 slaves under the leadership of Gabriel Prosser marched on Richmond, Virginia. Prosser and others had been planning their revolt for months and had a powerful collection of pikes, clubs, and swords. The Virginia government had been warned by two informers, and the militia quickly defeated the rebels. The majority escaped and returned to their plantations but many were arrested, and 35, including Prosser, were executed. Prosser and most of the others simply refused to speak but one of the leaders testified at his trial:

> I have nothing more to offer than what General Washington would have had to offer, had he been taken by the British officers and put to trial by them. I have ventured my life in endeavoring to obtain the liberty of my countrymen, and am a willing sacrifice to their cause; I beg, as a favour, that I may be immediately led to execution. I know that you have predetermined to shed my blood, why then all this mockery of a trial?[23]

Like Washington and other revolutionaries of the decades before, this slave was clear about his hopes and his belief that freedom was worth risking all.

The revolts continued in the succeeding decades. In 1810 a plot was discovered in Lexington, Kentucky. In 1811, 400 slaves revolted in New Orleans, Louisiana. In 1815 a white man named George Boxley attempted to lead a slave revolt.

And in 1822 Denmark Vesey prepared for the greatest slave revolt of the era. Veysey, with a large group of supporters who were well organized, planned to burn the military and financial center of the South, Charleston, South Carolina, to the ground, murder the white residents, and then seize the city's considerable stores of weapons and gold. They would then set sail for Haiti where they could begin a new life as free women and men. Veysey, who had purchased his own freedom in 1800, had been plotting his revolt for years. He was a bible-class leader in Charlestown for the African Methodist Episcopal Church, and he spoke of the biblical stories of moving from slavery to freedom with the passion of a latter-day Moses. He also spoke fluent French and was clearly influenced by the success of the Haitian revolt of 1804 that had permanently established the island's freedom, and which incidentally had exiled both white Haitian masters and some of their slaves to Charleston. No one really knows how close Veysey's efforts came to success. When they were betrayed on the verge of action, many estimated that Veysey's coconspirators numbered in the thousands. In stories whispered behind closed doors, Denmark Veysey and his many followers represented the ultimate terror to the white community and the ultimate symbol of freedom and hope to the African American world.[24]

In 1831 Nat Turner was more successful than Veysey. In August of that year he led a revolt in which over sixty whites in slave-owning families were killed in the first forty hours of their revolt. Terror spread throughout the South while hope grew quickly among Turner and his allies. The revolt was soon put down by state and federal troops. Over 100 slaves were killed in the fighting or executed after capture. Turner himself was captured in October and was hanged two weeks later on November 11. While he was awaiting trial, Turner was interviewed by his white court-appointed attorney, Thomas Gray, who subsequently published *Turner's Confessions*. The degree to which the voice of the *Confessions* is Turner's or Gray's will never be known.[25]

Nevertheless, some of Turner's words have an authentic ring. His hope for freedom was clearly based in a powerful spirituality. He reported having been a religious man from his earliest years, and his intense spirituality had been noted "by those by whom I had been taught to pray, both white and black." And Turner's prayers and meditations convinced him of two important things: "that I was ordained for some great purpose in the hands of the Almighty," and that the Almighty's purpose included freedom for American slaves and that "the great day of judgment was at hand."[26]

Clearly this spiritual core to his preaching was part of Turner's charisma. He gathered more and more fellow slaves who believed in him, and his impact was far greater than the immediate loss of life involved in his short-lived revolt. In the aftermath of the Turner revolt, more and more repressive laws were passed across the South. And the revolts continued. In 1853, 2,500 slaves were ready to revolt in New Orleans when they were betrayed, and an unnumbered group rose up in North Carolina in 1856. The hope of freedom remained a powerful, sometimes violent force as long as the much more violent institution of slavery itself existed.[27]

By the 1840s some among the free blacks of the North had also openly begun to call for the slaves of the South to revolt. David Walker, who had been born free in Ohio, wrote his *Appeal* in Boston in the late 1820s. In it, Walker set out his goal "To awaken in the breasts of my afflicted, degraded and slumbering brethren, a spirit of inquiry and investigation respecting our miseries and wretchedness in this Republican Land of Liberty!!!!!!" And while his investigation would review the history of slavery, ancient and modern, Walker kept coming back to his challenge. To white America he asked, will God "let the oppressors rest comfortably and happy always?" What sort of God would do that? He then asked, "O ye Christians!!! Who hold us and our children in the most abject ignorance and degradation, that ever a people were afflicted with since the world began—I say, if God gives you peace and tranquility, and suffers you thus to go on afflicting us, and our children, who have never given you the least provocation—would he be to us a God of justice?"

But the heart of Walker's *Appeal* was to his fellow African Americans. He said to them, "The whites want slaves, and want us for their slaves, but some of them will curse the day they ever saw us." His challenge was for them to join him in bringing that day as soon as possible. "Oh! My coloured brethren, all over the world, when shall we arise from this death-like apathy?—and be men!! You will notice, if ever we become men, I mean respectable men, such as other people are, we must exert ourselves to the full." In the face of slavery's horror, in the face of the reality that in many parts of the South blacks outnumbered whites, the time for rebellion, as far as Walker could see, had come.[28]

A decade later Henry Highland Garnet, who had been born a slave in Maryland in 1815 and escaped with his family in 1825, addressed the National Negro Convention. In his 1843 speech, "Address to the Slaves of the United States of America," Garnet did not mince words. He said to the slaves of the South:

> Brethren, arise, arise! Strike for your lives and liberties. Now is the day and the hour. Let every slave throughout the land do this, and the days of slavery are numbered. You cannot be more oppressed than you have been—you cannot suffer greater cruelties than you have already. Rather die freemen than live to be slaves. Remember that you are four millions!
>
> It is in your power so to torment the God-cursed slaveholders, that they will be glad to let you go free. . . . Let your motto be resistance! Resistance! RESISTANCE! No oppressed people have ever secured their liberty without resistance.[29]

For Garnet and Walker, and many others, the time was long past for aiding individual escapes or agitating for a constitutional end to slavery. An immediate and broad based slave rebellion, as had taken place in Haiti at the beginning of the century, was the key to liberty.

The most famous, if not the most effective, revolt of all took place at Harpers Ferry, Virginia, in 1859. On Sunday evening, October 16, 1859, John Brown along with fourteen other whites and five free blacks seized the federal armory in the crucial town of Harpers Ferry. For Brown and his followers the goal was to use the arms that they were seizing to support a revolution among the slaves. Every aspect of Brown's raid has been debated in the almost century and a half since it took place. There were no large-scale plantations nearby and not a single slave was actually freed by the raid. The military action did not seem to have been well planned. Brown's own statements on the purposes of the raid offered a mixed message. And when Brown's strongest supporters among northern abolitionists first heard the news, they tended to view the raid as, in Garrison's words, "wild, misguided, and apparently insane . . . though disinterested and well-intended."[30] And yet, John Brown's raid changed everything in the United States.[31]

The actual revolt was short lived. State and federal militia converged on Harpers Ferry and, after fierce fighting, it was over in less than a day. Several of Brown's comrades were killed, and Brown and others were arrested. Osborne Anderson, the only African American to escape the battle, remembered it well. Among other things, he had learned a lesson that day in class politics, "Hardly the skin of a slaveholder could be scratched in open fight; the cowards kept out of the way until danger was passed, sending the poor whites into the pitfalls, while they were reserved for the bragging and to do the safe but cowardly judicial murdering afterwards."[32]

The raid on Harpers Ferry sent a chill throughout the white South. With the emergence of the telegraph and faster printing presses, news traveled much faster in the South and in the North than it had only a few decades before. Especially in light of subsequent northern reactions to the raid, many white southerners became convinced that most northerners were in league with the abolitionists and those slaves who secretly harbored thoughts of revolt. The South quickly became an armed camp and secession from the union became a reality in many minds a year or more before the election of Abraham Lincoln.

In the North, after the initial confusion, the raid also began to galvanize a relatively wide spectrum of public opinion. The well-known author and abolitionist Lydia Maria Child offered to go to Virginia to nurse the wounded prisoner. Brown preferred to have his own wife with him, but Child's offer rebounded to the abolitionist cause when Virginia governor Henry A. Wise, in an attempt at gallantry, offered her protection on the visit while at the same time he charged her with being an accessory to the uprising. "I could not permit an insult even to a woman in her walk of charity among us," Wise wrote, "though it to be to one who whetted knives of butchery for our mothers, sisters, daughters and babes." In response Child continued her correspondence with the governor, which ended up being published and becoming a hugely popular abolitionist pamphlet. In response to the charge that northern women did not know how to care for the unfortunate as well as southern women, Child responded that, of course they did, but "here at the North, after we have helped the mother we do not sell the babies."[33]

Henry David Thoreau's "Plea for Captain John Brown" argued that the issue of Brown's violence could not be compared with the violence of slavery. He asked people to focus "not on the weapon but the spirit in which you use it." The pacifist William Lloyd Garrison, probably the nation's best-known white abolitionist, came in time to view the raid as "a desperate self-sacrifice for the purpose of giving an earthquake shock to the slave system." And many individual northerners came to believe that Brown was a hero and that the raid did, indeed, prove that the nation could not exist half-free and half-slave; a belief that translated into votes for the Republican nominee a year later.[34]

In the midst of all of this, Brown used the six weeks between his arrest and his execution on December 2, 1859, to extraordinary effect. Henry Mayer is right that the "last four weeks of John Brown's life witnessed a massive outpouring of sentiment—both spontaneous and orchestrated—perhaps never before lavished upon an individual American."[35]

Brown's extraordinary speech at his own trial and his response to his sentence, along with interviews he gave to the press and correspondence with friends and relatives, became some of the most widely read literature of the nineteenth century. He told the court:

> Now, if it is deemed necessary that I should forfeit my life for the furtherance
> of the ends of justice, and mingle my blood further with the blood of my children and with the blood of millions in this slave country whose rights are disregarded by wicked, cruel, and unjust enactments, I say, let it be done.

Prophetically he told a reporter from the *New York Herald*, "You may dispose of me easily, but this question is still to be settled—the negro question—the end of that is not yet."[36] That question was, indeed, not settled, though within a year the battle would be joined that would result in the end of the institution of chattel slavery. And in that much larger war, Union troops would march into battle singing:

> John Brown's body lies a-moldering in the grave
> But his soul goes marching on.

Whether he was seen as Don Quixote on a fool's errand or a freedom fighter ahead of his time, John Brown and his followers were a symbol of hope as much as those who had led the revolution of 1776. Within four years of his raid, the Emancipation Proclamation did accomplish the agenda for which he, and so many others, died.

NORTHERN WHITE ABOLITIONISTS

John Brown's raid and execution focused the nation on the issue of slavery in the fall of 1859 in an unprecedented way, but others had been laying the groundwork for that kind of national attention for decades.

When William Lloyd Garrison launched the first issue of *The Liberator* at the beginning of January, 1831, he was beginning a three-and-a-half-decade quest—often a lonely and dangerous quest—to make his hopes for an end to slavery a reality. In the lead editorial of the first edition of *The Liberator*, Garrison declared his commitment to the antislavery cause, "I am in earnest—I will not equivocate—I will not excuse—I will not retreat a single inch. –AND I WILL BE HEARD." In spite of many setbacks, he never backed down over the next thirty-five years, through the passage of the thirteenth amendment in December 1865. Garrison can hardly be called a community builder. He was a loner. He was difficult and he did not work well with others. Yet he kept a vision of a better society in front of a nation that did not want to hear about it for a third of a century.[37]

As Henry Mayer has noted:

When the twenty-five-year-old Garrison started his newspaper, Abraham Lincoln was a twenty-one-year-old sodbuster on the Illinois prairie, Jefferson Davis was a newly commissioned U.S. Army officer fighting the Sauk and Fox on the Wisconsin frontier, and Davis's West Point classmate Robert E. Lee was building federal batteries on the Georgia coast. Ulysses S. Grant and William T. Sherman were still schoolboys in Ohio, and Harriet Tubman was a ten-year-old field hand on a Maryland slave plantation. John Brown was teaching school and running a tannery in Pennsylvania, Stephen A. Douglas was reading law in western New York, Frederick Douglass was learning to read as an adolescent slave in Baltimore, and Harriet Beecher Stowe was teaching composition in her sister's Hartford Female Seminary. . . . With ferocious determination, Garrison broke the silence and made the public listen in a way that his predecessors had not.[38]

Mayer sometimes overstates Garrison's contribution—no one person can have the credit for the great abolitionist movement of the first half of the nineteenth century—but Garrison's role as a prophetic voice of conscience to a national community that did not want to listen can hardly be overstated.[39]

While he was hardly a communitarian, Garrison's hopeful vision of community was clear and well formulated. Garrison was plainly a believer in the "free labor" doctrine that would dominate the Republican party when it emerged decades after he began his work. He contrasted northern free labor and southern slavery. He did not, for the most part, care much about the views of others who saw northern free labor as its own kind of "wage slavery," though he did embrace the ten-hour day and attacked "our rich capitalists" after a tour of a Rhode Island cotton mill in 1832.[40]

If one reads *The Liberator*, one hears Garrison's call for a new spiritual identity for the United States. In the April 1831 issue he wrote, "Nothing but extensive revivals of pure religion can save our country. . . . All reformations, whether political, civil, or religious are . . . the result of long accumulating causes [and] are the harvests of the spiritual husbandmen who have tilled the ground and scattered the good seed." This was not the same kind of revival of pure religion advocated by the leading revivalists of the day, but the hopes of many exponents of evangelical religion had much in common with the voices of the abolitionists in antebellum America.[41]

Garrison was not a church member, though he preached in many churches and had a hand in the division of some denominations, including the Quakers, into abolitionist and nonabolitionist factions. He did say that his own views "harmonized" better with the Society of Friends than any other.[42] In many ways, however, Garrison modeled himself on his own image of an Old Testament prophet. He was not a coalition builder. He told one colleague, "There shall be no neutrals; men shall either like or dislike me." In many ways he saw the abuse that was heaped on him—and it was a considerable amount of abuse over many years—as proof of his own righteousness.[43]

One of Garrison's most radical statements was made at the annual Massachusetts Anti-Slavery Society picnic on July 4, 1854. At this sunny afternoon gathering in Framingham, Massachusetts, Garrison held up a copy of the hated Fugitive Slave Law, struck a match, and burned the paper. As it burned, Garrison the revivalist shouted, "And let all the people say, 'Amen.'" When the crowd roared its response, Garrison went further. He held up a copy of the United States Constitution—the document seen as almost quasi-sacred to many—and called it "the source and parent of the other atrocities," and set it on fire. "So perish all compromises with tyranny . . . And let all the people say, 'Amen.'"[44] No twentieth-century flag or draft-card burner (that I know of) was willing to emulate such a radical attack on the nation's foundation.

An irony of Garrison's abolitionism was that, for all of his radicalism, Garrison was also a pacifist. From the beginning to the end of his long and controversial career, Garrison insisted that as a pacifist he sought "to accomplish the great work of national redemption through the agency of moral power." While he argued that events from Nat Turner's bloody rebellion in 1831 to the 1837 murder of Elijah Lovejoy—an anti-slavery editor who was killed by a mob in Alton, Illinois, while he and his friends were engaged in an armed defense—were inevitable, he could never condone violence. Henry Mayer has noted what he called the "bitter irony" of Garrison's career, that "the end he most fervently desired—the abolition of slavery—came by means—the physical coercion of warfare—that, as a pacifist, he most consistently abhorred."[45] And yet, no one laid a more solid basis for the popular support of both the war and the Emancipation Proclamation, which finally gave the war its moral focus, than the intrepid editor from Boston.

Garrisonian abolitionists were not the only white advocates for the total abolition of slavery in the decades leading up to the Civil War, however. A group of evangelical Christians matched Garrison in their commitment to the cause. And an unlikely triumph for these abolitionists took place in Ohio at about the same time that Garrison was starting his paper in Boston.

Oberlin abolitionism and Oberlin perfectionism emerged from the work of a number of revivalists in the area of upstate New York known as the "burned over district" because of the heat of the religious enthusiasm generated there. Among the New York revivalists, the leading player throughout the 1820s was Charles Grandison Finney. Converted in Adams, New York, Finney left a successful law practice to begin his own career as a revivalist. Reminded of a pending case by one of his clients, Finney is supposed to have responded, "Deacon B———, I have a retainer from the Lord Jesus Christ to plead his cause, and I cannot plead yours."[46] For the next four decades, Finney would continue to plead the Lord's cause in America. He defined the cause as including both revivals and abolitionist activity. Finney's hopes for America included both individual conversions to Christianity and a national conversion to end slavery. He would never separate the two.

Among those converted by Finney himself, Theodore Dwight Weld stood out as both the most apt student and the one destined to move far beyond his mentor.[47] Weld had been converted during the Great Revival in Utica in 1825. He quickly became an important assistant to Finney, championed the right of women to speak in the revivals, and in 1827 began to study for the ministry. He also became deeply convinced of the evils of slavery and the need for immediate emancipation if the conversion of the nation was ever to mean social rather than merely personal transformation.[48]

Weld and a number of other Finney converts first went to Cincinnati, Ohio, to prepare for the ministry in a new Presbyterian seminary just being launched by a well-known New England preacher, Lyman Beecher. Beecher was a conservative abolitionist, more supportive of colonization efforts to return slaves to Africa than of securing their freedom in the United States.[49] By the time Weld arrived at Lane Seminary to study for the ministry in 1833, it was probably inevitable that he would clash with the school's president, just as Finney himself had clashed with Beecher over the proper forms of revivalism a decade before. Not long after his arrival at the seminary's campus, Theodore Dwight Weld wrote: "I am deliberately, earnestly, solemnly, with my whole heart and soul and mind and strength for the immediate, universal, and total abolition of slavery."[50] Through

Weld's influence, this position would quickly come to be shared by the majority of his fellow students.

Arthur and Lewis Tappan, successful New York merchants who had played such an important role in providing the funds for a variety of evangelical causes, especially antislavery, shared Weld's position on this matter. Lewis Tappan's biographer has correctly stated their expectations: "With Tappan paying their expenses, Weld and an eager band from Oneida Academy joined Beecher at Walnut Hills, which overlooked Cincinnati, the Ohio River, and the Kentucky slaveland beyond. From this source at Lane, the Tappan brothers expected an anti-slavery tide to roll eastward."[51]

Lyman Beecher's position was more than a little different. To the surprise of his Tappan benefactors, he would not agree with their single-minded devotion to the antislavery cause. Beecher was a reconciler, but this very concern with reconciliation betrayed the basic differences that existed between Beecher and Weld.[52] Beecher needed reconciliation between the most moderate and the most extreme abolitionists so that they could continue what he saw as the larger evangelical campaign to Christianize America. For Weld there was no larger campaign: righteousness was the issue. Thus, while both Beecher and Weld used much of the same evangelical language, and while both advocated a form of ministry that was actively involved in the issues of the day, the two differed radically on the proper focus and purpose of that activity.

Once he arrived in Cincinnati, Weld and his strongest allies quickly set about to convert the entire Lane student body. They talked with fellow students, reasoned with them about their doubts, and produced evidence of the horror of slavery and the sin of slaveholding. They planned their antislavery revival carefully and did not call a meeting until they were sure of some public converts.

Finally the time came for a public gathering, and for eighteen tumultuous evenings in February 1832 the debates were held. Weld and his fellow students were well prepared and marshaled their arguments about the horrors of slavery and the need for immediate emancipation. At the conclusion, nearly all of the Lane student body voted in favor of immediate abolitionism and against more gradual solutions to slavery.[53]

The student activists did not stop with debate. As Weld wrote to Lewis Tappan a month later: "We believe that faith without *works* is dead. We have formed a large and efficient organization for elevating the colored people in Cincinnati—have established a Lyceum among them, and lecture three or four evenings a week. . . . Besides this, an evening free school, for teaching them to read, is in operation.[54] Many of the trustees and the Cincinnati newspapers began to be very nervous and critical about this level of activism but that did not deter the students in the least.[55]

In October 1834, when Beecher returned to Cincinnati from a fundraising trip, he "found all in a flurry."[56] The trustees had passed a resolution "requiring that the Anti-Slavery Society and Colonization Society of the seminary be abolished."[57] In response, the students had left the campus. The students were still hopeful that Beecher would resign and join them. Instead, he tried to negotiate a settlement.[58] But it was far too late for negotiations. In spite of Beecher's pleas, the students did not return. From their temporary residence in Cumminsville, Ohio, they issued their own final words on the affairs of Lane Seminary.

In a forceful statement, the students insisted that to achieve the necessary preparation for the ministry they were led "to adopt this principle, *that free discussion, with correspondent effort is a DUTY, and of course a RIGHT.* . . . We applied it to missions, at home and abroad; and we *acted* immediately. . . . With the same spirit of free inquiry, we discussed the question of slavery." Of course the issue of slavery had caused a much more severe response from the trustees, compelling the students to say that as long as Lane maintained a rule on its books that limited the students' right to conduct their antislavery activity as they saw it, they could not remain and be true to their understanding of who a minister should be. They concluded:

> Finally, we would respectfully remind the trustees, that men, though students of a theological seminary, should be treated as men,—that men, destined for their service of the world, need, above all things, in such an age as this, the pure and impartial, the disinterested and magnanimous, the uncompromising and fearless,—in combination with the gentle and tender spirit and example of Christ; not parleying with wrong, but calling it to repentance; not flattering the proud, but pleading the cause of the poor.[59]

It was the end of the debate. The differences between the two factions, their different visions of the nature of the Christian ministry and their different hopes for the future of the United States, were too clear and too important for any reconciliation.

Having left Lane Seminary, the Lane Rebels, as they became known, moved on to other things. A year after leaving Lane, the students, along with their theological mentor Finney, were invited to essentially take over a floundering school farther north in the state.[60] The Oberlin Collegiate Institute had opened with two teachers and eleven students in 1833.[61] In the fall of 1835 the Lane Rebels became the new Theology Department at Oberlin.[62] The new arrivals had essentially refounded the institution when it was on the verge of collapse.[63] Before agreeing to move to Oberlin, the antislavery activists insisted that their friend from Cincinnati, Asa Mahan, be elected president of the school and that Charles Grandison Finney be elected professor of theology. The arrival of Charles Finney, the nation's best known revivalist, gave the school prestige and would influence its orientation for the next several decades.[64] The prospect of students, faculty, and Tappan money was more than the Oberlin trustees could reject.[65]

Theodore Weld did not accompany the Lane Rebels to Oberlin. For the rest of his life, he continued his own unique ministry as an antislavery organizer and activist.[66] Weld had been offered the theological professorship at Oberlin but had vigorously argued that Finney should play that role while he continued the antislavery organizing which was his primary vocation.[67] One of his first moves in his new position as agent for the American Anti-Slavery Society, however, took Weld back to Ohio. He needed agents to carry on the antislavery campaign in that state, and the natural place to turn was to his old allies. In August 1835 thirteen of the Lane Rebels met with Weld in Cleveland for two weeks and then scattered throughout the state as agents for antislavery. The pattern would be repeated as Weld became a virtual one-man employment agency for the antislavery cause.[68]

In May 1836, the American Anti-Slavery Society adopted a new campaign to evangelize the nation for abolitionism. The pamphlet campaigns of the last few years had not worked well. Written materials were too easy to destroy or ignore. What was needed were revivalists. Turning to biblical precedent, they voted to send out a mission of the seventy to convert the land. Funds would be raised to send out this number to preach the sin of slavery and the need for the repentance of abolitionism. Weld was commissioned to choose the agents.[69]

Weld turned to his old classmates, especially now that many of them were just on the point of seeking their first ministerial appointments. He traveled to Ohio to recruit. Eventually thirty of the fifty-four students who had signed the students' statement at Lane in 1834 became antislavery agents.[70] Some stayed for a few years and then moved on to other forms of ministry. Others spent their lives in the antislavery movement. Among them, they carried the mix of revivalism and activism that had emerged from Oberlin to all of the free states of the union. Weld's biographer has correctly described their form of ministry: "Rather than agents, the Lane rebels were evangelists of abolitionism, and their power to move communities was one with the power of Finney."[71] It was also a kind of evangelism not seen previously on the American stage. Unfortunately it was not seen again in the same form. But in the decades leading up to the Civil War, the Christian hope for a better future and the radical abolitionist demand that the future start immediately merged in a powerful and enduring mix.

"AND THE WAR CAME"

The causes and purposes of the Civil War have been debated from the time of the first Confederate shot on Fort Sumter to the present day, but the centrality of slavery to the conflict remains obvious. Many in the North may have fought to save the Union, but the Union would not have been threatened if southern slaveholders had not feared northern abolitionists. The South may have fought for states' rights, but states' rights would have remained a vague philosophical concept, worthy perhaps of argument in Congress or the local debating society but hardly rebellion if southerners had not come more and more to fear northern abolitionists and their potential alliance with southern slaves. Many actions by many people brought on the war, but virtually none of the actions would have taken place, or mattered, but for the issue of slavery.

At the beginning of the Civil War neither President Lincoln nor his generals had a clear policy regarding either the future of slavery in the states where it existed or the role of black soldiers in the conflict. The latter issue was addressed sooner than the former. Many blacks offered their services and rallied as those in Boston who said:

> Our feelings urge us to say to our countrymen that we are ready to stand by and defend our Government as the equals of its white defenders; to do so with "our lives, our fortunes, and our sacred honor," for the sake of freedom, and as good citizens; and we ask you to modify your laws that we may enlist,—that full scope may be given to the patriotic feelings burning in the colored man's breast.[72]

But it would take many months of war before any clear policy emerged.

In October 1861 the first recruitment of slaves fleeing across Union lines began when the secretary of war authorized General Thomas W. Sherman to "employ fugitive slaves in such services as they may be fitted for . . . with such organization as you may deem most beneficial to the service."[73] Sherman included combat among these "services." By the spring of 1862 an initially reluctant president had signed on to the policy and by the spring of 1863 Union generals were recruiting soldiers from among southern slaves wherever they could find them.

Once active recruitment of African American soldiers began, many signed up. By the end of the war military records showed that 93,000 black soldiers who had been recruited from the states of the Confederacy had served in the Union army, and an additional 40,000 from the border slave states, and 53,000 from the free states. Other blacks, free and former slaves, passed as whites and served in white regiments, and still others, such as Harriet Tubman, served as spies and unofficial agents of the Union army. Initially black Union soldiers suffered discrimination in pay and they—sometimes with their white officers—were shunned by white troops. Confederate president Jefferson Davis ordered that captured black troops be treated as rebellious slaves rather than captured soldiers. In spite of the terrible harsh conditions faced by all Civil War soldiers and the special mistreatment reserved for black troops, African Americans offered heroic service. Their hopes for victory were, after all, much greater than those of others. Saving the Union was minor compared to the promise of freedom that became increasingly clear, especially after President Lincoln finally issued the Emancipation Proclamation in the fall of 1862, stating that as of January 1, 1863

> All persons held as slaves within any state, or designated part of a state, the people whereof shall then be in rebellion against the United States, shall be then, thenceforward, and forever free.[74]

The timing might have been slow, the goals as much military as liberatory. But from then on there was no turning back.

Southern whites did all they could to keep slaves loyal to them and the Confederate cause. They withheld information whenever possible, spread wild tales of northern plans, and put slaves to work defending the Confederacy. Some slaves may have believed the stories and others may have been simply confused. But in spite of the South's best efforts, many slaves knew exactly what the war was about. That was why so many crossed enemy lines seeking freedom and in some cases a chance to serve the Union cause. One young slave, Susie King Taylor, who much later recorded her memoirs, remembered what it was like to hear about the coming of the Yankees in 1862:

> I had been reading so much about the "Yankees" I was very anxious to see them. The whites would tell their colored people not to go to the Yankees, for they would harness them to carts and make them pull the carts around in place of horses. I asked grandmother, one day, if this was true. She replied, "Certainly not!" that the white people did not want slaves to go over to the Yankees, and told them these things to frighten them. . . . I wanted to see these wonderful "Yankees" so much, as I heard my parents say the Yankee was going to set all the slaves free. Oh, how those people prayed for freedom! I remember, one night, my grandmother went out into the suburbs of the city to a church meeting, and they were fervently singing this old hymn,

> > Yes, we all shall be free,
> > Yes, we all shall be free,

Yes, we all shall be free,
When the lord shall appear.

When the police came in and arrested all who were there, saying they were planning freedom, and sang "the lord" in place of "Yankee," to blind any one who might be listening.[75]

By 1862 neither southern police officers nor southern slaves were able any longer to turn a blind eye to the powerful hope for freedom that was growing across the Confederacy.

The movement for women's rights and the antislavery movements were much more closely connected throughout the nineteenth century than many have recognized. Leaders in both were good friends and supported each other in many ways. With the coming of the war, women's rights leaders increased their antislavery activity while also linking it to their own concerns. Elizabeth Cady Stanton and Susan B. Anthony, in consultation with others, created a Women's Loyal League in 1861 to press for a constitutional amendment that would abolish slavery. Among the resolutions adopted at its founding meeting in May 1861 was a clear statement of the link between their concerns that, "There can never be a true peace in this Republic until the civil and political rights of all citizens of African descent and all women are practically established." This was followed by a pledge of, "our time, our means, our talents, and our lives, if need be, to secure the final and complete consecration of America to freedom." These women were quite clear on what this "complete consecration" meant. The members of the league scoured the nation getting signatures on petitions demanding immediate emancipation of the slaves. Ultimately 300,000 signatures were collected which, no doubt, helped push the ever cautious Lincoln toward his final Emancipation Proclamation.[76]

In one of her speeches about the work of the Loyal League, Susan B. Anthony provides a glimpse of the degree to which these feminists were far beyond the president in their commitment to equality.[77] For Anthony, Stanton, and other radical feminists, the goal could never be a return to the conditions before the war:

We talk about returning to the old Union—"the Union as it was," and "the Constitution as it is"—about "restoring our country to peace and prosperity—to the blessed conditions that existed before the war!" I ask you what sort of peace, what sort of prosperity, have we had? Since the first slave-ship sailed up the James River with its human cargo, and there, on the soil of the *Old* Dominion, it was sold to the highest bidder, we have had nothing but war. When that pirate captain landed on the shores of Africa, and there kidnapped the first stalwart Negro, and fastened the first manacle, the struggle between that captain and that Negro was the commencement of the terrible war in the midst of which we are to-day. Between the slave and the master there has been war, and war only, from the beginning. This is only a new form of the war. No, no; we ask for the no return to the *old* conditions. We ask for something better than the old. We want a Union that is a Union in fact, a Union in spirit, not a sham Union.[78]

The great hope for a new and just Union was the only cause for which Anthony was willing to urge action, as it would be for the next forty years of her career.

Anthony never did make her peace with Lincoln. At the end of the war she was furious that the president was considering the readmission of Louisiana to the Union without first giving the newly freed slaves of that state the vote. When news of the president's assassination reached her, she wrote to a friend, "And this blow fell just at the very hour he was declaring his willingness to consign those five million faithful brave, and loving loyal people of the south to the tender mercies of the ex slave lords of the lash—." In spite of the later mythology that sprang up around the martyred president, many of the abolitionists and feminists of the day shared the same judgment of President Lincoln.[79]

Perhaps William Lloyd Garrison said it best when, in his own eulogy for the president, he remembered Lincoln's maddeningly slow pace in moving toward emancipation. Lincoln, Garrison said, did not have much of a record as "either a philanthropist or a reformer, [but] no man ever did so large a business on so small a capital in the service of freedom and humanity." Lincoln had many faults, but it was his hand that signed the document ending slavery in the United States.[80]

Given his central, if sometimes ambiguous role, any discussion of the hopeful aspects of the history of the nineteenth century must include a discussion of the nation's sixteenth president. Abraham Lincoln is certainly a figure who elicits mixed responses—not only from Susan B. Anthony or William Lloyd Garrison but from anyone who reads his words and the record of his actions. Without question, Lincoln offered some of the grandest and most hope-filled rhetoric of any American ever. And he achieved great political power and used that power not only to speak but also to act. His condemnation of slavery, at times, could not have been clearer. Thus in 1858 he said: "As I would not be a slave, so I would not be a master. This expresses my idea of democracy. Whatever differs from this, to the extent of the difference, is not democracy."[81] Nevertheless, to the deep disappointment of other abolitionists, Lincoln the man clearly held personally racist views and Lincoln the politician was painfully cautious.

In all of his speeches prior to his election to the presidency, and continuing up to the Emancipation Proclamation in 1862, Lincoln made it clear that though he personally opposed slavery, and believed that the Constitution gave Congress the right to prohibit it in the territories, he did not think that the Constitution gave the president or the Congress the right to tamper with slavery in the states where it already existed. For abolitionists like Frederick Douglass, Susan B. Anthony, and William Lloyd Garrison, to say nothing of John Brown, this view was mere temporizing. Nevertheless, he also insisted that when the Declaration of Independence said "all men are created equal" (he did not even begin to engage the sexism of the founding document), he believed that it included African Americans as well as European Americans. Once the war began, unlike many northerners, he would not compromise with the South even if the war continued "until all the wealth piled by the bond-man's two hundred and fifty years of unrequited toil shall be sunk, and until every drop of blood drawn with the lash, shall be paid by another drawn with the sword." And he won and used the ultimate political power of the country to bring an end to slavery's two-hundred-and-fifty-year history in the lands of the United States.

At the end, a month before his assassination, Lincoln stood at the Capitol to give his second inaugural address as President of the United States. In that short speech he summed up the war that was just ending and his great hopes for the nation's future. The speech has properly become one of the nation's sacred documents, for it makes no pretense at avoiding the pain and cost that slavery had inflicted on the land and yet it voiced some of the grandest hopes for the future of the nation. In March 1865, Lincoln told the nation, "Both parties deprecated war; but one of them would *make* war rather than let the nation survive; and the other would *accept* war rather than let it perish. And the war came."

And at the war's end, he was quite clear just why it had come:

One eighth of the whole population were colored slaves, not distributed generally over the Union, but localized in the Southern part of it. These slaves constituted a peculiar and powerful interest. All knew that this interest was, somehow, the cause of the war. To strengthen, perpetuate, and extend this interest was the object for which the insurgents would rend the Union, even by war; while the government claimed no right to do more than to restrict the territorial enlargement of it. Neither party expected for the war, the magnitude, or the duration, which it has already attained. Neither anticipated that the *cause* of the conflict might cease with, or even before, the conflict itself should cease. Each looked for an easier triumph, and a result less fundamental and astounding. Both read the same Bible, and pray to the same God; and each invokes His aid against the other. It may seem strange that any men should dare to ask a just God's assistance in wringing their bread from the sweat of other men's faces; but let us judge not that we be not judged. The prayers of both could not be answered; that of neither has been answered fully. The Almighty has his own purposes. "Woe unto the world because of offences! for it must needs be that offences come; but woe to that man by whom the offence cometh!" If we shall suppose that American Slavery is one of those offences which, in the providence of God, must needs come, but which, having continued through His appointed time, He now wills to remove, and that He gives to both North and South, this terrible war, as the woe due to those by whom the offence came. . . . Fondly do we hope—fervently do we pray—that this might scourge of war may speedily pass away.

In his conclusion, Lincoln looked to the future. He held out a dream of reconciliation beyond the hopes of many, but not reconciliation at the cost of injustice.

With malice toward none; with charity for all; with firmness in the right, as God gives us to see the right, let us strive on to finish the work we are in; to bind up the nation's wounds; to care for him who shall have borne the battle, and for his widow, and his orphan—to do all which may achieve and cherish a just and a lasting peace, among ourselves, and with all nations.[82]

None of Lincoln's hopes were completely fulfilled. Reconstruction had much more malice and much less justice than his words led his fellow citizens to expect. But the dream of a nation united in justice and peace would not die.

The work of abolishing slavery ended with the words of Abraham Lincoln and the victories of the Union army. But the abolition of slavery had begun long before, in the courageous resistance of slaves who ran away, who rebelled, who fought for their freedom. It had begun in the organizing and the preaching and the actions of free blacks and their white allies. Many people, located in different places and times, made their contribution to the final fulfillment of the hope that slavery would, indeed, be abolished in America. And that hope was fulfilled.

CHAPTER FIVE

RECONSTRUCTION:
THE FIRST CIVIL RIGHTS ERA

FREE AT LAST, 1863–1865

ON JUNE 19, 1865, TWO MONTHS after Robert E. Lee's historic surrender at Appomattox Court House in Virginia, and fifteen hundred miles away, the Union army finally arrived in Texas. A detachment of Union soldiers under the command of Major General Gordon Granger landed at Galveston harbor. The last state of the Confederacy was finally under the flag of the United States once again. One of General Granger's first acts after he and his troops had landed was to read a series of official proclamations to the people of Texas. The most significant was General Order Number 3:

> The people of Texas are informed that in accordance with a Proclamation from the executive of the United States, all slaves are free. This involves an absolute equality of rights and rights of property between former masters and slaves, and the connection heretofore existing between them becomes that between employer and free laborer.

Finally, the sometimes seemingly impossible hopes of slaves and their allies for the past two hundred and forty-six years had been fulfilled. Slavery had ended across North America.[1]

June 19, 1865—Juneteenth as the holiday celebrating the event came to be called—represents an extraordinary time of hope and new beginnings. In the years and decades immediately following emancipation, Juneteenth became one of the most important holidays of the year within Texas's African American community. It was a time for barbecuing, rodeos, speeches, and other special symbols of celebration. Former slaves and their descendants gathered in parks and on farms across the state while many returned every year to Galveston to remember the date with prayers, speeches, food, and fundraising for the African American community. While the celebration declined in the early years of the twentieth century, Juneteenth resurfaced later and was declared an official state holiday in Texas in 1980.[2]

As word of Granger's order announcing and enforcing the Emancipation Proclamation spread across Galveston and then across all of Texas, jubilation, shock, and uncertainty followed. For some slaves, nothing mattered more than getting away from the plantation that had been the source of their degradation. They moved a short distance to be with friends and family or great distances to Louisiana, Oklahoma Territory, or the North. For others, the news that they could now be wage-earning employees was worth exploring. But for every slave in Texas, as for those who had been receiving the same news following the victories of the Union troops across the South for the previous two years, emancipation changed every aspect of life and made everything possible.

Similar celebrations had been taking place across the South even before the Emancipation Proclamation itself, when the Union armies freed slaves on the coast of South Carolina, in parts of Tennessee and Louisiana, and then during General William T. Sherman's march to Atlanta. And, as the historian Eric Foner has said, "The Emancipation Proclamation and the presence of black troops ensured that, in the last two years of the war, Union soldiers acted as an army of liberation."[3]

On February 18, 1865, the Union army took Charleston, South Carolina, the home of Fort Sumter where the war had begun. Among the triumphant soldiers marching into Charleston that day was the Massachusetts 54th Infantry, the African American unit, singing "John Brown's Body." An official celebration of the liberation of Charleston in March included four thousand African Americans. Schoolchildren marched with a banner "We Know No Master but Ourselves," and a group of adults carried a coffin with a sign "Slavery is Dead." One Union officer watching the flag raising at Fort Sumter said, "that now for the first time is the black man's as well as the white man's flag."[4]

Richmond, Virginia, the capital of the Confederacy, fell to Ulysses S. Grant's troops on April 3, and the celebration was filled with joy as those who had recently been slaves now prayed, danced, and sang "Slavery chain done broke at last." The next day President Lincoln himself walked the streets of the city, and one Richmond black told his former master, "There was to be no more Master and Mistress now, all was equal."[5]

In fact, many slaves across the Confederacy had not waited for the Union army. On Jefferson Davis's huge old plantation at Davis Bend on the Mississippi River, the president of the Confederacy and his brother, Joseph, had been known as kinder than some owners. Nevertheless, when Joseph Davis fled in 1862, the slaves took over the property and began running it themselves, much to the surprise of General Grant who arrived with the Union army in 1863.[6] And in spite of those planters who managed to stay out of the way of the Union troops, word passed quickly among the slaves. In Mississippi, while the war was still faraway, one black responded to a planter's greeting "Howdy, Uncle" with an angry "Call me Mister." On other plantations slaves simply refused to work unless they were paid, while still others moved on without any permission.[7]

Lincoln's Emancipation Proclamation in January 1863 and the December 1865 ratification of the Thirteenth Amendment to the United States Constitution, abolishing slavery forever, closed one chapter in the struggle for democracy while it opened another. Few moments in the nation's history could have been more hopeful than those days as the Civil War was ending and a new future was beginning, especially for the four million Americans who at the war's start had been held as the property of others. The frightening experiences of many African Americans through the years immediately after the war, and ultimately the tragic failure of Reconstruction itself in the 1870s and 1880s, have sometimes blinded historians to the hopes that emancipation initially brought. In the late 1860s and afterward, as their former owners tried to transform freedom into a wage slavery called sharecropping and as other whites sought to ensure their sense of superiority by a series of riots and terrorist activities, such as those by the Ku Klux Klan, hope dimmed dramatically. But at the time of emancipation, it could not have burned brighter.

Eric Foner, whose own studies vividly report the tragic disappointments of Reconstruction, nevertheless argues, "Despite the many disappointments that followed, this generation of blacks would always regard the moment when 'de freedom sun shine out' as the great watershed of their lives." Foner quotes Houston H. Holloway, a slave sold three times before his twentieth birthday in 1865, who recalled the day emancipation came to him in Georgia: "I felt like a bird out of a cage. Amen. Amen. Amen. I could hardly ask to feel any better than I did that day. . . . The week passed off in a blaze of glory." And six weeks later Holloway and his wife "received my free born son into the world."[8] Such changes could not but inspire the greatest of hopes.

In the aftermath of the Civil War women and men who had been the property of others found that they could buy property—land and homes. They could travel where they wanted without the hated passes from white masters. They could be reunited with family members from whom they had been separated against their will. People, whom only months before it had been illegal for others to teach to read and write, now became literate by the millions and became teachers, started their own schools, and opened colleges and universities. Slaves and free blacks who had never dreamed of voting became voters and officeholders as members of state legislatures, statewide officers, and members of the United States Congress. They passed laws creating a system of public education across the South and dreamed of a time when race would no longer be a factor in the opportunities available to African Americans in the economy, the culture, and the politics of the nation.

Reconstruction itself must be divided into the conservative phase of Presidential Reconstruction led by Andrew Johnson in 1865 and 1866, when the focus was on returning power to white Southern governments, and the happily more hopeful and radical phase of Congressional Reconstruction that began in 1867 and that by 1870 had led to the election of numerous African American officeholders and the creation of a range of African American–led institutions. Yet, even in the best of times, Reconstruction was always unraveling under the combined legal assault of conservatives from the North and South and the violence of groups such as the Klan. The withdrawal of federal troops following the election of 1876 accelerated the demise of Reconstruction, but it took two more decades before the full flowering of the Jim Crow separate and unequal South was in place.[9]

The forces of racism and reaction, allied to the fatigue and greed of others, were too great to allow the hopes of Reconstruction to be fulfilled. Nevertheless, for a brief moment after the Civil War, Reconstruction offered the most far-reaching hopes for change and a just and inclusive democracy ever dreamed of in the nation's history. The dreams were not realized. Vigilante violence across the South, corrupt politics at the local level and at state and federal capitals, compromise and abandonment—all served to undermine the dream. But the hopes of Reconstruction, the first great civil rights movement in the United States, must not be forgotten. There is perhaps no other era of American history for which historians need to attend as closely to E. P. Thompson's reminder "After all, we are not at the end of social evolution ourselves. In some of the lost causes of the people . . . we may discover insights into social evils which we have yet to cure." [10] In the dreams of Reconstruction, there was a vision of justice which indeed offers "insights into social evils which we have yet to cure." It is a vision well worth the attention of those who dare to hope in the twenty-first century.

"A WHOLE RACE TRYING
TO GO TO SCHOOL"

Looking back on the euphoric first days after emancipation, Booker T. Washington remembered: "Few people who were not right in the midst of the scenes can form any exact idea of the intense desire which the people of my race showed for education. It was a whole race trying to go to school. Few were too young, and none too old, to make the attempt to learn."[11] Education was important to the newly free men and women for many reasons, but it was terribly important to nearly all of them.

Northern whites who came to the South first with the Union army and then with the Freedmen's Bureau were continually amazed by the thirst of the freed blacks for education and literacy. One northern teacher, who had gone to Florida to teach, told of a sixty-year-old woman who, "just beginning to spell, seems as if she could not think of any thing but her books, says she spells her lesson all the evening, then she dreams about it, and wakes up thinking about it." Another elderly freedman in Mobile, Alabama, told a northern reporter, "he wouldn't trouble the lady much, but he must learn to read the Bible and the Testament." In Mississippi another elderly pupil focused more on this world than the next, telling a teacher, "I gets almost discouraged, but I does want to learn to cipher so I can do business." And perhaps summing up the others, a member of an education society in North Carolina said, "he thought a school-house would be the first proof of their *independence*."[12]

Seeing the schoolhouse as "proof of their independence" surprised numerous white observers, including Harriet Beecher Stowe, who in 1879 reported, "They rushed not to the grog-shop but to the schoolroom—they cried for the spelling-book as bread, and pleaded for teachers as a necessity of life."[13] In fact, the urgency would have been relatively easily comprehensible for anyone who examined the nature of Southern slavery during the previous half-century. James Anderson, the foremost historian of nineteenth-century African American education, has written:

During the three decades before the Civil War slaves lived in a society in which for them literacy was forbidden by law and symbolized as a skill that contradicted the status of slaves. As former slave William Henry Heard recalled: "We did not learn to read nor write, as it was against the law for any person to teach any slave to read; and any slave caught writing suffered the penalty of having his forefinger cut from his right hand; yet there were some who could read and write." Despite the dangers and difficulties, thousands of slaves learned to read and write. By 1860 about 5 percent of the slaves had learned to read. . . . No other class of native southerners had experienced literacy in this context. Hence emancipation extruded an ex-slave class with a fundamentally different consciousness of literacy, a class that viewed reading and writing as a contradiction of oppression.[14]

Seen in this context, "the spelling-book as bread" and "teachers as a necessity of life" makes great sense, for these were the clearest possible symbols of a new life of freedom.

Even before the end of the peculiar institution, one of the nation's most famous runaway slaves had explained the lessons that he had learned early in life about the power of literacy. While still a very young child of seven or eight, Frederick Douglass had been loaned by the owner of the rural Maryland plantation where he had been born to a family in Baltimore who wanted help in raising their young son. His new mistress had not previously owned slaves and saw no reason not to teach the alphabet to the young Frederick, along with her own son. In this home Douglass learned the alphabet and to spell a few simple words. The lessons, however, did not last long. As Douglass recalled:

> Just at this point of my progress, Mr. Auld found out what was going on, and at once forbade Mrs. Auld to instruct me further, telling her, among other things, that it was unlawful, as well as unsafe, to teach a slave to read. To use his own words, further, he said, "If you give a nigger an inch, he will take an ell. A nigger should know nothing but to obey his master—to do as he is told to do. Learning would *spoil* the best nigger in the world. Now," said he, "if you teach that nigger (Speaking of myself) how to read, there would be no keeping him. It would forever unfit him to be a slave."[15]

Few things appealed more to the child than being made unfit for his prescribed future. Things that had puzzled him as a child now made sense. "From that moment, I understood the pathway from slavery to freedom." In an odd way, the master had taught more than the mistress:

> The very decided manner with which he spoke, and strove to impress his wife with the evil consequences of giving me instruction, served to convince me that he was deeply sensible of the truths he was uttering. It gave me the best assurance that I might rely with the utmost confidence on the results which, he said, would flow from teaching me to read. What he most dreaded, that I most desired. What he most loved, that I most hated. That which to him was a great evil, to be carefully shunned, was to me a great good, to be diligently sought; and the argument which he so warmly urged, against my learning to read, only served to inspire me with a desire and determination to learn. In

learning to read, I owe almost as much to the bitter opposition of my master, as to the kindly aid of my mistress. I acknowledge the benefit of both.[16]

And with his new passion for study, Douglass made quick progress. During his seven years as a household servant in Baltimore, Douglass was given many errands to run, and most errands offered a chance to meet up with free white boys who would trade lessons for the bread that was made in the Auld home. By the time the young man Douglass made his escape to Massachusetts, he had the literacy skills that would make him one of the great orators and writers of the nineteenth century.[17]

If individual slave masters, like Mr. Auld, and the legislatures of every Southern state except Tennessee had made it illegal to teach a slave to read or write, they had also made literacy a most powerful symbol of freedom. Those who saw the first fruits of the combined hopes for freedom and literacy were amazed at the innovative ways the freedmen handled education. The task was extraordinary: in spite of the secret lessons won by Douglass and many others, at least 90 percent of the ex-slaves were illiterate in 1865. But change came quickly.[18]

Some of the earliest teaching was highly informal. Someone with a little literacy shared what he or she knew with others. A book would make the rounds. An officer of the Freedmen's Bureau described what he called the "wayside schools": "A negro riding on a loaded wagon, or sitting on a hack waiting for a train, or by the cabin door, is often seen, book in hand delving after the rudiments of knowledge. A group on the platform of a depot, after carefully conning an old spelling book, resolves itself into a class."[19] Such were the beginnings of the schools for freedmen. But more formal instruction quickly followed, and in some cases preceded, emancipation.

In the year the war began, Mary Peake, daughter of a free black mother and an English father, opened a school in Hampton, Virginia, before the first northern teachers arrived. The great educational experiment on the Sea Islands off the Carolina coast began operation with two schools taught by blacks before the first white teachers arrived. One of the Sea Island teachers was a cabinetmaker who apparently had been teaching a secret school at night for slaves for years.[20]

One of the closest white observers of schools that were operated independently by African Americans during and immediately after the Civil War was John W. Alvord, who was appointed first as inspector and later as general superintendent of schools by the Freedmen's Bureau. Alvord had been one of the Lane rebels in 1834. Now assigned the task of setting up schools across the South, Alvord recorded his initial surprise that they were already in operation when he arrived to start them. "Throughout the entire South," he reported, "an effort is being made by the colored people to educate themselves." Alvord found what he called a system of "native schools" and reported many examples. At Goldsboro, North Carolina, he found "two colored young men, who but a little time before commenced to learn themselves, had gathered 150 pupils, all quite orderly and hard at study." And, he continued, "no white man, before me, had ever come near them."[21] Indeed, Alvord found the story repeated again and again. He found that prior to the arrival of the army or northern teachers, schools were "making their appearance through the *interior* of the entire South." In his 1866 report, using information from his far-flung agents, Alvord estimated that there were "at least 500 schools of this description . . . already in operation throughout the South." And so, he concluded, "This educational movement among the freedmen has in it a self-sustaining element," not dependent on northern philanthropy in any form.[22]

Thanks to the work of James Anderson and others, the fact that the first schools in the South were founded by freedmen and free blacks is no longer subject to debate. Nevertheless, white agents of the Freedmen's Bureau and northern missionaries, white and black, also played an important role in the extraordinary literacy campaign that took place in the South in the late 1860s. W. E. B. DuBois described what he called "the crusade of the New England schoolma'am."

> Behind the mists of ruin and rapine waved the calico dresses of women who dared, and after the hoarse mouthings of the field guns rang the rhythm of the alphabet. Rich and poor they were, serious and curious. Bereaved now of a father, now of a brother, now of more than these, they came seeking a life work in planting New England schoolhouses among the white and black of the South. They did their work well. In that first year they taught one hundred thousand souls, and more.[23]

Sent by churches and the government, the best of these teachers became allies of the teachers who were already in the field and changed the region.

While the majority of teachers who went south were European American women, there were also free African Americans from the North who joined the missionary movement. Because of her extraordinary journal, Charlotte Forten was perhaps the best-known of these African American teachers. Born free in Philadelphia in 1837, Forten later moved to Salem, Massachusetts, where she taught in the Epes Grammar School in the late 1850s. As a teacher, a religious person, and an African American, Forten was anxious to teach in the schools for the recently freed slaves as quickly as possible.

Her opportunity came early in the war. One of the earliest experiments of the federal government in opening schools for the ex-slaves was in Port Royal, South Carolina, where the military had taken control of the coastal islands as part of the effort to blockade southern ports. On the Sea Islands the federal government sought to set up a model community for the former slaves even before the question of their postwar status had been settled, and schools were an essential element in that community. As noted above, the former slaves had started the first Sea Island schools on their own. But the Union army dramatically expanded the effort with the aid of teachers such as Forten.

Because Forten's journal was written at the time, and not as a reminiscence from later years, it gives the reader a glimpse of the urgency she and other teachers felt about their mission.

In early September 1862, while still waiting for an assignment, Forten reported, "Have been anxious and disappointed at nor hearing." A month later the news she wanted came. On October 21 she wrote: "To-day rec'd a note from Mr. McK.[im] asking me if I c'ld possibly be ready to sail for Port Royal perhaps tomorrow. I was astonished, stupefied, and, at first thought it impossible. . . . It will probably be the only opportunity that I shall have of going this winter, so at any cost I *will* go." [24]

A week later, her entry for October 27 reported, "I am in a state of utter bewilderment. It was on Wed. I rec'd the note. On Thursday I said 'good bye' to the friends that are so dear. . . . Enjoyed the sail down the harbor perfectly." And soon thereafter, "Mr. [John] H.[unn] came to our door to tell us that we were in sight of the blockading fleet in Charlestown harbor. Of course, we sprang to the window eagerly; and saw the masts of the ships looking like a grove of trees in the distance. We were not near enough to see the city. It was hard to realize that we were even so near the barbarous place." Before the end of October 1862, Forten was in the middle of the Confederacy, off the coast of South Carolina, with a mission to teach fellow African Americans. Indeed, she reported that she soon "began to feel quite at home in the very heart of Rebeldom; only that I do not at all realize yet that we are in S.[outh] C.[arolina]." [25]

Teaching was not always easy. In spite of her prior experience, Forten reported of one day, "Had a dreadfully wearying day in school, of which the less said the better." Nevertheless, the overall experience was quite extraordinary for this northern free woman.

The children are well-behaved and eager to learn. It will be a happiness to teach here. . . . We taught—or rather commenced teaching the children "John Brown" which they entered into eagerly. I felt the full significance of *that* song being sung here in S.[outh] C.[arolina] by little negro children, by those whom he—the glorious old man—died to save. Miss [Laura] T.[owne] told them about him. . . . Talked to the children a little while to-day about the noble Toussaint. They listened very attentively. It is well that they sh'ld know what one of their own color c'ld do for his race. I long to inspire them with courage and ambition (of a noble sort), and high purposes. It is noticeable how very few mulattos there are here. Indeed in our school, with one or two exceptions, the children are all black. . . . This eve. Harry, one of the men on the place, came in for a lesson. He is most eager to learn, and is really a scholar to be proud of. He learns rapidly. I gave him his first lesson in writing to-night, and his progress was wonderful. He held his pen almost perfectly right the first time. He will very soon learn to write, I think. I must inquire who w'ld like to take lessons at night. Whenever I am well enough it will be a real pleasure to teach them.[26]

And so her experience continued. She reported days of discouragement and days of great successes. But most of all she reported the hopes and joys of new freedoms won. On Thanksgiving Day, November 27, 1862, she attended church:

This morning a large number—Superintendents, teachers, and freed people, assembled in the little Baptist church. It was a sight that I shall not soon forget—that crowd of eager, happy black faces from which the shadow of slavery had forever passed. "Forever free!" "Forever free!" Those magical words were all the time singing themselves in my soul, and never before have I felt so truly grateful to God.[27]

These northern teachers, DuBois's "crusade of the New England school-ma'am," had been allowed to participate in one of history's truly hope-filled moments.

Forten was hardly alone. By 1870 there were several thousand teachers in the South divided between northerners—mostly whites—and southerners—mostly blacks. Many of them left valuable records. Maria S. Waterbury reported, "The instructions of the missionary society, are, 'go south about eight hundred miles, until you find the plantation school waiting for you.'" She more or less followed the instructions, faced down several angry mobs of whites, and at the end of the year she and a colleague reported, "We have taught over two hundred colored people, only two lady teachers. . . . We have lived in an old school building, used for a white school in slave times."[28] Through the courage of Forten, Waterbury, and thousands of others, Washington's "whole race going to school" had the teachers they needed.

While a majority of the teachers stayed for a year or two, some found their life's work in teaching in the new schools of the South. Laura M. Towne, Forten's white colleague on the Sea Islands, stayed on in the South for many years. In May 1871 she wrote to relatives in Massachusetts, "I do never intend to leave this 'heathen country.' I intend to end my days here and I wish to." Six years later, in November 1877, her enthusiasm was unabated, "if it were not for the almanac I should declare the last twenty years were only twenty months. Every year gets shorter too, and the next twenty may seem like twenty weeks. We have all had exceptionally happy lives, I think, so far, and I hope our years will grow only pleasanter and pleasanter, and I do not see why they shouldn't for a long time to come." What some viewed as sacrifice, others, in spite of danger and loneliness, found as the most fulfilling of a life's work. Towne did indeed stay another twenty years and more; she died in South Carolina in 1901.[29]

The arriving northern teachers had mixed experiences engaging with the former slaves who were already teaching across the former Confederacy. Nearly all were surprised by the degree of learning already taking place among people when they expected to find only illiteracy and degradation. Some adjusted quickly and became important allies. Others changed over time. And still others failed miserably to appreciate what they found.

The American Missionary Association was one of the leading religious organizations sending teachers south. One of its white teachers, William Channing Gannett, also understood perhaps better than most the tension between their valuable work and the need to respect the indigenous efforts. He reported "they have a natural praiseworthy pride in keeping their educational institutions in their own hands. There is jealousy of the superintendence of the white man in this matter. What they desire is assistance without control." Indeed, assistance without control was not just what was desired but what was needed if this hopeful experiment in education was to flourish and be sustained.[30] If everyone had understood Gannett's plea, the hopeful alliance of northern philanthropy and southern initiative might have flourished far more than it did.

Other northern missionaries were considerably less sensitive than Gannett, however. Rev. S. W. Magill, also representing the American Missionary Association, arrived in Savannah, Georgia, in the wake of Sherman's army. He found that local black ministers had already established the Savannah Educational Association, raised nearly $1,000, and enrolled 600 pupils in schools taught by fifteen black teachers. He also did not like what he found. He thought the black teachers were incompetent and the schools "radically defective." He reported, "It will not do to leave these people to themselves." Eventually, the Savannah Educational Association was forced to turn all of its resources over to the AMA, and its teachers were at best relegated to assisting white teachers. It was a tragic outcome to a well-meaning effort.[31]

Fortunately not all AMA representatives or their counterparts from other organizations were as insensitive as Magill, even if many were not as wise as Gannett or Alvord of the Freedmen's Bureau. Tensions between well-intentioned helpers and those they seek to help are not unusual throughout history. When the cultural differences and basic lack of information that both groups had about each other were as great as in the case of the northern teachers and the freedmen, it is amazing that the tensions were not greater. One wonders what the full story might have been behind a vote in a North Carolina convention of black citizens when a proposed resolution urging blacks to employ teachers of their own race wherever possible was tabled in favor of one thanking northern societies for their efforts.[32] In fact, both sentiments were probably widely shared across the convention and the region.

In time, however, African Americans, both newly free and those who had been born free, began to take charge of the schools of the South. In the process they laid the foundation for a public education system in the South where none had existed before. The ever observant John Alvord reported as early as 1866 "that the surprising efforts of our colored population to obtain an education is not spasmodic." And he continued, "They are growing to a habit, crystallizing into a system, and each succeeding school-term shows their organization more and more complete and permanent."[33]

Alvord and others in the Freedmen's Bureau were part of the process of organizing a system of public education. General Oliver O. Howard, the head of the Freedman's Bureau, greatly valued education and assigned all of his agents to work closely with the northern aid societies who were sending teachers south. The bureau also kept detailed records of the more well-established schools, plus reports like Alvord's on the more informal but probably more widespread educational efforts. The bureau also played a role in the founding of some of the black colleges in the South, including Atlanta, Fisk, Hampton, and Tougaloo, which were specifically designed to train teachers. And as early as 1869 the bureau was reporting that of the 3,000 teachers for the freedmen, the majority were now African American. Since this report did not include Sunday schools and other ventures where the black majority was even greater, this is a significant—and too often unnoticed—statistic.[34]

The move from informal patterns of education to structured systems of schools in cities, towns, and states began in the parts of the South where the Union army had its earliest victories. Major General Nathaniel P. Banks was the military leader of the Department of the Gulf that included Louisiana, Mississippi, Alabama, and Texas. In October 1863 Banks established schools for blacks in New Orleans, which had been held by Union troops since earlier that year. On March 22, 1864, he created a Board of Education to administer the black schools in New Orleans, and by the following fall the *New Orleans Tribune*, a black newspaper, reported that there were over 60 schools with "eight thousand scholars and more than one hundred teachers." In July 1864 the paper had also reported that schools had been extended beyond the city where teachers had been "sent to instruct black pupils in rural areas." When the Freedmen's Bureau took control of the school system in 1865, it included 126 schools with 19,000 students and 100 teachers.[35]

In Georgia in 1865 African American leaders formed the Georgia Educational Association. The association's goal was clear: "that the freedmen shall establish schools in their own counties and neighborhoods, to be supported entirely by the colored people." A year later, in the fall of 1866, they could report that they had financed—on their own or with outside support—96 of the 123 day and evening schools, and the association owned 57 school buildings. Their successes at such an early date were quite amazing. The *Loyal Georgian*, a black paper, reported that in Savannah 16 of the city's 28 schools were under the association's control, that is, "under the control of an Educational Board of Colored Men, taught by colored teachers, and sustained by the freed people."[36]

When Congress took control of the Reconstruction effort away from the more cautious President Johnson with the Reconstruction Act of 1867, the shift from military and Freedmen's Bureau control to state and local autonomy—with significant black involvement—expanded rapidly. The 1867 Act required all states of the former Confederacy to call state conventions to rewrite their state constitutions. The new constitutions were expected to include universal male suffrage, the exclusion of former Confederate officials from office, and the ratification of the Fourteenth Amendment. Johnson's version of home rule that had been instituted in 1865 and 1866 was discredited because it resembled the antebellum South in far too many ways; most of all, in the absoluteness of white rule and the exclusion of freedmen from both voice and benefits of government. The fact that fifty-eight members of the Confederate Congress, six Confederate cabinet officers, and the vice president of the Confederacy where all elected to Congress in 1865 and 1866 symbolized the failure of Johnson's policy to bring about meaningful change.[37]

The new conventions that met under the terms of the 1867 Reconstruction Act were quite different. Every one of them had black members and South Carolina's had a black majority. The new constitutions also provided for a system of public education in every southern state; none of them had such provisions prior to the war. During the radical phase of Reconstruction that followed, African Americans held public office across the South. While—contrary to some later mythology—there was no time when a southern state was controlled by a black majority, blacks did have significant influence in the legislatures and state capitals. When they allied themselves with reformist whites—many of whom were northern "carpetbaggers" or "scalawags" as pro-Reconstruction southern whites were called by their hostile neighbors—they were able to make significant changes in the laws of their states. And no change was more significant than the establishment of a system of public education. Even after the failure of Reconstruction, when state after state returned to white rule in the late 1870s and early 1880s, the public school system remained a part of the law and a part of the landscape where no such system had existed before. Public schooling is perhaps the proudest legacy of Reconstruction.[38]

In *Black Reconstruction in America*, W. E. B. DuBois wrote, "Public education for all at public expense was, in the South, a Negro idea."[39] He was not exaggerating. It is also true, as Eric Foner said more recently of the Reconstruction efforts in education and other areas that, "All witnessed dramatic departures from the traditions of the prewar South but in all, Republicans' achievements, while substantial, failed to live up fully to the lofty goals with which Reconstruction began."[40] With the end of Reconstruction, as white regimes took over the South state by state, disenfranchising blacks and their allies, the school systems atrophied. The systems remained but they were segregated, underfunded—especially for blacks—and far from what they should have been. But the hopes for literacy and universal education that had been so powerfully unleashed with emancipation also continued. They went underground and moved slowly. James Anderson has summed up the state of African American education in the half century that followed the end of Reconstruction with a reminder that:

> High schools were virtually nonexistent, and the general unavailability of secondary education precluded even the opportunity to prepare for college. The education of blacks in the South reveals that various contending forces sought either to repress the development of black education or to shape it in ways that contradicted blacks' interests in intellectual development. The educational outcomes demonstrate that blacks got some but not much of what they wanted. They entered emancipation with fairly definite ideas about how to integrate education into their broader struggle for freedom and prosperity, but they were largely unable to shape their future in accordance with their social vision.[41]

But as James Anderson has also noted, the seeds of something else were sown in these years. For all of the second-class status of black education for most of the following century, for all of the compromises that black educators had to make to simply continue their work in a hostile environment, they planted powerful seeds: "When their students helped launch the civil rights movement of the 1960s, the hard work of these educators seemed far more heroic in the hour of harvest than it did during the years of cultivation."[42] And that hour was, indeed, a flourishing of the hopes of 1865.

WHAT THE BLACK MAN WANTS/
WHAT THE BLACK WOMAN WANTS

Early in 1865, before the final Union victories that led to the South's surrender, Frederick Douglass appeared before a meeting of the Massachusetts Anti-Slavery Society. The society, with which Douglass had been so closely allied for so long, was at a crossroads. With the Emancipation Proclamation the Civil War had become a crusade to end slavery. And now the end was in sight—the end of the war and the end of slavery. The question for the society then was, what next? For many of its leaders, including the nearly iconic William Lloyd Garrison, the society had completed its mission and should disband. Others, including clearly Douglass, disagreed strongly.

In his speech Douglass outlined what he saw as the essential next step for the society and, much more important, for all African Americans and their white allies. The battle for freedom was not over; the hopes of the abolitionists had only begun to be fulfilled. So, Douglass argued, those who had for thirty years hoped and fought for the immediate, unconditional, and universal end of slavery now had a new mission, the "'immediate, unconditional, and universal' enfranchisement of the black man, in every State in the Union."[43] Without the vote, Douglass argued, the hope of emancipation was an empty promise. With the vote, emancipation would be complete and the victory of the war would be complete also.

While he was speaking to a very specific issue facing a specific group of abolitionists, Douglass was also speaking over their heads to the nation and to his fellow African Americans. The agenda, Douglass argued, must be the vote. There were at least three reasons why enfranchisement was essential to the meaning of emancipation. First, Douglass insisted, African Americans needed the vote because "it is our right," and "No class of men can, without insulting their own nature, be content with any deprivation of their rights." But there was more. The vote was essential to the continued self-image and education of the newly freed—and about to be freed—slaves. "Men are so constituted," Douglass said, "that they derive their conviction of their own possibilities largely from the estimate formed of them by others." Allow the freedmen to be treated as second-class citizens and they would become second-class citizens in their own minds, Douglass asserted. But finally, and most important, Douglass wanted the vote because the vote was the key to American democracy, because "ours is a peculiar government, based upon a peculiar idea, and that idea is universal suffrage." If African Americans lived in a monarchy, where many could not vote, the lack of a vote would not carry the same stigma, "but here where universal suffrage is the rule, where that is the fundamental idea of the Government, to rule us out is to make us an exception, to brand us with the stigma of inferiority, and to invite to our heads the missiles of those about us; therefore, I want the franchise for the black man."[44]

Douglass also had pragmatic reasons for urging a northern white audience to campaign for the vote for blacks. When the war was over, when Reconstruction began, northern Republicans would need the black vote in the South. Partly this was a matter of justice. As the war had progressed, the North had called on slaves to be their allies, resist the Confederacy, and enlist in the Union army. "Do you mean," Douglass asked incredulously, "to give your enemies the right to vote, and take it away from your friends?" But there was more than justice involved.

Douglass recognized, more quickly than most in the government, that the white South would not quickly reconcile to its multiple defeats—the loss of independence, the loss of the slaves, the loss of its economy. Once the leaders, the Davises and others, had been defeated, he warned, "there will be this rank undergrowth of treason." "Now, where will you find the strength to counterbalance this spirit, if you do not find it in the Negroes of the South?" Recognize us as equals, as allies, and the blood spilled in this terrible war will yield not just a limited freedom but justice. Fail to make the recognition, and you will defeat the purpose of the war and "the freedom of our people."[45]

Douglass's speech is a very important document. It lucidly states the beliefs of one significant group of African American leaders and their white allies, especially people such as Douglass himself and many of the most respected abolitionists. The dream of emancipation would not be complete with the end of slavery. The goal, they insisted, must always be full, free, and equal citizenship—symbolized most clearly in the vote and the right to participate in American society as free laborers and free citizens. That was the hope of the abolitionist movement, Douglass argued. With the Emancipation Proclamation, it had become the hope of the war. Now, it must be the hope and the goal of the peace that followed.

Three years later, under much more painful circumstances, Henry McNeal Turner made a similar point to the Georgia legislature. Turner was a leader of the African Methodist Episcopal Church who had gone to Georgia from his home in Washington, D.C., with the Union army. In 1867 he had been elected to Georgia's constitutional convention and then to the state legislature. In September 1868 the white majority of the legislature voted to expel him and the twenty-six other African American representatives. Turner had no intention of leaving quietly, and before he led the evicted delegates in their walk out of the chamber, he made a point very similar to Douglass's: Give us our rights as citizens and we will not ask for more. "Do we ask you for compensation for the sweat our fathers bore for you—for the tears you have caused, and the hearts you have broken, and the lives you have curtailed, and the blood you have spilled? Do we ask retaliation? We ask it not. We are willing to let the dead past bury its dead; but we ask you now for our RIGHTS." To remove our rights to vote and to be elected to office, he said, is to commit an "offence against God, against our humanity, and against our citizenship." "You may expel us, gentlemen, by your votes today; but while you do it, remember that there is a just God in Heaven." The issue for Turner, as for Douglass, was rights—especially the right to participate fully in the democratic process.[46]

Not everyone agreed with the Douglass and Turner perspective. Across the South many newly freed ex-slaves, contrary to Turner's assertion, did seek reparations. The promise of "forty acres and a mule," to be taken from land confiscated from plantation owners who had been traitors to the Union, swept the South as an almost millennial vision in the months immediately after the war. In Virginia, a freedman told a Union army officer, "If you had the right to take master's niggers, you had the right to take master's land too." In Alabama, a convention delegate reminded his audience that "the property which they hold was nearly all earned by the sweat of our brows." Another Virginia freedman, Bayley Wyat, protested the return of plantation land to its former owners, "We has a right to the land where we are located. For why? I tell you. Our wives, our children, our husbands, has been sold over and over again to purchase the lands we are now locates upon; for that reason we have a divine right to the land." Those closest to the land, those who had worked it for no pay and no reward, valued land and the promise of land ownership in ways that their more urban counterparts, black and white, could not understand.[47]

One of the most tragic cases of failed land redistribution took place in parts of Georgia and South Carolina. When General Sherman had made his famous march across these states he had set aside the "Sherman reservation" to resettle former slaves. After the war General Howard, as head of the new Freedmen's Bureau, issued an order instructing his agents to "set aside" forty-acre tracts for individual freedmen. The order was quickly followed and farming of the land began almost immediately. But President Andrew Johnson overrode Howard's order, issued pardons to former plantation owners, and ordered Howard to restore the land to its former owners, which meant taking it away from those who were currently using it. In October 1865 Howard himself made a painful journey to Edisto Island in South Carolina to announce the president's order. A committee of freedmen drafted their own powerful response:

General, we want Homesteads, we were promised Homesteads by the government. If it does not carry out the promises its agents made to us, if the

government having concluded to befriend its late enemies and to neglect to
observe the principles of common faith between its self and us its allies in the
war you said was over, now takes away from them all right to the soil they
stand upon save such as they can get by again working for *your late* and their
all time enemies . . . we are left in a more unpleasant condition than our
former. . . . You will see this is not the condition of really freemen.[48]

Redistribution of land, a place for each former slave to call their own, was also
part of the dream of Reconstruction, however marginalized in the succeeding
political resolution of the issues.[49]

And those who had long been campaigning for women's rights could not
accept Douglass's willingness to compromise on the rights of women to vote.
Douglass was clear, "I hold that women, as well as men, have the right to vote,
and my heart and my voice go with the movement to extend suffrage to
women." These were not just words. In the decade before and after battles
around the Fifteenth Amendment, Douglass proved his commitment to the
campaign for women's right to vote. But at the crucial time between 1865 and
1870, Douglass was willing to compromise. Yes, he recognized, "Women have
not this right." But, he asked, "Shall we justify one wrong by another?" For
Frederick Douglass the answer was that he was willing to divide the two issues
and say, "but that question [women's right to vote] rests upon another basis
than that on which our right rests."[50] It was a compromise that temporarily
but severely disrupted his lifelong friendship with Susan B. Anthony. It also
brought a sharp rebuke from another powerful former slave and abolitionist,
Sojourner Truth.

In a speech in 1867, at the height of the battle over whether the issue of
the vote for freedmen should or should not be tied to the vote for women,
Truth gave her own passionate response to Douglass and those who stood with
him. She told her audience that she too had been born a slave and rejoiced that
"They have got their liberty—so much good luck to have slavery partly destroyed; not entirely. I want it root and branch destroyed." And root and
branch destroyed, for Truth, meant the vote for all. Partial justice would not
do, "and if colored men get their rights, and not colored women theirs, you
see the colored men will be masters over the women, and it will be just as bad
as it was before." Using all of Douglass's arguments about rights, about self-
image, and about social consequences, Truth insisted on the right of women to
the vote. She concluded:

> I am above eighty years old; it is about time for me to be going. I have been
> forty years a slave and forty years free, and would be here forty years more to
> have equal rights for all. . . . I am glad to see that men are getting their rights,

but I want women to get theirs, and while the water is stirring I will step into the pool. Now that there is a great stir about colored men's getting their rights is the time for women to step in and have theirs.[51]

Truth's goal was not met in her lifetime or for a long time after. During the half century that separated the passage of the Fifteenth Amendment giving African American males the right to vote and the Nineteenth Amendment that gave women the vote, the rights of African Americans were systematically marginalized across the nation and most of all in the states of the former Confederacy. The right to vote, even more than the right to own land, was in the long run a dream deferred beyond the end of their lifetimes for the generation of African Americans who had participated in the great jubilee of emancipation itself. At the beginning, however, there was great hope. And that hope did not die. However much it went underground, however difficult the terrible years of segregation and economic and political marginalization, there were those who remembered the hopes of 1865 and were determined to see them fulfilled in time.

VOTERS AND LEGISLATORS

On January 21, 1870, the Mississippi state legislature elected Hiram R. Revels to the United States Senate. The election of a United States senator is not all that remarkable except for the fact that Revels was the first African American elected to the Senate and he was chosen to fill the unexpired term of former Senator—and then federal prisoner—Jefferson Davis. The Reconstruction legislature that elected Revels included forty blacks and one hundred whites. This was hardly the stereotypical black-dominated Reconstruction government that, in fact, never existed anywhere. Four days later the provisional military governor of Mississippi, General Adelbert Ames, signed the certification of Revels's election. The first African American ever elected to serve in the Senate, ironically was to fill the seat that had been vacant since Davis had resigned to become president of the Confederacy.[52]

Revels had been born free in Fayetteville, North Carolina, in 1827. Like many of the African American political leaders during Reconstruction, he had become a minister in the African Methodist Episcopal Church prior to the war and was serving as a pastor in Baltimore, Maryland, when the Civil War began. During the war Revels organized two all-black regiments for the Union army and served as their chaplain as well as teacher. At the war's end Revels went with his unit to Vicksburg, Mississippi, and then moved to Natchez. He was not initially a serious candidate for the Senate but his lack of ambition for the post made him a perfect compromise candidate. After his thirteen months in the Senate, Revels served for several years as president of the segregated black Alcorn University and pastor of the A.M.E. Church in Holly Springs, Alabama. He died in Aberdeen, Mississippi, in 1901.[53]

Revels's election was actually part of a series of compromises by which Mississippians—black and white—sought readmission to the Union. When the legislature met to conduct the election of new senators for Mississippi, they actually had three seats to fill. There were thirteen months left on Jefferson Davis's term. Then there was a full term for that seat and a full term for the other seat to which the state was entitled. Splitting the difference between pro-Union and pro-Confederacy, although not between the races, the legislature initially elected former Confederate general James L. Alcorn to begin serving the full six-year term in what had been Davis's seat. They also elected Union general and provisional governor Adelbert Ames to a full term. They then turned to the remaining thirteen months of the current term on what was to be Alcorn's seat. A century later, with senators elected by the full population, the obvious answer would have been to give Alcorn an early start. But in 1870 the Senate was elected by state legislatures, not by the public at large, and each term was considered on its own right. After thirteen ballots over three days, a candidate who had not originally sought the seat, Hiram Revels, won with eighty-one votes, a twenty vote majority. An exhausted legislature had made history.[54]

The battle over Revels's historic role did not end with his election. Senator Garrett Davis of Kentucky challenged his right to be seated. Since the Constitution clearly provides that each house of Congress may determine the right of its members to be seated, the issue was joined. Garrett Davis was not subtle in his racism although he and his opponents all clearly understood the historic nature of Revels's election. "Never before in the history of this government has a colored been elected to the Senate of the United States," Davis reminded his colleagues. But Revels's key defender, James Nye of Nevada, also understood history—especially the history of the recent war:

> This is his [Davis's] last battlefield. It is the last opportunity to make this fight. . . . In 1861 from this hall departed two senators who were representing here the state of Mississippi; one of them who went defiantly was Jefferson Davis. . . . Sir, what a magnificent spectacle of retributive justice is witnessed here today! In the place of that proud, defiant man, who marched out to trample under foot the Constitution and laws of the country he had sworn to support, comes back one of that humble race whom he would have enslaved forever to take and occupy his seat upon this floor.[55]

Nye's arguments won, and a month after his election Revels took the oath of office before the vice president and was seated. For the moment the anticipated "retributive justice" triumphed.[56]

Mississippi also sent the only other Reconstruction-era African American senator to Washington. Blanche K. Bruce was elected to a full six-year term in 1874. Bruce had been born a slave, but he had attended college and had established himself as a planter in Mississippi in 1868. Unlike Revels, he worked his way up the political ladder, serving as the sergeant-at-arms of the Mississippi state senate, assessor and sheriff of Bolivar County, and a member of the Board of Levee Commissioners of the Mississippi River. Not surprisingly, navigation on the Mississippi was a major concern of his during his Senate tenure, and he took a strong stand in the Senate against Chinese exclusion. Bruce was the last African American to serve in the Senate until Edward Brooke was elected from Massachusetts in 1966.[57]

Quite a number of African Americans served in the U.S. House of Representatives in the 1870s and 1880s. The same year that the Mississippi legislature elected Revels to the Senate, the constituents of his South Carolina district elected Joseph H. Rainey to the House, where he served three terms. Rainey and several other House members were more effective than their Senate counterparts. Rainey himself played an important role in arguing for the first major federal aid to education bill considered, although defeated, in Congress. Expanding to a national scale the same arguments used by African Americans in state legislatures across the South, Rainey told the House: "I would have it known that this ignorance is widespread; it is not confined to any one State. This mental midnight, we might justly say, is a national calamity, and not necessarily sectional. We should, therefore, avail power to avert its direful effects. The great remedy, in my judgment, is free schools, established and aided by the government throughout the land."[58] Commitment to education was clearly a hallmark of Reconstruction's advocates.

All told twenty-two blacks served in Congress in the years after the Civil War, including thirteen who had been born slaves. Between 1871 and 1873 South Carolina had three African American congressmen. In addition to Rainey, Robert C. De Large and Robert Elliott served in the same session. Several more African Americans were elected, including three House members and P. B. S. Pinchback as a senator from Louisiana, but racists like Kentucky's Garrett Davis used the confusion of Reconstruction to deny them their seats.[59]

At no time was Reconstruction smooth sailing for African Americans and their allies in government, education, or any other aspect of southern or national life. Nevertheless, for a brief period after the passage of the Congressional Reconstruction Act over President Johnson's veto in 1867, there was reason for some extraordinary hopes. If one looked around the nation on New Year's Day in 1873—the tenth anniversary of the implementation of Lincoln's Emancipation Proclamation—one could find things that seemed unimaginable a decade before. In Louisiana P. B. S. Pinchback was serving as the acting governor of the state. Ten African Americans from South Carolina, Georgia, Alabama, Florida, and Mississippi had recently served or were just about to take seats in the U.S. House of Representatives. In every southern state, African Americans played a major role in the state legislature and several held a variety of statewide offices. As John Hope Franklin and Alfred A. Moss have written, "The state constitutions drawn up in 1867 and 1868 were the most progressive the South had ever known. Most of them abolished property qualifications for voting and holding office; some of them abolished imprisonment for debt. All of them abolished slavery, and several sought to eliminate race distinctions in the possession or inheritance of property." In addition, all of the newly formulated constitutions and legislatures created public school systems and internal improvements designed to bring the South into the modern world. In spite of the difficulties past and future, it was hard not to hope in those heady days.[60]

HOPE BEYOND THE DARKNESS

The hopes of Reconstruction were defeated over several decades and by several different methods. Most significant was the pure violence of many white southerners who hid behind the chaotic conditions and poor communications to lynch, shoot, and intimidate blacks and their white allies. Former Confederate soldiers and others rallied to use extralegal means to restore the old order as nearly as possible. The Knights of the White Camellia, the Constitutional Union Guards, the Pale Faces, the Council of Safety, and the Knights of the Ku Klux Klan were among the paramilitary organizations organized during Reconstruction to terrify blacks and any whites who stood with them. Violence began in the immediate aftermath of the war and never really abated. In Louisiana a visitor reported, "they govern . . . by the pistol and rifle." A former slave in that state, Henry Adams, reported that "I saw white men whipping colored men just the same as they did before the war." In Texas an official of the Freedmen's Bureau reported that blacks, "are frequently beaten unmercifully, and shot down like wild beasts, without any provocation." A former slave, Susan Merritt from Rusk County, Texas, remembered seeing black bodies floating down the Sabine River and said, "There sure are going to be lots of souls crying against them [those responsible] in Judgment."[61]

While the majority of the violence, especially in the early years, was designed to drive the freedmen back into economic dependence and social inferiority, as Reconstruction progressed much of the violence turned specifically to denying the black vote. Blacks seeking to vote were met along the way to the polls or at the polling places by shotgun-carrying mobs who made it exceedingly clear that they should not proceed and who would not hesitate to kill resisters. A taste of what was coming took place in southwest Georgia in 1868 when 400 armed whites, led by the local sheriff, attacked a black election parade by shooting into the marchers and then chasing those who fled into the countryside, killing and wounding more than twenty blacks. One local leader who understood all too well what was happening said of the attackers, "We don't call them democrats, we call them southern murderers." The attack on the black vote in the decades that followed continued to rely on murder as much as legislation.[62]

Legislation disenfranchising freedmen went hand in hand with the violence, however. The outcome of the fateful presidential election of 1876 did not mark an immediate end to Reconstruction as it has sometime been viewed. As the report from Georgia in 1868 indicates, things were bad long before the compromise of 1876 and they continued to get worse for a long time afterward. But the outcome of the 1876 vote was nevertheless significant. At the Republican convention that nominated Rutherford B. Hayes, the aging abolitionist Frederick Douglass told the gathering that he was loyal and grateful to the party for emancipation, but the promises of land and full freedom had not followed. "You turned us loose to the sky, to the storm, to the whirlwind, and worst of all you turned us loose to the wrath of our infuriated masters."[63] The election's outcome did make things much worse. In return for support from Democrats in Congress regarding the contested electoral ballots that were essential to his victory over the majority vote winner (Democratic Samuel Tilden), Hayes and his handlers agreed to withdraw the remaining federal troops from the South. The last federal protection for Reconstruction was lost no matter what the laws of the land continued to say.

The withdrawal of federal troops heightened the power of terrorist organizations like the Klan. The expanding federal policy of pardoning Confederate leaders created a leadership class of unreconstructed Democrats. At the same time, some of the most vigilant Congressional Reconstructionists were passing from the scene, and their successors were much more pragmatic politicians wanting to return their focus to their own districts and to other issues. The combination of the loss of federal troop protections, and the declining federal interest in the issues of Reconstruction, along with the development of powerful southern white leaders, meant that many states were in a position to undo significant elements of the constitutions that they had adopted in 1867 and 1868. To the earlier terrorist campaigns to keep blacks from polls was now added a series of legal restrictions including poll taxes, literacy requirements that allowed local officials wide leeway in their judgments, white primaries, gerrymandered districts, and a range of other obscure regulations all designed to ensure that only whites actually voted. The U.S. Supreme Court threw out a number of suits under federal regulations designed to protect freedmen, ruling that while the Fifteenth Amendment prohibited discrimination "on account of race, color or previous condition of servitude," it did not guarantee anyone the right to vote. All in all, it was an ugly time in American politics.[64]

Disenfranchisement and segregation did not happen overnight. A few African Americans continued to be elected to Congress throughout the nineteenth century until George H. White of North Carolina, described prophetically by one African American newspaper as "the last of the Negro congressmen,"[65] bade a final farewell to the chamber in 1901 telling the House: "This, Mr. Chairman, this is perhaps the Negroes' temporary farewell to the American Congress. But let me say, phoenix-like, he will rise up someday and come again. These parting words are in behalf of an outraged, heartbroken, bruised and bleeding people, but God fearing people, faithful, industrious loyal people . . . rising people, full of potential."[66] The temporary farewell lasted for twenty-eight years until Oscar DePriest was elected to fill a seat from Chicago's African American community. And only after another civil rights movement did African Americans reach the number of representatives in the 1970s that they had in Congress in the 1870s.

Other forms of Jim Crow segregation and discrimination developed at a rapid pace during the late 1870s and the next two decades. Schools, public facilities, transportation, and most every other aspect of life were segregated. In addition to losing the vote, blacks were marginalized economically so that sharecropping became virtually the only option for large numbers of them. And a vicious campaign of lynching was launched to keep the rest of the system in place through fear and intimidation. Perhaps the capstone of what the great C. Vann Woodward called "the strange career of Jim Crow" was the U.S. Supreme Court's 1896 *Plessy v. Ferguson* decision that "separate by equal" facilities were quite acceptable under the United States Constitution.[67]

At such a time, hope in any form could seem a pipe dream. And for many it was. Yet, hope did not die. Just as George H. White promised the U.S. Congress that someday African Americans would rise, "phoenix-like," and be in Congress again, many others—politicians, ministers, educators, poets, just plain citizens—refused the corrosive effect of despair.

One of the greatest voices of hope in the late nineteenth century was Frances Ellen Watkins Harper. Harper was born free in Baltimore in 1825 but grew up surrounded by the slavery of her fellow African Americans. She began a career of writing and public speaking early, and in the years before the Civil War she traveled the country as a representative of the Maine Anti-Slavery Society. After the war she became both a Sunday school leader and a highly sought-after lecturer on race relations, women's rights, and temperance. Perhaps her most famous lecture of the time was "The Demands of the Colored Race in the Work of Reconstruction," but for Harper the issues of race, religion, suffrage, and temperance could not be divided. She was also a widely published poet, and her poetry reflected her toughness as when in "The Slave Mother" she reminded audiences

> Heard you that shriek? It rose
> So wildly on the air,
> It seem'd as if a burden'd heart
> Was breaking in despair.

Harper was determined to make white America look clearly at itself.[68]

As part of that effort, in 1890, when she was already sixty-five years old and one of the best-known writers in the nation, Harper set out to write her first full-length novel. She was determined to tell the story of Reconstruction to a nation that did not want to hear. The dominant literary voices reporting from the South at that time were writers such as Joel Chandler Harris and others of the so-called Plantation School, who described "a picturesque peasantry; their comic speech, their superstitions, their penchant for stolen watermelon or chicken."[69] Harper wanted to offer something radically different—a novel of both truth and hope. The result, *Iola Leroy or Shadows Uplifted* was published in 1892 and became the best-selling novel by an African American writer prior to the twentieth century.

Harper's novel begins in the midst of the great hopes of the Civil War and ends in the depths of the despair of the post-Reconstruction nation. In the aftermath of the war the book's heroine, Iola Leroy, a light-skinned former slave who had received a northern education, experiences many of the triumphs and tragedies of the newly freed slaves. Harper brilliantly uses the form of the novel to tell the story of what her own generation of African Americans experienced.

Because she is literate, the novel's central character is asked to be a teacher and then sees her schoolhouse burned to a smoldering ruin by angry southern whites. Nevertheless, she hears her students sing, "Oh, do not be discouraged, For Jesus is your friend," and as she watches their determination to rebuild says: "I am not despondent of the future of my people; there is too much elasticity in their spirits, too much hope in their hearts, to be crushed out by unreasoning malice."[70] Because she had been sold many times, she had lost track of her family, yet with the coming of freedom Iola Leroy was determined to find them and "bind anew the ties which slavery had broken."[71] In the novel's end, her mother and other relatives join in a happy reunion in which they partake "of that supper with thankful hearts and with eyes overflowing with tears of joy."[72]

Iola Leroy, like Frances Harper her creator, is no Pollyanna, however. While the novel tells of the triumph of hope over despair, it does so in the context of weaving in the full terror of slavery and the failures of Reconstruction. Late in the story another freed slave, Robert Johnson, one of the novel's main characters, muses: "But all the battles are not fought, nor all the victories won. The colored man has escaped from one slavery, and I don't want him to fall into another. I want the young folks to keep their brains clear, and their right arms strong, to fight the battles of life manfully, and take their places alongside of every other people in this country."[73] But Harper makes it clear that the victory Robert Johnson wants was not yet won. Iola herself is fired from one job and shunned at another because of her race. A white southerner says, "the negro . . . is perfectly comprehensible to me. The only way to get along with him is to let him know his place, and make him keep it." And Harper makes it clear that in the United States of the 1890s, the voice of the white racist was the winning voice of the day.[74]

Iola herself tells Dr. Gresham, the voice of white liberalism: "I do not think that you fully realize how much prejudice against colored people permeates society, lowers the tone of our religion, and reacts upon the life of the nation. . . . This prejudice against the colored race environs our lives and mocks our aspirations."[75] The good doctor continues to protest this analysis, but in the novel Iola is the voice of clear-eyed reality.

Nevertheless, *Iola Leroy* is a novel of hope. In her effort to inform an American public of the reality of the African American experience in the decades after slavery, to correct the terrible stereotypes of happy slaves and uncouth freedmen, and to point out the horrors of lynching and terrorism that had enveloped the South, Harper also, perhaps most of all, wanted to imbue her readers with hope. At the end of the novel she concludes with a note to the reader: "From the threads of fact and fiction I have woven a story whose mission will not be in vain if it awaken in the hearts of our countrymen a stronger sense of justice and a more Christlike humanity in behalf of those whom the fortunes of war threw, homeless, ignorant and poor, upon the threshold of a new era." And then she adds a poem:

There is light beyond the darkness,
Joy beyond the present pain;
There is hope in God's great justice
And the negro's rising brain.
Though the morning seems to linger
O'er the hill-tops far away,
Yet the shadows bear the promise
Of a brighter coming day.[76]

The power of that confidence in "the promise of a brighter coming day," not a corrosive and disempowering despair, is Harper's and her generation's gift to a future they would not live to see but which they never stopped hoping for.

1. Abigail Adams, who reminded her husband to "remember the ladies," while also critizing those slaveholding revolutionaries who "have been accustomed to deprive their fellow creatures" of liberty [permission of the Massachusetts Historical Society].

2. Thomas Paine, author of the incendiary pamphlet of the American Revolution, *Common Sense* [courtesy of the Massachusetts Historical Society].

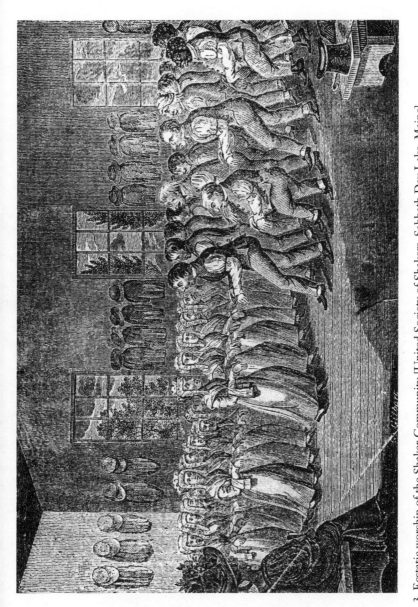

3. Ecstatic worship of the Shaker Community [United Society of Shakers, Sabbath Day Lake, Maine].

left 4. Harriet Tubman, Conductor par excellence of the Underground Railroad, who brought hundreds of slaves to freedom [courtesy of the Massachusetts Historical Society].

above 5. John Brown, whose efforts for a slave uprising gave hope to slaves and abolitionists [courtesy of the Massachusetts Historical Society].

6. Frederick Douglass, born a slave, became one of the nation's leading abolitionists, a leader of the Reconstruction era, and a defender of women's rights [courtesy of the Massachusetts Historical Society].

7. Elizabeth Cady Stanton, prime mover in the 1848 Seneca Falls Women's Rights Convention and a leading feminist throughout the nineteenth century [courtesy of the Massachusetts Historical Society].

8. Mother Jones leading striking coal miners and their families in Trinidad, Colorado [permission of Newberry Library, Chicago].

9. Eugene V. Debs, labor leader and Socialist party candidate for President giving a speech in opposition to World War I that resulted in a prison term [The Eugene V. Debs Foundation, Terre Haute, Indiana].

left 10. Jane Addams, founder of Hull House in Chicago and a voice for the most inclusive ideas of the progressive era [permission of The Newberry Library].

above 11. Nicola Sacco and Bartolomeo Vanzetti who hoped that their execution in 1927 would strike a blow "for tolerance, for justice, for man's understanding of man" [permission The Boston Globe via www.Merlin-Net.com].

left   12. Marcus Garvey, leader of the Universal Negro Improvement Association and a voice for African American empowerment in some of the most difficult days of the twentieth century [permission of the Photographs and Prints Division, Schomburg Center for Research in Black Culture, The New York Public Library, Astor, Lenox and Tilden Foundations].

above   13. Rev. Dr. Martin Luther King, Jr. [permission of the Northeastern University Library, Archives and Special Collections Department].

next page   14. Septima Clark (left) and Rosa Parks (right) two of the great leaders of the civil rights movement, in a quiet moment at the Highlander Center in Tennessee [permission of Highlander Research and Education Center].

CHAPTER SIX

FEMINISTS
AND SUFFRAGISTS

SENECA FALLS, 1848

ON JULY 20, 1848, SIXTY-EIGHT WOMEN and thirty-two men signed a Declaration of Principles as the capstone of their two-day meeting that had been called in the small town of Seneca Falls, New York, to discuss the rights of women. The document—which quite consciously copied the words and form of the Declaration of Independence—has become one of the grand documents in the history of the struggle of Americans for greater inclusion of people in the definition of liberty. This new declaration began just as the earlier declaration did, but with some subtle but significant alterations:

> When, in the course of human events, it becomes necessary for one portion of the family of man to assume among the people of the earth a position different from that which they have hitherto occupied, but one to which the laws of nature and of nature's God entitle them, a decent respect to the opinions of mankind requires that they should declare the causes that impel them to such a course.
>
> We hold these truths to be self-evident; that all men and women are created equal; that they are endowed by their Creator with certain inalienable rights; that among these are life, liberty, and the pursuit of happiness.

Then, just as Jefferson and his coauthors had listed their grievances against George III, those who gathered in upstate New York proceeded to offer their grievances against the men and the male dominated culture in which they lived:

The history of mankind is a history of repeated injuries and usurpations on the part of man toward woman, having in direct object the establishment of an absolute tyranny over her. To prove this, let facts be submitted to a candid world.

He has never permitted her to exercise her inalienable right to elective franchise.

He has compelled her to submit to laws, in the formation of which she had no voice.

He has withheld from her rights which are given to the most ignorant and degraded men both natives and foreigners.

Having deprived her of this first right of a citizen, the elective franchise, thereby leaving her without representation in the halls of legislation, he has oppressed her on all sides.

He has made her, if married, in the eye of the law, civilly dead.

The list continued. Its authors were being clear and specific in their bill of particulars. And they too concluded with a statement of their own commitment to the cause of women's rights, "Firmly relying upon the final triumph of the Right and the True, we do this day affix our signatures to this declaration." It was a commitment that many of those present would honor for the rest of their long lives.[1]

Elizabeth Cady Stanton, who was the prime mover in the Seneca Falls convention and the document that was issued by the group, described the informal beginnings of what became in retrospect the mythic Woman's Rights Convention at Seneca Falls, New York, in 1848. Stanton and her family had moved from Boston to rural Seneca Falls in 1847 because they thought it would improve her husband's health. After the initial romance of a new place, she found the management of a family, house, and farm both difficult and lonely. As she remembered: "Here our residence was on the outskirts of town, roads very often muddy and no sidewalks most of the way. Mr. Stanton was frequently from home. . . . Then, too, the novelty of housekeeping had passed away, and much that was once attractive in domestic life was now irksome."[2]

One day in early July 1848, she was invited to visit Lucretia Mott and poured out her discontent. Mott, and others present, seemed to have similar grievances. Stanton remembered the World Anti-Slavery Convention she had attended in 1840 with her husband, who had been one of the antislavery agents recruited from Oberlin. The group decided, "then and there, to call a 'Woman's Rights Convention,'" for the following week. With only a little overstatement Stanton remembered, "These were the hasty initiative steps of the most momentous reform that had yet been launched on the world—the first organized protest against injustice which had brooded for ages over the character and destiny of one-half the race."[3] The convention did, indeed, make its mark.

To Stanton's and Mott's surprise, the Woman's Rights Convention at Seneca Falls generated extraordinary attention. Initially most of the attention was negative. "With our Declaration of Rights and Resolutions for a text, it seemed as if every man who could wield a pen prepared a homily on 'woman's sphere.' All the journals from Maine to Texas seemed to strive with each other to see which could make our movement appear most ridiculous."[4]

Stanton had already experienced the hostility generated by her and her husband's radical antislavery activities. The new hostility was no less intense and was more surprising because it was unexpected. Like many reformers, if they are honest, she remembered, "If I had had the slightest premonition of all that was to follow that convention, I fear I should not have had the courage to risk it, and I must confess that it was with fear and trembling that I consented to attend another, one month afterward, in Rochester."[5] Sometimes the lack of knowledge is what allows great things to begin.

There were also important exceptions to the hostility. The abolitionist Frederick Douglass stuck by his support of the convention and so did most of the antislavery press. Women in other places—Massachusetts, Ohio, Indiana, Pennsylvania, as well as New York City, and Rochester in New York state—held their own conventions. And though they did not attend the Seneca Falls convention, the report caught the attention of other young women. Susan B. Anthony was a teacher who was active in temperance and antislavery reforms. From then on, for more than half a century, she would be Stanton's friend and fellow leader. Matilda Joslyn Gage had wanted to attend the convention, but she gave birth to a son the day before it began. Gage spoke at an 1852 convention in Syracuse and in later years worked closely with Stanton and Anthony in the leadership of the National Woman's Suffrage Association. Stanton, Anthony, and Gage also served as the editors of the first three volumes of the *History of Woman Suffrage*, published between 1881 and 1886.[6] The Woman's Declaration of Independence challenged the then accepted definitions of the good society and the loving community. It offered many women hope for a very different future and engaged a generation in a renewed effort to build that future.[7]

The 1848 convention of women at Seneca Falls was a very important milestone for the rights of women for many reasons. It was certainly not the first time women in the United States had begun to lobby for their rights. Abigail Adams's reminder to her husband, John, that the framers of a new government in 1776 should "remember the ladies" was far from the only time women of the revolutionary era hoped for, asked for, and demanded their rights. Women fought in the war for independence and other women fought for the

survival of their families during the hard years of the British siege of the colonial port cities. After the revolution, the new constitution for the state of New
Jersey gave women the vote although the provision was rescinded in 1807.[8]

But Seneca Falls represented something different. From then on the hope
for women's rights and women's votes would be institutionalized and consistent. Because it brought together such powerful women as Elizabeth Cady
Stanton, Lucretia Mott, and many others—soon joined by Susan B. Anthony,
Matilda Gage, and a generation of their peers—Seneca Falls provided the
foundation for a half century of camaraderie among the group that would lead
a long-term and eventually well-organized campaign for women's rights in
general and women's suffrage in specific. Because it issued a forceful statement, one that also received widespread, even if often hostile, recognition
around the nation, it framed the debate around women's rights for most of the
next century and gave ringing words to the hopes of many. And because it
linked veterans of the abolitionist struggle to the new cause, it represented a
hope for a unified vision of human freedom beyond the wildest dreams of the
nation's founders or of the earlier declaration that it so dramatically rephrased.

THE ALLIANCE:
ABOLITION AND SUFFRAGE

In the wake of the Seneca Falls convention, women's conventions were held all
over the nation in the following decade. At one of these subsequent meetings,
held in Akron, Ohio, in May 1851, the links of the abolitionist and feminist
movements were symbolized in a cogent short speech. As reported in *The
Anti-Slavery Bugle* in June, during the debates at the Akron convention, Sojourner Truth came forward asking, "May I say a few words?" Truth was already a nationally recognized figure. She had been born a slave in the Hudson
River Valley of New York state in 1799. She was freed from slavery by the
New York Emancipation Act of 1827, and she eventually took the name Sojourner Truth and traveled the nation demanding freedom for her fellow
Americans of African origin. In Akron she continued and expanded her demand for freedom. She told the convention:

> I want to say a few words about this matter. I am a woman's rights. I have as
> much muscle as any man, and can do as much work as any man. I have plowed
> and reaped and husked and chopped and mowed, and can any man do more
> than that? I have heard much about the sexes being equal. I can carry as much
> as any man, and can eat as much too, if I can get it. I am as strong as any man
> that is now. . . . And how came Jesus into the world? Through God who cre-

ated him and a woman who bore him. Man, where is your part? But the women are coming up blessed be God and a few of the men are coming up with them. But man is in a tight place, the poor slave is on him, woman is coming on him, he is surely between a hawk and a buzzard.[9]

Later published versions added the famous refrain "And ain't I a woman?" Whether or not that question was part of the original speech, Truth did more than ask that powerful question. She explicitly linked the campaigns of the slave and the woman, and she meant to be sure that the notion of liberty being limited to a few would stay "between a hawk and a buzzard" if she had anything to do with it.[10]

It is also important to note the vital connections that existed throughout the nineteenth century between the movement for women's rights and the movement for the abolition of slavery. These have too often been portrayed as separate and parallel movements. Sometimes they were. Sometimes the two movements battled over their differing interests. But for most of the nineteenth century nothing could have been further from the truth than the perception that abolition and feminism were hostile to each other. As Stanton noted, the idea for the convention itself came from the fact that she and her husband had been long-time abolitionists and had attended their share of abolitionist conventions. Henry Stanton had been one of the original Lane rebels, an evangelist for the antislavery cause. Frederick Douglass, well on his way to being one of the most prominent abolitionists of the century, attended the Seneca convention and supported the suffrage effort throughout his life, just as Stanton and Anthony remained ardent abolitionists and supporters of the rights of free blacks after the war.

Certainly there were stresses and strains between the two movements. After the Civil War, Anthony was exceedingly angry with Douglass when he supported male suffrage for African Americans prior to women's suffrage. Their friendship was ruptured for a time but eventually healed, and Douglass spent the last day of his life, February 20, 1895, with Anthony at a meeting of the National Council of Women.[11] But far more important than the deep personal friendship between these giants of the two movements was the fact that they and many of their supporters saw themselves as part of a larger whole—a campaign to make the full meaning of "all . . . are created equal" a part of the life of the United States.

Few others symbolized the powerful links between feminism and abolitionism as did the Grimké sisters from South Carolina, Sarah and Angelina. Born in 1792 and 1805 respectively to a prosperous and well-respected South Carolina slaveholding family, both women broke with their past, with their family, with slavery, and with the dominant understanding of the role of gentlewomen in society. While it was a difficult and lonely road, especially for Sarah who trod it first, by 1836 the two sisters had become the first two female agents of the American Anti-Slavery Society based in New York City. Angelina was the more confident and more effective public speaker while her older sister did more of the writing and eventually expanded feminist theory far beyond not only her younger sister but virtually any other writer of her time. In 1838 Angelina married another of the leading abolitionists, Theodore Dwight Weld. For most of the rest of their lives, Weld and the two sisters lived together in a household focused on their continuing campaigns for a nation free not only of slavery—though that was always a primary focus—but of the last vestiges of both racism and sexism.[12]

In 1837, a decade before the Seneca Falls convention, Sarah Grimké published *Letters on the Equality of the Sexes and the Condition of Women* in response to an attack from the Congregational clergy of Massachusetts on the antislavery lectures that she and Angelina had been giving throughout New England earlier in the year as part of their work for the Anti-Slavery Society. Grimké began her *Letters* with her basic assertion, "Here I plant myself. God created us equal."[13] She took the argument much further, however. Grimké, more than many writers of her own or later days, understood that her hope for freedom and equality needed to move beyond the assertion of her basic rights. It needed to include a clear analysis of why those hopes and those rights were systematically being frustrated. So Sarah Grimké continued:

> All history attests that man has subjected woman to his will, used her as a means to promote his selfish gratification, to minister to his sensual pleasures, to be instrumental in promoting his comfort; but never has he desired to elevate her to that rank she was created to fill. He has done all he could to debase and enslave her mind; and now he looks triumphantly on the ruin he has wrought, and says, the being he has thus deeply injured is his inferior.[14]

Whether it was the treatment of slaves by their masters or the treatment of women by men, Sarah Grimké looked unblinkingly at the depths of oppression and insisted that others who would join with her in hoping and working for change do the same.

Far ahead of other writers, Sarah Grimké made a distinction between the biological differences between women and men and the social and cultural interpretation of those differences in a given culture. She insisted that, "intellect is not sexed . . . strength of mind is not sexed; and . . . our views about the duties of men and the duties of women, the sphere of man and the sphere of woman, are mere arbitrary opinions, differing in different ages and countries, and dependent solely on the will and judgment of erring mortals."[15] Defining the differences in gender roles and potential as "mere arbitrary opinions" in a society that saw them as biologically determined for all time was a radical departure from the limits most nineteenth-century Americans, of both sexes, placed on their hopes and aspirations. As Gerda Lerner has noted, "Sarah defined the difference between sex and gender in terms which would not be as clearly stated again until the 20th century."[16]

Grimké's *Letters* concluded with a powerful appeal:

> I ask no favors for my sex. I surrender not our claim to equality. All I ask of our brethren is that they will take their feet from off our necks, and permit us to stand upright on the ground which God has designed us to occupy. . . . To me it is perfectly clear that WHATEVER IT IS MORALLY RIGHT FOR A MAN TO DO, IT IS MORALLY RIGHT FOR A WOMAN TO DO . . . she is clothed by her Maker with the *same rights*, and . . . the *same duties*.[17]

It was as powerful a statement of rights as any in an era of many such statements. And for the rest of their lives both Sarah and Angelina continued to make these assertions, for themselves and for all women, for slaves and for freed slaves. Though their work was forgotten for most of the century that followed, their lucid voices represented hope for a very different future.

REFORMER IN MANY FORMS

Shortly after the Seneca Falls convention, Elizabeth Cady Stanton became a proponent of another reform. Her cousin Elizabeth Smith Miller came to visit wearing something quite different from the long dress covering petticoats and a whale-boned bodice that was the expected clothing of any respectable woman of the time. The bloomer, as it came to be known because of the publicity given to it by Amelia Bloomer, assistant postmistress in Seneca Falls and editor of a widely read magazine, *Lily*, was a short skirt and loose trousers gathered at the ankle.[18] Stanton recorded her immediate reaction:

> To see my cousin, with a lamp in one hand and a baby in the other, walk upstairs with ease and grace, while, with flowing robes, I pulled myself up with difficulty, lamp and baby out of the question, readily convinced me that there was sore need of reform in woman's dress, and I promptly donned a similar attire. What incredible freedom I enjoyed for two years! Like a captive set free from his ball and chain, I was always ready for a brisk walk through sleet and snow and rain, to climb a mountain, jump over a fence, work in the garden, and, in fact, for any necessary locomotion.[19]

The bloomer later became an object of scorn. Certainly it is hard to compare a short skirt and pants with the right to vote. Yet the freedom as Stanton said, "to climb a mountain, jump over a fence, work in the garden" or to walk up stairs easily was not something to be dismissed lightly. In the movement toward freedom for women, the bloomer played an essential, if sadly temporary, role.

Lucy Stone was part of the same extended circle of feminists and abolitionists; she made what was probably her most unique contribution when she married Henry Blackwell but refused to take his name. At their wedding Blackwell and Stone jointly read a statement that said: "While we acknowledge our mutual affection by publicly assuming the relationship of husband and wife . . . we deem it a duty to declare that this act on our part implies no sanction of, nor promise of voluntary obedience to such of the present laws of marriage as refuse to recognize the wife as an independent, rational being, while they confer upon the husband an injurious and unnatural superiority."[20] Lucy Stone and Henry Blackwell continued their engagement in the issues that mattered to them and in maintaining their separate identities and names throughout their married lives.

Stone's act of defiance of tradition and the laws of the state of New York did not begin with her marriage. As a young student at Mount Holyoke Female Seminary (later Mount Holyoke College) Stone came into conflict with the school's founder, Mary Lyon, when Stone continued to distribute William Lloyd Garrison's *Liberator* in spite of a school ban on such radical action by the students. Stone subsequently left Mount Holyoke for the more congenial abolitionist pastures of Oberlin College. But even at Oberlin, the first college in the country to be both coeducational and open to students of all races, theory sometimes preceded practice. When Stone was named graduation speaker for her class she was also told that while she should write the speech, a male should deliver it. She refused to write what she could not speak.

As frustrating as Mount Holyoke and Oberlin were for women like Lucy Stone, they offered opportunities that were blocked elsewhere. At Oberlin, Stone became close to Antoinette Brown, who later became her sister-in-law when Brown married Samuel Blackwell. Brown also became one of the nation's first women ministers while Stone continued her career of feminist and abolitionist agitation. The theology of perfectionism, espoused by the famous nineteenth-century evangelist Charles Grandison Finney, and around which Oberlin was organized, gave both women the sense of hope that they could trust their own judgments about what would make the world a better place, even if their theological mentors disagreed with their conclusions.[21]

SUFFRAGE AND
SUSAN B. ANTHONY

No one came to represent the nineteenth-century campaign for women's right to vote more than Susan B. Anthony.[22] She was born in 1820, attended her first women's rights convention in 1852, and within a year had taken up her life's work. She was an acknowledged leader of the suffrage campaign from the 1850s until her death in 1906. Suffrage was her life and she made it a rich one.

After the Civil War, in 1868, Anthony and Stanton launched their own newspaper, *The Revolution*. In a letter to Anthony, Stanton described the importance of the name they had selected: "The establishing of woman on her rightful throne is the greatest revolution the world has ever known or will know." Anthony, Stanton, and their circle of allies were quite clear on the significance of the cause they espoused. Through their paper and their other efforts, Stanton and Anthony sought to reach a wider circle of women. *Revolution* included a column entitled "The Working Woman," and Anthony, in addition to editing the newspaper, also helped form the Working Woman's Association which focused specifically on the growing numbers of postwar women at work.[23]

In 1869 Anthony and Stanton also founded the National Woman Suffrage Association. Under slightly different names due to various splits and mergers, this organization, mostly under the leadership of Stanton and Anthony, continued the fight for a Constitutional amendment up to their final success in 1919. In the beginning, however, the NWSA was involved in a bitter battle with many of their closest friends. While many in the feminist and abolitionist movements, including Lucy Stone, Julia Ward Howe, Frederick Douglass, and William Lloyd Garrison, were prepared to support the Fifteenth Amendment, giving African-American men the right to vote, as an essential first step, Anthony and Stanton would not support any suffrage that did not include women. It was a hard moment as a unified vision of the future shattered on the issue of pragmatic politics.[24]

In November 1872, frustrated because the Constitution now gave the vote to African American men but not to women, and determined to continue the crusade for woman's vote whatever the cost, Anthony broke state and federal laws by casting her vote in the presidential election of that year. She simply showed up at her Rochester, New York, precinct, registered, and then cast her ballot before the bewildered officials could decide what to do. It was the only time in her life that she actually voted. Three weeks later she was arrested for voting, "without having the legal right to vote," and her crime became a cause célèbre. Freed on bail, she traveled the country, speaking about her case.[25] Indeed, her arrest gave her a way to focus the argument for suffrage more clearly and precisely than ever before. She told many an audience:

> I stand before you tonight under indictment for the alleged crime of having voted illegally at the last Presidential election. I shall endeavor this evening to prove to you that in voting, I not only committed no crime, but simply exercised my "citizen's right," guaranteed to me and all United States citizens by the National Constitution, beyond the power of any State to deny. . . .
>
> The preamble of the Federal Constitution says: *We, the people of the United States.* . . .
>
> It was we, the people, not we, the white male citizens, nor yet we, the male citizens, but we, the whole people, who formed this Union. And we formed it, not to give the blessings of liberty, but to secure them; not to the half of ourselves and the half of our posterity, but to the whole people—women as well as men. And it is downright mockery to talk to women of their enjoyment of the blessings of liberty while they are denied the use of the only means of securing them provided by this democratic republican government—the ballot.[26]

Part of Anthony's success was her ability to keep the issue very simple and very focused. For her "the only means" of securing democracy was "the ballot." She did not want to hear from those who saw the issue in more complex terms.

Anthony continued her stump speeches. If the Constitution was clear from the beginning, or at least after the Fifteenth Amendment, that "we the people" meant all the people, then:

> The only question left to be settled now, is: Are women persons? And I hardly believe any of our opponents will have the hardihood to say they are not. Being persons, then, women are citizens, and no State has a right to make any new law, or to enforce any old law, that shall abridge their privileges or immunities. Hence, every discrimination against women in the constitutions and laws of the several States, is to-day null and void, precisely as is every one against Negroes. Is the right to vote one of the privileges or immunities of citizens?[27]

If, as she suspected, she could never get the courts of New York to focus that clearly, she wanted to get the court of public opinion focused that way.

When she came to trial in June 1873, the judge refused to let her defend herself. Her only statement came the moment before sentencing, and she used it effectively to state her case. When the judge asked if she had anything to say, Anthony responded:

> Yes, your honor, I have many things to say; for in your ordered verdict of guilty, you have trampled underfoot every vital principle of our government.

My natural rights, my civil rights, my political rights, are all alike ignored. Robbed of the fundamental privilege of citizenship, I am degraded from the status of a citizen to that of a subject; and not only myself individually, but all of my sex, are, by your honor's verdict, doomed to political subjection under this so-called Republican government.[28]

The angry judge would not let her continue. But if Anthony had lost the specific case, she had gained a new level of public attention for her cause. And she never paid the fine!

Throughout the rest of her career, Anthony crisscrossed the nation speaking to every audience she could find for the cause of woman's suffrage. Her, "Women Want Bread, Not the Ballot," speech—the first line of which directly contradicted the title—was heard by many.[29] In response to the assertion that women would be happy if only their daily needs were met, Anthony responded, "I think I shall be able to prove to you that the only possibility of her securing bread and a home for herself is to give her the ballot." Power, as in the power of the ballot, always came first for Anthony. Thus she continued:

My purpose tonight is to demonstrate the great historical fact that disfranchisement is not only political degradation, but also moral, social, educational, and industrial degradation; and that it does matter whether the disfranchised class live under a monarchical or a republican form of government, or whether it be white workingmen of England, Negroes on our southern plantations, serfs of Russia, Chinamen on our Pacific coast or native born, tax-paying women of this republic. Wherever, on the face of the globe or on the page of history, you show me a disfranchised class, I will show you a degraded class of labor.[30]

Women's economic needs, women's social needs, women's ethical needs, all of these could only begin to be addressed for Anthony when women had the political power that came from the vote.

While Anthony became more and more well known and more and more effective in her speaking, campaigning, and lobbying, the basic themes of her work remained constant. In 1890 the National Woman Suffrage Association merged with the more cautious American Woman Suffrage Association to form the National American Woman Suffrage Association. Stanton served as its president for two years; Anthony then took over and served from 1892 until 1904, two years before her death.

The cause these women led made significant headway as a number of western states, beginning with the legislature of the Wyoming Territory, gave women the right to vote in 1870. Colorado, Utah, and Idaho followed.[31] During these same years, Anthony divided her time between speaking trips across the country and lobbying efforts in Washington. In 1900 she told a Senate committee considering one of the many suffrage amendments to come before the Congress between 1868 and 1919, "I want you to speak and act and report on this question exactly as if your half of the people were the ones who were deprived of this right to a vote and voice in governmental affairs."[32]

At the beginning of the new century, President Theodore Roosevelt expressed his own support for woman's suffrage although, to Anthony's great frustration, he refused to use his considerable political capital to move the issue. In 1905, a year before her death, Anthony met with Roosevelt at the White House. She pleaded: "Mr. Roosevelt, this is my principal request—it is almost the last request I shall ever make of anybody. Before you leave the presidential chair, recommend Congress to submit to the Legislatures a Constitutional Amendment which will enfranchise women, and thus take your place in history with Lincoln, the great emancipator. I beg of you not to close your term of office without doing this."[33]

Though Roosevelt and Anthony were close, he did not heed her request. Some months later, at the 1906 convention of the National American Woman Suffrage Association, Anthony heard the president's letter congratulating her on her eighty-sixth birthday read to the group. She took the podium and responded, "I wish the men would do something besides extend congratulations. . . . I would rather have him say a word to Congress for the cause than to praise me endlessly."[34] Her wish was not granted, and later that same year Anthony died, knowing that her life's work was not complete but full of hope for the future. In a little over a decade her hopes, so clearly focused and so long nourished, would be fulfilled.[35]

ELIZABETH CADY STANTON
AND THE WOMAN'S BIBLE

When she celebrated her eightieth birthday in November 1895, Elizabeth Cady Stanton was a nationally known figure. Whether or not people agreed with the militant push for women's right to vote that she, Susan B. Anthony, and others had been pursuing for half a century, it was impossible to ignore the campaign or its leaders. Stanton's religious views, however, were less well known. She had, in fact, been challenging the "misinterpretation" of Christianity that was used to keep women in their place for almost as long as she had advocated for women's rights. Thus in 1869 she had written in *The Revolution*: "The religious faith of woman has been so perverted and played upon, that she has really come to think that the chains that hold the mothers of the

race slaves to their own sons, were forged by the hand of the living God."[36]
But her heterodox religious views had not received nearly the attention of her
political views. That would soon change.

For Stanton, orthodox Christianity, as she had experienced it, was a
source of deep psychological pain for all involved and a major roadblock in the
campaign for women's equality. She recalled:

> I can truly say, after an experience of seventy years, that all the cares and anx-
> ieties, the trials and disappointments of my whole life, are light, when bal-
> anced with my sufferings in childhood and youth from the theological
> dogmas which I sincerely believed, and the gloom connected with everything
> associated with the name of religion, the church, the parsonage, the grave-
> yard, and the solemn, tolling bell. . . . The church, which was bare, with no
> furnace to warm us, no organ to gladden our hearts, no choir to lead our
> songs of praise in harmony, was sadly lacking in all attractions for the youth-
> ful mind. The preacher, shut up in an octagonal box high above our heads,
> gave us sermons over an hour long, and the chorister, in a similar box below
> him, intoned line after line of David's Psalms. . . . These old Scotch Presbyte-
> rians were opposed to all innovations that would afford their people paths of
> flowery ease on the road to Heaven. So, when the thermometer was twenty
> degrees below zero on the Johnston Hills, four hundred feet above the Mo-
> hawk Valley, we trudged along through the snow, foot-stoves in hand, to the
> cold hospitalities of the "Lord's House," there to be chilled to the very core
> by listening to sermons on "predestination," "justification by faith," and
> "eternal damnation."[37]

It was, indeed, not a happy memory.

It did not take the young Stanton long to move beyond all of this. Though
she remembered her sense of personal evil and her fear that the Devil "should
come one night and claim me as his own," she soon changed. "I was able to endure for years the strain of these depressing influences, until my reasoning
powers and common sense triumphed at last over my imagination." She was
determined that others not suffer as she had. From then on, "The memory of
my own suffering has prevented me from ever shadowing one young soul with
any of the superstitions of the Christian religion."[38] But at the end of her life
she did more. In 1895 she published *The Woman's Bible* and directly challenged
the religion of her childhood and especially the obstructions raised by organized religion and most of contemporary theology to the cause of women's
equality. Many of her suffrage colleagues were horrified. They did not want
new enemies among the religiously orthodox, and many were themselves
among the orthodox.

Stanton's closest friend and ally, Susan B. Anthony, continued her childhood connection with the Quakers. She did not care much, one way or the other, about Stanton's orthodoxy, but she viewed Stanton's plan for her *Bible* and her attack on the churches as a diversion from the only thing that really mattered: the vote. In 1895, Anthony wrote privately to Stanton:

> I simply don't want the enemy to be diverted from my practical ballot fight—
> to that of scorning me for belief one way or the other about the Bible—the
> religious part has never been mine—you know and I won't take it up—so long
> as the men who hold me in durance vile—won't care a dime what the Bible
> says—all the care for is what the Saloon says—So go ahead—in your own
> way—and let me stick to my own.[39]

A year later Anthony wrote even more sharply, "You say 'women must be emancipated from their superstitions before enfranchisement will be of any benefit,' and I say just the reverse, that women must be enfranchised before they can be emancipated from their superstitions."[40] Nevertheless, when Stanton's publication of the first short version of *The Woman's Bible* provoked a resolution of condemnation at the NAWSA, Anthony came to her defense. Although privately irritated, Anthony was not about to have her friend silenced or the organization divided. So Anthony said:

> The one distinct feature of our association has been the right of individual
> opinion for every member. We have been beset at each step with the cry that
> somebody was injuring the cause by the expression of sentiments which dif-
> fered from those held by the majority. The religious persecution of the ages
> has been carried on under what was claimed to be the command of God. I
> distrust those people who know so well what God wants them to do, because
> I notice it always coincides with their own desires . . . a Christian has neither
> more nor less rights in our association than an atheist. When our platform
> becomes too narrow for people of all creeds and of no creeds, I myself cannot
> stand upon it.[41]

Anthony's eloquence notwithstanding, she lost that vote.

In spite of the warnings and frustrations of some of her closest friends, Stanton persisted in her campaign and continued in all her later work to link women's freedom to vote with their freedom from religious oppression in any form. Though some could not accept her reasoning, Stanton was clear that the personal oppression of the religion of her childhood and the social and political repression of many religious institutions was inextricably linked with the oppression of women that the vote was supposed to end. And Stanton was confident in her own judgments. She asked, "Why should the myths, fables, and allegories of the Hebrews be held more sacred than those of the Assyrians and Egyptians, from whose literature most of them were derived? Seeing that the religious superstitions of women perpetuate their bondage more than all other adverse influences, I feel impelled to reiterate my demands for justice, liberty, and equality in Church as well as in State."[42] As predicted, this caused more opposition than even her suffrage activities. In the 1920s, after her death, her children republished her *Autobiography* but specifically excluded the material from the original 1897 edition that related to her religious views. Even after Stanton's great campaign for suffrage had been won, her religious views and her hopes for greater freedom in religion remained far too controversial for her own family.[43]

VICTORY AND ITS LIMITS

On August 26, 1920, the secretary of state of the United States announced that, with the ratification vote of Tennessee, the Constitution had been amended to say:

> The right of citizens of the United States to vote shall not be denied or abridged by the United States or by any State on account of sex.
>
> Congress shall have power to enforce this article by appropriate legislation.[44]

That fall, across the country, twenty-six million women were able to vote in the presidential election. One of them, Charlotte Woodward, at ninety-one, was the only surviving signer of the Seneca Falls Declaration of Sentiments of 1848. It had been seventy-two years since Elizabeth Cady Stanton and her allies had forthrightly proclaimed their hope for political liberty through the right to vote. But the hope that had animated the lives of generations of women had been fulfilled. Few victories were so clear-cut.[45]

The final push toward the passage of the suffrage amendment, like every previous step in the campaign, was marked by bickering, dramatic splits, and common purpose. Indeed, many historians argue that the splits were as important as the common purpose, for they allowed different women to work in different ways and with different allies toward the same goal.

Central to the campaign was the National American Women Suffrage Association (NAWSA). In 1915 Carrie Chapman Catt resumed the presidency of the NAWSA, which she had originally held with the retirement of Susan B. Anthony in 1904. Catt was an extraordinarily able leader. She had emerged in the leadership circles of the suffrage campaigns because of her work on state suffrage efforts in the 1890s. Her western roots helped, for suffrage had been most successful away from the east coast. But she also was a long-time ally of European suffragists, could court wealthy benefactors, and could talk politics comfortably with Emma Goldman and Charlotte Perkins Gilman. Upon resuming office in 1915, Catt mapped out a clearly focused campaign to gain an amendment to the Constitution within six years.[46]

To Catt's left were a number of more militant groups. Alice Paul had originally launched the Congressional Union within the NAWSA, but in 1915 she and the Union split off to help form the National Woman's Party, which planned much more direct assaults on politicians and political parties—at this point, especially the Democrats—who were resisting suffrage. While Catt had been one of the founders of the Woman's Peace Party in 1915 and had chaired its first convention, she broke with the movement once the United States entered World War I, seeking President Woodrow Wilson's continued support for suffrage. Others, including Jeanette Rankin, the first woman in Congress, and Jane Addams, took the much greater risk of sticking with their commitment to peace at a time when such views were seen as dangerously unpatriotic. Catt, on the other hand, demanded a suffrage amendment as a "war measure," to ensure a unified home front. In 1919 the Northeastern Federation of Colored Women's Clubs extracted a promise from Catt and the leaders of NAWSA that they would not agree to any compromise language in the constitutional amendment that could leave enforcement to the states. They knew all too well what southern state legislatures would do with the votes of African American women.[47]

In spite of these differences, there was solidarity across the lines. Jeannette Rankin, who had broken with Catt on the issue of the war, was the person who introduced the "Anthony Amendment," to the House of Representatives on January 10, 1918. The amendment passed the House 274 to 136, exactly the two-thirds majority needed for a constitutional amendment. The Senate moved more slowly, but with NAWSA's help, four antisuffrage senators were defeated in November of 1918, and the amendment was approved and sent on to the states in June 1919. State action came quickly, culminating with the vote of the Tennessee legislature little more than a year later, which gave the amendment its required thirty-sixth ratification. It was an extraordinary victory.[48]

The next steps in the campaign for true political equality were much more difficult. There were some immediate victories as politicians tried to respond to their expanded constituencies. In 1921 Congress passed the Sheppard-Towner Act, also known as the Maternity and Infant Act, that provided federal funds for prenatal and infant care. In 1922 the Cable Act also passed Congress, protecting the citizenship rights of American women who married noncitizens. By 1923 three women—all Republicans—were serving in the House of Representatives. At first, it seemed, suffrage was making real changes. But hopes for more far-reaching change demanded much greater organization and much more patience than any of the advocates for suffrage realized. And the 1920s were not good times for either careful organizing drives for the rights of citizens or for the patient focus on change displayed by Anthony, Stanton, and their many allies.[49]

In 1923 Alice Paul led the National Women's Party (NWP) in calling for a further amendment to the Constitution that would state, "Men and women shall have equal rights throughout the United States and every place subject to its jurisdiction." The Equal Rights Amendment was introduced in Congress the same year but has yet to be enacted.[50] But the time was not right and the NWP was not the right organization. Paul and the NWP leadership did not have the patience for the kind of grass-roots organizing that had led to the passage of the Nineteenth Amendment. And women in the 1920s were placing their hopes for a better future on many other kinds of activities. One well-known feminist, Crystal Eastman, supported the Equal Rights Amendment but also found it too narrow. Reflecting on the 1923 NWP convention that had endorsed the amendment, Eastman wished that there had been a much broader discussion of the issues facing women at the convention: "If some such program could have been exhaustively discussed at that convention, we might be congratulating ourselves that the feminist movement had begun in America. As it is all we can say is that the suffrage movement is ended."[51] In fact, as this and subsequent chapters will show, the feminist movement took many different turns and focused on the needs of many different women in the decades ahead, some quite narrow and cautious, others far more revolutionary than anything dreamed of by their predecessors.

"IF I CAN'T DANCE, I DON'T WANT TO BE PART OF YOUR REVOLUTION"

In *Living My Life*, Emma Goldman's extended autobiography, she describes a moment early in her career that is emblematic of her important contribution to twentieth century feminism. Working on New York's Lower East Side, she was helping to organize a strike of cloakmakers, young women in the needle trades. The young women met not only for long discussions but also for parties and dances. "At the dances," Goldman reported, "I was one of the most untiring and gayest." Not everyone agreed with Goldman's mix of radicalism and gaiety:

> One evening a cousin of Sasha [Alexander Berkman, anarchist leader and life-long friend and lover of Goldman's], a young boy, took me aside. With a grave face, as if he were about to announce the death of a dear comrade, he whispered to me that it did not behoove an agitator to dance. Certainly not with such reckless abandon, anyway. . . . I grew furious at the impudent interference of the boy. I told him to mind his own business, I was tired of having the Cause constantly thrown in my face. I did not believe that a Cause which stood for a beautiful ideal, for anarchism, for release and freedom from conventions and prejudices, should demand the denial of life and joy. I insisted that our Cause could not expect me to become a nun and that the movement should not be turned into a cloister. If it meant that, I did not want it. "I want freedom, the right to self-expression, everybody's right to beautiful, radiant things."[52]

It was a vision of the future filled with much more freedom and much more hope than that of many of Goldman's comrades, female and male.

The argument with the young revolutionary was as close as Goldman ever came to actually saying the famous line, "If I can't dance, I don't want to be part of your revolution." And it was close enough to the better-known statement to give the latter a ring of truth. Indeed, "if I can't dance," remains a good summary of Goldman's whole philosophy, and it has continued to live as a record of her contribution to both feminism and racial political action. As Leslie A. Howe, wrote, "One of the things that makes Emma Goldman stand out as an early feminist thinker, as well as a social revolutionary, is the fact that she is perhaps the only one to set forth a philosophy that accepts the body; indeed, celebrates it and its possibilities for enjoyment and the communion of two people."[53] While she was hardly as unique in her embrace of sexuality as Howe implies, Goldman's brand of hopeful and freedom-loving anarchism melded sexual freedom with a broader love of life and a commitment to human dignity that threatened many on the Left and the Right, but that also offered a model of a joy-filled life. No wonder Goldman's life and words have given so much hope to later generations who have studied her.

Emma Goldman was born in Kovno, Lithuania, on June 27, 1869, in a Jewish family torn by a father's violence and in a country torn by the deep Russian anti-Semitism and by the stirrings of revolutionary hopes on the part of anarchists, communists, and idealists of many stripes. In 1885, at the age of sixteen, Goldman and her older sister Helena managed to immigrate to the United States, settling in Rochester, New York, where Goldman worked long hours in the city's factories, married and divorced a fellow-worker, Jacob Kreshner, and in general found life almost as stultifying as it had been in Russia.[54] As she later described it, the one surprisingly bright light in her early life in America was her participation in the protests around the trial and eventual execution of the group that came to be known as the Haymarket martyrs. She first heard of their cause from the socialist Johanna Greie who lectured in Rochester. Greie told of the events of May 4, 1886, when a bomb at an anarchist rally for the eight-hour day killed seven Chicago police officers. In the aftermath, Illinois authorities arrested and eventually executed the anarchist speakers at the rally in spite of the complete lack of evidence that they had any involvement with the bomb itself. After Greie's speech, Goldman had a chance to meet her. As Goldman told it, Greie noted the young woman's sympathy for the cause and predicted, "I have a feeling that you will know them [the Chicago anarchists] better as you learn their ideal, and that you will make their cause your own."[55] If the story is true (Goldman described the event some forty years later) it was an accurate prophecy. Soon after, Goldman left her family to begin her life again in New York City.

As Goldman recalled, it was her arrival in New York City on a hot summer day in 1889 when she was twenty years old that was the real beginning of her life. "All that had happened in my life until that time was now left behind me, cast off like a worn-out garment. A new world was before me, strange and terrifying. . . . Whatever the new held in store for me I was determined to meet unflinchingly."[56] And she did.

Like many other young people arriving in New York, Goldman found that the city offered more than its share of hardships and of liberation. Goldman quickly became part of a group of young radicals, anarchists, and socialists. She met eighteen-year-old Alexander Berkman and they quickly became lovers and friends. Goldman remembered how, early in their friendship, she and Berkman shared the importance of the Haymarket events in their own development and agreed, "We are comrades. Let us be friends too—let us work together."[57] In spite of bitter disagreements, long separations, and divergent paths, it was a promise that they both kept.

From the beginning, however, the young Goldman sometimes found Berkman's political passions too narrow. She was also drawn to Fedya, a young artist friend, whom Berkman liked but found too bourgeois in his love of beauty. But for Goldman, "He had so much that Sasha lacked and that I craved. His susceptibility to every mood, his love of life and colour, made him more human, more akin to me. He never expected me to live up to the Cause. I felt release with him." She found herself wondering about "love for two or even for more persons at one time."[58]

It would be years later, hearing the lectures of a young Sigmund Freud in Vienna, that Goldman fully developed her own philosophical understanding of the revolutionary power of sexuality. "For the first time," she wrote of her encounter with Freud, "I grasped the full significance of sex repression and its effect on human thought and action. He helped me to understand myself, my own needs; and I also realized that only people of depraved minds could impugn the motives or find 'impure' so great and fine a personality as Freud."[59]

Goldman the anarchist became convinced that repression in any form was an enemy of the free world of which she dreamed. And sexual repression went more deeply than any other. A puritanical approach to life, whether it was the puritanism of small-town Rochester or that of either czarist or Bolshevik Moscow, limited the range of human experiences that enlarged and enriched life. She insisted: "Every stimulus which quickens the imagination and raises the spirits, is as necessary to our life as air. It invigorates the body, and deepens our vision of human fellowship. Without stimuli, in one form or another, creative work is impossible, nor indeed the spirit of kindness and generosity."[60] A revolution that did not lead to more freedom was not the kind of revolution that she would ever advocate. If she could not dance, she would not join.

Goldman's advocacy of birth control was always in the service of her larger mission. She insisted that women needed the freedom to control their own bodies and that birth control was a means to that end. Because birth control offered such basic freedoms to women, she strongly supported the practice. When she was arrested in 1916 for distributing information on contraception, she pleaded her own case and told the court that "if it was a crime to work for healthy motherhood and happy child-life, I was proud to be considered a criminal."[61] Evidently it was, for Goldman served a brief jail term, and her words aroused some of the greatest protests in her favor that she ever experienced. She parted company with Margaret Sanger and other birth control advocates, however, when she suspected that they saw birth control as *the* cause rather than one factor in a much larger cause of human freedom. She also distrusted what she saw as Sanger's tendency to see the cause as her own private venture and her failure to defend other family limitation proponents when they were arrested. "We were ready now," she said looking back to 1917, "to leave the field to those who were proclaiming birth control as the only panacea for all social ills."[62] For Goldman, the panacea was a much larger change in the whole nature of the social order.

The larger cause, for Goldman, was anarchism. Birth control, sexual freedom, socialism—all of these for her were part of a larger project, the full liberation of each individual from any form of interference by government, religious authority, or other cultural or political coercion. Anarchism was a rich and diverse philosophical movement in nineteenth-century Europe and, to a lesser extent, the United States. For Goldman anarchism meant: "The philosophy of a new social order based on liberty unrestricted by man-made

law; the theory that all forms of government rest on violence, and are therefore wrong and harmful, as well as unnecessary."[63] Goldman's anarchism was
strongly antistate and anticoercion of any kind. It was not, however, an ideal-
ization of the autonomous or lonely individual. Indeed, in the way she lived
her life and in the philosophy that she voiced, Goldman was deeply loyal to
both her friends and her social views. Most of all she had a powerful commitment to the free fellowship of individuals. In her 1917 book, *Anarchism and
Other Essays*, she wrote thoughtfully of the internal tensions within anarchism
and of the need to bridge the gap between the celebration of individual fulfillment and the building of a rich community life, without sacrificing either one:

> Peace or harmony between the sexes and individuals does not necessarily de-
> pend on a superficial equalization of human beings; nor does it call for the
> elimination of individual traits and peculiarities. The problem that confronts
> us today, and which the nearest future is to solve, is how to be one's self and
> yet in oneness with others, to feel deeply with all human beings and still re-
> tain one's characteristic qualities.[64]

A century later, reconciling individualism and community remains a vexing issue.

Goldman's advocacy of anarchism got her in far more trouble than her
commitment to individual freedom, sexual or otherwise. In 1892 Henry Clay
Frick, manager of Andrew Carnegie's steel empire, decided to cut wages and
break the union at the massive Homestead, Pennsylvania, Steel Works. When
the workers struck, Frick brought in a barge full of Pinkerton detectives and a
pitched battle ensued in which several workers and detectives were killed, followed by a long and difficult stand-off. In the middle of this tense situation,
Goldman and Berkman decided that dramatic action was necessary. As Goldman remembered:

> Words had lost their meaning in the face of the innocent blood spilled on
> the banks of the Monongahela. . . . everybody was considering Frick the
> perpetrator of a coldblooded murder. A blow aimed at Frick would re-echo
> in the poorest hovel, would call the attention of the whole world to the real
> cause behind the Homestead struggle. It would also strike terror in the
> enemy's ranks and make them realize that the proletariat of America had its
> avengers.[65]

Goldman and Berkman planned the assassination of Frick, and Berkman departed for Pittsburgh, leaving Goldman to be the defender of the noble cause
after his act. His parting words to her—romantic about both their relationship and their cause—were, "comrade, you will be with me to the last. You

will proclaim that I gave what was dearest to me for an ideal, for the great suffering people."[66]

In the end, Berkman wounded Frick but did not kill him. He was sentenced to twenty-two years and served fourteen before his release. Both Goldman and Berkman came to view the assault on Frick as an act of folly, but it changed their lives forever—Berkman's with a long prison term and Goldman's with a need to strike out on her own in new directions and to do more thinking for herself. It was the beginning of some of her most important work as an anarchist leader in the United States.

Goldman's American career came to an end in the anticommunist hysteria that followed World War I. Goldman, like most other anarchists and socialists, opposed the war and opposed any cooperation with the United States war effort. Goldman attacked President Wilson and military conscription:

> He had assured the world that America was moved by the highest humanitarian motives, her aim being to democratize Germany. What if he had to Prussianize the United States in order to achieve it? Free-born Americans had to be forcibly pressed into the military mould . . . to fertilize the fields of France. . . . No American president had yet succeeded in so humbugging the people as Woodrow Wilson, who wrote and talked democracy, acted despotically, privately and officially, yet managed to keep up the myth that he was championing humanity and freedom.[67]

Many may have agreed but it was not an acceptable public position to take in a nation focused on its war effort. Soon after the U.S. entered the war, Goldman along with Berkman, now released from prison, were both arrested and charged with conspiracy against the draft. Goldman was convicted of the charges and sentenced to the Missouri Penitentiary. She was released in September 1919, and deportation proceedings began almost immediately thereafter. In December 1919 Goldman, with Berkman and several hundred anarchists and others deemed dangerous foreigners—though many like Goldman had been in the United States for most of their lives—were deported to Russia.[68]

For American radicals of many persuasions, revolutionary Russia was the place to be in 1919. But for Goldman, the experience was ultimately both painful and disillusioning. The revolution she dreamed of was not the revolution she experienced. The Bolsheviks were no more open to individual freedom or to tolerance for those who disagreed with them than the American capitalists had been. The Russian intelligentsia, who had tended to support the revolution, the sailors of Petrograd whose uprising had started the revolution, and others who challenged Lenin and the Bolshevik authorities were ruthlessly stamped out. In *My Further Disillusionment in Russia*, Goldman recorded what she saw as the terrible mistakes of a revolution that had lost its soul.

> Not hatred but unity; not antagonism, but fellowship; not shooting, but sympathy—that is the lesson of the great Russian debacle for the intelligentsia as well as the workers. All must learn the value of mutual aid and libertarian co-operation. Yet each must be able to remain independent in his own sphere and in harmony with the best he can yield to society. Only in that way will productive labour and educational and cultural endeavour express themselves in ever newer and richer forms.[69]

It was a statement that well summed up all of her beliefs. While much romanticized and misunderstood, Emma Goldman remains an authentic American voice for a mix of "mutual aid and libertarian cooperation," of independence and the freedom to make individual decisions about how to best live in harmony with others and with the larger society. It is a powerful and hopeful vision for societies and the human endeavor.

MARGARET SANGER
AND BIRTH CONTROL

In her 1938 *Autobiography*, Margaret Sanger described the time when she changed the focus of her life, from a career as a nurse helping those who were suffering to a career as an activist committed to offering the hope that suffering could be avoided and pleasure honored as a natural right. In the summer of 1912 Sanger was pursuing her career as a visiting nurse, serving some of the poorest of New York City's residents. Again and again, as she visited the desperately poor of the Lower East Side, she heard the plea from women, "Tell me something to keep me from having another baby. We cannot afford another yet." All she could offer at the time was abstinence, *coitus interruptus*, perhaps a condom—none of which made any sense to these women, especially since these methods depended on the cooperation of men who were unlikely to give it. "What she was seeking," Sanger said of these women, "was self-protection she could herself use, and there was none." Or, at least none known to either Sanger the nurse or to the women she was supposed to help.[70]

As she continued to feel herself reproached by the situation of these women whom she had come to know and care for so much, things came to a head with one particular case:

> I was summoned to a Grand Street tenement. My patient was a small, slight Russian Jewess, about twenty-eight years old, of the special case of features to

which suffering lends a madonna-like expression. The cramped three-room apartment was in a sorry state of turmoil. Jake Sachs, a truck driver scarcely older than his wife, had come home to find the three children crying and her unconscious from the effects of a self-induced abortion.

Sanger and the attending physician treated the resulting infection that had nearly killed Mrs. Sachs. After three weeks of touch-and-go treatment in a sweltering apartment, the patient was out of danger. But the patient's anxiety told Sanger that the same danger would come again soon enough. When the recovering patient asked the doctor, "what can I do to prevent it?" he responded, "You want to have your cake and eat it too, do you? Well, it can't be done. . . . Tell Jake to sleep on the roof." Both Sanger and Sachs knew what this condemnation meant.

Three months later Sanger was summoned to the same apartment for the same reason. She got there quickly but, "Mrs. Sachs was in a coma and died within ten minutes. I folded her still hands across her breast, remembering how they had pleaded with me, begging so humbly for the knowledge which was her right." And as Sanger went home, she told herself, "never again." She knew then that "the doubt and questioning, the experimenting and trying, were now to be put behind me. . . . I went to bed, knowing that no matter what it might cost, I was finished with palliatives and superficial cures; I was resolved to seek out the root of evil, to do something to change the destiny of mothers whose miseries were vast as the sky." And she did.[71]

In the years and decades that followed her experience in that Lower East Side tenement, Sanger kept her promise of offering hope to women. She started out trying to discover what was known about limiting pregnancies. She found that there was very little, indeed, within the narrow world of the United States. Victorian prudishness had taken hold in the United States through the vigorously enforced Comstock laws, which after 1873 made it illegal to share any information or products designed to limit pregnancy. The great libraries of New York and Boston told her almost nothing. Perhaps symbolizing the connections between the multifaceted progressive agendas of the new century, it was the great labor agitator, Big Bill Haywood, who suggested that Sanger needed to go to France to find out what women on the continent knew that their American sisters did not. She embraced the idea and in October 1913, she and her husband, William, a painter, sailed to Europe.[72]

In Europe Sanger learned things that had been known in the United States a half century before. It seemed to her as she interviewed women in France that all of them had a sophisticated knowledge, passed down through the generations, of how to limit the size of their families. "Some of the contraceptive formulas which had been handed down were almost as good as those of today," Sanger said. "Although they had to make simple things, mothers prided themselves on their special recipes for suppositories as much as on those for *pot au feu* or wine." She also found government-sponsored birth control clinics that offered more scientific help. It was a startling discovery for her and she returned to the United States determined to share the word.[73]

Sharing the revelation of how to limit families was not easy in Sanger's home country. Nineteenth-century Americans had had quite a bit of information about family planning. In the 1830s douching after intercourse had been recommended by doctors and Charles Goodyear invented the rubber condom soon thereafter. By the 1850s chemically treated sponges were also on the market; even the *New York Times* advertised "Dr. Power's French Preventives," i.e., condoms.[74]

All of this valuable information and material became illegal to use, distribute, or describe, however, when a reformer of a very different sort, Anthony Comstock, head of the New York Committee for the Suppression of Legalized Vice, convinced Congress that contraceptives were obscene. The famed Comstock law, passed by Congress in 1873, left little to chance. It prohibited the use of the mail for: "Every obscene, lewd, or lascivious, and every filthy book, pamphlet, picture, paper, letter, writing, print, or other publication of an indecent character, and every article or thing designed, adapted, or intended for preventing conception or producing abortion.[75] The Comstock law and Anthony Comstock's forty-year advocacy of stricter and stricter federal and state regulation of all sexuality and information about sex had a dramatic effect. Information and devices that the Civil War generation had taken for granted were denied to their children and grandchildren, and were even less available to the great numbers of newer immigrants to the United States from the poorest parts of Europe.[76]

After her return from Europe, Sanger moved quickly to spread the gospel of family planning. At a gathering in her New York apartment, a few friends debated the name for her new movement: "We tried population control, race control, and birth rate control. Then someone suggested, 'Drop the rate.' Birth control was the answer: we knew we had it."[77]

In March 1914, Sanger began publishing a new magazine, *Woman Rebel*, in which she tried to include as much information as possible without running afoul of the Comstock laws. She did not succeed. The post office almost immediately found the magazine to be unmailable under the Postal Laws and Regulations. While she was fighting the battle about *Woman Rebel*, Sanger was also writing her more explicit booklet, *Family Limitation*, in which she set out to share all she knew about birth control. But her legal difficulties mounted quickly. Sanger was indicted on federal obscenity charges for *Woman Rebel*. Facing a risky trial, she left the country secretly before the end of 1914, arranging on her way to Canada for the publication of *Family Limitation* once she was outside of American jurisdiction. From Canada she sailed for England—a nation then at war—studying, writing, and preparing for her trial on her own schedule.[78]

In the years just before the United States entered World War I, Sanger began a long career of remarkable success. She returned to New York in 1915 and announced herself ready for trial, but the charges were eventually dropped. In 1916 she and her sister, Ethel Byrne, opened a clinic in Brooklyn and advertised "Safe, Harmless Information can be obtained of trained Nurses." The clinic was short lived, however. Within the month, Sanger and Byrne were arrested and the clinic closed.[79]

In the decades that followed Sanger worked unceasingly to make birth control both more widely available and more respectable. Building odd alliances, maintaining a dogged determination, living with contradictions of many sorts, Sanger did make slow but amazing progress. She focused on the single issue, avoiding any association that might divert her or her intended audience. She organized a birth control conference for physicians and researchers in New York City in 1921. She founded the American Birth Control League in the same year. In 1923 she opened a physician-run birth control clinic, thereby avoiding the crime of nurses dispensing birth control that had led to her arrest in 1916. She organized international conferences on birth control in New York in 1925, in Geneva in 1927, and in Zurich in 1930. In the 1930s she tested federal laws against the importation of foreign-made contraceptives and she won. In 1942 the American Birth Control League that she had founded in 1921 was transformed into Planned Parenthood with Sanger as honorary chair. She lived long enough to see the United States Supreme Court end all laws, state and federal, against contraceptives for married couples in *Griswold v. Connecticut* (1965), a decision extended to unmarried people in 1972.[80]

The crowning achievement in Sanger's career was the development of the birth control pill. In the 1950s, Sanger, first through a grant from Planned Parenthood, and then through her own independent links to wealthy benefactors, began to support the research of Gregory Pincus, a research scientist, and John Rock, a Catholic physician. In 1960 the Food and Drug Administration approved the first birth control pill and with it the freedom that Sanger had dreamed of—"self-protection she could herself use"—was a reality.[81]

Sanger was hardly a lone voice for birth control in the first half of the twentieth century. She owed a large debt, never fully acknowledged, to Emma Goldman, who was advocating birth control in the same circles that Sanger moved in, long before Sanger took up the cause. In the 1910s and 1920s, other people such as Robert Latou Dickinson and Mary Ware Dennet were sometimes Sanger's rivals for leadership in the movement. Dennett was especially critical of Sanger for her "medicalization" of contraception. Why give doctors so much power over women, Dennet asked, when as "Mrs. Sanger herself testified 'that the Clinical Research Department of the American Birth control League teaches methods so simple that once learned, any mother who is intelligent enough to keep a nursing bottle clean, can use them.'"[82]

Victories are not won by lone individuals. The wealthy Katherine Dexter McCormick—of Chicago's McCormick family—financed the movement including much of the research for which Sanger received the credit. Sanger was also nurtured by the interlocking reform movements that were changing the United States at the beginning of the twentieth century: socialism born of the labor movement and the bohemianism thriving in Greenwich Village. She did not come to her dream of liberating women in isolation. But Sanger's name, her continuous commitment over half a century, and her pragmatic optimism were essential ingredients in the victories that were won.[83]

The career that first convinced Sanger of the desperate need women had for a method of birth control that they could control themselves came through her work with a visiting nurse service started by Lillian Wald, New York's progressive settlement-house counterpart to Chicago's Jane Addams. Sanger's husband, William, shared the same radical reformist views. Married in 1902, they had three children and shared the same New York social circle as the journalist John Reed, who would chronicle the Russian Revolution with such enthusiasm, and Emma Goldman, who had championed women's reproductive rights, including the rights of single women, before Sanger had heard of the topic. Goldman, of course, went much further as perhaps the nation's best-known defender of anarchism, free love, and a more general rejection of bourgeois culture. For all Sanger's talk of her dramatic experiences as a nurse on the Lower East Side, which no doubt had a significant impact, it is hard to believe that the culture in which she lived, and especially the work of Goldman, did not have an at least equal impact.[84]

Sanger's personal life also reflected more of the spirit of her early years than she was sometimes willing to admit in later life. Unlike Goldman and others, she never attacked the institution of marriage. But she left William after their trip to Europe in 1913. In her personal life she enjoyed the freedoms she advocated, including a relatively well-publicized affair with the highly respected English psychologist and sex researcher Havelock Ellis, about whom Sanger said, "I have never felt about any other person as I do about Havelock Ellis." In the 1920s she was linked to the English writers' retreat at Wantley, designed to create a "morally unconstrained universe." Nevertheless, her personal life always seems to have taken a secondary position to her single-minded devotion to her cause.[85]

In time, however, Sanger also parted company with other radicals. As Margaret Marsh has argued, "Whatever Goldman's influence on Margaret Sanger, in the latter's hands birth control was transformed from one element of a larger philosophy into the essential precondition for women's freedom and independence."[86] Sanger herself said much the same thing, complaining that in their writings about women, "Feminists were trying to free her from the new economic ideology but were doing nothing to free her from her biological subservience to men, which was the true cause of her enslavement."[87] Sanger planned on a single-minded effort to end that source of enslavement.

Some of her old friends, Emma Goldman in particular, felt betrayed that while they had supported Sanger, she seemed to turn her back on them. She, on the other hand, felt that they were mixing too many issues and condemning themselves to failure on all fronts. Whatever the truth of the mutual disappointments, it is probably true that only a single-minded devotion to her cause could have allowed Sanger to accomplish all she did in her long life.[88]

A far more serious charge against Sanger concerns her lifelong flirtation with the eugenics movement. As M. E. Melody and Linda M. Peterson note, "Sanger spoke favorably about limiting the birthrate of the unfit from her earliest activist days to her last ones."[89] She was consistent on this point. In her 1938 *Autobiography* Sanger praised the immigration restriction of 1924 and condemned the failure to implement tougher immigration laws early in the century. "Had these precautions been taken earlier our institutions would not now be crowded with moronic mothers, daughters, and grand-daughters—three generations at a time, all of whom have to be supported by tax-payers who shut their eyes to this condition, admittedly detrimental to the blood stream of the race."[90] And in 1950 when Sanger, now the *grande dame* of the birth control movement, was given an award by Planned Parenthood, she attacked modern welfare programs that failed to weed out the "feebleminded and unfit." It is a sad but real part of the legacy of a woman who did so much to liberate her sisters.[91]

Looking back from what turned out to be the midpoint of her career, when Sanger published her *Autobiography*, she dedicated the book:

> To all the pioneers
> Of new and better worlds to come.[92]

Emma Goldman, Charlotte Perkins Gilman, John Reed, Big Bill Haywood, and the other radicals who had helped her along the way and then parted company could read their names in that dedication if they wanted to. But so could the unnamed women and men who had taken risks with Sanger, competed with her or supported her work, helped her coin the phrase "birth control" and then struggled to make it a reality. One thing they all shared was an abiding hope that the world could be made a better, freer, gentler, yet more passionate place, and an equally passionate commitment to making that hope a reality. It was a hope that has given an important if generally taken-for-granted freedom to so many citizens of the twenty-first century.

For all of their very real differences, Margaret Sanger, Emma Goldman, Alice Paul, Jeannette Rankin, Elizabeth Cady Stanton, Susan B. Anthony, and thousands and thousands of their sisters shared a very basic hope. Each in her own way dreamed of a day when women would be free of the wide-ranging forms of oppression—political, economic, religious, sensual, and sexual—that limited their freedom to live life to the fullest. And each in her own quite different way, helped make that hope a reality.

CHAPTER SEVEN

THE BEGINNINGS OF ORGANIZED LABOR

PRAY FOR THE DEAD AND FIGHT LIKE HELL FOR THE LIVING

ON MAY DAY 1930 MOTHER JONES, perhaps the nation's best-known labor organizer at the time, celebrated her one-hundredth birthday. At the celebration she made the last public speech of her life:

> America was not founded on dollars but on the blood of the men who gave their lives for your benefit. Power lies in the hands of labor to retain American liberty, but labor has not yet learned how to use it. A wonderful power is in the hands of women, too, but they don't know how to use it. Capitalists sidetrack the women into clubs and make ladies of them. Nobody wants a lady, they want women. Ladies are parlor parasites.[1]

The speech was vintage Mother Jones, a brief restatement of themes that she had been sounding for the last half century. Disdaining both middle-class pretensions and the failure of workers to seize what was rightfully theirs, Jones always insisted that laboring men and women could change their own destinies and the destiny of the nation if they would just be strong, be organized, avoid being sidetracked, and be willing to claim their power and their rights. And sooner or later, Jones was sure, this would indeed happen.

Maria Harris Jones (Mother Jones) was born in Cork, Ireland, in the early 1830s. Though she always claimed May 1, 1830, as her birthdate, she was actually born a good bit later. The records at St. Mary's Cathedral in Cork show that she was baptized there on August 1, 1837. But adding a few years to her age and claiming the worker's holiday of May Day as her birthday, like the black dresses she wore and the parallels she made with the another Mother Mary, only added to the luster of her persona.[2] And quite a persona it was.

Like many other immigrant families, hers settled first in Canada. She attended Normal School in Toronto in 1857 and 1858, taught at Monroe, Michigan, from 1859 to 1860, then worked briefly as a dressmaker in Chicago. She moved to Memphis, Tennessee before the end of 1860 and married George Jones in 1861. When her husband and children died in a yellow fever epidemic in 1867, she returned to dressmaking until the Chicago fire of 1871 destroyed her shop. From then on, union organizing and "raising hell" was her life. She actively supported several major nineteenth-century strikes and protests including the great railroad strike of 1877, the cause of the Haymarket radicals in 1886, the founding of the United Mine Workers of America in 1890, and the American Railway Union and the Western Federation of Miners in 1893. She organized for Coxey's Army, the 1894 national protest march on Washington that demanded jobs for those thrown out of work by the depression of that decade. In 1905–1906 she helped found the Industrial Workers of the World; pled for the rights of Mexican revolutionaries imprisoned in the United States in 1909; supported the women garment workers in New York City in 1910 and the Colorado mine workers at the time of the Ludlow massacre in 1914.[3]

When asked by a congressional committee in 1910 to state where she lived, she said with her standard flourish:

> I live in the United States, but I do not know exactly in what place, because I am always in the fight against oppression, and wherever a fight is going on I have to jump there, and sometimes I am in Washington, sometimes in Pennsylvania, sometimes in Arizona, sometimes in Texas, and sometimes up in Minnesota, so that really I have no particular residence. . . . No abiding place, but wherever a fight is on against wrong, I am always there. It is my pleasure to be in the fray.[4]

The statement was fairly accurate. For half a century she was a constant presence among the striking workers, especially the miners, across the country.

Meridel LeSueur recalled in 1990 the time she first saw Jones at a 1914 memorial march for workers killed by the Rockefeller-supported militia in Trinidad, Colorado.

> The only fighter I had seen like her was Eugene Debs, and I felt they were leaders of the future because they were the first people I had seen with love.

They were of, and came from, the wounds of the people, not as saviors from above or outside, but with speech and images of the American workers and farmers. They were the first so-called organizers I saw who embraced you. . . . She summoned the images of our life and silence and struggle, and invoked the muscular and impassioned fight and love for each other. We came alive as if touched by her mother flame. She seemed to nourish us, expel our fears, make fun of our so-called losing the strike. "You never lose a strike," she said. "You frighten the robbers and arm yourselves and your brothers." . . . She made us a family endangered, but powerful.[5]

Jones herself might have been embarrassed by some of LeSueur's words. She herself said, "Get it straight. I'm not a humanitarian—I'm a hell-raiser."[6] But this hell raiser, who somehow also projected love and courage, clearly empowered workers facing some of the most difficult situations in the United States a century ago. Her account of a few of those struggles gives a sense of her own hope for a better society—both the small society of the coal camp and the larger society of what a democratic United States should be.

Not a great deal is known about Mother Jones's life in the 1880s and early 1890s, although she was clearly involved as a participant or observer in some of the most militant labor organizing in the United States during those years. She claimed a role in the great railroad strike of 1877. She lived in Chicago in 1886 when the May 1 Haymarket anarchist rally for the eight-hour day led to a police riot, a bomb explosion that killed seven police officers, and eventually the execution of several anarchist leaders though there was never any link between them and the bomb.[7] She became a close friend of the great labor leader and socialist Eugene V. Debs and organized the welcoming committee for his release from his first prison term in 1896. And she supported another of the era's radicals, Julius Wayland, when also in 1896 he launched *Appeal to Reason*, soon to be an important radical newspaper. By 1900 she was surely a fixture in the American labor movement.[8]

Although she played a significant role in conventions of the United Mine Workers, the Industrial Workers of the World, and the Farm-Labor and Socialist parties, and testified before congressional committees and confronted governors and senators, Mother Jones's greatest role was in giving hope and power to workers for whom hope was an extraordinary risk. A Pennsylvania miner who later became a union official, John Brophy remembered Mother Jones from the 1890s:

She came to the mine one day and talked to us in our workplace in the vernacular of the mines. . . . She would take a drink with the boys and spoke their idiom, including some pretty rough language when she talked about the bosses. . . . She had a complete disregard for danger or hardship and would go in wherever she thought she was needed. And she cared no more about approval from union leaders than operators; wherever people were in trouble, she showed up to lead the fight with tireless devotion.[9]

Throughout the years the stories about Mother Jones were similar: she connected with workers in an amazing way, she was there when people were in trouble, and she was there to give courage and hope. The only way to organize people into a union, to convince them to take the terrible risks that joining a union or participating in a strike meant, was to exude extraordinary confidence and to paint a convincing picture of a better day to come.[10]

In the late 1890s the United Mine Workers began a series of strikes in the coal fields of Pennsylvania and West Virginia, the heart of industrial America. Jones was there in the middle of it all. The situation was quite desperate. The miners were terribly poor, easily divided by ethnicity, and the mine owners were determined not to have a union whatever the cost. In her *Autobiography* Jones told many stories from these years. One example gives a sense of her style. She had been working at another town when she was sent for by workers in Arnot, Pennsylvania, where a strike had been going on for several months. Under threats from the coal companies, many of the workers were ready to give up and go back to work. Starting out at bitter-cold daybreak, she went by horse and buggy from the nearest train station over rough mountain roads to Arnot. She arrived on Sunday afternoon and called a meeting.

> "You've got to take the pledge," I said. "Rise and pledge to stick to your brothers and the union till the strike's won!"
>
> The men shuffled their feet but the women rose, their babies in their arms, and pledged themselves to see that no one went to work in the morning.
>
> "The meeting stands adjourned till ten o'clock tomorrow morning," I said. "Everyone come and see that the slaves that think to go back to their masters come along with you."

During the night Jones was expelled from the coal company-owned hotel and ended up sleeping in the shack of one of the miners. As a result, her hosts were expelled from their rented shack in the morning. The mine owners clearly meant to play rough—but then so could Jones—who understood the value of drama as much as of direct confrontation. Her story continues:

> Then the company tried to bring in scabs. I told the men to stay home with the children for a change and let the women attend to the scabs. I organized an army of women housekeepers. On a given day they were to bring their

mops and brooms and "the army" would charge the scabs up at the mines. The general manager, the sheriff and the corporation hirelings heard of our plans and were on hand. The day came and the women came with the mops and brooms and pails of water.

I decided not to go up to the Drip Mouth myself, for I knew they would arrest me and that might rout the army. I selected as leader an Irish woman who had a most picturesque appearance. She had slept late and her husband had told her to hurry up and get into the army. She had grabbed a red petticoat and slipped it over a thick cotton night gown. She had tied a little red fringed shawl over her wild red hair. Her face was red and her eyes were mad. I looked at her and felt that she could raise a rumpus.

I said, "You lead the army up to the Drip Mouth. Take that tin dishpan you have with you and your hammer, and when the scabs and the mules come up, begin to hammer and howl. Then all of you hammer and howl and be ready to chase the scabs with your mops and brooms. Don't be afraid of anyone."

Up the mountain side, yelling and hollering, she had the women, and when the mules came up with the scabs and the coal, she began beating on the dishpan and hollering and all the army joined in with her. The sheriff tapped her on the shoulder.

"My dear lady," said he, "remember the mules. Don't frighten them."

She took the old tin pan and she hit him with it and she hollered, "To hell with you and the mules!"

He fell over and dropped into the creek. Then the mules began to rebel against scabbing. They bucked and kicked the scab drivers and started off for the barn. The scabs started running down hill, followed by the army of women with their mops and pails and brooms.

The demonstrating women with their mops and pails had turned the tide. And they did not stop there. "Every day women with brooms or mops in one hand and babies in the other arm wrapped in little blankets went to the mines and watched that no one went in. And all night long they kept watch. They were heroic women. In the long years to come the nation will pay them high tribute for they were fighting for the advancement of a great country." And they won the strike. For Jones, for the women, for the miners, it was a time of great rejoicing long remembered.[11]

Farther west, in the mountains of southeastern Colorado, coal miners and their families experienced some of the most brutal working conditions found anywhere in the United States. A strike in 1904 had been quashed by the Colorado Fuel & Iron Company, owned by John D. Rockefeller Sr. By 1913, with John D. Rockefeller Jr. now in charge, nothing had improved in the coal camps or the mines. Throughout that summer the United Mine Workers had been organizing secretly within the coal camps. The easily divided ethnic groups were becoming increasingly united. On September 15, 1913, 250 delegates from the mining camps gathered at Trinidad, Colorado, and voted for a strike demanding recognition for their union, a ten percent increase in wages, an eight-hour day, free choice of stores and doctors (rather than only company stores and doctors), and other reforms in their working conditions including enforcement of Colorado mining laws.[12] It was a courageous stance on the part of these downtrodden workers.

The next day, September 16, Mother Jones spoke to the convention, praising them for their vote and telling them to keep the faith. "Don't be afraid boys," she said. "Fear is the greatest curse we have." Beyond the call for courage, she also offered hope. "The miners have suffered, but it will have to come to an end for my boys. If your operators do not give to you that which is fair, then I say strike. . . . The time is ripe now." And she called on them all to stand by the courageous decisions they had made. "I want you to pledge yourselves in this convention to stand as one solid army against the foes of human labor. . . . We will fight until the mines are made secure and human life valued more than the props."[13]

The strike lasted fourteen months. It was long and bloody. In April 1914, the Rockefeller-controlled militia burned the coal miners camp in Ludlow, Colorado, killing thirty-two people, including eleven children huddled together for protection. Jones marched with the miners, planned with the miners, encouraged the miners, and served time in jail with the miners. The end was far from clear-cut. But Jones always took the long view. She told a Seattle, Washington, rally celebrating her release from jail in Colorado: "I have been a Socialist for more than twenty-nine years, but I am not one of those who believe that individual freedom is going to drop down from the clouds—while we sleep. The fight can be won, and will be won, but the struggle will be long and education, and agitation and class solidarity all must play a part in it."[14] Jones knew firsthand just how hard and long and painful the fight could be. She saw the courage and sacrifice of the women, children, and men of the Colorado coal camps and their counterparts around the country, and she shared their risks with them. She never lost hope that the fight could, indeed, be won.[15]

Mother Jones's most powerful weapon was her extraordinary ability to project hope even in what seemed to be the most hopeless situations. To the coal miners in Arnot, Pennsylvania, Clarksburg, West Virginia, or Trinidad, Colorado, to the dressmakers of New York City, to the streetcar workers in El Paso, Texas, or New York City, to the steel workers in Gary, Indiana, she carried the same message—the future is yours if you will but take it into your hands and mold it to your hopes. In July 1923, late in her long life, she addressed a conference of the National Farmer-Labor party in Chicago. She told the assembled delegates:

> Down in Johnstown, Pa., once . . . they asked me if I was a red. I said yes!
> They asked me if I was a Bolshevik, and I said 'yes,' . . . You must organize
> and use your heads . . . You have been letting bosses override you too long.
> You must clear out the crooked labor leaders among yourselves. All you need
> to do is to unite politically and you can have a thorough clean-up. You will be
> able to clean out the gunmen in the coal fields, particularly in West Virginia.
> It is time to get back to the spirit of the Revolutionary fathers. The produc-
> ers, not the meek, shall inherit the earth. Not today perhaps, nor tomorrow,
> but over the rim of years my old eyes can see the coming of another day.[16]

Not everyone could get away with mixing the revolutionaries of 1776 with the
Bolsheviks of 1917. But Jones saw consistency where others did not. She focused on building hope; hope that resistance on the part of oppressed people
could lead to their victory, and with the victory, a brighter future. And when
she spoke, others took heart and joined with her in her hope, and saw also
through her old eyes the coming of another day.

"CHEER UP MY BROTHERS, THE LONGEST NIGHT COMES TO AN END."

While Mother Jones won fame and was in her day one of the best-known
labor activists in the country, the miners and workers who formed the unions
remained nameless, then and now. Yet it was their hope and vision that transformed the nation. In the nineteenth century the vision often mixed the language of evangelical Christianity with that of labor militancy. An early issue of
The Labor Leader, a Massachusetts-based weekly labor publication dated August 27, 1887, carried an unsigned editorial note probably written by the journal's editor Frank K. Foster, that followed just this pattern: "A voice crying in
the wilderness has there been in all ages among the sons of men. The universal
aspiration of humanity for a higher social ideal has been, in one form or another, the theme of poet, prophet and philanthropist since time began." "The
universal aspiration of humanity for a higher social ideal," is clearly the hope
of this editor. And while the net is cast wide, the language is clearly that of
Christian hopes for the coming city of God:

> The "cross of the new crusade' is the cross of an old crusade, old as the pas-
> sions of the human heart. An idea may take different forms of expression and
> its ethical purport may be the same, and in whatever direction men may strive
> for this ambiguous thing we call social reform, if they mean anything at all,
> they but echo—be they Jew or Gentile, Greek or Christian, Deist or Atheist,
> Knight of Labor or Socialist—that carol of welcome, which was sung to greet

the coming of the Carpenter's Son in the centuries long gone by, "Peace on earth, good will toward men."

The sentinel on the social watch tower, with vision ranging world-wide and deep, unobscured the littleness of today . . . like St. Simon at death's door may exclaim, "The future is ours."[17]

The language was too religious for Mother Jones, but the conclusion was the same. And for thousands of unnamed workers, whether they used religious or secular language, the conclusion was the same: in joining the fight for the rights of workers everywhere they were making that most hopeful claim, "the future is ours."

A year later, Knights of Labor leader Charles Litchman wrote in a similar vein of religious hopefulness for the Philadelphia *Journal of United Labor:* "If you ask me to say how this system is to be changed, when the emancipation of the toiling millions on earth is to come, I can only say, 'I know not when it will come, but I know it will come,' because in the sight of God and God's angels the wrongs of the toiling millions on earth are a curse and a crime, and that as God is mercy and God is love, in His own good time the toiler will be free."[18] Such confidence that in God's own good time victory was inevitable made it possible to continue to struggle when all of the more immediate signs pointed only toward defeat. Knowing deeply in their hearts that the time would come when the capitalist system would be replaced was a powerful weapon indeed.

The March 29, 1894, issue of the *United Mine Workers' Journal* carried an article by an unknown coal miner from Newcomb, Tennessee, who called himself "Pumpkin Smasher." For this southern miner, the language was less religious but the confident hopefulness was the same: "Labor has made this country into a bed of roses so that a few may lie therein, and bask in the beautiful God-given sunshine, while the laborer or the creator of all this splendor is roaming in rags all tattered and torn. . . . Cheer up my brothers, the longest night comes to an end."[19] The faith that the world could, indeed, be made better—and be made better through the efforts of working men and women themselves—permeated all the early strikes and organizing activities that were the primary vehicle for mitigating the extreme hardships of industrialization. A new day was being born, and these unknown or now-forgotten heroes were confident that they were part of its advent.

The same religious hopefulness also helped the rank-and-file organizers give meaning to their work. They were spreading the new gospel just as the disciples of old had spread the Christian gospel almost two millennia earlier. The Amalgamated Association of Iron and Steel Workers' *National Labor Tribune* carried an unsigned note in its February 3, 1877, issue that vividly made the comparison.

Christianity was disseminated through the world eighteen hundred years ago by apostles and teachers, who traveled without pay, and for no other object than to spread the new gospel. . . . Armed with one thought, they traveled hither and thither, teaching and preaching wherever they could find listeners. In three centuries Constantine was a Christian and the religion of the crucified Nazarene was the religion of the Roman Empire.[20]

The implication that the faith of the American empire would undergo its own latter-day conversion based on the work of the labor missionaries was unmistakable.

Courage to endure the hardships of a strike or an organizing drive made no sense apart from hope that action on their part could make a difference. And for many workers, hope, courage, and confidence led to the success of some of the strikes and the greater success of the long-term efforts to organize the nation's workers so that they could protect their rights and build the labor movement they wanted. Labor organizers, especially in the early decades of the movement, saw organized labor as one essential element in the reorganization of a larger society along more egalitarian lines.

Not everyone shared the same level of comfort with the use of religious imagery to express their hopes for the future. Indeed, there was a strongly atheistic strand in the nineteenth- and early twentieth-century radical movements. Albert Parsons, one of the Chicago radicals who gathered in the International Working People's Association and who was ultimately executed as one of the Haymarket anarchists of 1886, insisted that "there is but one God—Humanity. Any other kind of religion is a mockery, a delusion, and a snare." Writing from jail while awaiting his execution, Parsons critiqued a review of social gospeler Richard Ely's pro-labor *Labor Movement in America* for claiming that religion was essential to reform. Parsons wrote: "Your reviewer says that when 'God is left out of any movement, there is very little of it left,' but nevertheless, the IWPA still insists that the labor movement is in fact capitalistic as long as the supreme, absolute right of man over himself is left out of it." Church, faith in a supreme being, or anything else that diverted women and men from their efforts to build a new world in the middle of the old smacked of a diversion, and therefore a crutch for capitalism, for radicals such as Parsons.[21]

The terms used and the degree of focus on the role of religious faith in labor's struggles varied greatly; nevertheless, the rise of organized labor is one of the clearest examples in American history of a vision of hope nurtured from the ground up. A handful of famous labor leaders—from Mother Jones, John L. Lewis, Walter Reuther—are the ones to receive notice in most of the history books. Many others who were famous in their own time—Terence V. Powderly,

Eugene V. Debs, Elizabeth Gurley Flynn, Big Bill Haywood—are virtually forgotten today. However, historians Herbert G. Gutman and E. P. Thompson have pointed out that unions were born and transformed the economic landscape because of the courage, commitment, and hopefulness of thousands and thousands of brave individuals more than because of any individual leaders.

Debs himself voiced a distrust of leaders: "I never had much faith in leaders. I am willing to be charged with almost anything, rather than to be charged with being a leader. . . . Give me the rank and file every day of the week."[22] E. P. Thompson has criticized the work of many other historians because of the tendency to "obscure the agency of working people, the degree to which they contributed, by conscious efforts, to the making of history." The Bread and Roses strike by the women who worked in the mills of Lawrence and Lowell, Massachusetts, the strikes by coal miners of Ludlow, Colorado, and at a hundred other western mines, and the great sit-down strikes in Detroit in the 1930s all began with local leaders and local militancy. The national leaders were brought in later. Such bravery does not emerge apart from hopefulness. In more cynical times it is hard to imagine the sacrifices of those who first organized, struggled, and died so that the workers of the nation could have basic rights to decent jobs, decent pay, and decent working conditions.[23]

THE LOWELL FACTORY GIRLS

Among America's earliest industrial workers, the women of the famous Lowell mills took the first steps at labor organizing and held some of the first strikes in the nation. The young women who worked in the factories in Lowell, Massachusetts, became the symbol of early nineteenth-century "factory girls," because Lowell was a show town and because of the success of the company newspaper, the *Lowell Offering*. In fact, during the early years of the nineteenth-century, similar factories staffed by young women developed in many parts of New England, first in Waltham in 1813, and soon in newer towns such as Lowell in 1823, and then in Manchester, Dover, and Nashua, New Hampshire, and Chicopee, Holyoke, and Lawrence, Massachusetts. In all of these towns, the textile industry grew and prospered based on the exploitation of young women who furnished the cheap labor that was essential to its success.[24]

In all these factories, most owned by the same small group of capitalists organized as the Boston Associates, the industrial revolution came to America. Francis Cabot Lowell and his colleagues wanted to avoid the squalid conditions of the English factories, and so instead of creating factory towns, they created tightly controlled boarding houses. And for the most part, they hired only single young women whose living conditions (and virtue) could be tightly controlled.

But while, at least in the early years, conditions may have been better than in the "dark satanic mills" of Manchester and Leeds, the work was hard, the hours long, and the conditions terrible at Lowell. As Philip Foner has argued:

> Quite a few of the female operatives, especially those associated with the *Low-ell Offering*, were convinced that the fame of Lowell gave standing and respectability to the women who worked for wages in factories, and this kept not a few from protesting about the conditions in the mills. But many of the level-headed Yankee girls quickly saw that the corporations were capitalizing on the favorable image of the factory girl created by the operatives' own efforts. It did not take long for them to realize that a favorable image was no compensation for exploitation.[25]

And with great courage, they responded. There were strikes in 1834 and 1836, and Lowell and Lawrence never stopped being seedbeds of militant labor activity in the century that followed.

A newspaper friendly to the women's cause, the *Dover [New Hampshire] Gazette*, not the *Lowell Offering*, gave the following report of the 1834 strike, one of the first in America:

> In consequence of the notice, given by the Agent to the Females, employed in the Manufacturing establishments in this town, that from and after the 15th instant, their wages would be reduced, to enable their employers to meet the *"unusual pressure of the times,"* the girls, to the number of between 600 and 700, assembled in the Court-House on Saturday afternoon, to devise ways and means to enable themselves to meet the *"pressure of the times"* anticipated from this threatened reduction.[26]

The first Lowell strike began the next Monday morning but did not last long. The company had far too much power and the women too little. Still the image of Lowell as a benevolent community run in the interests of its workers was broken forever. And the workers had made it clear that the economic problems caused by the *"unusual pressure of the times"* could not automatically be transferred to the workers "who were least able to bear it."[27]

A second strike took place two years later in October 1836. Harriet H. Robinson remembered the events: "When it was announced that the wages were to be cut down, great indignation was felt, and it was decided to strike, en masse. . . . The mills were shut down, and the girls went in procession from their several corporations to the 'grove' on Chapel Hill, and listened to 'incendiary' speeches from early labor reformers." Although the strike was again unsuccessful, it was a beginning not to be overlooked. Robinson remembered that when some had hesitated, she herself had led the young women from her floor out of the building. "As I looked back at the long line that followed me, I was more proud than I have ever been since at any success I may have achieved, and more proud than I shall ever be again until my own beloved State gives to its women citizens the right of suffrage."[28] Although she was writing a half century after the events, and although she would still have to wait another twenty years before women could vote in Massachusetts, Robinson's memory conveys both the pride and the political confidence that the labor movement generated and the link between labor and other reform efforts.

By the 1840s, things had become much tougher in Lowell and the other mill towns. The patina of benevolence that the mill owners had tried to maintain had worn off and the pretense was disappearing. At the same time, a depression in the New England farm economy meant that the option of simply quitting and returning home that had served as a pressure valve for discontent in the 1830s was fast disappearing. More and more of the young women stayed for longer and longer periods of time, not because things were so good in Lowell but because they had so few options.

As they stayed, the women built a community among themselves. Their letters, and especially their articles in publications like the *Voice of Industry* where they were able to express themselves freely, indicate the difficulties of their immediate experience and their hopes for the future. One woman, who signed herself Ada, spoke of both her frustrations and her hopes in biblical terms that would appeal to many of her counterparts:

> "Do unto others, as ye would that they should do to you," is a great precept, given to us by our great Teacher, as a rule and guide of action, towards all mankind. The Savior gave this for *practice;* he well knew what course of conduct would insure the greatest amount of happiness, to his creatures. . . . What but the neglect of this great principle, has brought into the world all this confusion, this disorder, this isolated state of interest, between man and man; all this monopoly and competition in business? And think you if all had "done unto others, as they would that they should do to them," if every man had "loved his neighbor as himself," that slavery would ever have existed, or oppression in any form? It could not have been.[29]

That 1846 vision of humanity free from oppression is also part of the hope that the Lowell factory girls gave to the future. It would blossom again a few miles away and sixty-six years later when a new generation led the great strike in the mills of Lawrence in 1912.

EARLY LABOR LEADERS

In a speech to a convention gathered in Chicago, Illinois, in the last months of the Civil War, William H. Sylvis—virtually forgotten today but the best-known labor leader in the country at the time—outlined what he saw as key to a better country: a recognition of the rights of organized labor, or, as he called it, co-operation, linked to a major increase in the wages of workers and a shorter work day. Only with much more money and much more free time, Sylvis insisted, could workers build the kind of just and humane culture that was morally demanded for the United States.

> A new idea has been born to the children of industry. "Co-operation" has dawned upon the world. "Co-operation" is the next great step; this taken, and we will have crossed the boundary which has so long separated man from his true destiny. This is the true remedy for the evils of society; this is the great idea that is destined to break down the present system of centralization, monopoly, and extortion. By co-operation, we will become a nation of employers—the employers of our own labor. The wealth of the land will pass into the hands of those who produce it. . . . The vile, the vicious, the evil-doers, and the idle of every class will be driven from society. . . . Such, Mr. Chairman, is destined to be the glorious future of the labor movement, wrought out by our remedies—brotherhood, combination, and co-operation.

But for Sylvis, this hoped-for future, wonderful as it was in his dream, was not inevitable. It was going to take hard work and courage to make it a reality. Success, he believed, "depends upon our own efforts. It is not what is done for people, but what people do for themselves, that acts upon their character and condition." Sylvis was confident of the outcome: "Yet the time is drawing nigh—a little bird whispers it in my ear—when the laborer, the workingman, no longer ignorant, brutalized, debased, shall rise, without impeachment of the claims of any, to the highest, best elevation of nature's aristocracy."[30] His Chicago speech clearly draws in the Protestant Christianity in which he was raised and lived. Unlike more the more secular later generation of union leaders, Sylvis was an active Methodist and Sunday school teacher as well as a labor leader. Here at the very beginning of the American labor movement was a leader confident of the ultimate victory.

Sylvis was born in Armagh, Pennsylvania, in 1828 to a wagon maker who was impoverished by the crash of 1837. Sylvis himself became an iron molder and in 1857 helped to lead a strike resisting a proposed decrease in wages in the shop where he worked. From that experience he quickly became a leader in the formation of a national union of iron molders. He fought briefly in the

Civil War, but by 1863 he was again engaged in union organizing. He was one of the early voices for the merger of all of the nation's unions into "one grand body" and helped organize the National Labor Union (NLU) which elected him as its president.[31]

As part of his effort to organize a truly national union, Sylvis, unlike most of his contemporaries, also worked tirelessly to overcome the great divisions of the nation by race and gender. Though he led the National Labor Union, Sylvis was frustrated that too many of his comrades did not truly believe in a racially inclusive union. In 1867, two years after the end of the Civil War and the end of American slavery, he and others issued an appeal to American trade unionists.

> Negroes are four million strong and a greater proportion of them labor with their hands than can be counted from the same number of any people on earth. Can we afford to reject their proffered co-operation and make them enemies? By committing such an act of folly we would inflict grater injury upon the cause of labor reform than the combined efforts of capital could furnish. . . . So capitalists north and south would foment discord between the whites and blacks and hurl one against the other as interest and occasion might require to maintain their ascendancy and continue their reign of oppression.[32]

The Executive committee of the NLU acted on Sylvis' appeal in December 1868 and voted that the next convention would invite all of those committed to the labor movement, "regardless of color or sex" to the next annual convention in Philadelphia scheduled for August 1869.[33]

When the delegates gathered as planned in Philadelphia they found themselves mourning Sylvis's death that had just occurred at the age of forty-one. In his honor, the union that he had founded did act on his appeal and voted, "The National Labor Union knows . . . neither color nor sex on the question of the rights of labor." African Americans and women took their seats at the convention in an unheard-of act of working-class unity. If only the majority of his successors in the labor movement had heeded Sylvis's prophesy the cause of labor might have succeeded more thoroughly and more quickly than it ever did in the United States. Nevertheless, it is important to note that for some, from the beginning, the vision of one big union for all workers was truly part of their plan.[34]

Sylvis and some of the other leaders of the National Labor Union were committed to the full inclusion of women in their ranks. The earlier 1868 convention, which met in New York City, had included a number of women delegates, and both Susan B. Anthony and Elizabeth Cady Stanton were actively involved—a reminder that suffrage, abolition, and the labor movement were much more closely linked in the nineteenth century than is often remembered. That convention had also agreed that their demand for the eight-hour work day include women's work as well as men's. They demanded equal pay for equal work, and the organization of trade unions among working women. It was the first time that any labor organization in the world had voted for equal pay for equal work, a vote that led Karl Marx to write:

> Great progress was evident in the last Congress of the National Labor Union in that among other things it treated working women with complete equality—while in this respect the English and the still more gallant French are burdened with a spirit of narrow-mindedness. Anybody knows, if he knows anything about history, that great social changes are impossible without the feminine ferment. Social progress can be measured exactly by the social progress of the fair sex.[35]

It was quite an endorsement of the National Labor Union and the vision espoused by the prophetic Sylvis.

Terence V. Powderly succeeded Sylvis as the nation's most widely recognized labor leader. In the 1870s and 1880s Powderly was the head of—or the Grand Master Workman of—the Knights of Labor, the most powerful union in the nation in the decades after the decline of the National Labor Union. Writing in 1889, while still at the height of his influence, Powderly expressed the need for unions in the increasingly industrialized and monopolized economy that was taking shape in the United States after the Civil War.

> The necessity for organization among producers becomes clearly discernible when one takes note of the tendencies toward centralization of power in the hands of those who control the wealth of the country. Combinations, monopolies, trusts, and pools, make it easy for a few to absorb the earnings of the workers, and limit their earnings to the lowest sum on which they can sustain life. Combination, in America, is heartless in the extreme. . . . And yet these combinations and pools are educators; they are teaching the American people that if a few men may successfully corner the results of labor, and the wealth to purchase them, there is no just reason why the many may not do so for the benefit of all, through agents of their own selection.[36]

Compared to many who followed him, Powderly was relatively conservative. He distrusted the anarchist and socialist wing of the labor movement, and while he supported the campaign for the eight-hour day in the 1880s, he distanced himself from anarchists such as those who led the 1886 May Day demonstration in Chicago's Haymarket Square. Nevertheless, to the industrial leaders of his day, Powderly was a truly dangerous man.

The report of his actions at the Knights of Labor's 1886 convention in Richmond, Virginia, speaks to the breadth of his concerns. In the aftermath of the end of Reconstruction, racism was rampant in the North as well as the South. Yet, at the Knights of Labor convention in the former capital of the Confederacy in October 1886, Powderly took a strong and principled stand, welcoming an African American delegate from New York to the convention and then inviting the delegate, Francis Ferrell, to introduce the Grand Master Workman himself for his speech at the convention. It was a symbolic act that brought a great deal of criticism of Powderly and the Knights of Labor. After the event, Powderly wrote a long article for the *Richmond Dispatch* in which he explained his actions and his reasoning.

> I stated to the meeting that it was at my request that Mr. Ferrell, a representative of the colored race, introduced me. . . . In acknowledging his introduction I referred to the prejudice which existed against the colored man. If previous to that day I had any doubts that a prejudice existed, they have been removed by the hasty and inconsiderate action of those who were so quick to see an insult where none was intended. . . . My sole object in selecting a colored man to introduce me was to encourage and help to uplift his race from a bondage worse than that which held him in chains twenty-five years ago—viz., mental slavery. I desired to impress upon the minds of white and black that the same result followed action in the field of labor, whether that action was on the part of the Caucasian or the Negro. . . . Both claim an equal share of the protection afforded to American labor, and both mechanics must sink their differences or fall a prey to the slave labor now being imported to this country.[37]

Powderly's actions came at one of the most racist times in American history, a decade after the last federal troops had been withdrawn from the South, and a time when the white establishment was bent on asserting its control over every aspect of life in the states of the former Confederacy. Following in the footsteps of William Sylvis two decades earlier, Powderly placed the nascent organized labor movement on the side of a fully inclusive union.

EUGENE V. DEBS

On Labor Day of 1895, Eugene V. Debs was serving the first of several terms in federal prison. He had been arrested for failing to abide by a federal court injunction to end the national railroad strike. But Debs was defiant. He was proud. And he was hopeful. From his jail cell, Debs wrote a letter to be read at a labor rally in his hometown of Terre Haute, Indiana. On that September day, ten thousand people heard his hope-filled words:

Labor is uniting in one solid phalanx to secure justice for labor. When this time comes and coming it is, peacefully, I hope, no judicial despot will dare to imprison an American citizen to please corporations. When this time comes, and coming it is as certain as rivers flow to the sea, bullion and "boodle" will not rule in congress, in legislatures, and in courts. Legislators and judges and other public officers will not be controlled, as many of them now are, by the money power. There is to come a day, a Labor day, when from the center to the circumference of our mighty republic, from blooming groves of orange to waving fields of grain, from the pine lands of Maine to the Pacific coast, the people shall be free, and it will come by the unified voice and vote of the farmer, the mechanic and the laborer in every department of the country's industries.[38]

The letter was vintage Debs, confident in the future and in the fact that the laboring women and men of the nation would create that bright future.

Eugene V. Debs was one of the great labor leaders, politicians, and moralists in American history. His vision of the workers of the nation united in one grand union and ultimately in one compassionate community of workers and citizens reflects a brand of tough-minded idealism that was powerful in the decades before the First World War. It is easy now to forget that as the presidential nominee of the Socialist party, Debs won 6 percent of the vote for president in 1912 while also making a respectable showing in 1904 and 1908. He received 3.5 percent of the vote in 1920 while serving a term in federal prison.[39]

Debs was born in 1855 in Terre Haute, Indiana. He received a better education at his parents' home and in school than many frontier youth but left school in 1870 to work for the railroad—a job that would change him and change the railroads forever.[40] Though he left his railroad job in 1874 he joined the Brotherhood of Locomotive Firemen in 1875. In a brief autobiographical statement given to the *New York Comrade* in April 1902, Debs recalled the beginning of his union career: "On the evening of February 27, 1875, the local lodge of the Brotherhood of Locomotive Firemen was organized at Terre Haute, Indiana, by Joshua A. Leach, then grand master, and I was admitted as a charter member and at once chosen secretary."[41] It was the beginning of a career that would take Debs to the leadership not only of the Brotherhood of Locomotive Firemen but of all of those who worked on the railroads. In 1893 he helped organize an industry wide union—the American Railway Union—which won its first major strike against the Great Northern Railroad in 1894. From then on, he was one of the nation's leading union figures. At this point in his career, Debs saw organization as the key. Those who owned the industries were clearly well organized. If the workers could do the same, then everything could change. As he described it, "My supreme conviction was that if they were not only organized in every branch of the service and all acted together in concert they could redress their wrongs and regulate the conditions of employment."[42] Events would soon teach him otherwise and lead him to expand his vision.

In 1894 it seemed that the American Railway Union was winning all of its battles. Never before had there been a victory like the settlement of the strike with the Great Northern Railroad. Then came the Pullman strike. Again the union was winning. Then everything changed:

> At this juncture there was delivered, from wholly unexpected quarters, a swift succession of blows that blinded me for an instant and then opened wide my eyes—and in the gleam of every bayonet and the flash of every rifle *the class struggle was revealed.* This was my first practical lesson in Socialism, though wholly unaware that it was called by that name. An army of detectives, thugs and murderers was equipped with badge and beer and bludgeon and turned loose; old hulks of cars were fired; the alarm bells tolled; the people were terrified . . . injunctions flew thick and fast, arrests followed, and our office and headquarters, the heart of the strike, was sacked, torn out and nailed up by the "lawful" authorities of the federal government; and when in company with my loyal comrades I found myself in Cook County jail at Chicago.[43]

Like many others before and after him, Debs found his 1894–1895 term in jail for refusing to end the Pullman strike an education more powerful than any other.

Debs went to jail in 1894 as a deeply dedicated and charismatic labor leader, but he left jail as a socialist who believed that organized labor by itself was not sufficient to bring about the changes he wanted for the country. "I began to read and think and dissect the anatomy of the system in which working men, however organized, could be shattered and battered and splintered at a single stroke," he recalled. It was an experience that changed him, and American radicalism, forever. In 1897 he led in the expansion of the American Railway Union into the Social Democratic party in the United States, which in 1900 became, simply, the Socialist party. The injunctions, the state violence, and the prison sentences may have broken the strike, but not the faith of Debs or his comrades. In his own estimation, this too was an essential victory: "The American Railway Union was defeated but not conquered—overwhelmed but not destroyed. It lives and pulsates in the Socialist movement, and its defeat but blazed the way to economic freedom and hastened the dawn of human brotherhood."[44]

Debs spent the rest of his life campaigning to hasten this dawn of human brotherhood. He ran as the Socialist presidential candidate and received nearly 100,000 votes and changed the dialogue of American politics. In 1905 he helped found the Industrial Workers of the World with a goal of "one big union" for the whole nation. He also continued as Socialist leader and standard bearer.

In what may have been his finest hour, Debs campaigned vigorously against U.S. entry into World War I and against the war after the United States did enter it. His speech at Canton, Ohio, in June 1918 (described in more detail in the next chapter) was a calculated challenge to the 1917 Espionage Act, passed to silence or jail opponents of the war. Days after giving the speech Debs was arrested for violating the act. He was tried and sentenced to ten years in prison. He began serving his term in 1919, after the war had ended, was still nominated by his party in 1920, gaining 900,000 votes. He was pardoned by President Warren Harding in 1921.

Although he refused to join the American Communist party—he disapproved of their secrecy—he remained a radical socialist to the end of his days. When he heard of the October Revolution in Russia in 1918, Debs wrote, "From the crown of my head to the soles of my feet I am a Bolshevik, and proud of it." He argued with Lenin and with the Communist International but still wrote in 1922 that, no matter "what its mistakes have been, nor what may be charged against it, the Russian revolution . . . is the greatest, most luminous and far-reaching achievement in the entire sweep of human history."[45]

During the first two decades of the twentieth century, Debs offered an alternative vision of what the United States could be to that which dominated the press and the major political parties. In accepting the 1904 nomination of the Socialist party to run for president against Theodore Roosevelt and the Democratic nominee, Alton B. Parker, Debs reminded the audience that for all of Roosevelt's exuberant progressivism, the Republican president had defended court injunctions against strikes and had said at one point that "he would have such as Altgeld, [the Governor of Illinois who pardoned the last of the Haymarket rebels], Debs and other traitors lined up against a dead wall and shot." At the same time Parker, whose nomination the 1900 Democratic nominee William Jennings Bryan called a betrayal of labor, was known most of all for his close links to the Rockefellers and Standard Oil. But then, Debs asked, what else could one expect from the capitalist system? He proposed another system, one that offered a different vision.

The Socialist Party comprehends the magnitude of its task and has the patience of preliminary defeat and the faith of ultimate victory.

The working class must be emancipated by the working class.

Woman must be given her true place in society by the working class.

Child labor must be abolished by the working class.

Society must be reconstructed by the working class.

The working class must be employed by the working class.

The fruits of labor must be enjoyed by the working class.

War, bloody war, must be ended by the working class.

These are the principles and objects of the Socialist Party and we fear-lessly proclaim them to our fellowmen.[46]

With such speeches Debs carried the message of socialism around the nation.

In spite of many setbacks—defeats, terms in prison, and a series of painful splits within the socialist movement that sometimes pitted him against some of his closest erstwhile allies—Debs kept the vision alive. As he often acknowledged, he made his own share of mistakes and compromises. The movement in which he participated had more than its share of internal and external enemies. After his release from federal prison in 1921, Debs often seemed beset with a kind of melancholy. But in spite of it all Debs managed to maintain the vision, the hope that someday—not in his lifetime, perhaps, but not too far in the future—the free, caring, and socialist society of which he dreamed would come to be.

Three years before his death, in one of his last major public speeches, Debs addressed a 1923 campaign rally in Harlem for African American Social-ist party candidates in New York City. He reminded his audience of the ways that racism had undermined the socialist movement in the past. He reminded them of his own deep frustration when white railway workers had refused to welcome African American workers into the union and then were surprised when "they expected the colored porters and waiters to stand by them" in a strike. Debs also reiterated another of his longstanding themes, that leaders could never do for people what the people could do for themselves. He was not there as a savior or a leader. "I want to speak to you very plainly tonight," he said, "especially you colored people, and have you understand that it is not in my power to do anything for you but to take my place side by side with you. . . . But while I can do nothing for you there is nothing you cannot do for yourselves." But in solidarity he asked his audience to join with him in looking to and working for the future.

> Everywhere the awakening workers are lifting their bowed bodies from the earth—those toiling and producing masses who have been the mudsills of soci-ety through all the ages past. They are learning at last how to stand erect and hold up their heads and press forward toward the dawn, keeping step to the in-spiring heartthrobs of the impending Social revolution. They are of all races; they are of all colors, all creeds, all nationalities. . . . And in that crowning hour men and women can walk the highlands side by side and enjoy the enrapturing vision of a land without a master, a land without a slave; a land radiant and re-splendent in the perfect triumph of the brotherhood of all mankind.[47]

For Debs, there was indeed no limit to the hope that the future held.

ROSE SCHNEIDERMAN

While Debs traveled the country preaching labor solidarity and revolutionary socialism, other socialists stayed closer to home, organizing the workers of their immediate vicinity in an effort to build a lasting and powerful union. Rose Schneiderman wrote her autobiography in 1967 when she was an old and much-respected voice of the labor movement. The book is most interesting for its focus on the early years of the century. Between 1880 and 1920 there was a massive exodus of Jews from Russia and eastern Europe; the majority of whom came to New York City. Many found work in the garment industries. Marginalized in American society as immigrants, as non-English speakers, and as non-Christians, they worked long hours for exceedingly low pay. Social reformer Jacob Riis described the prevalent working conditions that he observed in the garment trades:

> Five men and a woman, two young girls, not fifteen, and a boy who says unasked that he is fifteen, and lies in saying it, are at the machines sewing knee pants. . . . The floor is littered ankle-deep with half-sewn garments. . . . The faces, hands, and arms to the elbows of everyone in the room are black with the color of the cloth on which they are working. The boy and the woman alone look up at our entrance. The girls shoot sidelong glances, but at a warning look from the man with the bundle [the contractor] they tread their machines more energetically than ever. . . . They are "learners," all of them, says the woman, who proves to be the wife of the boss, and have "come over" only a few weeks ago. They turn out 120 dozen knee pants a week. They work no longer than to nine o'clock at night, from daybreak.[48]

In this seemingly hopeless situation, labor unions offered a powerful kind of hope.

Late in the nineteenth century, a number of organizing drives took place in the garment industry. Usually structured along ethnic lines and often led by women, these efforts began to change the working conditions and the power relationships in the garment industry. Schneiderman describes the mix of naiveté and confidence that led to her first, albeit small scale, union effort. She and her co-workers were frustrated by the fact that they were individually responsible for owning a sewing machine, that they suffered significant downtime due to the poor management of the work, and that they were basically pieceworkers at the mercy of their bosses: "Bessie Braut pointed out all these things and more, insisting that it was possible for us to have these hardships corrected if we complained as a group. An employer would think twice before telling a group what he would not hesitate to tell an individual employee. . . . Bravely we ventured into the office of the United Cloth Hat and Cap Makers

Union and told the man in charge that we would like to be organized." Told that they would need twenty-five signatures before they could be chartered, they simply "waited at the doors of the factories and, as the girls were leaving for the day, we would approach them and speak our piece. . . . Within days we had the necessary number, and in January 1903 we were chartered as Local 23, and I was elected secretary."[49] The creation of the union and Schneiderman's election as an officer began a process that would offer a significant education and a major change in the direction of her life.

Her role in the union brought both changes and joy.

> It was such an exciting time. A new life opened up for me. All of a sudden I was not lonely anymore. I had shop and executive board meetings to attend as well as the meetings of our unit. I was also a delegate to the Central Labor Union of New York, which was a remarkable experience for me. The central body was in many ways an educational organization. It met every Sunday afternoon, and at each meeting there was a speaker who would discuss some question of current interest. I always listened eagerly and continued to do so years later when I returned as the delegate of the New York Women's Trade Union League.[50]

In time, Schneiderman and her co-workers knew that they had to put their new union into action, to see if they could, in fact, make a difference for themselves. "That June we decided to put our strength to the test. In the summer the men usually worked only half-day on Saturdays, which was pay day. But even when there was no work we women had to hang around until three or four o'clock before getting our pay." Schneiderman headed a committee to present their case to the boss. "He didn't say outright that he agreed; he wouldn't give us that much satisfaction. But on the first Saturday in July, when we went for our pay at twelve noon, there it was ready for us."[51] Having tasted the fruits of victory, Schneiderman was hooked on the union cause. In one form or another, union activism would dominate the rest of her life.

The more she did within the union movement, the more she realized that the union had become her home. It was a place of learning, of socializing, and of fun. May Day, the great worker's holiday, was their holiday, "We took the day off on our own, receiving no pay. I was elected delegate from my union. We women rode in the parade in a wagon, for it was not considered ladylike to participate on foot. It was an exciting and heartwarming day and I enjoyed it tremendously." But there was more to the movement than parades and friendship.

If the union meant anything, it meant solidarity, taking risks for themselves and for other workers. Not surprisingly, Schneiderman's life evolved to include strikes, picket lines, and speeches to other union audiences. She recalled her first speech to striking workers. One of the employers had moved his business across the Hudson River, to Bayonne, New Jersey, to escape the union. "We felt that if one employer was allowed to operate a nonunion shop," she recalled, "he could easily undersell union firms and they might be tempted to follow his example. . . . A mass meeting of the strikers was scheduled." On the way to the rally, Schneiderman was asked to be one of the speakers. "I was scared stiff. What was I to say? . . . When I was called on to speak, my knees turned to putty. I doubt whether I lasted more than five minutes and I don't believe I deserved the enthusiastic applause they gave me. But even if it was undeserved, it felt good."[52] And the experience confirmed Schneiderman on the course her life was taking.

The strikes that were carried out across the New York garment industry in the first years of the twentieth century culminated in a major strike in 1909, which led to the beginnings of union recognition in the industry. The unions not only improved income and working conditions, they played a very important role in the development of Jewish community life. In addition to seeking better working conditions, as Schneiderman's story shows, the union itself also provided community among the workers. Often more secular than religious, the first generation of Jewish immigrants found opportunities for philosophical discussions and active engagement in socialism, anarchism, and social reform. The union brought broader horizons and participation in a wider world.

The tragic 1911 fire at the Triangle Shirtwaist Company in which 146 workers—mostly young Jewish and Italian women—were killed because the owners had blocked the exits to the factory revealed the horrendous working conditions that persisted even after the advent of the unions in the garment trades. The size of the death toll and the sheer horror of the Triangle Shirtwaist fire made it a turning point in the lives of many New York reformers and unionists. It brought the reality of life in the garment industry home to many. Schneiderman, by then a well-known women's trade union leader, was one of speakers at the memorial meeting for the victims. She knew the reality of what women workers faced in New York too well to be surprised by what had happened. In the immediate face of the tragedy, Schneiderman spoke with more anger than hope: "This is not the first time girls have been burned alive in this city. Every week I must learn of the untimely death of one of my sister workers. Every year thousands of us are maimed. The life of men and women is so cheap and property is so sacred! . . . I can't talk fellowship to you who are gathered here. Too much blood has been spilled. . . . It is up to the working people to save themselves."[53]

Yet, even in her anger, Schneiderman did see the key to a more hopeful future. Sounding a lot like Debs, she was clear that outside helpers and reformers were not going to do what was needed. "It is up to the working people to save themselves." And in that spirit she dedicated the rest of her life to that effort. The tragedy of the Triangle fire did hasten the development of both stronger unions and the legislation of safer working conditions in the garment industry.

Schneiderman went on to be a leader of the Women's Trade Union League and was always known as a fiery speaker who could inspire a militant hope in others. During the term of office of New York governor Al Smith—who came to admire her greatly—she became a leader in the fight for an eight-hour working day for women.[54] Standing up for herself and a few co-workers and then joining the union movement had expanded her horizons and her hopes for the future for herself and her society far beyond what she had ever considered as a young person.

THE INDUSTRIAL WORKERS
OF THE WORLD

While labor was getting itself better organized in the urban northeast, some of the most hard-fought and bitter union drives took place out in the rural west. The Western Federation of Miners was founded in Montana in 1893 and fought against some of the most violent antilabor tactics ever used in the United States. Its leaders were used to police violence, arrest, and murder—either by hired thugs or, as in the case of the legendary hero Joe Hill, by the company-controlled courts. Throughout its first decade of existence, leaders of the Western Federation of Miners had sought to expand their work to include all of the various industries of the region, but with limited success. By 1905 they were able to join with several other streams of American radicalism, including the Socialist party under the leadership of Eugene V. Debs and the independent radicalism of Mother Jones, to create the most radical, and in some ways the most hope-filled, union in the nation's history, the Industrial Workers of the World (IWW).[55]

On June 27, 1905, over two hundred delegates gathered in Chicago to found the Industrial Workers of the World. Usually known as the Wobblies, the rank-and-file members of the IWW along with their leaders offered an often-romanticized but actually hard-headed attack on all aspects of American capitalism. The Wobblies represented a dream of worker solidarity in the service of a better future for all. The first speaker at the convention was the legendary Big Bill Haywood, one of the leaders of the Western Federation of Miners and a symbol of tough and courageous organizing. Among the other speakers was Daniel DeLeon, now generally forgotten but in his day the American radical most admired by Lenin, Lucy Parsons, militant widow of one of the Haymarket martyrs of 1886, and, of course, Debs and Mother Jones. It was quite a collection of the American left. Haywood opened the convention, addressing the audience as "Fellow Workers," and went on to state his view that they were gathered there, "to confederate the workers . . . into a working class movement that shall have for its purpose the emancipation of the working class from the slave bondage of capitalism." The time for compromises had passed, for Haywood. Debs expressed the hope that the time had come for the various factions of the labor and socialist movements to unite "and begin the work of forming a great economic or revolutionary organization of the working class so sorely needed for their emancipation."[56] The time to begin building the new world was at hand.

The convention adopted a constitution that included in its preamble their vision of what was to come:

> It is the historic mission of the working class to do away with capitalism. The army of production must be organized, not only for the every-day struggle with capitalists, but also to carry on production when capitalism shall have been overthrown. By organizing industrially we are forming the structure of the new society within the shell of the old.[57]

The constitution was a direct challenge not only to the capitalists who dominated America in 1905 as never before, but to the more cautious trade unionism of the American Federation of Labor, which might match the IWW on the "every-day struggle" front but which had no ideal of "forming . . . the new society." That new society, and nothing less, was the IWW goal.

Later in 1905, in a speech to a gathering of workers in Chicago, Debs outlined his own commitment to the IWW and his hopes for what it could accomplish. He reiterated that "the unity of labor, economic and political, upon the basis of the class struggle, is at this time the supreme need of the working class." He was clear: economic unity in labor unions, especially single-trade unions, was insufficient. He had learned years before that the corporate world could easily use state power to crush any union and, as a result, trade unions working alone were always going to be limited to the role of amelioration and cooperation with big business. On the other hand, for all of his political efforts within the Socialist party, Debs also knew that electoral politics alone, without the parallel, deep organizing of the working class, would always be marginalized by the power of capital. But if the workers of the nation could truly come together, could transcend the divisions of their different trades, their different ideologies, and their differences in race, language, ethnicity, and gender, then something very different could be built even within the shell of the old order. So he predicted:

In every mill and every factory, every mine and every quarry, every railroad and every shop, everywhere, the workers, enlightened, understanding their self-interest, are correlating themselves in industrial and economic mechanism. They are developing their industrial consciousness, their economic and political power; and when the revolution comes, they will be prepared to take possession and assume control of every industry. With the education they will have received in the Industrial Workers they will be drilled and disciplined, trained and fitted for Industrial Mastery and Social Freedom.[58]

The future, he was telling his fellow-workers once again, was theirs to create.

The future was destined to be more difficult to attain than Debs, Mother Jones, Lucy Parsons, Big Bill Haywood, or any of the estimated million IWW members in its relatively short history ever dreamed. The IWW was attacked by the press, the corporate world, and the government as few organizations ever have been. Even more seriously, from the beginning it was riven with ideological splits, personality tensions, and terrible factional divisions. By the 1920s the IWW was hopelessly split by the U.S. government's wide-ranging attacks on radicals following World War I and by the ideological divides of its own communist and noncommunist factions.

Big Bill Haywood's own career symbolized much of this difficult road. In 1910 he left the United States for the first time to attend the Second Socialist International meeting in Copenhagen, Denmark. At that meeting he began lifelong friendships with union leaders and radicals from around the world, including Rosa Luxemburg and V. I. Lenin. When he returned to New York City, Elizabeth Gurley Flynn—another great in turn-of-the-twentieth-century labor organizing—introduced him to a mass meeting and welcomed him home. Haywood replied that "while I fully appreciated the splendid reception they were giving me, I had really not been away from home. In all my travels I had been with the working class in different countries."[59] Today such language from a labor leader would sound somewhere between corny and simply unbelievable. But in 1910 Haywood meant it and the crowd believed him. That sense of connection—of a bond and solidarity—among all of the working people of the world was the basis of sacrifices and commitments that transformed much of the world in the early years of the century. It was the beloved community for many who participated and for others who do not know the history but reap its benefits. Like Debs, Haywood was also a victim of the wartime 1917 Espionage Act and the post–World War I red scare. Unlike Debs, he saw no value in an extended federal prison term. While awaiting sentence, he quietly left the United States for the new Soviet Union. He is one of two Americans—the other is journalist John Reed—buried in the Kremlin Wall.

Given the internal and external devastation of the early 1920s, the IWW was never again a powerful force. But for fifteen years leading up to World War I, the IWW led strikes, organized workers, and offered solidarity and courage to people facing extraordinary difficulty. It is perhaps fitting that the IWW lives on primarily in the legends of its heroes and in the songs of its still-published *Song Book*.[60]

Joe Hill, an IWW organizer, executed in Utah in 1915 on framed-up murder charges for his involvement in a strike of the copper workers, wrote many of the IWW's songs and became himself the stuff of song and legend. Joe Hill reminded workers of the promises made by preachers of the standing order who offered them:

> You will eat, bye and bye,
> In the glorious land above the sky;
> Work and pray, live on hay,
> You'll get pie in the sky when you die.

And for those willing to take the risk of asking for pie now, Joe Hill also offered the way, the IWW way, of course.

> If the workers took a notion
> They could stop all speeding trains;
> Every ship upon the ocean
> They can tie with mighty chains.
> Every wheel in the creation
> Every mine and every mill;
> Fleets and armies of the nation,
> Will at their command stand still.[61]

Through these songs and legends, the IWW provided hope far beyond their immediate history.

BREAD AND ROSES:
THE LAWRENCE STRIKE OF 1912

In the years immediately after its founding, the IWW gave much more immediate hope and assistance to downtrodden workers. On New Year's Day 1912, a new Massachusetts law took effect that limited the work week to fifty-four hours, a cut of two hours from the fifty-six-hour norm in the mills of Lawrence. The companies happily complied with the law and cut the wages of their workers accordingly. When the first pay envelopes of the new year were distributed on January 12, the workers in plant after plant looked at the pay cut and walked off the job. Thus was launched one of the most heroic and most romanticized of all American strikes.[62]

The situation in Lawrence in 1912 was truly terrible. Workers lived in extremely congested housing and worked under miserable conditions. A medical examiner's report said, "thirty-six out of every hundred of all men and women who work in the mill die before or by the time they are 25 years of age." Poor housing, inadequate diet, the inability to afford warm clothing, as well as the working conditions in the mills led to this horrendous death rate. The cut, any cut, in pay would only make these conditions worse. For the management, however, there seemed little reason to worry. The workers of Lawrence were mostly recent immigrants, spoke forty-five different languages, were divided into different crafts, and had little union allegiance. Of the 30,000 mill workers in Lawrence in 1912, only 2,500 were union members and these were split between the craft-oriented American Federation of Labor and the "one big union" of the Industrial Workers of the World, which sought to unite all of the workers in the different trades in one militant union that would defend all of its members. In such circumstances, cutting the pay to correspond to the cut in hours seemed to management both prudent and safe. Things, however, did not turn out that way.[63]

In the days just before the new pay period, Italian, Polish, and Lithuanian workers had already agreed to strike if their pay was cut. When they opened their envelopes on January 12, the mostly Polish weavers at the Everett Cotton Mill walked off their jobs. Others followed quickly, so that an estimated 14,000 workers were on strike by the end of the first day.

While they had previously been split, the workers of Lawrence quickly came together under the leadership of the IWW which preached unity and which evidenced the most confidence in their united efforts. It is important to remember, however, that the original decision to walk off their jobs was local and immediate, not the result of any outside organizing drive. Elizabeth Gurley Flynn, then a twenty-one-year-old IWW organizer, but also one of the most recognized and feared voices of labor in the country, played a major role in the strike. She remembered:

> The small pittance taken from the workers by the rich corporations, which were protected by a high tariff from foreign competition, was the spark that ignited the general strike. "Better to starve fighting than to starve working!" became their battle cry. It spread from mill to mill. In a few hours of that cold, snowy day in January, fourteen thousand workers poured out of the mills. In a few days, the mills were empty and still—and remained so for nearly three months.[64]

It was an amazing and heroic act. The hard part, of course, was maintaining what they had begun. To do this, workers in Lawrence, through the IWW local, asked for help from the national union. And they got it—from the IWW and from some of its most important strategic allies. Joseph J. Ettor of the IWW along with Arturo Giovannitti of the Italian Socialist Federation came within days. Lawrence, with its many Italian immigrants, would be among many other things the place where grass-roots American radicalism and the radicalism of nineteenth-century revolutionary Italy came together in an effective coalition for the first time. The *Federazione Socialista Italiana del Nord America* (FSI) had been organized among various revolutionary Italian immigrant groups in 1902 and had quickly linked its efforts with the IWW. But it was in Lawrence that the alliance became real. As writer Michael Miller Topp has said, "the Lawrence strike imbued the impoverished, neglected immigrant workers who participated with a sense of hope and a sense of dignity that had rarely been a part of their lives."[65]

Flynn gives a sense of what Ettor and Giovannitti, with their IWW and FSI backgrounds, brought to Lawrence:

> They could speak eloquently in both English and Italian. Giovannitti, who was the editor of the Italian labor paper *Il Proletario*, was a poet and a magnificent orator. Ettor was an able organizer, a smiling, confident, calm man, who moved quickly and decisively. He selected interpreters to bring order out of this veritable tower of Babel. They organized mass meetings in various localities of the different language groups and had them elect a Strike Committee of men and women, which represented every mill, every department, and every nationality. They held meetings of all the strikers together on the Lawrence Common (New England's term for park or square), so that the workers could realize their oneness and strength."[66]

Under their leadership, the strikers were organized into rotating picket lines buttressed by regular meetings of the workers in which they were addressed in their different native languages. Ettor and Giovannitti understood what it took to keep the spirits of the workers high. And they did so in spite of increased police brutality and the presence of army units of the state militia. In response to a city ordinance banning gatherings in front of any of the mills, the strike leaders devised a new tactic, one now familiar to many: a moving picket line in which strikers kept walking in a continuous line around the mills, but not stopping which would violate the law.[67] It was just this sort of creativity that kept the strike going.

Things turned much more violent at the end of the month. On January 29 Anna LaPizza, an Italian woman, was shot while walking through a picket line on the way to visit friends. She died instantly. Nineteen witnesses testified that they had seen a soldier shoot LaPizza, but Ettor and Giovannitti were arrested for inciting the murder. They were effectively removed from the strike leadership and placed in jail on charges that could lead to the death penalty, a danger not unfamiliar to IWW organizers. But in Lawrence, all of the strikers themselves faced similar dangers, from the police and military violence and from the fact that they, in their poverty, had absolutely no reserves on which to draw.[68]

Others came quickly to take the place of Ettor and Giovannitti, including two of the best-known IWW leaders, Big Bill Haywood and Elizabeth Gurley Flynn. The courage of the IWW was shown in the speed with which, following the arrest of one, another person rose up to take their place. The organizing continued. Flynn described the message that she and Haywood brought, the IWW philosophy with its mix of socialism and old-fashioned American patriotism.

> We talked to the strikers about One Big Union, regardless of skill or lack of it, foreign born or native born, color, religion, or sex. . . .
>
> We spoke of their power, as workers, as the producers of all wealth, as the creators of profit. Here they could see it in Lawrence. Down tools, fold arms, stop the machinery, and production is dead—profits no longer flow. We ridiculed the police and militia in this situation. "Can they weave cloth with soldiers' bayonets or policemen's clubs?" we asked. "No," replied the confident workers. "Did they dig coal with bayonets in the miners' strikes or make steel or run trains with bayonets?" Again the crowds roared "No." We talked Marxism as we understood it—the class struggle, the exploitation of labor, the use of the state and armed forces of government against the workers. It was all there in Lawrence before our eyes. We did not need to go far for the lessons.
>
> We talked of "Solidarity," a beautiful word in all the languages. Stick together! Workers, unite! One for all and all for one! An injury to one is an injury to all! The workers are all one family! It was internationalism. It was also real Americanism—the first they had heard. "One nation indivisible, with liberty and justice for all." They hadn't found it here, but they were willingly fighting to create it.[69]

If they workers had not found one nation, indivisible, with liberty and justice for all, they certainly meant to create it in Lawrence through their actions in the strike.

For all the fame of leaders like Haywood and Flynn, the success of the strike came from the continued commitment and hope of thousands of workers. Leaders such as Haywood and Flynn succeeded because they spoke so effectively to these commitments and hopes. When a judge charged that the strike leaders were manipulating the workers, and especially the women, putting them at the front lines, one woman delegate to the strike committee challenged him: "I want to say to the press that the women strikers are not being egged on by anyone or forced to go upon the picket line, as Judge Mahoney has said, but that we go there because that is but duty. We are not listening to anyone skulking in the background, as the judge has stated, and if we did, we would have gone into the mills long ago." At one point, even the ever-conservative American Federation of Labor accused the IWW of putting women in the front, to which Flynn responded, "The IWW has been accused of putting the women in the front. The truth is, the IWW does not keep them in the back and they go to the front." When given the chance, women and men, from all of the different languages, nationalities, trades, stood together and stuck together through the long and difficult months of the strike because they were animated by a vision of something better for themselves and their children.[70]

One particularly effective technique that the strikers developed as the time wore on was to send their children to other cities, in part for safe keeping and a more normal life, but also in part because the crusade of these children created enormous public sympathy for the strike in other parts of the country. As Flynn described the move:

> A proposal was made by some of the strikers that we adopt a method used successfully in Europe—to send the children out of Lawrence to be cared for in other cities. The parents accepted the idea and the children were wild to go. On February 17th, 1912, the first group of a hundred and fifty children were taken to New York City. A small group also left for Barre, Vermont. A New York Committee, headed by Mrs. Margaret Sanger, then a trained nurse, and chairman of the Women's Committee of the Socialist Party, came to Lawrence to escort them. (She has since become world renowned for her advocacy of birth control.) Five thousand people met them at Grand Central Station. People wept when they saw the poor clothes and thin shoes of these wide-eyed little children.[71]

Other groups of children were sent out. Then, late in February 1912, the police and military decided that this too must be stopped. Flynn described what happened next:

> At the railroad station in Lawrence, where the children were assembled, accompanied by their fathers and mothers, just as they were ready to board the train, they were surrounded by police. Troopers surrounded the station outside to keep others out. Children were clubbed and torn away from their parents and a wild scene of brutal disorder took place. Thirty-five frantic women and children were arrested, thrown screaming and fighting into patrol wagons.

They were beaten into submission and taken to the police station. There the women were charged with "neglect" and improper guardianship and ten frightened children taken to the Lawrence Poor Farm. The police station was besieged by enraged strikers. Members of the Philadelphia committee were arrested and fined. It was a day without parallel in American labor history. A reign of terror prevailed in Lawrence, which literally shook America.[72]

The attack on the departing children also helped to turn the tide of public opinion in the nation. People who had been bystanders or hostile to the strike decried the attack on children and their parents. Newspapers began to shift the tone of their reporting. A congressional investigation began. Through it all, the workers themselves held firm, and eventually the mill owners gave in.

In his autobiography, Haywood himself, never one to get carried away with his enthusiasm, described the hope-filled end of the strike.

> The strike committee had its last meeting after a sub-committee had gone to Boston and made a settlement with William Wood of the American Woolen Company. The report of the sub-committee was received with long cheers. The strike was off, if the settlement should prove satisfactory to the majority of the workers of all the mills involved, and there was no reason to suppose they would not be satisfied. I appealed to the committee and the strikers that filled the hall, to hold their union together, as there would be a time when they would have to strike again, if Ettor and Giovanitti were not released from prison. I helped twenty-three members of the strike committee to climb up on the platform. They were all of different nationalities, and we sang the "International" in as many different tongues as were represented on the strike committee.
>
> When the strike was settled, early in March, it was a sweeping victory for the workers. Hours of labor were reduced, wages were increased from five to twenty per cent, with increased compensation for overtime, and there was to be no discrimination against any person who had taken part in the strike. The strike had been a magnificent demonstration of solidarity, and of what solidarity can do for the workers.[73]

It appeared that hope, when mixed with courage, commitment, and solidarity really could make a difference both in the daily lives of working women and men and in the kind of nation that they envisioned for the future.

The success of the Lawrence strike was an extraordinary step forward for the IWW, for workers across the United States, and for a different vision of what the future could hold for those on the very bottom of the American industrial order. As Flynn said of the men and women—especially the women—she met in Lawrence, "This was more than a union. It was a crusade for a united people—for "Bread and Roses."[74] According to tradition, it was during the first days of the strike, as working women, some with their babies in their arms, marched through the streets of Lawrence with signs reading, "We Want Bread and Roses, Too," that the name by which the strike is remembered today was coined. In time they sang the song by which the strike is most remembered:

> As we come marching, marching
> In the beauty of the day
> A million darkened kitchens
> A thousand mill lofts gray,
> Are touched with all the radiance
> That a sudden sun discloses
> For the people hear us singing:
> "Bread and Roses! Bread and Roses!"[75]

The song, with its vision of greater days secured through the suffering and militancy of Lawrence's women, is one of labor's great contributions to the history of hope. It can, indeed, appropriately stand for the hopes of generations of labor organizers and labor union members who took extraordinary risks to make those hopes a reality.

CHAPTER EIGHT

THE MANY FACES
OF THE PROGRESSIVE ERA

JANE ADDAMS AND
THE PROGRESSIVE MOVEMENT

IN 1909 JANE ADDAMS, one of the nation's prominent progressive voices,[1] published *The Spirit of Youth and the City Streets.* In that book she called on the nation, and especially progressive leaders in education, the church, and the social settlement movements not only to improve the conditions under which urban young people lived but—what was much more radical—to engage young people in the effort to improve life for themselves and for all of society. She concluded:

> All of us forget how very early we are in the experiment of founding self-government in this trying climate of America, and that we are making the experiment in the most materialistic period of all history, having as our court of last appeal against that materialism only the wonderful and inexplicable instinct for justice which resides in the hearts of men,—which is never so irresistible as when the heart is young. We may cultivate this most precious possession, or we may disregard it. We may listen to the young voices rising clear above the roar of industrialism and the prudent councils of commerce, or we may become hypnotized by the sudden new emphasis placed upon wealth and power, and forget the supremacy of spiritual forces in men's affairs. . . . We may either smother the divine fire of youth or we may feed it. We may either stand stupidly staring as it sinks into a murky fire of crime and flares into the

intermittent blaze of folly or we may tend it into a lambent flame with power to make clean and bright our dingy city streets.[2]

Her words capture Addams's style as well as her philosophy. Here she clearly states her always confident hope that the future could be radically better than the present and her equally confident assertion that the future she hoped for could only be built with, and never for, the people whom she sought to serve— the young, the poor, the immigrants who came to her Hull House, and those in similar neighborhoods of poverty across the nation.

Jane Addams, born to a comfortable life in 1860, had moved to Chicago in 1889 and with her friend Ellen Starr had opened Hull House, one of the nation's earliest social settlement houses. The idea of settlement houses had begun in England with Toynbee Hall in London, and was spreading to a number of American cities in the 1880s. A small group of social reformers, often young people from comfortable backgrounds, settled in a home in a poor neighborhood and sought to offer help and uplift for the poor through new ideas and social services. Ultimately Hull House in Chicago, though not the first American settlement house, would become the model for all others.[3]

From the beginning, Addams made it evident that she was there to be a part of the community, not to offer help from above. She knew that she was living there as much to help herself as to help her economically poorer neighbors. "In those early days," she recalled, "we were often asked why we had come to live on Halsted Street when we could afford to live somewhere else." But Addams, Starr, and others who soon joined them quickly came to feel accepted. "In time it came to seem natural to all of us that the Settlement should be there. If it is natural to feed the hungry and care for the sick, it is certainly natural to give pleasure to the young, comfort to the aged, and to minister to the deep-seated cravings for social intercourse that all men feel."[4] Also from the beginning, Addams and her colleagues developed their creed that they were not there for sacrifice or for service out of obligation, but for building a community that included themselves and their neighbors.

Perhaps these first days laid the simple human foundations which are certainly essential for continuous living among the poor: first, genuine preference for residence in an industrial quarter to any other part of the city, because it is interesting and makes the human appeal; and second, the conviction, in the words of Canon Barnett, that the things which make men alike are finer and better than the things that keep them apart, and that these basic likenesses, if they are properly accentuated, easily transcend the less essential differences of race, language, creed, and tradition.[5]

Addams lived where she lived and as she lived "because it is interesting" and she shared with her neighbors "finer and better things" that united them than any that might divide. This assertion remained for the next forty-five years as the hallmark of Addams's brand of progressivism.

One of Addams's great strengths was her ability to laugh at herself and to learn from her mistakes. As an example, she reported an effort early in the life of Hull House to improve eating habits in their neighborhood. One of the Hull House residents went to Boston for training in ways to prepare cheap and nutritious meals, and the Hull House kitchen began to serve as a model and to turn out prepared soups and stews for the neighborhood. The food was not uniformly appreciated, however. As Addams recalled, "We did not reckon, however, with the wide diversity in nationality and inherited tastes . . . perhaps the neighborhood estimate was best summed up by the woman who frankly confessed that the food was certainly nutritious, but that she didn't like to eat what was nutritious, that she liked to eat 'what she'd ruther.'"[6] It was a defeat that Addams also turned into a lesson as Hull House became more and more appreciative of ethnic diversity and of the strengths and uniqueness of the different cultures represented in turn-of-the-century Chicago's poorest neighborhoods.

Hull House did much more than provide services to the poor. It also took the side of the poor in labor and legal disputes. While services were respected or at least tolerated, with some kindly derision, the direct involvement in labor and legal issues provoked open hostility. During a strike in a local shoe factory, Addams reported that the strikers realized that those most likely to give up on the strike were the young women who feared being tossed out of their rooming houses for lack of rent money. One of the women said, "Wouldn't it be fine if we had a boarding club of our own, and then we could stand by each other in a time like this?" Addams and her colleagues took up the challenge and launched a cooperative women's boarding house next door to Hull House. With this effort, and the national impact of the Pullman strike in which Addams again sided with the workers, she also noticed a change. Indeed, the "situation changed markedly after the Pullman strike, and our efforts to secure factory legislation later brought upon us a certain amount of distrust and suspicion; until then we had been considered merely a kindly philanthropic undertaking whose new form gave us a certain idealistic glamour. But sterner tests were coming."[7] And come they did.

One of Addams's early experiences with the hatred that her brand of progressivism could stir up came at the time of President McKinley's assassination in 1901. McKinley's murderer was a self-described anarchist and anarchists all over the country, including Emma Goldman, were immediately arrested as potential conspirators. Given Hull House's close connections to European immigrant communities, especially refugees from the early stirrings of revolution in Russia, there were many Russian anarchists associated with Hull House. One of them, the editor of a small anarchist newspaper, was immediately arrested in Chicago. Addams first protested his arrest to the mayor of Chicago and then went to visit the prisoner to assure him of the concern of his friends and family. The result was widespread denunciation of Addams and Hull House, for as she said, "The public mind at such a moment falls into the old medieval confusion—he who feeds or shelters a heretic is upon prima facie evidence a heretic himself—he who knows intimately people among whom anarchists arise is therefor an anarchist." And certainly many in Chicago developed exactly that view of Hull House. After all, as Addams also noted, "At times of public panic, fervid denunciation is held to be the duty of every good citizen, and if a Settlement is convinced that the incident should be used to vindicate the law and does not at the moment give its strength to denunciation, its attitude is at once taken to imply a championship of anarchy itself."[8] Addams was no anarchist. But she was determined to both befriend and seek to understand the anarchists with whom she associated. It was a principled stance that got her into deep trouble throughout her life.

Addams would face even deeper challenges. In 1915 Addams was one of the leaders in the creation of the Woman's Peace Party which sought to advocate, for "the mother half of humanity," in opposition to war generally and to the United States entry into World War I specifically. The Peace Party also sent a delegation to the International Congress of Women in The Hague that sought to show women's solidarity around the world in spite of the war then raging. Addams said of The Hague meeting that "The whole enterprise has about it a certain aspect of moral adventure." The adventure became much tougher in 1917 when the United States entered the war on the side of the allies and when the U.S. government began to treat all forms of dissent as subversion if not treason. While Carrie Chapman Catt, the original chair of the Woman's Peace Party, and many others resigned to support the president and the war, Addams and a minority stood firm in their opposition to the carnage in Europe. It was a courageous and dangerous thing to do and some former friends never forgave Addams. She was now classed with the dangerous subversives—people like Debs and Goldman—as never before.[9]

In time, Addams came to be respected for her stance. After the war, in 1919, Addams helped to found the Women's International League for Peace and Freedom and in the 1920s traveled the world in the name of peace. The first American woman awarded the Nobel Peace Prize, she received it in 1931, over a decade after she had been denounced by the American Legion as "un-American" and by the Daughters of the American Revolution as "a factor in the movement to destroy civilization and Christianity."[10] Fortunately her earlier experience with attacks by Chicago's elite had prepared her for these criti-cisms. But it required the long view to hold firm.

While Addams became increasingly a national and international figure, one of the greatest contributions of Addams and her Hull House colleagues was their determination to continue to live with and learn from their immedi-ate neighbors. Addams and her co-workers never wavered in their belief that hope for social progress could only be discovered by tapping into the wisdom of those most in need. One of Hull House's most effective residents, Julia C. Lathrop, was appointed as a Cook County visitor whose assignment was to visit the poorest residents of the Hull House neighborhood. Lathrop saw these visits not as a time to check up on people but rather to learn from them. Later, as a member of the Illinois State Board of Charities, Lathrop sought to transform the charitable institutions of the state based on what she had learned. Addams commented, "Perhaps her most valuable contribution toward the enlargement and reorganization of the charitable institutions of the State came through her intimate knowledge of the beneficiaries, and her experience demonstrated that it is only through long residence among the poor that an official could have learned to view public institutions as she did, from the standpoint of the inmates rather than from that of the managers."[11] It was a view that compelled the residents of Hull House always to base their designs for the future on the lived experiences of people rather than on finely devel-oped social theories.

Based on these experiences Addams wrote *The Spirit of Youth and the City Streets*. In that book, which Addams said was her favorite, she made a number of assertions that seem surprising for a volume written almost a hundred years ago. She began by celebrating young people's sexuality as a source of joy and energy, and not as something to be denied. She wrote with frank appreciation of "this fundamental sex susceptibility which suffuses the world with its deep-est meaning and beauty, and furnishes the momentum towards all art."[12] She condemned the "separating of education from contemporary life," and chas-tised both schools and industry for the failure to draw on the imagination that is fired when young people are able to focus their creative energies on solving real problems and doing real and meaningful work.[13] In an interesting exam-ple of what happens when young people also understand the meaning of their work, she described the pride of an African American girl (Addams used the then-current word colored) especially pleased with a design she was embroi-dering because, as the girl said, "Of course, I like it awfully well because it was first used by people living in Africa where the colored folks come from."[14] In one telling paragraph she critiqued both traditional and progressive forms of education, describing the need to celebrate with a little child who calls a house of cardboard a castle but to challenge an older youth to "call attention to the quality of the dovetailing in which the boy at the manual training bench is engaged. . . . At one point the child's imagination is to be emphasized, and at another point his technique is important."[15] In her celebration of youthful sexuality, in her critique of meaningless schooling and meaningless work, in her celebration of an African American girl's interest in Africa, and in her call for an integrated kind of education for young people, Addams was years ahead of most educators and commentators on youth.

Most of all, however, *The Spirit of Youth and the City Streets* reflects Addams's own brand of progressivism, one in which the hope for building a better world is always firmly based on enlisting the best aspirations and ideas of those who will inhabit that world. She affirmed young people's anger as well as their aspirations as a positive reality. "Youth's divine impatience with the world's inheritance of wrong and injustice makes him scornful of 'rose water for the plague' prescriptions, and he insists upon something strenuous and vital." And she called for a new form of democracy that would enlist urban youth in both the definition and the implementation of democracy. The old forms may not hold, but the quest for a living democracy was vibrant. "To fail to recognize it in a new form, to call it hard names, to refuse to receive it, may mean to reject that which our fathers cherished and handed on as an inheritance not only to be preserved but also to be developed."[16] To say that democracy was not static but ever changing and ever in need of development made Addams a subject of great distrust by those who benefited most from the status quo. But for the young people of Chicago and other great industrial areas of the country, especially poor and marginalized young people who saw themselves excluded from democracy as it was defined in the United States in 1909, Addams's definition of an evolving and expanding democracy was at the center of a progressivism that truly rested on a never-ending commitment to progress.

At the conclusion of *Twenty Years at Hull House*, Addams summed up her hopes for a future built on the combined wisdom of all of the nation's diverse citizens. She insisted that "The Settlement casts aside none of those things which cultivated men have come to consider reasonable and goodly, but it insists that those belong as well to that great body of people who, because of toilsome and underpaid labor, are unable to procure them for themselves." It was the Settlement's aim to make sure that the finer things of life—art, culture, and a genuine humanity—belonged to all people. She also asserted repeatedly that the culture that mattered was the one that was actually produced by all people, not merely one that was a gift of the elite. Indeed, "those 'best results of civilization' upon which depend the finer and freer aspects of living must be incorporated into our common life and have free mobility through all elements of society if we would have our democracy endure." In this way she meant to "socialize democracy" and create a new society in which not only were the needs of all citizens met but also the contributions of all citizens valued.[17] It was, indeed, a powerful and far reaching social vision.

PROGRESSIVE JOURNALISM

One of the most prominent of the early progressive journalists, Jacob Riis was born in Denmark in 1849. He came to the United States in 1870, working first as a carpenter then making a name for himself as a police reporter for the *New York Tribune*. In the late 1880s Riis began using new techniques of flash powder photography to take pictures of the homes and work places of New York City's poorest residents. His photographs led to a lecture series with the New York City Mission Society and, in 1890, to the publication of his most famous work, *How the Other Half Lives*. Written originally as text to accompany his pictures, it quickly took on a literary life of its own. Riis described poverty clinically, and though he certainly did not identify with the poor, he made it far more difficult for New York's prosperous to ignore the other city that was in their midst. While the volume has many detailed reports on what life in poverty was like, the introduction set the tone for what follows. Riis began, "Long ago it was said that 'one half of the world does not know how the other half lives.' That was true then. It did not know because it did not care." Riis was not sure that he could make the people who represented the top half of society care, but he was absolutely determined that as a result of his work they would know.[18]

For Riis, poverty was not an accident and it was not the fault of the poor. Poverty and all of the crime that went with it were a direct result of "greed and reckless selfishness." The former police reporter told his audience: "By far the largest part—eighty per cent, at least—of crimes against property and against the person are perpetrated by individuals who have either lost connection with home life, or never had any, or whose homes *had ceased to be sufficiently separate, decent, and desirable to afford what are regarded as ordinary wholesome influences of home and family*."[19] As long as the terrible housing conditions of the tenements continued, New Yorkers, rich and poor, could hope for little change. But there were things that could be done. "The remedy that shall be an effective answer to the coming appeal for justice must proceed from the public conscience," Riis said. "Neither legislation nor charity can cover the ground. The greed of capital that wrought the evil must itself undo it, as far as it can now be undone. Homes must be built for the working masses by those who employ their labor; but tenements must cease to be 'good property' in the old, heartless sense."[20] Only when such investments were made unprofitable could conditions in New York, and the nation's other great cities, begin to change, Riis believed.

For Riis a new level of commitment by those who were part of the better-off half of society was the key to building a world that was more caring, and more humane, for all its citizens. Riis, despite his journalistic cynicism, never stopped believing that if the majority of people really understood the nature of the problem of poverty, they would begin, slowly perhaps but also surely, to bring about the changes that were needed for a more humane future.

Jacob Riis was among the best-known of the many muckraking journalists. He was far from alone. Thousands of articles, written by dozens of authors, filled the progressive press in the decades around the turn of the twentieth century. While a few of the so-called muckrakers—such as Riis, Henry Demarest Lloyd and Ida Tarbell who exposed big business, and Lincoln Steffens who described corrupt politicians—became celebrities, many more quietly worked at their trade. They exposed working conditions for children, migrant laborers, and sharecroppers. They described unsanitary housing and food preparation. And with the support of Presidents Theodore Roosevelt, William Howard Taft, and Woodrow Wilson, as well as many in Congress and state legislatures across the country, they helped change the laws and working and living conditions of thousands.[21]

Among these progressive journalists, Ernest Poole is interesting because he switched careers from settlement house worker to muckraking journalist. From 1902 to 1905 he lived at University Settlement House in New York City and, while participating in the life of that extended community, also wrote articles and pamphlets like the best of the progressive journalists. In an article in *McClure's Magazine*, one of the leading progressive journals, Poole not only described the lives of the boys who sold newspapers and carried messages on the streets of New York but also discredited the Horatio Alger myth that these boys thereby learned the ways of enterprise and rose to high positions in the capitalist world.

> We all glance in passing at the shrewd little newsboys, peddlers, messengers, and boot-blacks that swarm by day and night through every crowded street of busy New York. We catch only a glimpse. The paper is sold in a twinkling, and like a flash the little urchin is off through the crowd. We admire his tense energy, his shrewd, bright self-reliance. We hear of newsboys who in later life have risen high; and we think of street work, if we think of it at all, as a capital school for industry and enterprise.

But Poole insisted, "Those who follow deeper are forced to a directly opposite conclusion. The homeless, the most illiterate, the most dishonest, the most impure—these are the finished products of child street work." Far from the Horatio Alger myth, the child labor of these boys was a breeding ground for crime and for hopelessness and ill health, he reported.

Investigating the lives of newsboys and street messengers, Poole found a life that cut them off from home, offered no useful skills, and subverted their morality and their health. He continued:

> The street's improvidence is a natural result of its irregularity. For many this nervous irregular life is sustained and poisoned by hastily bolted meals, with often double a man's portion of coffee, cigars, and cigarettes. . . . Smoking is almost universal, and coffee is used to an amazing excess. I know over a hundred boys who average at least three huge bowls each night, and some who often drink six at supper. In thousands of cases, too, the work makes the sleep irregular. Several hundred at least sleep all night on the streets, in stables, condemned buildings, and halls of tenements, waiting until after midnight when the lights are all out. . . . Gambling and improvidence go together. Most street workers are inveterate players at the game of "craps." This whiles away the time between the irregular working periods, and often runs well up into the dollars. In one of the large messenger offices on Broadway it is common for boys to lose the entire week's earnings in the hall and stairway before reaching the street.

The result, Poole made quite clear, was that while the newspapers and the companies dependent on night messengers were thriving, those children who did the footwork were being punished by the greed of a society that cared nothing for them and created myths to assuage its own guilt.[22]

Lincoln Steffens, progressive journalist *par excellence*, wrote about the depths of municipal and state political corruption across the United States for *McClure's* and other magazines as a stimulus to reform. For Steffens, and others like him, the hope for the future was that once the public did understand the reality of municipal corruption, they would demand action. In many cases, the hope was fulfilled. The early decades of the twentieth century did witness significant efforts to end the kind of "boss rule" that dominated many American cities.

At the same time, Steffens, more than many, understood the complexity of urban life. As he explained in his *Autobiography*, the business elite who were at the forefront of campaigns to end municipal corruption often had no understanding of or commitment to the urban poor. And, the "corrupt boss" was often the only friend a poor person could find. Steffens described a visit to Boston at the invitation of Edward Filene and other municipal leaders who wanted his help in improving their city. They wanted to get to the bottom of

Boston's problems and they thought no one could do this better than Steffens. In starting his investigation, Steffens asked these assembled leaders, "Who was the worst, the most impossible, man in Boston?" "Martin Lomasny" (well known ward boss of the city's West End), they said, all in quick agreement. Steffens decided to pay a visit to Lomasny and found himself in an interesting conversation. Steffens asked Lomasny, "What do you do about the petty crooks?" Pretending to be cross, Lomasny responded cagily at first, but when pressed, defiantly admitted that he went to see the district attorney or the police or the judge and got them off repeatedly.

> "Yes, I do," he said, dropping his feet and facing me with three fingers thrust under my nose. "Three times."
>
> I laughed. "Ah, now, don't you sometimes do it four times?"
>
> He was defying me. "Seven times? Martin, don't you even get 'em off seventy times seven times?"
>
> "Yes, I do," he burst. "I never quit some of 'em, not the way you do."
>
> "Of course," I said, "You stick, but tell me, how do you justify it to yourself, saving these hopeless crooks over and over and over again when you know they'll come back and do it over and over and over again!"
>
> I did not expect him to answer this question. It was more of an exclamation on my part, but he did answer it; inarticulate people can sometimes express themselves.
>
> "I think," said Martin Lomasny, "that there's got to be in every ward somebody that any bloke can come to—not matter what he's done—and get help. Help, you understand; none of your law and your justice, but help."[23]

It was a sentiment that Jane Addams could understand, even if many other progressives could not. Law and justice were important. But for someone on the very margins of society, someone barely hanging on, what they needed was help, and they needed it immediately, not in some distant future. Until that help could be provided in more legitimate ways, the bosses such as Lomasny who knew how to offer it, would continue their hold no matter what the more distant—and all too often indifferent—law and justice advocates said or did. For Steffens, it was only when those who dominated American society came to terms with the needs met by the likes of Martin Lomasny that the rest of their efforts at reform could be realized.[24]

THE SOCIAL GOSPEL

In an era when newspaper reporters used the printed word to expose the ills of urban and industrial America and to call for reform, a young Congregationalist pastor in Topeka, Kansas, did essentially the same thing in fictionalized form. *In His Steps* by Charles M. Sheldon was published in 1897. Sheldon wrote one of the best-selling novels of its time. It told the story of a fictionalized minister, Henry Maxwell, in a fictional town of Raymond, who is moved by a labor leader's comment that "it was hopeless to look to the church for any reform or redemption of society" to ask if the statement is, indeed, true.

Maxwell decides to put the question to the test. In a Sunday morning sermon he asks his congregation what he thinks is a simple, basic question:

> What would be the result, if in this city every church member should begin to do as Jesus would do? . . . What would Jesus do in the matter of wealth? How would he spend it? What principle would regulate His use of money? Would he be likely to live in great luxury and spend ten times as much on personal adornment and entertainment as He spent to relieve the needs of suffering humanity? How would Jesus be governed in the making of money? Would he take rentals from saloons and other disreputable property, or even from tenement property that was so constructed that the inmates had no such thing as a home and no such possibility as privacy or cleanliness? What would Jesus do about the great army of unemployed and desperate who tram the streets and curse the church, or are indifferent to it, lost in the bitter struggle for bread that tastes bitter when it is earned, on account of the desperate conflict to get it. Would Jesus care nothing for them? Would he go His way in comparative ease and comfort? Would he say it was none of His business? Would he excuse Himself from all responsibility to remove the causes of such a condition?[25]

The sermon and Rev. Maxwell's continued insistence on asking the same question—"What Would Jesus Do?"—transforms both the life of the town of Raymond and the life of Maxwell himself. In Sheldon's story, it marks the beginning of a total social transformation to a new more just and more humane world.

In His Steps struck a chord in turn-of-the-century America. The hope that Sheldon offered, that by asking that simple question "What Would Jesus Do?" society could begin to be transformed, led to the sale of 15 million copies of his novel. It also led to people across the country to ask the same simple question and to answer, sometimes in small ways but also at times in larger and more powerful ways. At a time when Protestant Christianity, often a highly individualized version of Protestantism at that, still dominated American culture and when the pressing needs of the society were growing greater and greater, it was a book that was a social phenomena and one that made a difference. Those who care about the causes of hope in society dismiss it at their peril.[26]

In His Steps was far from the only religious response to the emerging needs of the fast-changing nation. For the most part, the Progressive movement was a fairly secular affair. Jane Addams had specifically distanced Hull House from the religious connections of its English predecessor, Toynbee Hall. Most of the journalists, educators, organizers, and others who worked to improve the lives of those most marginalized in industrial America also saw themselves in fairly secular terms, although their language sometimes betrayed the more religious themes of their younger years. But within the nation's religious communities, progressivism also took hold and flourished. Religious leaders of various theological views were joined in believing that their faith offered a hope for the future—not just a pie-in-the-sky future but here and now. Among Protestants, Catholics, and Jews, representing the principle religious traditions of the nation at the time, there were those who embraced the social gospel—the view that improving society was both the right thing for religious people to do and, indeed, that it was God's will.

George D. Herron, Sheldon's contemporary and also a Congregationalist minister, led a virtual revival movement, or what he called the "Kingdom movement," following the 1890 publication of a speech that made him famous, "The Message of Jesus to Men of Wealth." He spoke in churches and on college campuses around the country in the decade that followed. In his early years Herron was more individualistic than later social gospel figures. He stressed self-sacrifice and voluntary stewardship as a way to improve the general society. In his 1899 book *Between Caesar and Jesus*, Herron said: "We cannot honestly imagine one in Christ's state of mind, one feeling as Christ felt, one coming at the world from his point of view, giving himself to acquiring individual wealth. Strictly speaking, a rich Christian is a contradiction of terms."[27] For Herron there was not a lot of wiggle room, although he still focused primarily on the morality of the individual who held the wealth.

Around the turn of the century Herron joined the Socialist party and became a stronger and stronger advocate of Christian socialism. It was a stance that marginalized him from many others in the social gospel movement, but it gave his message a clarity that was impossible to miss. In *The Christian State: A Political Vision of Christ* (1895) Herron wrote:

> The only hope of the people for either industrial or political freedom lies in their taking lawful possession of the machinery, forces, and production of great industrial monopolies. Through the instrumentality of the state the people, constituted in the realized democracy of a social commonwealth, could organize their social economy in justice, that would insure work and bread for all who would work, as well as make common to all many social

benefits now exclusively enjoyed by the privileged few; and would find some service that would give a measure of profit and hope to even the weakest.[28]

For Herron it was simple—the political vision of Christ meant taking control of the means of production. Karl Marx could hardly have said it better.

While Washington Gladden, a long-time pastor in Columbus, Ohio, and Richard T. Ely, an economist at Johns Hopkins, the University of Wisconsin, and then Northwestern University, did as much as any individuals to develop the idea of a social gospel, Walter Rauschenbusch's name is probably more linked to the social gospel movement than any other. Rauschenbusch grew up in Rochester, New York, an area in which abolitionism and feminism had laid the groundwork for church involvement in social issues. However, it was his own ministry in the small Second German Church of New York City that led him, like Jacob Riis and Jane Addams, to see the issues of poverty and oppression firsthand. In the 1890s he wrote—in an article that was not published until the 1960s—"Christianity is in its nature revolutionary." He continued: "The prophets were the revolutionists of their age. They were dreamers of Utopia. They pictured an ideal state of society in which the poor should be judged with equity and the cry of the oppressed should no longer be heard; a time in which men would beat their idle swords into ploughshares and their spears into pruning hooks, for then the nations would learn war no more."[29] It was, indeed, an ancient hope that Rauschenbusch and his colleagues sought to infuse into the modern industrial world.

While his early work reflected much of the optimism of his time, *A Theology for the Social Gospel*, which he published in 1917 in the midst of World War I, reflects the sobering impact of the war on theology and social ethics. In it Rauschenbusch argued: "The social gospel seeks to bring men under repentance for their collective sins and to create a more sensitive and modern conscience. It calls on us for the faith of the old prophets who believed in the salvation of nations."[30] The theological hope that the ancient concept of sin could be broadened from meaning individual flaws to include social institutions that oppressed others, and that "the permanent institutions of human society" could be redeemed and transformed from individualistic to social uses was at the very heart of the social gospel movement.

When the aging Walter Rauschenbusch published *A Theology for the Social Gospel*, a young Reinhold Niebuhr had just begun his own pastoral ministry in a small Evangelical and Reformed congregation in Detroit. By midcentury Niebuhr would emerge to be considered by many one of the great theologians of the twentieth century. He and other "Christian realists" transformed American Protestant theology by adding a note of caution, not about the need for social reform but about the continuing sinfulness in all human affairs that made difficult all grand plans to improve the world, including the plans of Rauschenbusch and other advocates of the social gospel with whom Niebuhr otherwise would agree. But in the early years of the century, Niebuhr was not dealing with theological debates but with the day-to-day reality of parish ministry in a rapidly changing working class in the most industrial of American cities, Detroit. The journal he kept of those years casts a useful light on the impact of the social gospel in the grass-roots reality of parish life.

In 1926, Niebuhr wrote in his journal of a colleague who had lost his job because of his political views.

> A letter from Hyde brings the sad news that C_____ has lost his pastorate. I am not surprised. He is courageous but tactless. Undoubtedly he will regard himself as one of the Lord's martyrs. Perhaps he is. Perhaps loyalty to principle will always appear as tactlessness from the perspective of those who don't agree with you. But I agree with C_____ and still think him wanting in common sense. At least he is pedagogically very awkward. . . .
>
> Of course it is not easy to speak the truth in love without losing a part of the truth, and therefore one ought not be too critical of those who put their emphasis on the truth rather than on love. But if a man is not willing to try, at least, to be pedagogical, and if in addition he suffers from a martyr complex, he has no place in the ministry.[31]

Many a parish-based effort to make the world a better place that began with great hopes has floundered on similar shoals. Reality would, indeed, have been served well if more in the ministry had paid greater attention to Niebuhr's call for pedagogical wisdom. The comment was typical Niebuhr: insightful on both the difficulty of preaching a social gospel in an individualistic nation and the need to be wise in how one approaches the issue so that one could avoid being "pedagogically awkward."

On an earlier occasion, in 1923, Niebuhr had written of what he saw as a basic problem, in the parish and on the world stage then being vacated by the leaders of World War I: "There doesn't seem to be very much malice in the world. There is simply not enough intelligence to conduct the intricate affairs of a complex civilization."[32] All of Niebuhr's writings were tempered by the same caution—usually a fairly gentle caution—that building the future one wanted was usually more difficult than one might expect. So in 1928 he wrote:

> The whole Christian adventure is frustrated continually not so much by malice as by cowardice and reasonableness. Of course everyone must decide for himself just where he is going to put his peg; where he is going to arrive at

some stable equilibrium between moral adventure and necessary caution. And perhaps everyone is justified if he tried to prove that there is a particular reasonableness about the type of compromise which he has reached. But he might well learn, better than I have learned, to be charitable with those who have made their adjustments to the right and to the left of his position. If I do not watch myself I will regard all who make their adjustments to my right as fanatics and all who make them to the left as cowards.[33]

In the hands of some of Niebuhr's latter disciples, this caution about where to stand on the difficult issues of the time led to a virtual paralysis. For Niebuhr himself, who in his last days was protesting the U.S. involvement in Vietnam, it was a caution not to take one's position as the only correct one while nevertheless always engaging with serious social issues of the day with a moral courage that would have made Rauschenbusch very proud.

While the term social gospel tended to be popular among Protestants and while some of its most vocal proponents, such as Rauschenbusch himself, tended to be distrustful of Catholics, a similar focus on social issues and on the needs of society swept Catholic America with at least as much impact as the social gospel had on Protestant America. One of the most consistent advocates of the rights of Catholic workers to organize to defend their rights was James Cardinal Gibbons, the long-time archbishop of Baltimore and nominal leader of American Catholics. At a time when most European Catholic leaders were focused on their fear of the anticlericalism and socialism of European labor movements, Gibbons defended the American labor movement and the role of Catholics in it to a wary Vatican.

In his autobiography, *A Retrospect of Fifty Years*, Gibbons argued that in the United States the rise of monopolies with their "heartless avarice which, through greed of gain, pitilessly grinds not only men, but even the women and children in various employments," demanded action. It was clear to him that "it is not only the right of the laboring classes to protect themselves, but the duty of the whole people to aid them in finding a remedy against the dangers with which both civilization and social order are menaced by—avarice, oppression and corruption."[34]

Gibbons was also clear about the remedy. He endorsed labor unions in general and the Knights of Labor specifically. He defended the rights of Catholics to belong to these unions and to unite with Protestants and others in organizing and leading them. He assured the Vatican that, though American Catholics were exposed not only to Protestants but to "atheists, communists, and anarchists," these were simply among "those trials of faith which our brave American Catholics are accustomed to meet almost daily," and there was no need to fear for the outcome. By the time he wrote his autobiography in 1916, the Vatican had embraced Gibbons views, but when he had first espoused them and when in 1887 he took his arguments to Rome itself, there was considerable doubt about the reception he would receive. It took courage for Gibbons to say what he did and to stand in solidarity with the American Catholics who were organizing through the Knights and other labor organizations.[35]

A Catholic priest in New York, Edward McGlynn went much farther than Gibbons. McGlynn preached that "It is not for nothing that He who came to save the souls of men did so much to minister to the relief of their bodily wants." For McGlynn, the way that Jesus would want to deal with the bodily wants of New Yorkers in the late nineteenth century would be to embrace the campaign of Henry George for a single tax. So McGlynn got very specific in his gospel.

> How are we going to give back to the poor man what belongs to him? How shall we have that beautiful state of things in which naught shall be ill and all shall be well? Simply by confiscating rent and allowing people nominally to own if you choose, the whole of Manhattan Island. . . . And how are we going to do that? By simply taxing all this land and all kindred bounties of nature to the full amount of their rental value.[36]

A 100 percent tax on property and the threat of confiscation was too much for a Vatican still reeling from the confiscations of church property by the Italian revolutionary movement. In 1887, the same year that Gibbons made his appeal to Rome, McGlynn was excommunicated. He was restored five years later, however, and kept preaching the same gospel until his death in 1900. It was a much more radical Catholicism than that of Gibbons. But it too struck a chord among those who hoped that the day would soon come when it would be recognized, as McGlynn preached, that the earth and all its wealth belonged equally "to the human family, to the community, to the people, to all the children of God."[37]

In 1891 a change in perspective from the Vatican itself came with Pope Leo XIII's encyclical *Rerum Novarum*, which showed deep concern for social welfare. Throughout the early years of the twentieth century there was a growing openness on similar issues by a number of American Catholic bishops. The nation's Catholic bishops came together during World War I to focus on issues of social welfare. These meetings were formalized after the war as the National Catholic Welfare Conference and Msgr. John A. Ryan drafted the document that was adopted by the conference in 1919 as "The Bishops' Program of Social Reconstruction." "The ending of the Great War has brought peace," it said. "But the only safeguard of peace is social justice and a contented people. . . . Great problems face us. They cannot be put aside; they must be met and solved with justice to all."[38]

The document went on to call for "social reconstruction" in considerable detail, including specific pleas that concerned the maintenance of wages, housing, a legal minimum wage, and social insurance. The document also affirmed the right of labor to organize and to deal with employers through their representatives.[39]

The 1919 program called for many social changes only dreamed of by reformers of earlier decades, but it also came at the price of a diminished sense of hope for larger social changes. Like much of organized labor, especially within the American Federation of Labor, Catholic social advocates turned away from the redistributive hopes of McGlynn toward more prosaic ideals. Socialism, they feared, meant "bureaucracy, political tyranny, the helplessness of the individual." Nevertheless they clearly affirmed "that the laborer is a human being, not merely an instrument of production; and that the laborer's right to a descent livelihood is the first moral charge upon industry." In the post-war world of 1919 these were still radical words and they provided a foundation for much Catholic activism in the decades that followed.[40]

For the nation's growing Jewish community, the focus on political debates in the Progressive Era remained mostly in quite secular venues. Irving Howe has written sensitively of the primary concerns of the immigrant generation of Jews in New York and elsewhere:

> The soaring new faith of the immigrant world was socialism—a vision of human fraternity that would bring to an end the exploitativeness, the inhumane competitiveness, the moral frigidity associated with capitalism. We're not inclined to go along with facile analogies between religious faith and secular politics; still there does seem good reason to say that something of the messianic fervor of religious fathers was appropriated by radical sons and daughters. For Jewish socialism was far more than a politics—it was a gleaming faith, at once splendid and naïve in its dreams of perfection and brotherhood.[41]

Socialism and socialist organizations of many varieties filled the place of more traditional religious assemblies for many within the eastern European immigrant communities.

For some immigrant Jews, this socialist faith also led to times of both spiritual and ethical conflict. I. Benequit, who wrote his memoirs in Yiddish, told of his own crisis as he began to work his way up in the garment industry. He had gone from working in another's shop to owning his own.

> During the time I had the shop the shirtmakers founded a union. My friends would needle me for considering myself a radical—an anarchist, yet—and not only do I not belong to the union, I've gone the other way, hiring people. What came mildly from friends came as "enemy of the workers," "parasite," from strangers. They claimed I lived off others' labor, but I knew I made no more than my workers, who earn more from me than elsewhere; and that I worked a lot harder. Nevertheless the words were painful and I debated with myself—am I a socialist? Do I believe in the anarchist ideal? Either I stay a contractor and give up my ideals or leave contracting and remain true.[42]

For Benequit, the ideals won. Benequit left contracting, joined the union, and was soon leading a strike in the garment district. Such was the living faith of socialism and the social gospel of at least this one man who took the ethical implications of his decisions very seriously even if he had left the more traditional rituals of faith behind when he came to America.

But socialism, powerful as it was, did not replace religion for everyone in the immigrant Jewish community. With the massive immigrations of 1880 to 1920 came the rapid growth of synagogues. And among the leaders of these religious communities were rabbis who also took their own version of the social gospel very seriously. In 1928, the Central Conference of American Rabbis, an organization of Reform Judaism, reported through its Commission on Social Justice in words that paralleled the 1919 words of the Catholic bishops and the Protestant social gospel preachers. These rabbis positioned their call for justice squarely within their tradition:

> Deriving our inspiration for social justice form the great teachings of the prophets of Israel and the other great traditions of our faith, and applying these teachings concretely to the economic and social problems of today, we, the Central Conference of American Rabbis, make this declaration of social principles. . . . We regard those tendencies to be unjust which would make the fundamental goal of industry the exploitation of the material world on the basis of unbridled competition and the unlimited and unrestricted accretion of goods in the hands of a few while millions are in want.

They also made it clear that workers had the right to organize to defend their God-given rights, rights that many in their congregations had been exercising robustly for decades. "The same rights of organization which rest with employers," they affirmed, "rest also with those whom they employ. . . . Workers have the same inalienable right to organize according to their own plan for their common good and to bargain collectively with their employers through such honorable means as they may choose."

Finally, they insisted that all citizens needed to recognize that "Contribution to the common good and not the selfish service of a class is the touchstone of all moral endeavor." The development of a society based on this touchstone was the only way in which their ancient traditions could be truly honored.[43]

Henry M. Sheldon, Walter Rauschenbusch, Reinhold Niebuhr, Cardinal Gibbons, Father McGlynn, the leaders of the Central Conference of American Rabbis, and many who worshipped with them shared a hope that the plea of the ancient prophets, "let justice roll down like waters," could be realized in the midst of industrial America. Their hopes were often tempered by their increasingly sophisticated understanding of human sinfulness and also by their inevitable alliance with those who contributed the most to their institutions. Nevertheless, a generation of American religious leaders and communities participated actively in a wide variety of expressions of a hopeful social gospel which added religious fervor to progressivism.

THE REVOLUTION OF THE TEACHERS

In 1899 John Dewey, still a relatively young professor of philosophy at the University of Chicago, wrote *The School and Society*. In that volume he stated distinctly his own hopes for the transformation of the schools and, ultimately, for the place of the schools in the transformation of the larger society. For Dewey and many of his fellow educational progressives, one of the chief problems of the school was the boredom created by its almost complete isolation from the rest of society and especially from the activities of adults, which children, in fact, found so interesting that they emulated them in much of their play. Dewey advocated bringing this real world into the classroom and making it the stuff of the curriculum.

> To do this means to make each one of our schools an embryonic community life, active with types of occupations that reflect the life of the larger society and permeated throughout with the spirit of art, history, and science. When the school introduces and trains each child of society into membership within such a little community, saturating him with the spirit of service, and providing him with the instruments of effective self-direction, we shall have the deepest and best guaranty of a larger society which is worthy, lovely, and harmonious.[44]

By engaging children in the life of the world, by creating real democracies in the school classrooms, Dewey argued, young people would be offered the best possible preparation not only for the world of work and for understanding work, but for engaged citizenship in a vibrant democracy that could be made more "worthy, lovely, and harmonious" as a result. This, at its best, was the faith and the hope of progressive education.

Dewey understood all too well that most people asked much less of the schools than the creation of a worthy, lovely, and harmonious society. They wanted to know how their own children were progressing. "We are apt to look at the school from an individualistic standpoint, as something between teacher and pupil, or between teacher and parent," Dewey said in *The School and Society*. Moreover, "That which interests us most is naturally the progress made by the individual child of our acquaintance." This was fair enough as a beginning, but Dewey extended these ideas.

> What the best and wisest parent wants for his own child, that must the community want for all of its children. Any other ideal for our schools is narrow and unlovely; acted upon, it destroys our democracy. . . . Here individualism and socialism are at one. Only by being true to the full growth of all the individuals who make it up, can society by any chance be true to itself. And in the self-direction thus given, nothing counts as much as the school, for as Horace Mann said, "Where anything is growing, one former is worth a thousand re-formers."[45]

Here was a vision of the future in which the school would nurture all of society's children in such a way that not only would all be served but all would become the agents of a continual process of building a better society. It was an audacious hope and it inspired many in the decades that followed.

References to Progressive education often bring to mind the name of John Dewey and sometimes also a stereotype of ill-fated efforts to focus so much on the needs and wants of the individual child that teaching and learning got short-changed. While John Dewey was a central figure in the progressive education movement, and while some progressives—a minority I would argue—did veer into the swamp of so much permissiveness that they forgot they were educators, progressive education was much more than all of that. Lawrence A. Cremin, in his study of progressivism in education, comes much closer to an accurate understanding of the movement. "The word *progressive* provides the clue to what it really was: the educational phase of American Progressivism writ large. In effect, progressive education began as Progressivism in education: a many-sided effort to use the schools to improve the lives of individuals."[46] And, it must be added, a fierce confidence that such an effort could succeed—for students, teachers, and the larger society.

In fact, progressive education meant many different things to different people. For some business-oriented reformers, it meant reorganizing schools to be more businesslike with centralized administrations and bureaucratic top-down modes of decision making. For militant teachers, it meant the exact opposite: a restructuring of schools to give teachers more voice and more influence in all aspects of education, moving them from being mere cogs to the center of the action. For yet others, the focus was not structure at all, but the child him- or herself. For these child-centered progressives, what schools needed was a shift in emphasis from the curriculum and teaching to the learner and the complex process of learning and truly knowing. For yet others who called themselves progressives, progressivism meant making education scientific and especially including scientific measurement—usually through standardized testing—into the life of schools. Finally, for social radicals, progressive education meant transforming both the school and the larger society, using the school to build in microcosm the kind of larger society that, in Dewey's words, was worthy, lovely, and harmonious. With all these and yet other educators calling themselves progressives, it is, indeed, fair to say that the term progressive education is too broad to have meaning. Exploring the complex relationships among these different progressive educators is also beyond the scope of this book. But a history of hope—of those people in the history of the United States who have spoken and acted in the passionate belief that their words and actions could help others both visualize and build a better tomorrow—would not be complete without attention to a few of the progressive educators who dreamed great dreams for themselves, the children, and the role of the schools, and who more effectively than many helped turn those dreams into realities.[47]

In 1904 Margaret Haley stood before the National Education Association (NEA) to propose a union for teachers. In her speech "Why Teachers Should Organize," she projected her hopes for the future of the teaching profession and called on the NEA—then dominated by male superintendents and academics—to join her in the quest to fulfill those hopes. When she spoke to the NEA, Haley was already the best-known teacher advocate in the United States. Founder and leader of the Chicago Teachers Federation, she was a powerful and effective voice for the rights of teachers. She told the delegates to the association's 1904 meeting precisely what the problem was and what needed to be done to fix it.

Nowhere in the United States today does the public school, as a branch of the public service, receive from the public either the moral or financial support needed to enable it properly to perform its important function in the social organism. The conditions which are militating most strongly against efficient teaching, and which existing organizations of the kind under discussion here are directing their energies toward changing, briefly stated are the following:

1. Greatly increased cost of living, together with constant demands for higher standards of scholarship and professional attainments and culture, to be met with practically stationary and wholly inadequate teachers' salaries.

2. Insecurity of tenure of office and lack of provision for old age.

3. Overwork in overcrowded schoolrooms, exhausting both in mind and body.

4. And, lastly, lack of recognition of the teacher as an educator in the school system, due to the increased tendency toward "factoryizing education," making the teacher an automaton, a mere factory hand, whose duty it is to carry out mechanically and unquestioningly the ideas and orders of those clothed with the authority of position, and who may or may not know the needs of the children or how to minister to them.

The individuality of the teacher and her power of initiative are thus destroyed, and the result is courses of study, regulations and equipment which the teachers have had no voice in selecting, which often have no relation to the children's needs, and which prove a hindrance instead of a help in teaching.[48]

If these needs were addressed, Haley told the NEA, then teachers would be freed from being a "mere factory hand" and turned into respected professionals ready and able to make their full contribution to the future of the schools and the education of the next generation. If these needs were not addressed, Haley also warned, no other actions could suffice to improve the schools.

Of course, Haley understood that teachers needed to be the primary agents of addressing these concerns and improving their own lot. And she knew the vehicle by which teachers could do so was a labor union of teachers. She reminded her audience that, "The organization of these workers for their mutual aid has shortened the hours of labor, raised and equalized the wages of men and women, and taken the children from the factories and workshops. These humanitarian achievements of the labor unions—and many others which space forbids enumerating—in raising the standard of living of the poorest and weakest members of society are a service to society which for its own welfare it must recognize." A union of teachers could do the same for the schools; indeed it was already beginning to do so in Chicago.

The battle for the rights of teachers—to improve their own lot and to improve the schools—was part of a much larger struggle that Haley saw underway in the United States. "Two ideals are struggling for supremacy in American life today: one the industrial ideal, dominating through the supremacy of commercialism, which subordinates the worker to the products and the machine; the other, the ideal of democracy, the ideal of the educators, which places humanity above all machines, and demands that all activity shall be the expression of life. . . . If the school cannot bring joy to the work of the world, the joy must go out of its own life, and work in the school as in the factory will become drudgery." Either schools would be an essential building block in a wider and more expansive democracy or they would be a barrier to that democracy. In Haley's view there was no middle ground. So, she concluded, "Today, teachers of America, we stand at the parting of the ways: Democracy is not on trial, but America is."[49]

Although her 1904 speech was the most powerful and well-known statement of her beliefs, it was far from her only word on the subject. For decades Margaret Haley fought to change the nature of the teaching profession, to organize teachers into unions, and through the unions to make the schools more humane and democratic places and servants of a more humane and democratic society.[50]

A quarter century after Haley's speech, in the midst of the Great Depression, George Counts went further than either Dewey or Haley had, stating his hopes for what teachers and schools could do to build a better future. In a series of speeches to teacher's unions, Counts called on their members to "Dare to Build a New Social Order." He reminded the teachers of the 1930s, "that the educational problem is not wholly intellectual in nature." It was also frankly political. Counts insisted that until progressive educators were willing to enlist children themselves in a struggle for a better world, in politics, they were failing to offer them a proper education.

> Our Progressive schools therefore cannot rest content with giving children an opportunity to study contemporary society in all of its aspects. This of course must be done, but I am convinced that they should go much farther. If schools are to be really effective, they must become centers for building, not merely for the contemplation, of our civilization. This does not mean that we should endeavor to promote particular reforms through the educational system. We should, however, give to our children a vision of the possibilities that lie ahead and endeavor to enlist their loyalties and enthusiasms in the realization of that vision.[51]

It was not enough, Counts insisted, for educators to teach the great debates of the day. For Counts, the heart of education lay in the struggle to shape a new world in the place where teachers have the most opportunity to do it—their own classrooms.

Counts was deeply frustrated that progressive education had seemed to settle for so much less. He found himself increasingly frustrated with the fact that the child-centered wing of progressivism was drowning out all of the rest. "Like a baby shaking a rattle, we seem to be utterly content with action, provided it is sufficiently vigorous and noisy," he said. "The weakness of Progressive Education thus lies in the fact that it has elaborated no theory of social welfare, unless it be that of anarchy or extreme individualism."[52] Counts wanted much more of teachers. And if teachers did not rise to the challenge, Counts warned, they would be seen by their students and by society as people who were "moved by no great faiths . . . touched by no great passions." So, Counts asserted: "We cannot, by talk about the interests of children and the sacredness of personality, evade the responsibility of bringing to the younger generation a vision which will call forth their active loyalties and challenge them to creative and arduous labors."[53] Schools, Counts said, must be not only democratically administered and teach the values of a democratic society, they must—in the experience they offer their students—be vehicles for building a truly democratic culture in this country if they are to merit the term democratic schools.

Counts's words, in *Dare the School Build a New Social Order?* and in the journal that he edited, *Social Frontier,* certainly represented some of the most radical and daring efforts to expand the hopes of progressive educators to include envisioning a very different society for all Americans. But while Counts may have gone farther than others, there were many within the progressive education community—teachers, union leaders, philosophers—who shared his belief that the educational process could be made more engaging and more democratic, and that in the process the society in which the school operated could also become a more dynamic and engaged democracy.

John Dewey announced quite early in his career a similar belief that the link between democracy and education goes very deep. For a democracy, the commitment to education involves enlightening citizens and, far more importantly, it involves the continuous restoration and recreation of the idea of democracy itself as a potent source of energy and vision. Dewey wrote in 1897: "By law and punishment, by social agitation and discussion, society can regulate and form itself in a more or less haphazard and chance way. But through education society can formulate its own purposes, can organize its own means and resources, and thus shape itself with definiteness and economy in the direction in which it wishes to move."[54] The ethical belief that this was the right thing to do and the faith that it could be done through the efforts of educators and their allies was at the core of all the best hopes of the movement known as progressive education.

PEACE IN A TIME OF WAR

In the spring of 1918 the nation's best-known socialist leader gave a speech to a large assembly in a park in Canton, Ohio. In the midst of World War I, with patriotism rising high and fear of subversives in the air, Eugene V. Debs outlined his own brand of patriotism and courted the charge of subversion if subversion meant opposition to capitalism and a capitalist war. For Debs, the speech was not merely one more opportunity to attack the bloody workings of capitalism. In spite of the terrors of the war itself and the national hysteria about subversion, Debs focused on his hopes, on his absolute belief that a new day was dawning and it was up to his fellow workers to open their eyes and see the light. The choice he offered workers was the age-old choice between light and darkness:

> Socialism is a growing idea; an expanding philosophy. It is spreading over the entire face of the earth. It is as vain to resist it as it would be to arrest the sunrise on the morrow. . . . It is the mightiest movement in the history of mankind. . . . It has given me my ideas and ideals; my principles and convictions, and I would not exchange one of them for all of Rockefeller's blood-stained dollars. (Cheers.) It has taught me how to serve—a lesson to me of priceless value. It has taught me the ecstasy in the handclasp of a comrade. It has enabled me to hold high communion with you, and made it possible for me to take my place side by side with you in the great struggle for the better day . . . to know that I am kin to all that throbs; to be class-conscious, and to realize that, regardless of nationality, race, creed, color, or sex, every man, every woman who toils, who renders useful service, every member of the working class without an exception, is my comrade, my brother and sister—and that to serve them and their cause is the highest duty of my life. (Great applause.)[55]

This was the socialist movement to which Debs had given his life, and he was proud and grateful for his part in it, proud and grateful to call all there with him his comrades, his brothers and sisters.

While the heart of the speech that Debs gave that day in Canton was an appeal to workers to join the Socialist party, he also made it clear what he thought of the war then underway and of the United States' decision to enter the war. He had no use for either side, for he knew that "the purpose of the Allies is exactly the purpose of the Central Powers, and that is the conquest and spoilation of the weaker nations that has always been the purpose of war." And why should the working class take part? He reminded them, "that the working class who fight all the battles, the working class who make the supreme sacrifices, the working class who freely shed their blood and furnish the corpses, have never yet had a voice in either declaring war or making peace. It is the ruling class that invariably does both."[56] Apparently that was enough for the authorities to indict Debs.

To make such a speech in the heartland of the United States was not an easy or simple thing to do. Debs certainly knew that he was courting arrest under the nation's wartime subversion statutes. At the beginning of the speech he paid homage to socialists already in jail because of their opposition to the war and joked with his audience that "I may not be able to say all I think," but he assured them that "I would rather a thousand times be a free soul in jail than to be a sycophant and coward in the streets."[57] And yet, he invited his audience to stand with him in this critical time. Arrests might come. Setbacks might come. But the hope of the future was apparent to him and he returned to it as his main theme:

> Yes, in good time we are going to sweep into power in this nation and throughout the world. We are going to destroy all enslaving and degrading capitalist institutions and re-create them as free and humanizing institutions. The world is daily changing before our eyes. The sun of capitalism is setting; the sun of Socialism is rising. It is our duty to build the new nation and the free republic. We need industrial and social builders. We Socialists are the builders of the beautiful world that is to be. We are all pledged to do our part. We are inviting—aye challenging you in the name of your own manhood and womanhood to join us and do your part.
>
> In due time the hour will strike and this great cause triumphant—the greatest in history—will proclaim the emancipation of the working class and the brotherhood of all mankind. (Thunderous and prolonged applause.)[58]

For early twentieth-century America, this was, indeed, the vision of hope for a new community of freedom and mutuality in the United States.

The emancipation of the working class and the unity of the human race did not happen with the speed or inevitability that Debs imagined that beautiful spring morning. He was arrested soon after giving the speech, tried, and on September 12 convicted of violating the 1917 Espionage Act with the speech. He told the jury hearing the case that he would not deny any of the speech. "I admit being opposed to the present social system. I am doing what little I can, and have been for many years, to bring about a change that shall do away with the rule of the great body of the people by a relatively small class and establish in this country an industrial and social democracy." If that was a crime, he pleaded guilty.[59]

Debs appealed his conviction to the Supreme Court. He argued that when the Constitution said, "Congress shall make no law . . . abridging the freedom of speech," the Constitution meant what it said. The Court did not agree and Debs's conviction was upheld. He used his sentencing hearing not to appeal for clemency but to make a final forceful statement of his views. He began,

Your Honor, years ago I recognized my kinship with all living beings, and I made up my mind that I was not one bit better than the meanest on earth, I said then, and I say now, that while there is a lower class, I am in it, while there is a criminal element I am of it, and while there is a soul in prison, I am not free.

Debs insisted that those with whom he stood in solidarity also knew that no matter what happened to him personally, the future was assured: "They feel—they know, indeed—that the time is coming, in spite of all opposition, all persecution, when this emancipating gospel will spread among all the peoples, and when this minority will become the triumphant majority and, sweeping into power, inaugurate the greatest social and economic change in history."[60] A powerful faith had sustained Debs and his fellow socialists for years and, he was confident, would sustain him in the jail term he was facing.

Debs was sentenced to ten years in federal prison on the espionage charge. He served two years and was pardoned by President Warren Harding in 1921. The socialist movement was splintered by the redbaiting attacks of federal and state governments, by the prosperity of the 1920s, and by its own factional disputes. The Debs who emerged from federal prison was a much more somber figure. Still, the vision that Debs and his socialist comrades held high during the early years of the twentieth century has continued to inspire their successors. Sometimes they have been a very small group; at other times, in the 1930s and 1960s, the socialist movement grew much larger. Throughout the twentieth century Debs's vision of a society governed by the recognition that "regardless of nationality, race, creed, color, or sex, every man, every woman who toils, who renders useful service, every member of the working class without an exception, is my comrade, my brother and sister" inspired hope and commitment.

Debs was not the only American prosecuted for opposition to World War I. There had been a brisk debate about the war prior to the U.S. entry, and more than fifty members of the House of Representatives, including the first woman in Congress, Jeannette Rankin, as well as several senators, among them the progressive stalwart Robert M. LaFollette, voted against the declaration of war in the spring of 1917. But once the country was at war, the government of Woodrow Wilson came down viciously on any opposition. As Debs noted, other socialists were jailed and more would be at the war's end; some who opposed the war, including Jane Addams, were attacked as "reds" and subversives. Careers and reputations were ruined.[61]

In the years leading up to the war, the Anti-Enlistment League sought to encourage young men to refuse to serve if war came. Between 1915 and 1917 the league received 3,500 signatures on a pledge that read, "I, being over eighteen years of age, hereby pledge myself against enlistment as a volunteer for any military or naval service in international war, either offensive or defensive, and against giving my approval to such enlistment on the part of others."[62] The goal was both resistance and pressure on the United States to stay out of the war.

Once war came, a military draft replaced the calls for volunteers. Some young men refused to serve on religious grounds of pacifism, some on the platform that Debs and others espoused, that it was not their war. The religious pacifists were offered alternative service. The political dissenters were jailed, some for terms of 20 to 25 years; there were also 142 life sentences and 17 death sentences. All the death sentences were later commuted and the last of the prisoners were released in November of 1920. The harshness of the initial sentences indicated both the fear and the anger of a government at war as well as the courage and confidence of those who were willing to risk challenging that government.[63]

In November 1915 the American Union Against Militarism was founded in New York; among its leaders were some of the nation's prominent reformers, including Rev. John Haynes Holmes, Lillian Wald, Jane Addams, Max Eastman, Amos Pinchot, Rabbi Steven S. Wise, and Norman Thomas. In time, under the leadership of Roger Baldwin, who served a year in prison for his own refusal to participate in the war, this organization became the nucleus of the American Civil Liberties Union.[64]

Members of the Socialist party and the Industrial Workers of the World, and other radicals, socialists, and anarchists, were both the heart of the antiwar effort and those most brutally attacked for their antiwar stance. In the summer of 1917 twelve hundred members of the IWW in Arizona were rounded up and abandoned in the middle of the Arizona desert. In Montana an IWW organizer was lynched. In September 1917 every IWW meeting hall in the country was raided under orders from the U.S. Attorney General A. Mitchell Palmer, and a number of radicals including Big Bill Haywood and Elizabeth Gurley Flynn were arrested. Haywood eventually fled to the Soviet Union. Emma Goldman and Alexander Berkman were also arrested and deported to the Soviet Union. Clearly the government was determined to break the back of the antiwar effort and to use the wartime patriotism to crush radicalism in every form. In the short run it was a successful effort. It would be a long time before the power and confidence of the prewar radical movements in the nation were seen again.[65]

Socialists opposed not only World War I, they opposed all wars that they saw as merely battles of the international elites with the workers used as cannon fodder. Quakers, always part of a pacifist tradition, opposed World War I as they would any war. Many religious leaders also opposed the war, including Unitarian John Haynes Holmes, Rabbi Stephen S. Wise, and the Baptist Harry Emerson Fosdick. In 1917 Fosdick wrote:

> One who knows what really is happening on European battlefields to-day and calls war glorious is morally unsound. . . . War now is dropping bombs from aeroplanes and killing women and children in their beds; it is shooting, by telephonic orders, at an unseen place miles away and slaughtering invisible men; it is murdering innocent travelers on merchant ships with torpedoes from unknown submarines; it is launching clouds of poisoned gas and slaying men with their own breath. War means lying days and nights wounded and alone in No-Man's land; it means men with jaws gone, eyes gone, limbs gone, minds gone.[66]

Fosdick would allow no romance. For him the war, and the U.S. involvement in it, was evil pure and simple. The only hope for the future was an end to such evil and such madness, not any effort to paint it as either glorious or as productive.

Whether it was Eugene V. Debs and countless other socialists and Wobblies refusing to be part of a war that they saw as only serving their masters and undermining working-class solidarity around the world, or individual pacifists risking social rejection and harsh jail sentences, or preachers like Harry Emerson Fosdick refusing to be part of any glorification of war, during World War I countless people held up the hope that peace could prevail and that wars could be brought to an end. In the court proceeding relating to his own refusal to serve in World War I—the beginning of a lifetime career defending those most despised in American society because of their views—Roger Baldwin said:

> I am opposed to this and all other wars. I do not believe in the use of physical force as a method of achieving any end, however good. . . . Though at the moment I am of a tiny minority, I feel myself just one protest in a great revolt surging up from among the people—the struggle of the masses against the rule of the world by a few, profoundly intensified by the war. It is a struggle against the political state itself, against exploitation, militarism, imperialism, authority in all forms.[67]

Baldwin's would remain a minority though powerful view. He and many others represented a hope for a better day of freedom from violence, exploitation, and injustice in every form.

CHAPTER NINE

HOPE IN HARD TIMES

THE CASE OF SACCO AND VANZETTI, 1920–1927

WHEN EUGENE V. DEBS WAS RELEASED from the federal prison in Atlanta in December of 1921, one of his very first actions, before he boarded the train that was to take him to freedom, was to take the five-dollar bill, which he and all prisoners received at their release, and send it to the new committee that had been set up to defend two recently arrested anarchists, Nicola Sacco and Bartolomeo Vanzetti. It was the kind of act of solidarity for which Debs was so widely admired. It was also a symbolic passing of the torch from a leader who had dominated the first two decades of the twentieth century to a group gathered around two men whose case would embody the hopes and fears of many in the third decade of the century.[1]

The case of Sacco and Vanzetti signified different things to different people. For anarchists and other radicals, including Debs, they were fellow revolutionaries, comrades deeply committed to radically changing the political and economic structure of the United States and the world. For Italian-American immigrants, they were symbols of the oppression that they all faced in trying to make a place for themselves in the new world and of the hopes for a better day. For civil libertarians and for the descendants of abolitionists and suffragists, their case represented American justice at its worst, a continuation of all of those cases from the 1857 Dred Scott decision that legalized slavery in the territories, to the 1896 *Plessy v. Ferguson* case legalizing racial segregation, to the court-sanctioned force-feeding of suffragists early in the twentieth century and the red scare of 1918 and 1919. If the case could be won, if the voices of Sacco and Vanzetti could be heard and their freedom won, then—for different constituencies—a blow could be struck for anarchism, or for the rights of every immigrant, or for the civil liberties of every American citizen.[2]

In the middle of it all were the two men. Nicola Sacco was born in Torremaggiore, in southern Italy, in 1891. He immigrated to the United States in 1908 and worked in a shoe factory in Milford, Massachusetts. He was married in 1912, and a son, Dante, was born in 1913 and a daughter, Ines, in 1920. Bartolomeo Vanzetti was born in Villafalletto, in northern Italy, in 1888. He also came to the United States in 1908 and worked as a laborer, first in New York City and later in Massachusetts, where he held a number of jobs including that of a fish vendor. In the United States both men, like many other immigrants of their generation, were attracted to radical politics and became dedicated anarchists.

Sacco and Vanzetti first met through their involvement in the anarchist movement in 1917 and became good friends. They were both arrested on the evening of May 5, 1920, for the robbery and the murder of a paymaster and guard of a shoe factory in South Braintree, Massachusetts. They were tried in the midst of the antiradical hysteria that was sweeping the country and convicted in July 1921. After a long series of appeals, all of which were paralleled by massive public protests managed by a well-organized defense committee, their conviction was upheld by the Massachusetts Supreme Judicial Court in April 1927. They were sentenced to death by their trial judge, Webster Thayer. After a further review of the case by a commission of Harvard president A. Lawrence Lowell, M.I.T. president Samuel W. Stratton, and retired judge Robert Grant, Massachusetts Governor Alvan T. Fuller denied the appeal for clemency. They were executed at Charlestown Prison on August 23, 1927.[3]

Given the symbolism surrounding the case, Sacco and Vanzetti have been painted as many different kinds of people. They themselves were quite clear who they were and where they placed their own hopes. In a joint letter to their defense committee on August 4, 1927, they said, "We die for Anarchy. Long live Anarchy." As Sacco told his daughter, "the nightmare of the lower classes saddened very badly your father's soul." And Vanzetti wrote, with anarchy, "the social wealth would belong to every human creature." In common with other anarchists they believed that it was society's institutions—government, the church, and especially the idea of private property—that led to the oppression of the many by the few. The head of their defense committee, Aldino Felicani, made it clear "that he did not believe in marriage nor the church, and that he did not believe in authority or the observance of the laws of the State, that he was an anarchist." If those institutions of the state could be abolished, these anarchists were confident that women and men would find a way to live together in equity and peace. They were not pacifists. They believed that revolutionary violence was probably essential to accomplishing their cause. But as their statements and letters from prison show, they were also both extraordinarily gentle men who cared deeply about those around them and about the society in which they lived.[4]

In a February 27, 1924, letter to one of his staunchest supporters, Alice Stone Blackwell—daughter of the nineteenth-century feminists and abolitionists Lucy Stone and Henry Blackwell and a symbol of the defense committee's link to these earlier movements—Bartolomeo Vanzetti laid out distinctly many of his beliefs about anarchism, his hopes for the future, and his position on a number of issues. Although he hated violence, he also saw its necessity. He wrote, "I abhor useless violence. I would [shed] my blood to prevent the shedding of blood, but neither the abyss nor the earth, nor the heavens, have a law which condemns the self-defense." Revolutionary violence certainly could be self-defense, for the attack of the rich on the poor was continuing. "Authority, Power, and Privilege would not last a day upon the face of the earth," he declared, "were it not because those who possess them, and those who prostitute their arms to their defense do suppress, repress, mercilessly and inescapably every effort of liberation of each and all the rebels." Given that situation, given that those in power "never had pity for our children, our women, our dear, poor old fathers and mothers—and they never will have it," the struggle needed to continue. But Vanzetti made it equally clear that he hated violence.

> The more I live, the more I suffer, the more I learn, the more I am inclined to forgive, to be generous, and that the violence as such does not resolve the problem of life. And the more I love and learn that "the right of all to violence does not go together with liberty, but that it begins when liberty ends." The slave has the right and duty to arise against his master. My supreme aim, that of the Anarchist is, "the complete elimination of violence from [human relations]."

Even when justified, violence was the enemy of liberty. His supreme aim, as an anarchist, was the elimination of all forms of violence, but especially the violence of the oppressors against the oppressed.

The issue for him, after all, Vanzetti reiterated to Blackwell, was his dream of a different future:

> To be possible, we must have freedom and justice. Now we have the opposite of them, because through errors and consequent aberrations, men have risen as tyrants, deceivers and exploiters of other men, believing to gain their personal, familiar and cast welfare by such a deed. Through both tyranny and

servitude, we have lost our capacity of liberty and we are making life ever-more miserable, operating our own ante-destruction.

In his own way Vanzetti was anticipating later twentieth-century revolutionary theory. The lack of freedom and justice came not only from the tyrants; through servitude also women and men had lost their capacity to think and dream as free people, had lost their capacity for liberty. The key to freedom was freedom, the key to liberty was liberty, and he and his fellow anarchists would not rest until that door was unlocked. "Until not a man will be exploited or oppressed by another man, we will never bend the banner of freedom." With this commitment, he also knew what he hoped for. The details of his own case were secondary to him. The injustice and mistreatment he experienced were secondary to him.

> The only vengeance which could placate me is the realization of freedom, the great deliverance which would beneficiate all my friends as well as all my enemies: All. But till that, the struggle goes on, till we are breath to breath with the enemy fighting with short arms, till then, to fight is our duty, our right, our necessity. . . . Either we must go on and win, or we must ask for an armistice. And who will grant it to us? Since the enemy has no scruples nor pity, to ask pity of him is to encourage him to slander our fellows, to try to grant to him the immunity for his crime against us.

For all his implacable opposition to his oppressors, Vanzetti in the end wanted the realization of freedom for all, his friends and his enemies. For if the divide of oppressed and oppressor were abolished, if anarchism could come, then both could grow in the new liberty that he dreamed.[5]

There is little reason to doubt the sincerity of Vanzetti's words. Unlike their defenders, neither Sacco nor Vanzetti had much hope that their case could be won. In the same letter Vanzetti said of Judge Thayer, "No matter how much sympathy I try to bestow upon him, or with how much understanding I try to judge his actions, I only and alone can see him a self-conceited narrow-minded little tyrant. . . . He is a bigot, and therefore cruel."[6] Those were hardly the words of someone trying to curry favor with the courts. On the night of his execution, Nicola Sacco expressed a similar view. In reporting their last interview, William G. Thompson, who had worked hard to win freedom for the two, reported Sacco's gentleness with him:

> It was magnanimous in him [Sacco] not to refer more specifically to our previous differences of opinion, because at the root of it all lay his conviction, often expressed to me, that all efforts on his behalf, either in court or with

public authorities, would be useless, because no capitalistic society could afford to accord him justice. I had taken the contrary view; but at this last meeting he did not suggest that the result seemed to justify his view and not mine.[7]

It was the magnanimity of someone supremely confident of his own view of the world and of what the future eventually held. It was also the magnanimity of an extraordinarily gentle soul.

Given the public attention that the case received and the symbolic power it acquired, it is not surprising that many people hung other interpretations and hopes on the two men. While, as good anarchists, Sacco and Vanzetti had no use for religion, they were portrayed as Christ-like by many, perhaps most powerfully by Ben Shahn who painted "the Passion of Sacco and Vanzetti" and for whom they were another example of redemptive suffering. For others their execution was the end of hope. Katherine Anne Porter, waiting with the crowd outside of Charlestown Prison, said that she felt as if "we were all of us soiled and disgraced and would never in this world live it down."[8] Roberta Strauss Feuerlicht tells of her Jewish-immigrant parents waiting on the tenement steps in the Lower East Side of New York and weeping together when news of the execution reached them.[9] For many who had fought so hard for their defense—hoping that they could strike a blow for anarchism, hoping that the world of the immigrants would be redeemed, hoping that the American judicial system would be proved just—it seemed that hope died that August evening.

In the end, however, Sacco and Vanzetti themselves gave the world a clear statement of their own hopes, of the meaning of their case, their lives, and their cause. In May 1927, just after their final death sentence, Vanzetti told Philip Stong, a young journalist who visited him in the Dedham jail, how he wanted to be remembered:

If it had not been for these things, I might have lived out my life talking at street corners to scorning men. I might have died, unmarked, unknown, a failure. Now we are not failures. This is our career and our triumph. Never in our full lives could we hope to do such work for tolerance, for justice, for man's understanding of man as now we do by accident. Our words—our lives—our pains—nothing! The taking of our lives—lives of a good shoemaker and a poor fish-peddler—all! That last moment belongs to us—that agony is our triumph.[10]

It was a triumph in the midst of despair that has kept the hope of a better, gentler, freer future alive for three-quarters of a century.

MARCUS GARVEY
AND THE UNIVERSAL NEGRO
IMPROVEMENT ASSOCIATION

While in the 1920s many, especially in the new urban European immigrant communities of the United States, pinned their future hopes on the ultimate victory of Sacco and Vanzetti; other urban Americans placed their hopes elsewhere. The economic changes surrounding World War I had encouraged a massive migration of African Americans from the rural South, where agriculture no longer needed their labor and where harsh segregation seemed destined to last forever, to the urban North, where job opportunities existed and where segregation, while still omnipresent, seemed at least marginally less brutal. In these northern urban communities of African Americans a new culture was being born and the hope for the future was taking different forms.

For a generation of African-Americans, no one better articulated their hopes than the charismatic Jamaican leader Marcus Garvey. Garvey was born in Jamaica in 1887, where he attended school and then became a printer and officer of the printer's union. In 1910 he visited other nations of the Caribbean and in 1913 and 1914 spent time in London studying British colonialism in the West Indies and around the world. In 1914 he returned to Jamaica and devoted the rest of his life to being an organizer, writer, and speaker for his cause—celebrating and encouraging the racial pride and the economic and political self-determination of people of African origin.

Garvey established the Universal Negro Improvement and Conservation Association and African Communities League—the full name of the UNIA—in Jamaica in August 1914. From the start, Garvey conceived very broad purposes for the organization.

> To establish a Universal Confraternity among the race; to promote the spirit of pride and love; to reclaim the fallen; to administer to and assist the needy; to assist in civilizing the backward tribes of Africa; to assist in the development of Independent Negro Nations and Communities; to establish a central nation for the race; to establish Commissaries or Agencies in the principal countries and cities of the world for the representation of all Negroes; to promote a conscientious Spiritual worship among the native tribes of Africa; to establish Universities, Colleges, Academies and Schools for the racial education and culture of the people; to work for better conditions among Negroes everywhere.[11]

At a time when nearly all of Africa and his own homeland of Jamaica were colonies of European powers, at a time when blacks in the United States faced

some of the most violent bigotry in the form of segregation, economic marginalization, political disenfranchisement, and brutal lynchings, it took an extraordinary leap of faith to even begin to envision the future that Garvey outlined.

Garvey came to the United States for the first time in the spring of 1916,
two years after the formation of the UNIA and at a moment in U.S. history
when both the nation and the position of the African American community
within the nation were changing rapidly. Within a few years Garvey's hopes
and ideas would seem a perfect match for many of the uprooted of African descent in the United States. While he immediately set about trying to build the
American branch of his Jamaica-based UNIA, he had only modest success in
the first couple of years. With the end of World War I, however, things
changed rapidly for Garvey and his cause. Many African Americans, including
another significant leader, W. E. B. DuBois, had supported Wilson's war effort
in the hope that they would be rewarded in the postwar years. The support
was appreciated but the rewards for the African American community failed to
materialize. African American troops had experienced segregation and second-
class status in the army, but a warm welcome in Europe itself, especially in
France, where many for the first time experienced a level of social equity that
made it all the more difficult to return to the segregation of their homeland.
During and after the war the northern cities that had seemed to hold new
hopes were racked by race riots. In 1917 in East St. Louis, Illinois, at least
forty African Americans were murdered by whites angry about blacks getting
jobs in wartime industries. The riots continued elsewhere across the country.
In the summer and fall of 1919, while white radicals were being arrested and
deported, blacks were being attacked in many places, including Washington,
D.C. In Chicago a riot that began with a drowning of an African American
youth in Lake Michigan on July 27, 1919, led to days of violence and at least
thirty-eight African American deaths, hundreds of injuries, and the burning of
many homes. In the South the Ku Klux Klan was reborn and lynchings were
increasing. It was an ugly time across the nation.[12]

In this desperate situation, Garvey's message of rejecting integration with
white America and turning instead to self-help, self-determination, and African
nationalism struck a powerful chord, especially among many of the poorest and
most marginalized blacks. Whereas the National Association for the Advancement of Colored People and the National Urban League were seen as elite, the
Universal Negro Improvement Association was seen as universal by many. At
the beginning of 1918 the New York branch of the UNIA had about 1,500
members; during the next three years it grew with amazing rapidity, so that by
1920 Garvey was claiming a membership of two to four million in thirty
branches across the country. While Garvey and the organization were never

strong on record keeping or organizational details, there is no question that many thousands—probably half a million people—joined the UNIA and many more were responding positively to the hopes offered by Garvey.[13]

Garvey was extraordinarily consistent in outlining his own hopes for the future of the African race. During this period of his greatest success Garvey outlined "The Future As I See It." The UNIA, Garvey said, asserted, "the readiness of the Negro to carve out a pathway for himself in the course of life." This independent pathway involved no "hating other people," but it did clearly involve independence, separation, and taking responsibility for their own fate.

> We are organized for the absolute purpose of bettering our condition, industrially, commercially, socially, religiously and politically. We are organized not to hate other men, but to lift ourselves, and to demand respect of all humanity. We have a program that we believe to be righteous; we believe it to be just, and we have made up our minds to lay down ourselves on the altar of sacrifice for the realization of this great hope of ours, based upon the foundation of righteousness. We declare to the world that Africa must be free, that the entire Negro race must be emancipated from industrial bondage, peonage and serfdom; we make no compromise, we make no apology in this our declaration. We do not desire to create offense on the part of other races, but we are determined that we shall be heard, that we shall be given the rights to which we are entitled.[14]

Through the UNIA, Garvey insisted, Africans from around the world would establish their independence as a nation and as a people. It would take courage; it would take a rejection of the blandishments of integrationists for whom Garvey had no use. The future for Garvey was not coexistence in the United States or anywhere else, but rather an African homeland, governed by Africans for Africans.

> Men of the Negro race, let me say to you that a greater future is in store for us; we have no cause to lose hope, to become faint-hearted. We must realize that upon ourselves depend our destiny, our future; we must carve out that future, that destiny, and we who make up the Universal Negro Improvement Association have pledged ourselves that nothing in the world shall stand in our way, nothing in the world shall discourage us, but opposition shall make us work harder, shall bring us closer together so that as one man the millions of us will march on toward that goal that we have set for ourselves.[15]

Here was hope, indeed.

John Cartwright, the Martin Luther King Jr. Professor Emeritus at Boston University, has said that the great choice facing African Americans, and probably many other marginalized groups in the United States, is between wanting in (seeking integration and full citizenship) and wanting out.[16] Garvey clearly was the voice of wanting out through rigidly separate social and economic development and ultimately through a return to the ancestral lands of Africa. In surprising ways Garvey saw himself as an heir to the ideas of the more accommodationist Booker T. Washington, though Garvey placed *much* more emphasis on the separate social development advocated by Washington than on any of Washington's talk of unity. Certainly Garvey was an unyielding foe of the integrationists of the NAACP and especially W. E. B. DuBois who fully returned the hostility. Garvey declared, "Let the Negro have a country of his own. Help him return to his original home, Africa, and there give him the opportunity to climb from the lowest to the highest positions in a state of his own." Garvey also warned white America that this was an appeal for justice and, if not heeded, then "the nation will have to hearken to the demand of the aggressive 'social equality' organization, known as the National Association for the Advancement of Colored People, of which W. E. B. DuBois is leader, which declares vehemently for social and political equality."[17]

Garvey was at the height of his popularity in the early 1920s. In 1919 the UNIA purchased a large auditorium at 114 West 138th Street in New York City's Harlem, which served as the organization's permanent headquarters and rallying point. In August 1920 the UNIA hosted a massive international convention that adopted a Negro Declaration of Rights. A UNIA parade in Harlem presented the organization at its most colorful, with the men of the African Legion in uniform and a delegation of 200 women of the Black Cross Nurses marching with many others in a show of strength and pride. Delegates came from Africa as well as from all of the Americas and 25,000 gathered in Madison Square Garden on August 2, 1920, for the beginning of the convention. Garvey told the Madison Square Garden rally: "We are the descendants of a suffering people; we are the descendants of a people determined to suffer no longer. . . . We do not desire what has belonged to others, though others have always sought to deprive us of that which belonged to us. . . . If Europe is for the Europeans, then Africa shall be for the black peoples of the world. We say it; we mean it . . . it is time for the 400,000,000 Negroes to claim Africa for themselves.[18] It was a powerful claim and it gave people a sense of strength, pride, and confidence that was sadly lacking in the United States of the 1920s.

There would be other successes, but that convention was the high point of the movement. Garvey was deeply committed to economic self-determination. Anticipating by a quarter century the efforts of the Nation of Islam, the UNIA set up cooperatives in the African American community to sell groceries, clothing, and other services. The crown jewel of the economic development effort, the Black Star Line, was also Garvey's downfall. The line was launched in 1920 and eventually owned a number of ships. Garvey was determined to develop an international shipping company that would carry passengers and freight between the United States, the islands of the Caribbean, and Africa, and make money for its investors. Selling stock at $5 per share, Garvey eventually collected over $750,000, perhaps much more. It was an extraordinary outpouring of hope and confidence from a terribly poor community. The project was also a disaster. Whether through mismanagement or corruption, or probably a good bit of both, the shipping line totally floundered.

The Black Star Line's business plans were attacked by blacks as well as whites. As early as December 1920, W. E. B. DuBois published a detailed indictment of the management of the Black Star Line based on his own analysis of its financial reports. With the rapid collapse of the Black Star Line came the collapse of the rest of Garvey's U.S.-based efforts. He was arrested for using the mails to defraud, selling Black Star stock through "fraudulent representations" after he knew that the line was bankrupt. He was tried in federal court, convicted, and sentenced to five years in federal prison in 1923. He had two more years of freedom while the case was on appeal, but in February 1925 he began serving his term in the Atlanta Federal Penitentiary; where Debs had also served. In November 1927 President Calvin Coolidge commuted Garvey's sentence but had him deported immediately to Jamaica. For the next decade Garvey continued to build the UNIA in Jamaica and traveled through much of the world, but his power and prestige were gone. He died in London in 1940 and was buried there; in 1964 his remains were returned to Jamaica and reburied in the Marcus Garvey Memorial in Kingston.[19]

While he was serving time in the federal penitentiary in Atlanta in 1925, Garvey wrote an editorial for the UNIA newspaper, *The Negro World*, urging his followers to "forget and cast behind . . . hero worship and adoration of other races, and to start out immediately, to create and emulate . . . our own saints, create our own martyrs, and elevate to positions of fame and honor black men and women who have made their distinct contributions to our racial history." He continued:

> We must inspire a literature and promulgate a doctrine of our own without any apologies to the powers that be. The right is ours and God's. Let contrary sentiment and cross opinions go to the winds. Opposition to race independence is the weapon of the enemy to defeat the hopes of an unfortunate people. We are entitled to our own opinions and not obligated to or bound by the opinions of others.

Let the sky and God be our limit, and Eternity our measurement. There is no height to which we cannot climb by using the active intelligence of our own minds. . . . Remember, we live, work and pray for the establishing of a great and binding RACIAL HIERARCHY, the founding of a RACIAL EMPIRE whose only natural, spiritual and political limits shall be God and "Africa at home and abroad."[20]

The spirit of that editorial—the call for the African American community to have its own saints, its own literature, its own ideas, as well as its own land—was Garvey's greatest gift of hope to the African American community at a time when hope was a very scarce commodity.

Marcus Garvey's business dealings were shaky at best, yet he launched a spirit of self-help and self-dependence that flourished later in the century. His confidence that African Americans and African Caribbean peoples would be welcome in a postcolonial Africa was not confirmed by many Africans, and few African Americans really wanted to move. Nevertheless, he anticipated black pride and African nationalism by more than a quarter century. He organized the first nationwide mass movement of African Americans. Perhaps the greatest tribute to him is the fact that so many leaders of the later civil rights movements, especially leaders in the urban North, will in moments of quiet reflection trace their earliest interest in their own rights and their earliest assertions of their own pride as Africans to a parent, grandparent, or other family member or friend who was a Garveyite in the 1920s.[21] It is a powerful legacy indeed.

W. E. B. DuBois

W. E. B. DuBois was perhaps Marcus Garvey's toughest critic. DuBois looked to a future based on a different foundation than Garvey's. Garvey was right: DuBois would not rest until he had found full citizenship, full equality, and the right to make his full intellectual and political contribution within the American culture that had been so oppressive to him and his ancestors for three centuries.

William Edward Burghardt DuBois was never a voice of the grassroots of the African American community, yet he is acknowledged by many as the greatest African American intellectual of the twentieth century, the person who described black life as it was in the early years of the century and did so much to expand what it could be. Slowly and painfully—and with many different allies—he laid the basis for the great civil rights movement of the 1960s. DuBois's own life spanned the century before the movement. He was born three years after the end of the Civil War, in 1868, and died, literally, on the eve of the great March on Washington in 1963.

DuBois was born and grew up in the small town of Great Barrington, Massachusetts, in a nearly all white community far from the heartland of African Americans. He left the North for the first time to attend Fisk University in 1885, where he learned much from his academic experience and from his immersion in the life of the segregated South. He remembered his departure: "I was going to the South, the South of slavery, rebellion and black folk; above all, I was going to meet the colored people of my own age and education, of my own ambition." After studying at Fisk, DuBois returned to Massachusetts and took a second baccalaureate degree at Harvard in 1890. He studied in Berlin and received his Ph.D. from Harvard in 1895. The primary work of the rest of his life was as an academic. He taught at Atlanta University from 1897 to 1910, served as editor of the NAACP's journal, *The Crisis*, from 1910 to 1934, and again taught at Atlanta University from 1934 to 1944. In 1944 he rejoined the NAACP and in the 1950s, having decided to dedicate "the remaining years of [his] active life" to fighting racism and colonialist imperialism, he clashed increasingly with the United States government as another round of anti-Communist hysteria was at its height. In 1961 he moved to Ghana where he died three years later at the age of ninety-four.[22]

For all of his extraordinary output, DuBois's best-known work remains one published in 1903, very early in his life, *The Souls of Black Folk*. In the forty years between the end of slavery and the publication of that book, the bright promises of freedom had faded to the ugly mix of rigid segregation, political disenfranchisement, economic depravation, and a harsh racism that permeated the culture of the country, South and North, all reinforced by lynchings, riots, and other forms of violence. DuBois was determined to use education and scholarship to fuel the process of changing all of that, starting with a description that would make it impossible for white or black America to ignore the reality.[23]

DuBois began *Souls of Black Folk* with the prophetic words, "the problem of the Twentieth Century is the problem of the color line."[24] The book, part poetry and part prose, is an attack on what he saw as the frustrating and ultimately destructive caution of Booker T. Washington, a historical analysis of the work of the Freedmen's Bureau, and a sociological study of the turn-of-the-century South. At its heart, however, is DuBois's analysis of what it means to be black in America.

[T]he Negro is a sort of seventh son, born with a veil, and gifted with second-sight in this American world—a world which yields him no true self-consciousness, but only lets him see himself through the revelation of the other world. It is a peculiar sensation this double-consciousness, this sense of always looking at one's self through the eyes of others, of measuring one's soul by the tape of a world that looks on in amused contempt and pity. One ever feels his two-ness,—an American, a Negro; two souls, two thoughts, two unreconciled strivings; two warring ideals in one dark body, whose dogged strength alone keeps it from being torn asunder.[25]

In that passage DuBois described a reality experienced by many who had lived it but not named it.

In expressing that reality, DuBois was also exposing black America to a dangerous hope. He wrote, "The history of the American Negro is the history of this strife,—this longing to attain self-conscious manhood, to merge his double self into a better and truer self."[26] One southern newspaper of the day warned, "This book is dangerous for the Negro to read, for it will only excite discontent and fill his imagination with things that do not exist, or things that should not bear upon his mind." [27] That was exactly what DuBois intended, to do the dangerous work of raising hopes and filling people's imaginations with things that might exist if their hopes could be fulfilled.

In 1905 DuBois along with William Monroe Trotter of Boston and others called a meeting of African American leaders determined to move beyond the caution of Washington. They met at Niagara Falls, Canada, and created what became known as the Niagara Movement, a group committed to aggressive action for full freedom of speech, suffrage, and basic human rights for all African Americans. When the group met again in 1906, DuBois wrote a preface to their resolutions that described the current state of the nation: "In the past year the work of the Negro hater has flourished in the land. Step by step the defenders of the rights of American citizens have retreated. . . . Never before in the modern age has a great and civilized folk threatened to adopt so cowardly a creed in the treatment of its fellow-citizens, born and bred on its soil."[28] The Niagara Movement meant to challenge and change that and do so quickly.

In 1909 a group of white reformers, including the social worker Mary White Ovington and Oswald Garrison Villard, grandson of William Lloyd Garrison, also realizing the seriousness of what was happening in the country, called a meeting "for the discussion of present evils, the voicing of protests, and the renewal of the struggle for civil and political liberty." The radicals of the Niagara Movement were invited and the majority, led by DuBois, attended and together they created the National Association for the Advancement of Colored People. The integrated organization pledged themselves to end all forms of segregation, to complete enfranchisement of African Americans, and to equal educational opportunity. Incremental as the initial NAACP goals may seem in retrospect, in America in 1909 they represented a radical hope that only a few people, black and white, were willing to announce.

DuBois himself always lived in tension with the NAACP, sometimes pushing it to go farther and faster than the organization was willing to go, at other times, especially as editor of its journal, *The Crisis*, serving as its primary spokesperson. But in his work with the NAACP, in his work as a scholar, in his life as a public speaker and prodder of others, and finally as an exile in Africa, DuBois always held to his absolute commitment to freedom and equity without compromise.[29]

The last chapter of *Souls of Black Folk* is devoted to what DuBois called "the Sorrow Songs," the songs by which slaves and their descendants shared their pain and their grief, maintained the music and rhythm of Africa, and shared their hope for a new day to come, in this world or the next. "They that walked in darkness sang songs in the olden days—Sorrow Songs—for they were weary at heart," DuBois said. He knew that as a young man living in the North, far from the land in which the songs were born, they touched him deeply. They connected him to something ancient in his own family and his race. "The songs are indeed the siftings of centuries; the music is far more ancient than the words, and in it we can trace here and there signs of development." The music allowed the African chant to stay alive in an American "voice of exile." Yet it was not just the music. The words too were important; words of pain and words of hope; poetic words that had helped shape a people. And so, DuBois concluded, it would be through these words of pain and hope that the future might yet be won.

> Even so is the hope that sang in the songs of my fathers well sung. If somewhere in this whirl and chaos of things there dwells Eternal Good, pitiful yet masterful, then anon in His good time America shall rend the Veil and the prisoned shall go free. Free, free as the sunshine trickling down the morning into these high windows of mine, free as yonder fresh young voices welling up to me from the caverns of brick and mortar below—swelling with song, instinct with life, tremulous treble and darkening bass. My children, my little children, are singing to the sunshine, and thus they sing:

> > Let us cheer the weary traveler,
> > Cheer the weary traveler, Let us
> > Cheer the weary traveler A-
> > Long the heavenly way.

> And the traveler girds himself, and sets his face toward the Morning and goes his way.[30]

THE NEW DEAL

In the fall of 1929 the American economy fell apart. The crash of the Wall Street stock market on Black Tuesday, October 29, was the powerful symbol of the crisis, but in reality a sizable number of Americans, perhaps as many as half—farmers and farm workers, factory workers, and others—had been living on the edge of poverty throughout the 1920s, while the basic underpinnings of the American economy, including banking and international trade, were surprisingly fragile. When the economy came apart, it came apart thoroughly and, unlike other business downturns, things continued to get worse and worse. By 1932 farms across the country had been foreclosed—and more would have been had not armed groups of farmers banded together to prevent the sales—factories were closed across the country, one out of three people were out of work and many were living in shanties or Hoovervilles on the edges of the nation's cities, the unemployed were riding the rails or waiting on bread lines, and the entire banking system seemed on the verge of collapse.[31]

In that desperate situation, probably the most desperate economic moment in American history, Franklin Delano Roosevelt defeated the incumbent president, Herbert Hoover, by a landslide. And at his inauguration on March 4, 1933, the new president told the nation:

> This is preeminently the time to speak the truth, the whole truth, frankly and boldly. Nor need we shrink from honestly facing conditions in our country today. This great Nation will endure as it has endured, will revive and will prosper. So, first of all, let me assert my firm belief that the only thing we have to fear is fear itself—nameless, unreasoning, unjustified terror which paralyzes needed efforts to convert retreat into advance.[32]

In that speech, Roosevelt did not merely excoriate "fear itself," however. He stated clearly that he was ready to act. He also made it clear, in language no political leader of any party would use today, who was to blame for the current crisis. Roosevelt said of the industrial and business leaders:

> Nature still offers her bounty and human efforts have multiplied it. Plenty is at our doorstep, but a generous use of it languishes in the very sight of the supply. Primarily this is because rulers of the exchange of mankind's goods have failed through their own stubbornness and their own incompetence, have admitted their failure, and have abdicated. Practices of the unscrupulous money changers stand indicted in the court of public opinion, rejected by the hearts and minds of men.[33]

In the days and weeks that followed, Roosevelt proclaimed a New Deal in American political life and began use his executive authority to take drastic action while also proposing one piece of economic legislation after another to a cautious Congress.[34]

Roosevelt had a magnetic, optimistic personality and he made effective use of the relatively new media of the radio with frequent "fireside chats" and press conferences. The bank holiday that he declared on his third day in office was the beginning of rebuilding the nation's banking system. His administration quickly began a series of programs to control the banks and the stock market and to foster agricultural and industrial recovery. The National Recovery Act of June 1933 was more than symbolism; it set a minimum wage and minimum prices, outlawed child labor, and guaranteed organized labor the right to organize in new occupations. The "We Do Our Part," NRA signs that sprouted in windows across the nation were, in themselves, symbols of hope.[35] And perhaps the New Deal's greatest legacy was in the area of social insurance for retired and unemployed citizens. The Social Security Act of 1935 created the pension system on which nearly all Americans now rely for support in their retirement. This too is a direct result of the New Deal.[36] Perhaps never before or since has a president's personal optimism and activism done so much so quickly to give hope to millions.

One of the great ironies is that for all of the ways in which Roosevelt's own actions and the New Deal that he led changed the country, they did not end the Great Depression. While banks were stabilized and programs like the Civilian Conservation Corps provided work to some of the unemployed, and the role of the federal government in all aspects of the American economy expanded dramatically, the American economy was still in bad shape throughout the decade of the 1930s. Only with the beginning of the war economy in the late 1930s and its massive new federal spending that created jobs in industry after industry did the Great Depression really come to an end.

Historians in the 1930s and in every decade since have argued about the nature of the New Deal; to what degree it truly changed and improved the lives of working Americans and to what degree it protected capitalism from much more far-reaching changes that were being advocated by many. The radical southern activist and educator Myles Horton was probably very close to the truth when he described the New Deal as a time when, "Franklin Roosevelt would force the capitalists to take some bitter pills and get themselves in control again." But he was also right in saying that such a description represented a retrospective analysis. At the time, Horton, like many other radicals and like many average citizens, found great hope in the president's words and deeds. "We had an uncritical feeling that we could change the system, based partly on a lack of understanding of the power of capitalism. . . . Those of us who supported Roosevelt didn't think we were backing a guy who would be carrying a bunch of pills around for the system. In doing it he did a lot of good things, but he had to have the forces of labor to do what he wanted to do."[37] As Horton also noted, throughout the Depression years, while the federal government was a source of hope and support to many, the sources of hope in hard times were numerous and some of the most powerful had little to do with the direct sponsorship of the federal government and much more to do with others who were willing to take direct action themselves.[38]

ORGANIZED LABOR:
THE CIO AND THE GREAT SIT-DOWN
AT FLINT

Many in the labor movement had decidedly mixed feelings about Roosevelt and the New Deal. There is no question that the National Industrial Recovery Act of June 1933, the primary purpose of which was to stabilize prices, also—at Roosevelt's insistence—included a clause recognizing workers' rights to bargain collectively through unions. This was followed by the Wagner Labor Act of 1935 that further guaranteed unionized workers rights that they had never held before, including collective bargaining without interference and the right to strike. For the next decade workers and unions could be relatively sure that at a minimum the federal government would not directly intervene in a strike on the side of management as they had done many times during the previous half-century. But many wanted and expected so much more. And relatively quickly they decided that they needed to act to make their hopes a reality.[39]

No group of Americans set to work more quickly or effectively than the workers in some of the nation's basic industries, especially the steel, electrical, and automobile industries. In 1935 when the Wagner Act was passed guaranteeing all workers the right to bargain collectively and to strike, only about ten percent of American workers were labor union members, mostly in the better-off craft unions of the American Federation of Labor (AFL). A number of union leaders within the AFL, most notably John L. Lewis of the United Mine Workers of America, Sidney Hillman of the Amalgamated Clothing Workers, and David Dubinsky of the International Ladies' Garment Workers Union, pushed hard for the AFL to begin to organize the unorganized and to do so along the lines of the IWW decades before. Lewis and his colleagues wanted industrial unions that would organize all of the workers in an industry, whether in steel or automobiles or textiles—rather than the much smaller craft unions of the AFL that organized one trade—the carpenters, the plumbers, the electricians—at a time. But the leadership of the AFL would have none of it; they had organized the elite of the work force and they meant to protect their workers.

In a bitter split, Lewis, Hillman, Dubinsky, and others called a meeting of a new organization, the CIO, the Committee for Industrial Organization. At the October 1935 meeting of the AFL in Atlantic City, William Hutchenson of the Carpenter's Union called Lewis a 'big bastard" and a "Red." Lewis, in a step he later admitted he had carefully planned, walked across the stage and punched Hutchenson in the nose. A clearer symbol of the split would have been hard to find. Nevertheless, for a little while longer, Lewis and his colleagues continued to proclaim their intent to organize "the unorganized workers in the mass production and other industries upon an industrial basis . . . to bring them under the banner and in affiliation with the American Federation of Labor." But by the time they said this, in November of 1935, everyone knew that their emphasis was on the first half of their statement— that they were going to organize the unorganized in industry after industry with or without the blessing of the AFL. Soon thereafter, the Committee for Industrial Organization became the Congress of Industrial Organizations, a million-member competitor to the AFL.[40]

John L. Lewis, founding president of the CIO, could be tough, arbitrary, arrogant, self-absorbed, and exceedingly difficult to deal with. He also was able to spark hope in the minds of the nation's workers as no one since Debs and Mother Jones had been able to do. In July of the crucial year 1936 Lewis said:

> Let him who will, be he economic tyrant or sordid mercenary, pit his strength against this mighty surge of human sentiment now being crystallized in the hearts of thirty millions of workers who clamor for the establishment of industrial democracy and for participation in its tangible fruits. He is a madman or fool who believes that this river of human sentiment, flowing as it does from the hearts of these thirty millions, who with their dependents constitute two-thirds of the population of the United States of America, can be dammed or impounded by the erection of arbitrary barriers of restraint.[41]

It was Lewis's genius to both understand and lead what he knew was by 1936 a "mighty surge of human sentiment" that was about to change much of the industrial heartland of America.

In a matter of a few months after the first meeting of the CIO in November 1935, workers began joining by the thousands and, even before they had joined, launched a new CIO-style strike—the sit-down strike. Instead of walking off the job and onto the picket lines, as they had since the days of the Lawrence strike at the turn of the century, CIO-inspired workers simply stopped work and sat down where they were. In doing so they guaranteed that they could not be replaced by scabs and that they were hard to attack without also attacking the machinery that they were guarding. They were also much more comfortable inside the plant than outside. It turned out to be a brilliant shift in tactics. There had been a few sit-down strikes before, including one inspired by the IWW in 1906, but in general the sit-down was a new tactic and it took the nation, and the workers in the basic industries, by storm.[42]

The first big sit-down strike took place in Akron, Ohio, at the Firestone Tire Plant No. 1 on January 29, 1936. The workers, some of whom had already joined the CIO and others who were only thinking about it, had agreed, with successful secrecy, that at 2 A.M. on the night shift they would stop the assembly line and sit down where they were. At one moment the workers simply stopped. After the noise of the assembly line stopped one worker was reported to have said, "Jesus Christ, it's like the end of the world." It was the end of the world for industrial giants used to having their way with no need to negotiate with their workers regarding the speed of the line, job security, the rate at which workers would be paid or promoted, or their right to organize a union. The Firestone workers stayed where they were for three days and they won their strike, the end of a speed-up, and the right to a CIO union. The sit-down was clearly a winning strategy. It offered hope for victories when there had been only defeats. The idea spread like wildfire.[43]

Workers across the country tried the same tactic. The CIO reported a surge of telephone calls, "We've sat down! Send someone over to organize us!" From September 1936 through the following spring, 485,000 workers were reported to have engaged in sit-down strikes. The CIO, which had begun with one-million members in its six founding unions, doubled to two-million members in six months. A United Auto Workers song gave a sense of the confidence and joy of the moment:

When the speed-up comes, just twiddle your thumbs,
 Sit down! Sit down!
When the boss won't talk, don't take a walk,
 Sit down! Sit down![44]

For most assembly line workers in the 1930s, the primary complaint was not salary per se. As one Chevrolet worker told a National Recovery Administration investigator in 1934, "Of course, we make enough to live on while we are working, but we don't work enough time."[45] Irregular employment and constant layoffs undermined workers incomes and, even more, undermined their sense of security. There might be enough work, and enough income, in any month. But no one working in the steel or auto industry or in the other mass production industries could ever rest secure. "People were longing for some kind of security in their work," one local organizer for the auto workers said, and the CIO was the vehicle for providing it.[46]

Along with insecurity, workers on assembly lines complained about constant speed-ups. Indeed, most of those who participated in the sit-down strikes of 1936 and 1937 said the speed-up was the primary reason for their strikes. In an assembly-line industry the pace of the line ruled everything else. As a Buick worker complained to a federal investigator, "We didn't even have time to go to the toilet. . . . You have to run to the toilet and run back. If you had to . . . take a crap, if there wasn't anybody there to relieve you, you had to run away and tie the line up, and if you tied the line up you got hell for it." A straw boss at Chevrolet complained, "they keep rushing me to crowd the men more." But few supervisors complained. A Flint Chevrolet worker remembered, "The supervisors that they chose at that time were just people with a bullwhip, so to speak. All they were interested in was production. They treated us like a bunch of coolies. 'Get it out. Get it out. If you cannot get it out, there are people outside who will get it.' That was their whole theme." One of the leaders of the sit-down at Flint's Fisher Body No. 2, the scene of some of the toughest fighting over a sit-down, said it most clearly, "I ain't got no kick on wages, but I just don't like to be drove."[47] It was the hope that they could gain more control over their work and their work lives, and the absolute commitment that they were going to accomplish their goal no matter what the cost, that inspired the courage of workers who stopped the line, sat down where they were, and prepared to defend themselves and their position come what may.

In the winter of 1936–1937, a lot came the way of the sit-down strikers. On December 30, 1936, workers in two of General Motors' main production units, the huge Fisher Body Plant No. 1 and the smaller neighboring Fisher Body Plant No. 2 stopped the line and sat down where they were. By January 4, 1937, workers were sitting in at GM plants in Cleveland, Ohio, Atlanta, Georgia, Anderson, Indiana, Norwood, Ohio, and Kansas City, Missouri, as well as in the huge Flint plants. It was the beginning of a long cold winter of struggle that eventually won recognition of the United Auto Workers by General Motors. But as they began the new year of 1937 inside the plants, the GM workers were by no means sure of victory. All they could be sure of was that a battle lay ahead.[48]

On January 11, with the sit-down still in full force, the first big battle came. The temperature in Flint had dropped to 16 degrees Fahrenheit. The workers in the smaller Fisher Body No. 2 plant were getting cold and discouraged. Early in the afternoon the GM management turned off the heat in the plant

which up to that point had been left on. A short time later plant security officers removed a ladder to the second floor which had been used to get in and
out. Then at 6 P.M., for the first time company police blocked a delivery of
food. Things were going to get desperate very quickly. Soon a group of about
thirty strikers went to the main gate and broke through a police lock to get to
the picket line of supporters outside. For a brief moment strikers and supporters celebrated and sang together. But the company police called the Flint police
to report that they were in danger, and before the strikers could return to the
plant, a phalanx of Flint police attacked them with tear gas and also fired tear
gas into the plant. Strikers responded by throwing door hinges, bottles, and
stones, "popular ammunition" as they called it, at the attacking police. It was a
battle royal or as the UAW came to call it "the Battle of the Running Bulls." In
time the wind shifted and blew the tear gas back on the police; that and the
continuing hail of missiles from the plant drove them back, but also infuriated
them and they began shooting at strikers and pickets. It was a terror-filled
evening but amazingly no one was killed, though many were injured by the battle or the profuse tear gas. The young wife of one striker, Genora Johnson, who
was herself on the picket line, said later, "I did not know fear. I knew only surprise, anguish, and anger." At the time of the police attack she had yelled at the
police, "Cowards, Cowards! . . . Shooting unarmed and defenseless men." She
also told the other women on the picket line to stand firm, although she warned
that if the police were cowardly enough to shoot unarmed men, they would also
shoot women picketers. At the same time, Victor Reuther, one of three Reuther
brothers among the leaders of the UAW organizers kept encouraging the strikers from a sound truck. Another union official said Reuther's voice provided
"one steady unswerving note. . . . It dominated everything! . . . [It was] like an
inexhaustible, furious flood, pouring courage into the men." The courage of
Reuther, Johnson, and the workers who stood on the picket lines and in the
plant was an extraordinary expression of hope that won the day. In spite of the
tear gas, the bullets, and the violence, the sit-down was not dislodged. Still, it
would be another month before the strike ended.[49]

Everyone in the union and in the General Motors management agreed on
one thing, the key to the strike was the ability of those conducting the sit-in to
successfully continue it. GM was banking on their failure, the UAW was
counting on their success. Most of those engaged in the sit-in were not yet
union members and few of them had ever been involved in a strike, much less
a protracted sit-in, before. In the GM factory the nature of the line had tended
to keep workers separated from each other and to keep morale low. With
amazing speed all of that changed with the sit-in. A community was formed
out of the courage, hope, and desperation that had made the sit-in happen.

The workers recorded later that they quickly felt a powerful new sense of solidarity. As one said, "It was like war. The guys with me became my buddies."
The workers elected a strike committee and set up a tight structure of self-
governance. They held daily mass meetings and they sang together. Singing
workers may seem sentimental, but in the cold winter of 1937 it gave the
workers great power as they sang:

> Solidarity forever
> Solidarity forever
> Solidarity forever
> For the Union makes us strong.

The union, and their own action, did make them strong.[50]

The strikers created committees for all of their needs—a committee to secure food and contact with the outside, a committee for contact with the national union representatives, a security committee that patrolled the plant and
more than once caught supervisors attempting to listen in. They also remained ready to defend themselves if they were attacked by police or company
security forces. They improvised weapons of many of the auto parts that were
available to them and the two- to three-pound car-door hinges worked especially well. At one point while Roy Reuther was visiting Fisher Body No. 1 to
bolster the strikers' morale, he also told them to remember that "every thing
hinges on the hinges." Workers also linked their need for discipline with their
need for humor. They created their own court and made sure that it was as entertaining as it was efficient. Strikers that did not perform their assigned duties
were assigned extra duties. But a striker who forgot his credentials was sentenced to give a speech to the assembled workers and to make sure it was
funny. Logistical support tested the workers and the union. Feeding two thousand strikers three meals a day stretched the union kitchen and those who
moved the food in; but they did it for almost two months. Family support was
also essential. Some families did ask husbands and fathers to leave and some
did. More common was the letter of one wife to her husband, "Honey I miss
you dreadfully but I know you are fighting for a good cause." And one husband's letter to his wife that read, "I could of come out wend they went on
strike. But hunny I just thought I join the union and I look pretty yellow if I
didn't stick with them." And while workers did come and go, the majority returned and the strike stuck.[51]

The strike had many leaders: CIO and UAW organizers who came to
Flint, grass-roots leaders who emerged from within the union, and strike committees in each of the plants. Among those leaders were the three brothers

who all played essential roles in the Flint sit-down and who subsequently became among the nation's most important labor leaders—Walter, Roy, and Victor Reuther. All three had been "born in the labor movement"; their father was an organizer for the United Brewery Workers and they had all been involved in Socialist activities of one sort or another. They had worked in the auto industry in Flint—Walter was fired from Ford in 1933 for being an "agitator"—and they had also studied the labor movement at what would become Wayne State University in Detroit, and Roy also studied at Brookwood Labor College in Katonah, New York, a hotbed of progressive labor organizing that was critical of the AFL's caution. They did not come to the winter of 1936–1937 unprepared. Throughout the strike the brothers seemed to be everywhere—Victor as the leader of those who successfully battled the police attack on Fisher Body No. 2, Roy as the builder of morale and the one to remind them to take care of the hinges, and Walter bringing reinforcements from nearby locals to augment the Flint strikers.[52]

The national unions—the United Auto Workers and the CIO—made it clear that the strikers in Flint were not alone. John L. Lewis wired them that they were

> undoubtedly carrying through one of the most heroic battles that has ever been undertaken by strikers in an industrial dispute. The attention of the entire American public is focused upon you, watching the severe hardships you are suffering in order to demonstrate the strength of labor in the present struggle to organize for the purpose of obtaining a decent standard of living. For every working man in America, every worker and representative of labor in this country owes a debt of gratitude to each of you and I trust that this knowledge will cheer you through your long weary hours of waiting for the honorable settlement which in the nature of things must inevitably come.[53]

For workers who had seen themselves as isolated from each other and certainly from the main currents of Michigan, not to say America, these were heartening words.

And through it all they sang. They sang "Solidarity forever." They made up their own songs:

> Oh Mr. Sloan! [chairman of General Motors] Oh Mr. Sloan!
> Everyone knows your heart was made of stone,
> But the Union is so strong
> That we'll always carry on.
> Absolutely, Mr. Travis! [head of the UAW]
> Positively, Mr. Sloan![54]

Negotiations began in mid-January then broke off. Other workers took over a Chevrolet plant and expanded the sit-in. The negotiations began again. Both the Roosevelt administration and the governor of Michigan urged the negotiations forward and generally supported the union's rights, but the union was in the lead. On February 11 a settlement was reached. General Motors recognized the UAW's right to represent its members, something the company had sworn never to do. It promised to negotiate in good faith on all of the issues that the strikers had put forward and that there would be no punishment of workers because of their "former affiliation with or activities in" the sit-down. The union promised to end the strike and the sit-in and to work cooperatively to return to regular work as soon as possible. One of the men in Fisher No. 1, John Thrasher, recalled the strange feeling of packing up the prosaic things of what had been his home for a month and a half, "house slippers, extra shirt, sox and underwear; razor and shaving equipment; two books, a reading lamp; and the picture of my wife that hung above my bed," and preparing to march in triumph from the plant. He reflected, "The first victory has been ours but the war is not over. We were strong enough to win over the combined forces of our enemies and we shall continue to win only if we remember that through solidarity we have been made free. Now the door is opening."[55] The United Automobile Workers journal said of the February 11 settlement, "The greatest strike in American history has been victoriously concluded." One striker said it more modestly, "Even if we got not one damn thing out of it other than that, we at least had a right to open our mouths without fear."[56] It was, indeed, an extraordinary victory for courage over fear and for hope over despair.

The GM settlement was not the end of the battle to organize the major industries. It was, as Thrasher had said, only the "door opening." Far fiercer fighting took place between the UAW and Ford before Ford recognized its union. And in other industries in the 1930s there were equally tough battles. But the Flint, Michigan, strike settled the basic issue. Workers with enough resolve and enough hope could win. It was a lesson of great power.

MARY MCLEOD BETHUNE, A. PHILIP RANDOLPH, AND THE MARCH ON WASHINGTON

America was a deeply segregated nation before, during, and after the Great Depression. Black and white, Asian and Latino, Americans all suffered during the terrible years of the 1930s, but for the most part they suffered separately. Franklin Roosevelt never demonstrated a deep commitment to the cause of African Americans, although after his inauguration his wife, Eleanor Roosevelt, began taking very strong stands on issues of race, supporting the anti-lynching bill then in Congress and ensuring the appointment of African Americans to powerful positions within the New Deal administration. Like the workers in Flint, the African American community did not wait for the New Deal, but used the opportunities that the New Deal sometimes made possible to further an agenda that had been developing for decades.

No one was more effective in engaging the New Deal to press for African American equality than Mary McLeod Bethune. One of seventeen children born to former slaves in South Carolina in 1875, she was the child sent to school to prepare to teach the others. She used her education in seminary, bible school, and mission school to accomplish her goals and to prepare to be a missionary to Africa. The focus of her work quickly shifted to her own country, however. Bethune was proud of being a descendant of Africans. She opened a school for girls in Daytona, Florida, in 1929 that would become Bethune-Cookman College. Throughout her life, ensuring a quality education for African Americans was one of her passions.[57]

During the 1920s Bethune developed a more widely recognized national profile. She became president of the National Association of Colored Women and used the NACW to advocate for a federal antilynching bill, to help women gain new skills in agriculture and in industry, and to support black women in attending college. Through the NACW she also began her international efforts lobbying for women's rights in Puerto Rico, Haiti, and Africa. Frustrated by what she saw as the conservatism of the NACW, in 1935 she launched the more radical and aggressive National Council of Negro Women. At Eleanor Roosevelt's urging, Bethune was appointed as the director of the Negro Division of the National Youth Administration, where she was able to direct some of the NYA's considerable resources toward creating jobs for African American youth. She also successfully pushed the NYA to create a special scholarship program for African American college students. Bethune used her position in the federal government and her links to Eleanor Roosevelt to unite other African Americans in the Roosevelt administration. She was recognized as a leader of what became known as Roosevelt's Black Cabinet, and she organized a Federal Council of Negro Affairs to ensure that blacks in and out of the administration spoke with one voice. Bethune's own voice was heard. When in 1941 Secretary of War Henry L. Stimson called a conference on organizing women for the war effort and failed to invite black women, she wrote to him, "We are not humiliated. We are incensed."[58] Bethune could be gentle, but she also made it very clear she was not ever going to be ignored.

In 1935 the NAACP awarded Bethune the Springarn Award for her lifetime achievement and she used the occasion of that award to state some of her own hopes and commitments: "The creed of freedom has not yet been written. . . . Let us as workers under this banner make freemen spread truth about economic adjustment; truth about moral obligation; truth about segregation; truth about citizenship; truth about home building; yes, truth wherever truth is needed. Then our lives may be lived with freedom and we shall be what ourselves demand us to be."[59] Bethune never stopped believing in this dream. Twenty years later, in the last months of her life, she wrote in *Ebony* magazine, "The Freedom Gates are half ajar. We must pry them fully open."[60]

On the West Coast, Japanese Americans also organized for their civil rights. In 1938, Ruth Kurata and other Japanese delegates demanded that the Young Democrats of California call for federal laws against racial discrimination and establish their own anti-discrimination council. In 1939, progressives within California's Japanese American community petitioned for state laws for equal rights in housing and employment.[61]

In 1941, as the nation's industrial strength expanded to meet the needs of the looming war effort, and as the Depression passed and unemployment declined, African Americans continued to see themselves excluded from the new prosperity. It was one thing to be out of work when no one had a job. But when more white Americans were employed and were making more money than ever before, the meaning of economic segregation became clearer. As more African Americans sought change, A. Philip Randolph, long-time president of the Brotherhood of Sleeping Car Porters and the nation's most respected African American labor union leader, proposed a massive march on Washington. According to Randolph's plan, 50,000 to 100,000 blacks would march in the nation's capital to demand that the government protect their rights to their fair share of the many new jobs in the wartime economy, which the government was funding. The march was called for July 1, 1941.

As the plans developed, it became clear that the march would be a powerful event, and many people within the administration began to panic. They challenged Randolph's patriotism—How could he do such a thing with war imminent? What will they think in Berlin? Randolph's logical response was, "Oh, perhaps no more than they already think of America's racial policy." Friends within the administration tried to persuade Randolph to postpone the march, but even after a meeting with President Roosevelt, he persisted. The only grounds on which the march could be called off, he said, would be a government order "with teeth in it" that would truly protect the economic rights and opportunities of African Americans in the new industries that were quickly developing and offering so much opportunity to others. In the end, Randolph won. On June 25, 1941, Franklin Roosevelt signed Executive Order 8802 that said, "there shall be no discrimination in the employment of workers in defense industries or Government because of race, creed, color, or national origin. . . . And it is the duty of employers and of labor organizations . . . to provide for the full and equitable participation of all workers in defense industries, without discrimination because of race, creed, color, or national origin."[62] As part of the order, the Fair Employment Practices Committee was set up to ensure that everyone, and especially defense contractors, met their new obligations. It was the order "with teeth in it." The march was called off. To many African Americans at the time, Executive Order 8802 was an economic Emancipation Proclamation. And as with the first Emancipation Proclamation, resistance was strong and ways to resist and undermine the order were many. But Randolph had issued a serious challenge to the government: there would be no turning back on the road to freedom.[63]

A year later, with the United States at war, Randolph called a Policy Conference of the March on Washington Movement in Detroit. He continued to make it clear that there could be no compromise. "Unless this war sounds the death knell to the old Anglo-American empire systems, the hapless story of which is one of exploitation for the profit and power of a monopoly-capitalist economy, it will have been fought in vain," he told the conference. "We must do much more than defeat Nazism. We must also promise that we will not return to the pre-war status quo in either American racism or British imperialism." The people, he continued, "want something more than the dispersal of equality and power among individual citizens in a liberal, political, democratic system. They demand with striking comparability the dispersal of equality and power among the citizen-workers in an economic democracy that will make certain the assurance of the good life—the more abundant life—in a warless world."[64] The dream of Garvey and DuBois, and of Debs and Reuther, Randolph insisted, must be realized for all Americans, and especially for African Americans. Long before Martin Luther King Jr. declared a poor people's march, the dream of an inclusive economic democracy had been proclaimed by Randolph.

HIGHLANDER FOLK SCHOOL AND MYLES HORTON

Many years later, Myles Horton looked back on his decision to create the Highlander Folk School, later known simply as Highlander, in Tennessee. He remembered thinking about the problems facing the country in 1929, especially those experienced by the people of the rural southern mountains, and coming to the conclusion that, "if I was to use education to play any role in changing society, I would have to work with that segment of society that had the power to change society." And he knew where that power, real power to make real change, rested. "It was a very simple matter to know that this segment was composed of working-class people. . . . I made a decision to work with people from the bottom, who could change society from the bottom." To start anywhere else, Horton reasoned, was to create a situation where the real power to change would forever remain with those who already had power. And the kind of changes Horton envisioned, more than anything else, involved changing who had the power in America and how they used that power.[65]

Nevertheless, Horton also understood that not all powerless people had the same potential to bring about change. If he was committed to change, to truly bottom-up change, then he also had to focus on those people who could be expected to make change.

> It made no sense, however, to work with poor people who had given up hope. Only people with hope will struggle. The people who are hopeless are grist for the fascist mill. Because they have no hope, they have nothing to build on. If people are in trouble, if people are suffering and exploited and want to get out from under the heel of oppression, if they have hope that it can be done, if they can see a path that leads to a solution, a path that makes sense then they'll move. But it must be a path that they've started clearing. They've got to know the direction in which they are going and have a general idea of the kind of society they'd like to have. If they don't have hope, they don't even look for a path. They look for somebody else to do it for them.[66]

These thoughts reflected the strategies that Horton would use for the rest of his life and the philosophy of education and social change that would govern him and Highlander for the rest of the twentieth century.

Myles Horton was born in Tennessee in 1905 to a family that had lived in the Appalachian mountains for generations. As he remembered, "We didn't think of ourselves as working-class, or poor, we just thought of ourselves as being conventional people who didn't have any money." He did, however, grow up with parents and grandparents who had pretty strong notions of right and wrong and that in general, "poor people were good and rich people bad." His life philosophy was shaped very strongly by those early years in ways that never changed. His family were Cumberland Presbyterians, and he remembered beginning to question Presbyterian theology. "One day I went to my mother and said, 'I don't know, this predestination doesn't make any sense to me, I don't believe any of this. I guess I shouldn't be in this church.' Mom laughed and said, 'Don't bother about that, that's not important, that's just preachers' talk. The only thing that's important is you've got to love your neighbor.' She didn't say, 'Love God,' she said, 'Love your neighbor, that's all it's about.'" And that remained the focus for Horton. As time went by, religion became less and less important for him, although he always worked closely with religious as well as non-religious people, but love remained central.[67]

As clear as Myles Horton's basic philosophy was, filling in the details took time. In spite of the general poverty, Horton's church encouraged him to attend Cumberland University in Lebanon, Tennessee, which he did from 1924 to 1928. During these years and the following year he also traveled the mountains working for the Student YMCA. The work, more than the college, taught him important lessons about equality, about the violence that poverty did to people, and about listening to people rather than talking at them. In an essay from the 1920s he described what he had been learning:

> For generations men and women have been coming to the Southern Mountains to help us.... There has been advancement, of course, in some instances exceptional advancement, but as a whole, we are still "poor whites," waiting to be helped. It is now time to realize that this will always be true, unless we use our own resources; our intellectual resources within and material resources about us. We must discard out blind faith in help from powers that be—whether manna from heaven, or Red Cross flour.[68]

A solid foundation of economic and social justice could only come, Horton was sure, if the same people who would live with the results built it.

As his ideas were taking shape, Horton went north to study at Union Theological Seminary in New York City in 1929. He studied with and became close to Reinhold Niebuhr, who had by then moved from his pastorate in Detroit to teach social ethics at Union. Horton joined the Socialist Party, picketed for the International Ladies' Garment Workers' Union, was hit on the head by a mounted policeman at a May Day parade, and participated in endless seminars and late night discussions among the seminary's and the city's Depression-era radicals. The following year he continued his studies in Chicago where he had similar experiences at the University of Chicago and was mentored by Jane Addams. From there he went to Denmark to study the Danish folk school movement on which he intended to model his own school. And finally, at the end of 1931, he realized that he had studied long enough; it was time to go back to Tennessee and make it happen.[69]

The core of making it happen for Horton was the creation of a place—Highlander—"a place where people could learn how to make decisions by actually making decisions." Classes and workshops might be offered. Highlander staff would lend their time to educational and organizing drives. At the core would always be the philosophy that as people came together, they could solve problems by thinking and talking them through as a group that they could never solve separately. And the focus of all of this problem solving was "bringing about a new social order."[70]

Highlander had several physical homes, the first of which was a farm near Monteagle, Tennessee. Many people—from old Industrial Workers of the World (Wobblies) and friends from New York and Chicago, to local people who wanted to join in a discussion of local problems or simply participate in the square dancing or receive piano lessons for their children—came through Highlander. Eleanor Roosevelt was there more than once. But Highlander's greatest impact was in its links with two of the great political movements of the twentieth century: "the labor movement of the 1930s and 1940s, and the civil rights movement of the 1950s and 1960s." In its unique way, Highlander was a school for both.[71]

In part because of the IWW influence, some of the people at Highlander began talking about the importance of "one big union," an industrial union, as a way to meet the challenges of the Depression, challenges that the elite craft unions of the AFL clearly were not meeting. It was not surprising that when the CIO was organized as a national union based on the industrial model in the mid-1930s, its leaders turned to Highlander to help with organizing in the South. Horton remembered a call from an officer of the Amalgamated Clothing Workers, one of the founding CIO unions, who said, "We don't know anybody down there," and soon Highlander was the official CIO education center for the entire South.[72]

Zilphia Horton, Myles's first wife, and others on the Highlander staff began collecting oral histories of union activity in the rural South dating back to the Knights of Labor in the 1880s. They also collected folk music and protest music and, like the sit-down strikers at Flint, they came to understand the power of music. Zilphia Horton described a strike of the South Carolina CIO Food and Tobacco Workers Union in Daisy, Tennessee, in 1945:

> We were marching two-by-two with the children in the band. They marched past the mill and 400 machine gun bullets were fired into the midst of the group. A woman on the right of me was shot in the leg, and one on the left was shot in the ankle. . . . Well, in about five minutes a few of us stood up at the mill gates and sang, "We shall not be moved, just like a tree planted by the water . . ." and in ten minutes the marchers began to come out again from behind barns and garages and little stores that were around through the small town. And they stood there and WERE NOT MOVED and sang. And that's what won their organization.[73]

It took courage to sing like that, but it worked.

Like the later civil rights movement, the southern labor movement was not all singing and marching. There was also a lot of tough, hard, dangerous, and discouraging work. Highlander had strong support, however. When the American Legion went after the school, the Chattanooga Central Labor Union supported them with a resolution "condemning such attacks on the Highlander Folk School as an indirect attack on the Chattanooga labor movement and the organized labor movement in general." Clearly, Highlander made a difference.[74]

For Highlander, there could never be any compromise on the issue of race. They certainly found allies in the labor movement who agreed with them. Labor unions have rightly been accused of racism throughout their history, but there were also always important exceptions that have been too easily overlooked. Local labor leaders associated with Highlander were among these important exceptions, but it was difficult. "Once people took the position of working on the basis of equality in their union," Horton wrote, "they had to face a lot of opposition from their rank-and-file members, their families and the Klan. But it wasn't just the Klan, it was society in general that opposed them. The church people and the business people opposed them, so they had to be very strong. Actually, the Klan was less of a problem for them than were the other community pressures."[75] It was when they went to church or the neighborhood bar or their children went to school and were taunted that union women and men committed to equity faced their greatest challenges. But then, Horton noted, these were people who had learned to deal with conflict and risk, and some of them became the core of the later civil rights movement in the South.

The second problem, especially after World War II, was the constant red-baiting that the more radical union members experienced, as did the staff at Highlander. The Packinghouse Workers Union had an especially strong nondiscrimination stance and an especially close relationship with Highlander. In 1951 the CIO demanded that all of its unions include an anticommunist clause in their charter. Ralph Helstein, president of the Packinghouse Workers, in consultation with Horton, refused. The union survived in spite of threats from the CIO. But for most unions, by the 1950s the need to shed the image of radicalism meant that their crusading spirit also declined and with it Highlander's enthusiasm for partnership with them. The emphasis shifted to a new movement that was consistent with Highlander's deepest core principles.[76]

The connection to the civil rights movement began in a similar way to the links with organized labor. From the beginning, Highlander had been racially integrated. They only worked with unions committed to the full and equal inclusion of black and white workers. They simply violated all of the laws of Tennessee requiring segregation of all living and dining facilities. In conversations during their work with the CIO they came to the conclusion that, "we'd get only so far before we'd run up against the playing off of blacks against whites. It was a barrier that stopped us from moving toward our goal of economic democracy. We began to pull together at Highlander the people we knew in the labor movement and outside. . . . We had begun to build a network prior to the civil rights movement, but of course we didn't create the civil rights movement any more than we created the industrial union movement."[77] But when the movement came, Highlander was ready as were few other places.

As a result of a United Nations workshop at Highlander in 1955—one of many times that Eleanor Roosevelt was there—representatives from the Sea Islands off the coast of South Carolina and Georgia raised an issue closer to home. South Carolina, like most Southern states, had a literacy clause for voters, designed to keep blacks from voting, and it was working in the Sea Islands because many of the black residents were illiterate. Septima Clark, a former teacher who had been fired for her membership in the NAACP, was also attending the UN workshop and took on the job of leading a Citizenship Program on the Sea Islands. Literacy programs fit naturally with the Highlander philosophy. Horton said, "Becoming literate was only a part of the larger process. We tried to fit literacy into a program that would be clear enough to be effective, and one the people could run themselves." Empowering local people was not just providing a service. Clark understood that these literacy programs, the first Citizenship Schools, needed to be comfortable; for people for whom schooling had been uncomfortable, this meant holding the programs in places that did not look or feel like schools. Bernice Robinson, one of the first teachers in the Sea Islands, began her classes by saying, "I am not a teacher, we are here to learn together." And rather than textbooks that tended to demean adults because of their childish approach, she started the literacy program with the UN Declaration of Human Rights and the South Carolina state constitution. "Along with becoming literate, they learned to organize, they learned to protest, they learned to demand their rights, because they also learned that you couldn't just read and write yourself into freedom. You had to fight for that and you had to do it as part of a group, not as an individual." Here, indeed, was a program that could and did serve many liberating purposes.[78]

Under the direction of Septima Clark and Bernice Robinson, Citizenship Schools expanded across the South. Horton recognized that Clark and Robinson had advantages that he and other Highlander staff did not have. First, they were African American themselves and the trust that they established came much more easily. Clark also understood people's impatience, and Horton recognized that his tendency to always ask questions and to want people to think through all aspects of a problem could be frustrating to people. He said of

Clark, "She was less interested in asking questions.... Her approach was much more popular than mine. People want help. They don't want you to ask them a lot of questions."[79]

At first all of the teachers came to Highlander to be trained, but as time went by Clark and Robinson started regional centers, first in Louisiana and Georgia, then in all parts of the South, to prepare future Citizenship School teachers. Finally, in 1961, Highlander turned the whole Citizenship School program over to the Southern Christian Leadership Conference (SCLC), led by Martin Luther King Jr. Septima Clark along with Andrew Young (who had recently joined the Highlander staff) both shifted to the SCLC staff. For the next several years, Citizenship Schools continued to be a very important part of the civil rights movement. The schools taught illiterate or barely literate African Americans to read and write sufficiently to pass state literacy tests that were consciously designed to exclude them. Under Septima Clark's leadership, the Citizenship School always did more. They taught people to be proud and to be militant in their continued efforts for change. They taught people to ask questions such as "Do you have an employment office in your town?" or "How come the pavement stops where the black section begins?" As Septima Clark said, the key was "asking questions like that, and then knowing who to go to talk to about that, or where to protest it."[80] Passing the literacy test and gaining the right to vote was an essential first step, and only a first step, in a very long road to freedom.

The Citizenship Schools were far from Highlander's only link to the civil rights movement. Martin Luther King Jr. was there many times, a fact that was used against both King and Horton at various points. The Student Nonviolent Coordinating Committee (SNCC) emerged in part from a student meeting at Highlander.[81] A connection that would eventually overshadow all the others—although no one realized it at the time—began when a young Rosa Parks attended a workshop at Highlander. Parks was the executive secretary of the NAACP in Montgomery, Alabama. She had been sponsored for the workshop by E. D. Nixon, the Alabama state president of the NAACP and vice president of the Brotherhood of Sleeping Car Porters, and by Virginia Durr, a white Montgomery citizen also deeply committed to ending segregation. At the end of the workshop Parks said she was not sure what she would do with what she had learned when she returned home to the "cradle of the Confederacy," but a short time later she made up her mind. One day, when her feet were tired, she refused to move. She was arrested, and the great Montgomery Bus Boycott had begun.[82]

When the Citizenship Schools were moved from Highlander to the SCLC, Horton gave a farewell speech in which he tried to place the Citizenship School movement in the larger context of education for freedom. He said,

To get something like this going in the first place you have to have a goal. That goal shouldn't be one that inhibits the people you're working with, but it should be beyond the goal you expect them to strive for. If your goal isn't way out there somewhere and isn't challenging and daring enough, then it is going to get in your way and it will also stand in the way of other people. Since my goal happened to be a goal of having revolutionary change in this country and all over the world, it's unlikely to get in the way in the near future.[83]

But it would give hope to many people for a very long time.

CHAPTER TEN

THE CIVIL RIGHTS MOVEMENT

"I HAVE A DREAM," 1963

THIRTY YEARS AFTER A. PHILIP RANDOLPH first proposed a march on Washington, and one hundred years after Abraham Lincoln had signed the Emancipation Proclamation, on August 28, 1963, over 200,000 Americans marched in the nation's capital and then stood in front of the Lincoln Memorial to hear the speeches. The keynote address of the March on Washington for Civil Rights was delivered by Martin Luther King Jr., already the nation's most charismatic and respected leader of the civil rights movement. In words that have become immortal, King declared his hope for America. "Go back to Mississippi; go back to Alabama; go back to South Carolina; go back to Georgia; go back to Louisiana; go back to the slums and ghettos of the northern cities," King told the marchers, "knowing that somehow this situation can, and will be changed. . . . Let us not wallow in the valley of despair," he said. Hope was coming.

> So I say to you, my friends, that even though we must face the difficulties of today and tomorrow, I still have a dream. It is a dream deeply rooted in the American dream that one day this nation will rise up and live out the true meaning of its creed—we hold these truths to be self-evident, that all men are created equal.

King knew that the dream would need to become a reality in some of the nation's most difficult places; in Mississippi, "a state sweltering with the heat of injustice," and in Alabama, "with its vicious racists." Yet it was right there in places like Mississippi and Alabama that King believed that, "little black boys and black girls will be able to join hands with little white boys and white girls as sisters and brothers." That was his hope and his dream.[1] Thus, in the hundred-year-old cadences of traditional black preachers, using words from Katherine Lee Bates, Thomas Jefferson, the biblical prophet Isaiah, and his own experience, King preached hope as hope had never been preached, before or since, in this weary land. King insisted hope was power, the dream would give life to the fulfillment of the dream. Hope would lead to renewed energy and to direct action.

Martin Luther King's words, especially his "I Have a Dream" speech, have been repeated so often that they have become part of the American literary idiom. Removed from their context, King's words sometimes seem to have their power diluted. In August 1963 it took extraordinary courage and vision to make that speech not only because, as he would be five years later, civil rights workers and leaders were being killed in America but also because many would think such hopes foolish and empty.

Although the civil rights movement had certainly made some progress and was receiving much more national attention than it had during the 1950s, progress came with a very high price tag and the hope for more progress was hard to muster. In 1963 "Bull" Connor, the head of the police department in Birmingham, Alabama, had ordered a violent attack with fire hoses and police dogs turned on peaceful demonstrators. Medgar Evers, the NAACP field secretary in Jackson, Mississippi, was murdered on his front porch in June. Riots erupted in northern cities in July. Who knew what was coming next?

King himself, in a less frequently quoted part of the speech, reminded his audience of all that was wrong with America. He noted that they were gathered on the hundredth anniversary of the Emancipation Proclamation, "But one hundred years later, the Negro still is not free . . . one hundred years later, the Negro lives on a lonely island of poverty in the midst of a vast ocean of material prosperity; one hundred years later the Negro is still languished in the corners of American society and finds himself in exile in his own land."[2] All was not well, all was not hopeful, in America as King spoke. The dream was not a description of America as it was. The dream that King preached that summer day was a dream that would only be fulfilled by much more work, courage, and bloodshed.

THE LONG ROAD TO
BROWN V. BOARD OF EDUCATION

On what seemed one of the most hopeful days in American history, May 17, 1954, the United States Supreme Court announced its unanimous decision in the most significant case they had faced in many years. Chief Justice Earl Warren wrote the opinion of a unanimous court:

> We conclude that in the field of public education the doctrine of "separate but equal" has no place. Separate educational facilities are inherently unequal. Therefore we hold that the plaintiffs and others similarly situated for whom the actions have been brought are, by reason of the segregation complained of, deprived of the equal protection of the laws guaranteed by the Fourteenth Amendment.[3]

The legal foundation of segregation had been cracked beyond any possible repair by the *Brown v. Board of Education* decision. It had been a long road to that day.

Segregation and discrimination, economic marginalization, and political disenfranchisement had been part of the reality faced by most African Americans for decades following the end of slavery and the Civil War. With the collapse of Reconstruction in the 1870s and 1880s, the white power structure of the South seemed determined to force African Americans to the margins of society—in terms of their role in the economy, the political structure, educational opportunity, or simply the right to conduct their day-to-day lives with a modicum of respectability. As Thurgood Marshall, the chief architect and lead counsel for the NAACP in the Brown case, said, the bright hopes of Reconstruction "were actually thwarted by the conspiracy between Northern capitalists and others to bring 'harmony' by leaving the Negro and his problems to the tender mercies of the South."[4]

The National Association for the Advancement of Colored People (NAACP), which had been born out of the merger of W. E. B. DuBois's Niagara Movement and an alliance of white progressives in the early years of the twentieth century, became in the middle decades of the century one of the most powerful forces for change and for hope in the African American community. Throughout the 1930s, 1940s, and 1950s, NAACP was often a whispered word in black communities in the South even as the organization was gaining membership and strength throughout that region and the nation. In the early 1950s Anne Moody, then a high school student in Centerville, Mississippi, first heard the acronym NAACP from an angry white woman for whom she worked. When she asked her mother what NAACP meant, her mother responded, "Don't you ever mention that word around Mrs. Burke or no other white person." A teacher was more forthcoming. In response to Moody's questions, her homeroom teacher told her, "You see the NAACP is trying to do a lot for the Negroes and get the right to vote for Negroes in the South." She also warned Moody, "I shouldn't be telling you all of this. . . . It could cost me my job." And it probably did. The teacher was gone the following year, just as Septima Clark had been fired in 1954 from her teaching job in South Carolina for her membership in the organization. But for Moody, as for Septima Clark, the link to the NAACP was the start of a movement in their own lives that led them into the heart of the major civil rights struggles of the 1950s and 1960s.[5]

Early in its history the NAACP took a leading role in condemning the wave of lynchings that were prevalent across the South in the first half of the twentieth century. It also focused its efforts on both economic and legal attacks on segregation, although within the organization, the legal efforts always received more attention than the economic. The NAACP had more than its share of divisions and tensions also. DuBois had resigned as editor of its journal, *The Crisis*, in 1934, after twenty-four years in that position, because of his frustration with what he saw as the excessive caution of the NAACP top leadership. Despite the caution that frustrated DuBois and others, the NAACP came to focus on a strategy of court actions that would have a far-reaching impact in American society; that would, indeed, destroy the legal foundations on which segregation was built.[6]

In the 1930s the NAACP began to give major attention to the issue of school segregation in public schools, colleges, and universities. As a first step in a long-term strategic effort initially designed by executive secretary Walter White and the NAACP's legal strategist Nathan Ross Margold, the organization began to challenge the equal part of separate but equal, bypassing state legislatures and governors with a series of federal court cases. In a 1938 case, *Missouri ex rel. Gaines v. Canada, Registrar of the University, et al.*, the U.S. Supreme Court ruled that Lloyd Gaines could not be rejected by the University of Missouri Law School on the basis of his race unless the university could offer him an equally good legal education within the state of Missouri. To offer legal education to whites but not to blacks, or to force blacks to leave the state for their education, Chief Justice Hughes said, "is a denial of the equality of the legal right to the enjoyment of the privilege which the State has set up, and the provision for the payment of tuition fees in another State does not remove the discrimination."[7] It was the first step in what would be a very long march over the next two decades.

Two brilliant lawyers took charge of the NAACP strategy—Charles W. Houston, then the dean of the Howard University Law School, and his recent student, the young Thurgood Marshall. When Houston retired in 1938, Marshall, then just thirty years old, became the NAACP chief counsel. In this position, which he held for twenty-three years, he would be the principal leader of the legal challenges to segregation. In 1961 he left the NAACP to serve on the U.S. Court of Appeals, and from 1967 to 1991 he was an associate justice of the U.S. Supreme Court.[8]

The Houston-Marshall strategy was simple—chip away at segregation in every possible way. In *Alston v. School Board of the City of Norfolk* in 1940, they won a ruling that separate salary schedules for black and white teachers violated the Fourteenth Amendment. In *Sweatt v. Painter* in 1950 they won another significant case when the Supreme Court ruled that though the state of Texas offered separate law schools for blacks and whites, the two were not substantially equal. And in *McLaurin v. Oklahoma State Regents*, also in 1950, the court ruled that segregating graduate students in the same program violated their equal protection rights under the Fourteenth Amendment. With each case segregation was becoming more expensive for southern states and the arena in which it could be exercised, smaller and smaller.[9] The time was coming for a direct challenge to *Plessy v. Ferguson*, the 1896 case that had legalized segregation in the first place.

While the NAACP lawyers were planning national strategy and Supreme Court cases, grass-roots activists were also busy on their own. In the spring of 1951, a group of students at the all-black R. R. Morton High School in Farmville, Virginia, had called a student assembly on their own. Led by a sixteen-year-old junior, Barbara Johns, the niece of Vernon Johns, the militant minister who had preceded Martin Luther King Jr. at the Dexter Avenue Church in Montgomery, they called a strike to protest conditions at their high school. While the white school in Farmville had comfortable facilities, some of the R. R. Morton classes were held in tar-paper shacks, its students had to wear coats throughout the classes, and its teachers had to gather wood for the wood stoves. The authorities had long promised new facilities, but the promise was continually postponed. The students wanted something better.

Only after going on strike did the students appeal to the NAACP. The national organization, thinking they were dealing with adult community leaders and not students, sent word that they would consider taking the case, but only if the challenge was for completely integrated schools. After realizing how far they had come, the students agreed. One of the local preachers told the adults of Farmville's black community, "Anybody who would not back these children after they stepped out on a limb is not a man." Quite a few women and men among the adults agreed. Thus was launched one of the five cases that would be consolidated on their way through the appeals process and be tried as *Brown v. Board of Education* during the Supreme Court's 1953–1954 term. Grass-roots activism and courageous local leadership were linked, as they always had to be, with the legal skills and national vision of leaders such as Thurgood Marshall and the national officers of the NAACP in this effort.[10]

In designing the final attack on segregated schools, Marshall and his colleagues developed a two-part strategy. On the one hand, they used the long string of cases they had already won, especially the Sweatt case in which the court came close to saying that separate was inherently unequal, to convince the Court that by its own precedents—the Supreme Court's favorite reason for any action—*Plessy v. Ferguson* had to be reversed. And at the same time, they built a case on the work of scholars, especially the work of psychologist Kenneth Clark, who had studied at Howard along with Marshall in the 1930s, to show the psychological damage of legal segregation on children. If the damage was clear, the NAACP team argued, then segregated facilities also inherently undermined the equal protection promised to all Americans by the Fourteenth Amendment to the Constitution.[11]

While the Brown case was pending before the Supreme Court in the spring of 1954, Thurgood Marshall was invited to deliver a series of lectures at Dillard University in New Orleans, Louisiana. In one of those lectures he outlined his own deeply held belief that segregation had to be attacked in every possible way:

> Historically, we have to ask whether or not, even as we stand today, our country can afford to continue in practicing *not* what they preach. Historically, the segregation patterns in the United States are carry-overs from the principles of slavery. They are based on the exploded theory of the inferiority of the minority group. . . . All of us know that segregation traditionally results in unequal facilities for the segregated group. . . . Finally, segregation leads to the blockage of real communication between the two groups. In turn, this blockage increases mutual suspicion, distrust, hostility, stereotypes, and prejudices.[12]

Marshall hated segregation. For him it was a badge of slavery, of inferiority, of inequality, and of suspicion and distrust. He meant to end it and, on the level of Constitutionally defined principle, he did.

The court accepted the NAACP strategy fully. In spite of the efforts by the counsel for the four states involved—led by the 1924 Democratic nominee for president John W. Davis—to frame the argument otherwise, the unanimous decision said that the question was quite clear: "We come then to the question presented: Does segregation of children in public schools solely on the basis of race, even though the physical facilities and other 'tangible' factors may be equal, deprive the children of the minority group of the equal educational opportunities? We believe that it does."

The justices gave two basic reasons for their decision. First, there were the intangible but quite clear violations of constitutional protection that were inherent in all legalized segregation and in the legal precedent of earlier court cases. So they said: "In Sweatt v. Painter, in finding that a segregated law school for Negroes could not provide them equal educational opportunities, this Court relied in large part on 'those qualities which are incapable of objective measurement but which make for greatness in a law school.'" And if they applied to a law school, they applied just as much to an elementary school. The precedent was clear.

In addition, the nine justices attended to the psychological arguments put forward by Marshall and Clark. Indeed, Clark's influence was apparent when they wrote: "Segregation of white and colored children in public schools has a detrimental effect upon the colored children. The impact is greater when it has the sanction of law; for the policy of separating the races is usually interpreted as denoting the inferiority of the Negro group. A sense of inferiority affects the motivation of a child to learn." And, the matter of motivation was also the proper province of constitutional protection. The issue, it seemed, could not have been more surely resolved.[13]

The foundation of segregation was shattered but the pieces were very much still in place. There were those at the time who thought that with the Brown case the whole battle against racism was about over. Kenneth Clark, whose testimony on the psychological damage inflicted on black children by segregation was central to the case, recalled ruefully:

> I was full of optimism at the time of the *Brown* decision. Thurgood Marshall and the other lawyers, and my social science colleagues, whom I involved in working with me, thought this was going to be a turning point. How naïve I was! . . . At long last America would have some way of getting out of its moral schizophrenia. I thought that within ten years or so, America would be free of it. I'm telling you this as an example of my naiveté. I expected southern states to resist, but I thought that their resistance would decrease and that we were on the road to some sort of functional democracy.[14]

It would take more than a federal court order, more than Marshall, or Clark, or any of the participants in the Brown case even dreamed, before the court's promise and the legal work of two decades began to make a difference in the day-to-day lives of many people. It took a shift in the focus from the courts to the streets, from standing up in court to sitting down on buses and at lunch counters, and the terrible risk of registering to vote in the face of hostile mobs, in order to shift the culture that was central to the maintenance of the racial segregation endemic in the United States in the middle of the twentieth century.

Robert Moses, who led some of the toughest voter registration drives in Mississippi in the 1960s, observes accurately of the Brown case, "Indeed, the 1954 Supreme Court decision was one important victory won by civil rights advocates." But advocacy by some for the rights of others was part of the problem for Moses. "And perhaps because it was primarily won by advocates, it proceeded 'with all deliberate speed,'" which was very slowly indeed. Change came when something else happened, he writes, "when sharecroppers, day laborers, and domestic workers found their voice, stood up, and demanded change." Then, and only then, did real change come; then it was "that the Mississippi political game was really over . . . and the century-long game of oppression through denial of the political franchise ended."[15] None of this meant that the Brown case was unimportant; on the contrary, it was terribly important. The Brown decision meant the legal foundation of segregation could not survive. The hopes of many people that the federal courts would be on their side was beginning to bear fruit. But it would take other people and other kinds of actions to build the hoped-for new structure of a less racist and more democratic society. Brown was an essential step—though only a step—that gave hope to others that their own steps too could bring about powerful changes and that, indeed, as Martin Luther King would later say, "Let us realize that the arc of the moral universe is long but it bends toward justice."[16]

MONTGOMERY, ALABAMA

On the afternoon of December 1, 1955, a year and a half after the Supreme Court's *Brown* decision, Rosa Parks finished her work day at the Montgomery Fair department store and began her bus ride home. She took a seat toward the front of the prescribed "Negro section" in the back of the bus. A few blocks later, when more whites boarded the full bus, the driver, J. P. Blake, following the local law, moved the line between the sections so that all of the whites could have seats. He told the four blacks who were in the front row of their section that they needed to give up their seats and move further back, which also meant standing. When none of them moved, Blake warned them, "You better make it light on yourselves and let me have those seats." Three of the blacks then moved. Rosa Parks stayed where she was. "Are you going to stand up?" Blake asked. Parks said, quite simply, "No."[17] Parks was arrested on the bus. Though none of the participants in the little drama on the Cleveland Avenue bus would have guessed it at the time, the world was never the same again.[18] Perhaps the mercurial Eldridge Cleaver said it best, "Somewhere in the universe, a gear in the machinery shifted."[19] A new and very powerful hope was born. It had been a long gestation.

Having arrested Parks on his own authority, Blake summoned the Montgomery police who took her to the city jail on North Ripley Street, and officially booked, fingerprinted, and jailed her. After a long wait she was allowed to call home and told her mother that she had been arrested and was in jail. Parks's mother immediately got in touch with E. D. Nixon, the acknowledged leader of Montgomery's nascent civil rights movement. Nixon, then fifty-six, had been president of Montgomery's local chapter of the NAACP and the Alabama state chapter. He worked as a porter on the railroad and was most proud to be the vice-president of the Alabama branch of the Brotherhood of Sleeping Car Porters, the most powerful black-led union in the United States. He had joined the Brotherhood of Sleeping Car Porters in 1927 after hearing a speech by the union's founder, A. Philip Randolph. And under Randolph's influence, he helped organize the Alabama chapter of the NAACP in 1928. He had been one of Randolph's supporters in the plans for the 1941 March on Washington. Active in unionism and civil rights, he was not a newcomer to political organizing or to making tough decisions.[20]

Nixon also knew almost all of Montgomery's leaders, black and white. As author Taylor Branch said of him, "He was famous to Montgomery Negroes as the man who knew every white policeman, judge, and government clerk in town, and had always gone to see them about the grievances of any Negro who asked him for help. Nixon seldom got anything close to justice, but he usually got something."[21] When Nixon called the jail this time, he could not get anything except anger. He asked Clifford and Virginia Durr, two of the handful of Montgomery whites who were also civil rights activists, to join him, and the three went to the Montgomery jail to sign the bond for Rosa Parks's release. Within a few hours of her arrest Parks was free and at home with her husband, Raymond, and her mother, Leona Edwards McCauley, in the apartment they shared in the Cleveland Courts housing project.[22]

Early in the evening of her arrest the entire matter could have ended. The court would probably have let her off with a small fine and the segregated world of Montgomery could have returned to normal. While rumors abounded, only a handful of people actually knew what had happened that afternoon. In the next few hours, however, several fateful decisions were made that changed the course of history. As Nixon and the Durrs talked with Rosa Parks, her husband, and her mother, the question they faced was obvious. Was this the test case they had all been waiting for? In *Brown v. Board of Education* the year before, the Supreme Court had ruled that segregation was illegal in education. But what about transportation? The segregated buses of Montgomery and the rest of the South were a daily affront. At least two other women had been arrested in Montgomery in the previous few months for refusing to move. In March a high school student, Claudette Colvin, had been arrested when she refused to give up her seat. But when Nixon, the Durrs, and the other civil rights leaders had discovered Colvin's short-fused temper, her tendency to profanity, and the fact that she was pregnant and unmarried, they decided that the Colvin case was not the right one for the test they needed. In October Mary Louise Smith also failed to pass the propriety test though some, including the leaders of the influential Women's Political Council, were unhappy with the continued waiting. But with Rosa Parks, there was no reason to wait any longer. If she were willing, if she could overcome her husband's fear that, "The white folks will kill you, Rosa," there could not be a better person for the test case they all anxiously sought.[23]

In later years Rosa Parks would become one of the most famous Americans of her century. But in 1955 she was already known and respected in the small world of Montgomery's African American community. She was the secretary of the local chapter of the NAACP and quite close to Nixon and its other leaders. She had been the one to sign Martin Luther King Jr.'s appointment letter when the new pastor in town joined the executive committee of the local NAACP chapter a few months before. She was not part of Montgomery's middle-class African American elite, but she was respected for her poise and quiet confidence. She was married and active in a church. And her work as a seamstress at a department store and for white families had gained her the respect of Montgomery's working families, which a more prominent person might not have had.[24]

Rosa Parks was born in Tuskegee, Alabama, on February 4, 1913. Her family, like nearly all African Americans of the time, were sharecroppers. The world she was born into was not only poor and segregated, it was filled with terror. The month she was born, the NAACP journal, *The Crisis*, recorded sixty-three lynchings of blacks in 1912. She was always a "good girl." Her family subscribed to Booker T. Washington's belief in self-help, personal cleanliness, and morality. She remembered, "The church, with its musical rhythms and echoes of Africa, thrilled me when I was young." And the church remained central to her all her life. Her grandfather had been a follower of Marcus Garvey until he was ejected from a Montgomery County meeting of the Universal Negro Improvement Association for being too light-skinned. Parks also remembered sleeping on the floor beside her grandfather's rocking chair where the old man sat with a shotgun across his lap while the Klan paraded on the street outside. "I remember thinking," she later said of that evening, "that whatever happened, I wanted to see it."

The family moved to Montgomery where Parks grew up. While always quiet and friendly, Parks had a proud and stubborn streak. She recalled as a child being pushed off the sidewalk by a white boy and, in a dangerous violation of the rules of the day, she pushed him back. "A white woman was standing not too far from us. She turned out to be his mother, because she said she could put me so far in jail that I never would get out again for pushing her child. So I told her that he had pushed me and that I didn't want to be pushed, seeing that I wasn't bothering him at all."[25] Later reporters have sometimes made Parks a bit too mild. "I didn't want to be pushed" was always part of her make-up.

In 1931 she met a local barber, Raymond Parks, and they were married in 1932. She said of her husband, "I was very impressed by the fact that he didn't seem to have that meek attitude—what we called an 'Uncle Tom' attitude—toward white people."[26] Indeed, Raymond Parks had been among the charter members of the Montgomery branch of the NAACP. He and then Rosa became very active in the campaign to free the Scottsboro Boys, nine African American boys who had been arrested on trumped up charges of raping white women. The case with its many injustices dominated much of the racial atmosphere of the 1930s and certainly shaped Rosa Parks's later life.[27]

In the 1940s Rosa Parks became secretary of the local chapter of the NAACP and began her close association with E. D. Nixon. During World War II she had become active in a campaign for the vote; like the Scottsboro cause, a dangerous one to advocate in Alabama at the time. In the 1940s the top two issues on the NAACP chapter's agenda were the right to vote and the desegregation of the city buses. Parks first tried to register to vote in 1943 and was told she did not pass the literacy test. The same thing happened in 1944. In 1945 she hand-copied every question on the literacy test while she was taking it, in an obvious first step toward a legal challenge to the test. Apparently the authorities wanted to avoid a legal challenge more than they wanted to avoid Parks's vote. She received her registration in the mail and began voting with the Alabama gubernatorial election of 1946.[28]

The bus laws were also high on her agenda. Parks was actually put off a Montgomery bus in 1943 for refusing to follow the rules of the day that said an African American should pay at the front, then get off, and reboard at the back door. The driver of that bus was J. P. Blake, the same driver whom she met on the Cleveland Avenue bus twelve years later. Parks remembered him well. She said of the Montgomery drivers, "Not all of them were hateful, but segregation itself is vicious, and to my mind there was no way you could make segregation decent, nice or acceptable."[29]

In the late 1940s and early 1950s Parks became increasingly active in civil rights matters. At an NAACP leadership training seminar in 1946 she met Ella Baker who was then the national director of the NAACP branch offices and later the godmother to the founding of the Student Nonviolent Coordinating Committee (SNCC). Parks continued to work to defend young black men accused of rape, advised the local NAACP Youth Council, and kept in close contact with other NAACP offices. Parks, Nixon, and the Durrs were part of a small but growing group of African American leaders and their white allies who in February 1954 had informed Montgomery city officials that the segregation rules on the buses were their greatest complaint. In the summer of 1955 Virginia Durr nominated Parks to attend Highlander workshops focused on desegregation. "I was forty-two years old, and it was one of the few times in my life up to that point when I did not feel any hostility from white people," Parks said of Highlander. "I experienced people of different races and backgrounds meeting together in workshops and living together in peace and harmony. I felt that I could express myself honestly, without any repercussions or antagonistic attitudes from other people."[30] Parks had seen the future she wanted.

Given her extraordinary background and the planning that was taking place in Montgomery, many have wondered if Parks's action that December day had itself been planned. The answer from everyone involved, most of all from Rosa Parks herself, was no. She had not planned any dramatic stand for herself, certainly not on the day she went to work in the morning and made history in the afternoon. But her personal history for the previous two decades, as well as the history of her city and country, had prepared her far better than any other citizen for what happened. Author Douglas Brinkley has speculated that running into J. P. Blake again, twelve years after the 1943 incident, precipitated Parks's action.[31] Martin Luther King saw it as part of a much bigger picture. In *Stride Toward Freedom* he wrote:

> She was not "planted" there by the NAACP, or any other organization; she was planted there by her personal sense of dignity and self-respect. She was anchored to that seat by the accumulated indignities of days gone by and the boundless aspirations of generations yet unborn. She was a victim of both the forces of history and the forces of destiny. She had been tracked down by the Zeitgeist—the spirit of the time.[32]

Parks herself told the Highlander executive committee a few months later, "There had to be a stopping place, and this seemed to have been the place for me to stop being pushed around and to find out what human rights I had, if any."[33]

Once Parks had made her two fateful decisions, first to remain seated and then, later that evening, to offer her arrest as the test case, things moved very quickly. The focus of the first conversations that Thursday evening at Rosa Parks's home and church were on the legal challenge. Parks, Nixon, and the Durrs agreed that a young African American lawyer, Fred Gray, with whom they all worked closely, should be her attorney, but that they would contact the national NAACP legal defense fund led by Thurgood Marshall for support. The Parks defense team for the test case challenging the segregation of the buses in Montgomery as a violation of the U.S. Constitution was in place before midnight.[34]

The second development came almost as quickly. Among his first moves as Parks's attorney, Fred Gray called Jo Ann Robinson, a member of the faculty at Alabama State College and a leader of the generally middle-class but quite militant Women's Political Council. Robinson had heard rumors and when Gray called her at 11:30 that evening, she had already begun thinking that the council should call a one-day bus boycott on Monday, the day of Parks's trial. When Gray asked, "Are you ready?" Robinson replied that she was very ready. Pretending that they needed to grade papers, Robinson and a few friends met in her Alabama State office at midnight. They drafted a leaflet that began:

> Another Negro woman has been arrested and thrown into jail because she refused to get up out of her seat on the bus and give it to a white person. . . .
> Until we do something to stop these arrests, they will continue. . . . The next time it may be you, or you or you. This woman's case will come up Monday. We are, therefore, asking every Negro to stay off the buses on Monday in protest of the arrest and trial.

They then reproduced the leaflets on the mimeograph machines at Alabama State in the middle of the night.

The women knew they needed to act quickly so that the source of the leaflets would not be known. Alabama State was the black college, completely dependent on the white legislature for its funding. They did not want the source of the leaflets traced, and they wanted them ready for quick distribution. Robinson called Nixon about three in the morning on Friday. She found him awake and in the middle of his own planning. Nixon quickly supported Robinson's idea for a boycott; he had been thinking of something similar himself. By dawn on the morning after Parks's arrest, the bus boycott was arranged, though at that point it was planned for one day, not the long year that it eventually lasted.[35]

Not long after talking with Robinson, Nixon began calling the local ministers. The new minister at Dexter Avenue was third on his list. As King remembered it, Nixon skipped any preliminaries and began, "We have taken this type of thing too long already," concluding, "I feel that the time has come to boycott the buses. Only through a boycott can we make it clear to the white folks that we will not accept this type of treatment any longer." King asked for time to think it over before he endorsed the boycott but agreed to host a planning meeting at Dexter Avenue on Friday afternoon. Soon after, Ralph Abernathy, pastor of First Baptist and already King's closest friend among the Montgomery clergy, was on the phone and persuaded King to support both the test case and the boycott. Before dawn on Friday, December 2, the court challenge had been planned, the boycott announced, and King was on board with the campaign.[36]

King's *Stride Toward Freedom* offers a compelling account of the next few days. On Friday afternoon the planning meeting at King's Dexter Avenue Church included a large number of ministers as well as a good number of other leaders in the African American community. It was, by all accounts, a chaotic meeting, but the results were clear. Everyone agreed that the boycott should take place on the following Monday and that a great deal of planning was needed over the weekend to make it a reality. One committee began contacting all of the black taxi companies to ask them to offer rides for the cost of bus fare. Another including King drafted a second, shorter leaflet that said simply:

> Don't ride the bus to work, to town, to school, or any place Monday, December 5.
>
> Another Negro woman has been arrested and put in jail because she refused to give up her bus seat.
>
> Don't ride the buses to work, to town, to school, or anywhere on Monday. If you work, take a cab, or share a ride, or walk.
>
> Come to a mass meeting, Monday at 7:00 P.M. at the Holt Street Baptist Church for further instructions.

Both Robinson's and the minister's leaflets were distributed widely and the white *Montgomery Advertiser* inadvertently helped the campaign along by publishing news of the plan on its front page on Saturday. The news was meant for the white community, but it also meant that everyone in the black community, including the many people who did not ever receive a leaflet, knew about the boycott.[37]

Monday morning was a tense time for all of the leaders of the proposed boycott. King said that if 60 percent of the black community stayed off the buses that day, it would be a victory. He and his wife waited and watched the bus stop that was directly in front of their house. King recalled: "I was in the kitchen drinking my coffee when I heard Coretta cry, 'Martin, Martin, come quickly!' I put down my cup and ran toward the living room. As I approached the front window Coretta pointed joyfully to a slowly moving bus: 'Darling, it's empty!' I could hardly believe what I saw." The boycott was a success. Nearly all of Montgomery's blacks stayed off the buses all day. It was a victory beyond the wildest expectations of the organizers. As King said, "The once dormant and quiescent Negro community was now fully awake."[38]

As King drove around Montgomery that day, he saw a determination in the black community that he had never seen before. "They knew why they walked, and the knowledge was evident in the way they carried themselves." At 9:30 that Monday morning Rosa Parks went on trial at the police court with Fred Gray as her counsel. The judge found her guilty of "disobeying the segregation law" and fined her ten dollars plus four dollars in court costs. Parks appealed. The case could not have been more clear cut. If the judge had dismissed the case, if the conviction had been for "disorderly conduct," or some similar offence, appeals might have been more difficult. As it was, Parks, Gray, and their supporters had just what they wanted, the perfect test case with the right client.[39]

That Monday afternoon another planning meeting was held to prepare for a meeting at Holt Street Baptist and to decide on the next steps. Martin Luther King Jr., then twenty-six years old and barely one year into his position as pastor of Dexter Avenue Baptist Church, was elected president of the as-yet-unnamed organization. Some have speculated that the older ministers recognized King's promise, while others have guessed that the more seasoned preachers simply wanted to stay out of harm's way. Perhaps they also wanted to have a minister in the top position or simply to block E. D. Nixon. As Taylor Branch wrote in *Parting the Waters*, perhaps "his chief asset was his lack of debts or enemies."[40] Later in the same meeting they decided at Ralph Abernathy's suggestion to call themselves the Montgomery Improvement Association (MIA). They debated whether to extend the boycott beyond its one successful day and agreed to let the temper of the evening meeting at Holt Street decide for them.[41]

King's election as president of the MIA meant that he would be the main speaker that evening. He saw a difficult challenge in that speech: "How could I make a speech that would be militant enough to keep my people aroused to positive action and yet moderate enough to keep this fervor within controllable and Christian bounds?"[42] It was a dilemma that King would face not only that night but for the rest of his life. He had little time to prepare, but when he saw the crowd in the church and gathered outside, "The enthusiasm of these thousands of people swept everything along like an onrushing tidal wave." King began by reporting what had happened to Rosa Parks. Then he explored the meaning of her act:

> But there comes a time that people get tired. We are here this evening to say to those who have mistreated us so long that we are tired—tired of being segregated and humiliated; tired of being kicked about by the brutal feet of oppression. . . . For many years, we have shown amazing patience. . . . But we come here tonight to be saved from that patience that makes us patient with anything less than freedom and justice.[43]

The response told King that his audience was with him, that something very important was happening as his words connected with the change in the hearts and minds of Montgomery's African American community.

King continued reminding his audience of the justice of their cause and of their need to stick to it. He also urged them to remember to "Love your enemies." This was to be a campaign of love and dignity and militancy. He concluded: "If you will protest courageously, and yet with dignity and Christian love, when the history books are written in future generations, the historians will have to pause and say, 'There lived a great people—a black people—who injected new meaning and dignity into the veins of civilization.'"[44] And from then on he was the acknowledged voice of the protest in Montgomery and soon in the nation. He had had very little time to prepare that speech, just as Rosa Parks had little time to ponder her decision to refuse to move. And yet, like Parks, King had been preparing for that moment all of his life. When the crisis came he was ready.

The next item on the agenda that evening was Ralph Abernathy's proposed resolution that the boycott continue until the demands were met. The initial demands were moderate—courteous treatment by the bus operators and the seating of passengers on a first-come first-served basis, whites from the front, blacks from the back. Segregation itself was not yet challenged, only the kind of humiliating enforcement experienced by Parks when she was told to give up her seat. The demands for more would come later. But from that evening it was clear—it was not to be a one-day boycott. People would wait as long as it took. When the vote came, everyone stood in favor of the motion. As King said, "The people had expressed their determination not to ride the buses until conditions were changed."[45]

Something had happened in those few short days to give hope to a community that had virtually given up on hope and determination to a people who had been seen by their oppressors as lacking the will to fight for justice. Later that evening King recalled thinking that the victory of Montgomery had already been won, a victory much larger than the immediate situation. "The real victory was in the mass meeting, where thousands of black people stood revealed with a new sense of dignity and destiny." And so in *Stride Toward Freedom* he said of that evening in December 1955: "That night we were starting a movement that would gain national recognition; whose echoes would ring in the ears of people of every nation; a movement that would astound the oppressor, and bring new hope to the oppressed. That night was Montgomery's moment in history."[46] It was one of the greatest victories for hope in the history of the United States.

The days and weeks and months ahead have been romanticized in hindsight, but for most of the participants most of the time, there was little romance in what was ultimately a year-long boycott of the Montgomery buses by the black community. King recounted the combination of careful and detailed logistical planning and inspirational preaching and praying that were essential to the movement's success. The day after the December sermon that solidified his role as the leader of the Montgomery movement, King remembered, "I woke up Tuesday morning urgently aware that I had to leave the heights and come back to earth. I was faced with a number of organizational decisions. The movement could no longer continue without careful planning." As president of the MIA King formed a number of committees, one to coordinate the taxis and later the car pools, one to raise funds, and one to plan strategy. He understood that he needed to tread carefully: "As in all organizations, the problem of conflicting egos was involved." King also moved to increase the outside support and eventually used some of the funds to hire a full-time staff for the MIA. And he continued the terribly difficult work of keeping the movement together. As he understood all too well, "The biggest job in getting any movement off the ground is to keep together the people who form it." Indeed, most great movements flounder on just such a problem. But in large part because of King's work the MIA succeeded. He knew: "This task requires more than a common aim: it demands a philosophy that wins and holds the people's allegiance; and it depends upon open channels of communication between the people and their leaders. All of these elements were present in Montgomery."[47] The philosophy of nonviolent resistance and Christian love emerged from the churches and gained strength as it held people together and as it showed that strength in the face of legal authorities that had kept the African American community in place for generations. The careful tactical planning and the lofty ideals were part of a whole piece. And the piece held.

On many occasions defeat and worse seemed more likely than even the most marginal sort of victory. In the first few days the boycott had been made possible by the unanimous support of the black taxi drivers, all of whom drove people for the same ten-cent fare that the bus company charged. But quickly the police commissioner issued an order that the taxi companies had to charge their regular minimum forty-five-cent fare for every ride. As King said, "This brought an end to the cheap taxi service." And it created the much more complex and usually chaotic car pooling on which the boycott depended for the next several months.[48] During the first weeks there were efforts by the MIA, the city leaders, and the bus company to negotiate a settlement, but they were too far apart; the city leaders, sensing both the danger of the boycott and the weakness of the organization, quickly hardened their position and made stronger alliances with the racist White Citizens Council. As a negotiated settlement became less likely, the MIA leaders took the bold step of approving the plan put forward by Fred Gray to file a second legal challenge—not merely the Rosa Parks appeal but a wider federal suit against the entire system of segregated buses in Montgomery. They knew it would create additional hostility in the white community, but they also knew it would ultimately receive quicker and surer action within the federal courts. They were right on both counts.[49]

By the third week in January, as the city authorities' positions hardened, they made life difficult for the boycotters. Policemen stopped car-pool drivers on every pretext. Jo Ann Robinson, author of the first leaflet, received seventeen tickets during the first few months—for going too fast, too slow, or failing to signal. On January 26 King himself was arrested—for the first of what would be many times in his career—on a charge of driving thirty miles an hour in a twenty-five mile zone. He was taken on a lonely and frightening ride and imprisoned with a good many of his followers. Not long after, King's house was bombed while he was leading one of the evening services. Coretta and their first baby, Yolanda, were unhurt, but things were getting very close to home. A few days later another bomb exploded in E. D. Nixon's yard. King's father begged him to come home to Atlanta until things cleared up, but King stayed.

In late February 1956, more than two months into the boycott, a grand jury issued indictments for all of the boycott leaders and King was among more than twenty ministers booked. In all, over ninety leaders were arrested. And the pressure continued in many other ways. Employers, both businesses and families hiring servants, threatened to lay off workers who would not take the bus to work. Having forced the taxis to stop charging a lower fare for the boycotters, the city authorities then challenged the MIA's right to operate its own fleet of cars. In the fall the city brought what would ultimately be a successful suit to ban the car pools and impose a fine on the MIA for lost revenue. Fred Gray, a minister as well as a lawyer, had his draft deferment revoked. Others were threatened in many different ways. For the thousands of Montgomery's African American citizens, every day was exhausting, wondering if the car pool would work, walking to and from work and shopping and any other errand that needed their attention. At no point was victory at all certain.[50]

At the same time, the nation's black leadership was far from united in its support of what was happening in Montgomery. Roy Wilkins, the longtime national leader of the NAACP, kept his distance and regularly argued with King over fundraising. He did invite King to address the NAACP convention in San Francisco, but when the NAACP field director from Mississippi, Medgar Evers, invited King to Mississippi and told the convention how important nonviolent direct action was, Wilkins and the NAACP leadership resisted. The delegates were with King, but the leadership was not. Wilkins and Thurgood Marshall openly criticized King and the idea of direct action, preferring to stick with the court cases they had been winning with growing speed.[51]

In light of the barely contained local violence, the constant tension within the community, and the lack of early national support, it took courage to continue, but the boycotters did, through the winter, the spring, the hot summer, and the coming of another winter. They continued the evening meetings, they preached and prayed and told stories. They celebrated the courage of those who would not give up, such as an old woman known as Mother Pollard who had refused suggestions from her friends that her age exempted her from the boycott. "My feets is tired, but my soul is rested," she was reported to have said.[52]

And the tide did begin to turn. The mass indictments of the boycott leaders in February brought the first of what became continuing national media attention to Montgomery, nearly all of which favored the boycotters over the city leaders. In part because of the attention, fundraising became easier and King found himself becoming a national celebrity and a very successful fundraiser. The aged W. E. B. DuBois wrote that though he still had his doubts, if King's passive resistance could undermine American racism, it would be a way to conquer war itself. On June 4 a three-judge appeals court ruled in favor of the suit that had been filed in February. Although the case was immediately appealed to the Supreme Court, a federal authority had ruled that Montgomery's bus segregation was unconstitutional. And finally, on November 13, 1956, while King sat in a Montgomery court convinced he was about to lose the city of Montgomery's call for an injunction against the car pools, the United States Supreme Court affirmed the appeals court ruling. As one observer said in the courtroom that day, "God Almighty has spoken from Washington, D.C.!" King himself remembered, "At this moment my heart began to throb with an inexpressible joy. The darkest hour of our struggle had indeed proved to be the first hour of victory." After nearly a year of extraordinary courage and perseverance, the Montgomery boycott had won.[53]

It took another month for the official court action to be transmitted to Montgomery, and in the meantime the city did win its injunction. For the last few weeks everyone walked, but by then they also knew they had won. Early in the morning of December 21, 1956, a year and three weeks after Rosa Parks had sat down and refused to move, King, Gray, Abernathy, and a few others, followed by reporters, boarded the first bus of the day. "We are glad to have you," the polite driver said, and a new era began.[54]

Resistance was not over. On December 23 a shotgun was fired into King's home, but again no one was hurt. On Christmas eve, a fifteen-year-old girl was beaten by whites while waiting for a bus. Snipers shot at integrated buses. Early in the morning of the new year, 1957, Ralph Abernathy's home and church were bombed, as were a number of other churches and homes of leaders around Montgomery. Two weeks later King's home was bombed again, this time more seriously, though no one was home at the time. Also in January 1957, a gathering of some of the leading civil rights leaders from the region and the nation met in Atlanta and created a new organization, the Southern Christian Leadership Conference (SCLC), electing King as its president. By then King was a national figure, civil rights was part of the national consciousness, and the buses of Montgomery were forever integrated.[55]

Few victories were as clear cut as those of December 1956. Much hard work, pain, and terror lay ahead. Sometimes every victory of the civil rights movement seemed more difficult than the one before. Each step met terrible hatred and resistance. There would be great defeats as well as grand victories. And yet, after Montgomery there was no turning back. Something had changed—in the souls of a great many African Americans and their supporters, in the laws of the land, in the way the culture of the United States defined itself. Hope was on the march in a new way.

THE STUDENTS AND THE SIT-INS

When Martin Luther King began his ministry in Birmingham in 1954, and when Rosa Parks kept her seat in 1955, no African American under the age of ninety remembered the joys of emancipation and none under the age of seventy could remember a time when the right to vote or speak or live with a modicum of security had been real. In every era of American history there have been efforts to romanticize both slavery and life in the free but segregated South. Anne Moody's powerful autobiography, *Coming of Age in Mississippi* tells the story much more accurately. She describes the grinding poverty of farming—on someone else's farm—linked with an ongoing campaign of terrorism whose purpose was to keep African Americans like her "in their place."

A wave of terrorism hit Moody's home town of Centerville, Mississippi, in the mid-1950s. One night she was awakened by screams and smoke. The home of a nearby family had been burned to the ground with the family still inside. "All that was left," she wrote, "were some iron bedposts and springs, a blackened refrigerator, a stove, and some kitchen equipment." It was a terrifying sight, made all the more terrifying as it became clear that the fire had been deliberately set to send a message to the black community of Centerville. "We sat in the car for about an hour, silently looking at this debris and the ashes that covered the nine charcoal-burned bodies. . . . I shall never forget the expressions on the faces of the Negroes. There was almost unanimous hopelessness in them."[56] In a nation that tolerated not only segregation but also the state terrorism of the local sheriff and the blind eye of a federal government whose leg-islative arm was dominated by representatives of the South, what could one do?

Nevertheless, it was in the middle of that terrifying and "almost unanimous hopelessness" that the greatest movement of hope in American history was born. After the Supreme Court's 1954 decision outlawing segregation in schools and after the success of the Montgomery boycott in 1956, white terrorism increased dramatically. In their final gasps, it seemed that the segregationists were determined to stamp out hope. But their time had passed, it was too late. The civil rights movement did not begin because one day Martin Luther King and other preachers began to preach a new kind of sermon, important as those sermons were. It did not begin because courageous lawyers such as Thurgood Marshall spent their lives developing a legal strategy to undermine the structure of segregation, although those cases were terribly important. The civil rights movement really began because in small towns and farms all across the South a generation of young people, such as Anne Moody, and a few of their elders, such as E. D. Nixon and Rosa Parks, began to say they just wouldn't take it anymore. In the 1950s, while Dwight Eisenhower was president and most of America seemed caught in a state of frozen content, segregation came to an end in the hearts and minds of a people a decade or more before it ended in practice.

Anne Moody was a good example of those changes. Though her parents and teachers taught her to be careful and to accept the world in which she lived, she could not do it. The change in her began with small steps. During her junior year in high school, the white woman whose house she cleaned asked her what she thought of school integration. At first she pretended not to understand, but when pressed she answered, "I don't know, Mrs. Burke. I think we could learn a lot from each other." Once the words were out of her mouth, she was terrified at what she said. Nevertheless, as she reflected she knew that, "courage was growing in me too. Little by little it was getting harder and harder for me not to speak out."[57]

By 1960 the courage and hope of the nascent civil rights movement was bearing fruit in hundreds of different places and in different ways. On February 1, 1960, four freshmen at North Carolina Agricultural and Technical College sat down at the lunch counter of the Woolworth's store in downtown Greensboro, North Carolina, and asked very politely for service. And again the universe shifted. These four African American students were challenging one of the most sacrosanct rituals of the segregated South. This was much more than sitting in mixed company on a bus. The lunch counter protest involved the social rituals of a meal. It was far from the first time African Americans had sought to break the color barrier at a lunch counter or a restaurant.

But the timing was right this time. Nineteen students joined the sit-in the next day and on the third day they numbered eighty-five. This was not a well-planned event. The established civil rights leaders, whether preachers or lawyers, the SCLC or the NAACP, had not been involved in the discussions that led to the action and, indeed, knew nothing of it until after the fact. They had to struggle to decide whether they wanted to support, ignore, or lead the sit-ins. But it didn't matter what they did. Something new was happening in America and young students were at the forefront.[58]

The sit-ins that started in Greensboro spread like wildfire across the South. The ease with which a sit-in could be organized, the freedom that the students had from the need for careful planning which sometimes almost seemed to paralyze their elders, and the confusion that they caused in the white establishment all added fuel to the movement.[59]

Before February had ended, there had been sit-ins in thirty-one cities across eight southern states. One of the largest and longest took place in Nashville, Tennessee. James Lawson, a long-time advocate of nonviolent resistance on the Gandhian model, had been leading workshops in nonviolent tactics in that city for some time. When word of the Greensboro actions reached them, over 500 students met with Lawson and others to discuss what to do. Lawson argued for time to do careful preparation and training, but the students were ready for action. In the end, Lawson joined them and began preparing them on the spot. The next morning, Saturday, 500 well-dressed African American college students walked into downtown Nashville and sat down at lunch counters in all of the major stores. Clearly this was a force to be reckoned with.[60]

After some initial confusion the Nashville authorities began to crack down. On Saturday, February 27, the police allowed a mob to beat many of the demonstrators and then arrested seventy-seven blacks and five whites including future movement leaders John Lewis and Diane Nash. In court on Monday, Nash announced that, "We feel that if we pay these fines we would be contributing to and supporting the injustice and immoral practices that have been performed in the arrest and conviction of the defendants." She, Lewis, and fourteen others were jailed, soon to be joined by more than sixty others. The mayor sought compromise and agreed to appoint a biracial committee to look at segregation in the stores. The appointment of the committee was a victory long sought by Nashville's older civil rights leaders and it had been won by the students.[61]

Almost alone among the established civil rights leaders, King endorsed the sit-in movement. Fred Shuttlesworth, one of the leading preachers within the SCLC, contacted the organization's executive director Ella Baker to say, "You must tell Martin that we must get with this." King agreed. It was a turning point in his career. While many of King's peers were not sure what to make of the sit-ins and the NAACP Legal Defense Fund was not willing to defend those arrested, King made up his mind. Less than a month into the movement he endorsed it, saying that it was "destined to be one of the glowing epics of our time." In a rally in Durham, North Carolina, he said to the students, "What is fresh, what is new in your fight is the fact that it was initiated, led, and sustained by students. What is new is that American students have come of age. You now take your honored places in the world-wide struggle for freedom."[62] These were words of both respect and endorsement. King seemed to see in the sit-ins what he had been seeking since the bus boycott three years earlier, a way to directly but nonviolently confront segregation. The students had found it for him.

Having endorsed the sit-in movement, King found himself defending the movement even to many of his traditional allies. In November 1961 he spoke to an interracial group who were committed to civil rights but wary of the speed with which the students were moving. He told his audience to look at the power for good in a movement that believed "that there is within human nature an amazing potential for goodness. There is within human nature something that can respond to goodness."[63] He also told his liberal audience that they needed to look carefully at the key components of the student movement. First, it was a revolt against the "negative peace . . . in which the Negro patiently accepted his situation and his plight." "It is also," King said, "a revolt against what I often call the myth of time . . . individuals in the struggle must come to realize that it is necessary to aid time." But most of all, King saw the student actions as "a movement based on faith in the future. It is a movement based on a philosophy, the possibility of the future bringing into being something real and meaningful. It is a movement based on hope."[64] And hope, for King, meant that much was possible. "With this faith in the future, with this determined struggle, we will be able to emerge from the bleak and desolate midnight of man's inhumanity to man, into the bright and glittering daybreak of freedom and justice." Like all of King's speeches it was a dynamic one. But even more than others, it was a courageous one, for King was endorsing something over which he had virtually no control and trusting that students he did not know would lead him and others to where they needed to be.[65]

Anne Moody's account of the sit-ins in Jackson, Mississippi, a few years later gives a good sense of the tenor of the sit-in movement. From beginning to end, the sit-ins were led by young people. Endorsements such as King's were gratifying but not essential. More and more young people were becoming more radical and more courageous. They would no longer wait for their elders to give them permission or to try to stop them.

In the late spring of 1963 a group of Tougaloo College students decided it was time for a sit-in at the lunch counter of the local Woolworth's store. Anne Moody and two others were to make the first move. They had entered the store from different directions to keep the authorities off-guard and at 11:15 that morning the three sat down together and asked to be served. When the waitress told them the Negro lunch counter was in the back, they said, "We would like to be served here." The waitresses and most of the other customers quickly disappeared. Initially, a few whites in the store offered words of encouragement, but the mood changed quickly. As white students from the local high school arrived at noon, they were first surprised, then started chanting antiblack slogans and making threats, and the mood became more tense. The three students started to pray:

> We bowed our heads, and all hell broke loose. A man rushed forward, threw Memphis from his seat, and slapped my face. Then another man who worked in the store threw me against an adjoining counter. Down on my knees on the floor, I saw Memphis lying near the lunch counter with blood running out of the corner of his mouth. As he tried to protect his face, the man who'd thrown him down kept kicking him against the head. If he had worn hard-soled shoes instead of sneakers, the first kick probably would have killed Memphis. Finally a man dressed in plain clothes identified himself as a police officer and arrested Memphis and his attacker.

After the arrest of one of the students, the crowd continued to attack the other two. They hit them, tried to drag them out of the store and shouted "Communists, Communists, Communists" at them. The two remaining demonstrators were joined by two others. Moody continued: "There were now four of us, two whites and two Negroes, all women. The mob started smearing us with ketchup, mustard, sugar, pies, and everything on the counter. Soon Joan and I were joined by John Salter, but the moment he sat down he was hit on the jaw with what appeared to be brass knuckles. Blood gushed from his face and someone threw salt into the open wound." Eventually the president and the chaplain from Tougaloo College rescued the demonstrators and took them to NAACP headquarters. But the same scene would be repeated again and again in Jackson and across the South.[66]

The story of the sit-ins is a story of extraordinary courage. It is important to remember that the civil rights movement was not just a matter of marches, demonstrations, and singing protest songs in church basements. These things helped keep the movement's spirit strong. But many people took the kinds of beatings that Moody described, and many were killed, including Rev. George W. Lee and Jack Smith in Mississippi in the 1950s; Herbert Lee in Amite

County, Mississippi in 1961; Louis Allen in the same area in 1963; Carol Denise McNair, Cynthia Wesley, Addie Mae Collins, and Carole Robertson, four little girls in a Sunday school classroom in Birmingham, Alabama, in 1963; and Andrew Goodman, James Chaney, and Michael Schwerner on a highway in Mississippi in 1964; Viola Liuzzo on the road to Selma, Alabama, in 1965; as well as leaders from Medgar Evers to Malcolm X to Martin Luther King Jr. There are thirty-nine names on the Civil Rights Martyrs monument in Montgomery, Alabama, and it is only a partial list.[67] The price of freedom in this as in every other cause was extraordinarily high, yet the movement persisted in spite of it. And in spite of all the risks it also changed the lives of all who participated. As Moody remembered: "But something happened to me as I got more and more involved in the Movement. It no longer seemed important to prove anything. I had found something outside myself that gave meaning to my life."[68] The hope and the sacrifice changed the United States. It also changed and enriched the lives of everyone who was part of it.

MISSISSIPPI

If Martin Luther King's speech at the 1963 March on Washington was the one that was most remembered, the speech by John Lewis, who was chairman of SNCC, the Student Nonviolent Coordinating Committee, was the most controversial at the time. Among other things, Lewis included in his speech a call for a new political future for African Americans: "The party of Lincoln is the party of Goldwater. The party of Kennedy is the party of Eastland. Where is our party?"[69] A year later the Republican Party would nominate Senator Barry Goldwater of Arizona, leader of its conservative wing who would be one of those voting against the Civil Rights Bill of 1964, for president. And Senator James Eastland, segregationist Democrat of Mississippi, had used his position as chairman of the Judiciary Committee to kill all but one of the 121 civil rights bills to come before Congress in the previous decade.[70] There was good reason for Lewis to say what he did, but within a year Lewis and the young people at the core of SNCC had the beginnings of the answer they sought. They had created the Mississippi Freedom Democratic Party and had changed the politics of the Democratic Party not only in Mississippi but nationally.

There is a direct chain of events from the sit-ins that began in Greensboro, North Carolina, in early 1960 to the arrival of the Mississippi Freedom Democratic Party delegation that sought to claim the seats allocated to Mississippi at the national Democratic Party Convention in Atlantic City, New Jersey, in August of 1964. The first key link in that chain was the courage and hope of young people, mostly African American college students, joined on occasion by high school students, who were ready to act while their elders continued to consider. The second link in the chain was the emergence of some remarkable leaders of courage and vision including students such as John Lewis, Robert Moses, Charles Sherrod, and Diane Nash who made powerful alliances with civil rights veterans including Ella Baker and Medgar Evers. The third essential link was the alliance that was forged between these young people and grass-roots activists in some of the most out of the way places in the South, including Amzie Moore of Cleveland, Mississippi, C. C. Bryant of Pike Country, E. W. Steptoe of Amite County, and the extraordinary Fannie Lou Hamer of Sunflower County, as well as hundreds of others whose courage has not been recorded as it should be.[71]

No one did more to shape the philosophy of SNCC in its early years and set the tone for its efforts in Mississippi in 1963 and 1964 than Ella Baker. Baker had been director of the state branches for the NAACP in the 1940s, when she had met Rosa Parks, but had left in frustration over the elitism of the organization. Martin Luther King recruited her to be the acting executive director of the Southern Christian Leadership Conference but she also found herself deeply frustrated by the male dominance and hierarchical nature of the minister-led SCLC. Her own philosophy was much more deeply egalitarian. She was convinced, as Bob Moses said, of her idea of leadership, that "it should emerge from the community and be helped in its growth by grass-roots organizers," a view that "clashed with SCLC's idea of projecting and protecting a single charismatic national leader."[72] As Baker herself said: "My basic sense of it has always been to get people to understand that in the long run they themselves are the only protection they have against violence or injustice. . . . People have to be made to understand that they cannot look for salvation anywhere but to themselves."[73] And in the student-led sit-in movement, Baker sensed that she had found like-minded souls.

Cheered by the beginning of the sit-in movement in February, 1960, Baker had worked hard and successfully to get Martin Luther King to endorse the movement. At the same time, she wanted to be sure that the students were not co-opted by SCLS or any other main-line organization. While still serving as the acting executive director of SCLC, Baker gathered some of the sit-in students for a conference at Shaw University in Raleigh, North Carolina, on Easter Weekend of 1960. She recalled, "Just as the sit-ins had skyrocketed or escalated without rhyme or reason, so too the response to the concept of a conference escalated beyond our expectations." James Lawson, who had played a major role in the sit-in movement in Nashville and had been expelled from the Vanderbilt University divinity school for his efforts, was another participant at the Raleigh conference. He told the students that their actions were "a judgment upon middle-class conventional, halfway efforts to deal with radical social evil." The students themselves voted to form their own organization rather than affiliate with either the SCLS or the NAACP. Thus, SNCC was born.[74]

The hopes that animated SNCC during the early years of its existence and that gave rise to the extraordinary activities that took place in the state of Mississippi in 1963 and 1964 were well summarized by another line in the speech that John Lewis had prepared for the March on Washington. Lewis planned to voice the student hopes for something far wider than the demands and dreams of other speakers. "We all recognize," the manuscript for Lewis's speech said, "the fact that if any radical social, political and economic changes are to take place in our society, the people, the masses must bring them about. In the struggle we must seek more than mere civil rights; we must work for the community of love, peace, and true brotherhood. Our minds, souls, and hearts cannot rest until freedom and justice exist for all the people."[75] Here was a dream of a very different America being voiced by one of the youngest speakers at the march. In fact, the dream was too radical for the others, and Lewis was forced to delete this paragraph and others from his speech before he was allowed to appear on the platform that summer day.

When a recent Hamilton College graduate, Bob Moses, arrived in Atlanta in the summer of 1960 to volunteer for SCLC during his vacation from his job as a teacher in New York City, he found himself becoming one of the first itinerant organizers for SNCC. As Moses started to travel through the rural south that summer, he met some amazing people who lived far from the centers of what had been civil rights activity up to that point, and who had been waiting for the right moment. Moses described one meeting:

> One of my most important contacts on the trip was forty-nine-year-old Amzie Moore, president of the Cleveland, Mississippi, branch of the NAACP and vice president of the state's conference of NAACP branches. He was the only adult I met on this trip who had clearly fixed the students in his sights. It was as if he had been sitting there in Cleveland watching the student movement unfold, waiting for it to come his way, knowing it had to eventually come, and planning ways to use it in light of his fifteen year effort, since World War II, at making changes in the cotton plantation land of the Mississippi delta.[76]

Moses would encounter more people like Moore in time, and in each case he found the same mix of courage, staying power, and hopeful confidence that the changes were, indeed, coming, even in Mississippi.

Moses learned that while Moore favored the legal work of the NAACP that focused on school integration, integration was not his priority. His real passion was the vote. Living in a congressional district that was two-thirds black, it was obvious to Moore what the vote could do for his community. Moses wrote to the SNCC office in Atlanta, "Amzie thinks, and I concur, the adults here will back the young folks but will never initiate a program strong enough to do what needs to be done." Thus was born SNCC's focus on grass-roots organizing and massive student involvement focused on the vote.[77]

The result was the development of several new tactics within the civil rights movement. In the spring of 1961 CORE (the Congress of Racial Equality, founded in the 1940s) began the Freedom Rides. They were soon joined by SNCC in arranging for integrated teams to ride Greyhound and Trailways buses through the South to test the new federal integration rules for interstate transportation. Blacks and whites sat together throughout the buses and ignored the "Colored" and "White" signs in the bus stations. In Anniston, Alabama, riders on both buses were badly beaten and the Greyhound bus was burned to a charred hull by white rioters who included at least one FBI informant. The Kennedy administration sought to defuse the direct confrontations of the Freedom Rides by launching the Voter Education Project thinking that a focus on the vote would be less confrontational than public facilities. They were wrong in their supposition, but they did provide important resources to CORE, SNCC, and others who wanted to focus on the vote in any case.[78]

The viciousness of the attack on the Freedom Riders made international news. SNCC continued to focus on both direct action and voter registration. For those working on the vote, it was hard, painful, slow going. Moses, who had returned full time to Mississippi in 1961, was beaten several times, jailed, and threatened. Close confederates were killed.

In September 1961 Herbert Lee, a supporter of the voter registration effort in Amite County, Mississippi, was shot by E. H. Hurst, a white state representative and father-in-law of one of the men who had beaten Moses earlier in the summer. Hunt admitted that he had shot Lee but claimed it was in self-defense and was never prosecuted for the murder. For Moses, the guilt of knowing that his organizing probably precipitated Lee's murder was exacerbated when Lee's widow walked up to him at the funeral and said, "You killed my husband." Moses said, "It is one thing to get beaten, quite another to be responsible, even indirectly, for a death. If we hadn't gone into Amite to organize, Herbert Lee wouldn't have been killed. I was sure of that." Two years later Louis Allen, a witness to Lee's murder, was also murdered after offering to testify for the prosecution. When he had asked for federal Justice Department protection, Allen had been told, "We can't protect every individual Negro in Mississippi."[79]

Even when the threat of violence and murder was not imminent, the work crawled. African Americans who had lived with segregation all their lives were reluctant to challenge the system. Again and again, Moses and the others heard things like "Don't want none of that mess here, boy," or "Now ya'll be careful foolin' around with that white folks' business." It was hard to keep trying in light of such discouragements. But all of this was the price paid by those who dared to hope for change in Mississippi in the early 1960s.[80]

Looking back, Moses reflected on the kind of change it took inside a person in order for someone to think of taking the first step toward the voter registration office, even if that person turned the idea down cold the first time it was suggested: "I liked to think I got anyone I spoke with imagining himself or herself at the registrar's office. Getting someone to make this kind of mental leap, even for a moment, had to be considered an achievement in the Black Mississippi of those days where even the idea of citizenship barely existed."[81] In the early 1960s more and more people were making that leap. They were registering. They were becoming participants and leaders in a movement for change that would transform the politics of the state and the nation.

In the winter of 1963–1964 a plan took shape within SNCC to bring a thousand college students, whom everyone knew meant mostly white students, to Mississippi to help with the voter registration effort and to focus national attention on the denial of voting rights in Mississippi. The plan was not without opposition as many of the African American SNCC field organizers worried that the generally unconscious elitism and racism of the students would undermine the growing strength of the black community by superimposing a white leadership group. On the other hand, grass-roots leaders such as Fannie Lou Hamer argued that the students were needed, besides, "If we're trying to break down this barrier of segregation, we can't segregate ourselves." In time, the violence of the white attacks on the voter registration effort settled the issue. Something more was needed and the arrival of a thousand students for the Mississippi Freedom Summer of 1964 was certainly something more.[82]

The Freedom Summer project was linked closely to the development of the Mississippi Freedom Democratic Party (MFDP) organized to challenge the official all-white Mississippi delegation at the August 1964 Democratic Convention at which Lyndon Johnson was to be nominated for reelection. In early August, just weeks before the national convention, hundreds of newly registered voters from around Mississippi met in Jackson and launched the party, electing sixty-eight delegates to represent Mississippi when the Democrats gathered in Miami later that month. Newly registered black voters had already attempted to attend local Democratic Party meetings and had uniformly been turned away. The determination of the Mississippi Democrats to maintain a segregated party was both the moral and the legal basis of the MFDP's challenge to demand the Mississippi seats. Joseph Rauh, counsel for the United Auto Workers, had agreed to serve as legal counsel for the MFDP and promised, with what turned out to be unwarranted optimism, that, "if the Mississippi delegation is challenged, they will be unseated."[83]

It was not to be. Although the challenge failed and the MFDP delegation ultimately rejected the compromise offered by the convention, it did succeed in raising the denial of voting rights in Mississippi to a new level of national attention. And it made Fannie Lou Hamer, a forty-seven-year-old Mississippi sharecropper, a national voice. Hamer's story was similar to thousands of other blacks in the deep South. "My life has been almost like my mother's was," she said, "because I married a man who sharecropped." There was little reason for Hamer to think it might change until one day in 1962, when she attended a mass meeting and heard about a campaign to register people like her to vote.

> Until then I'd never heard of no mass meeting and I didn't know that a Negro could register and vote. Bob Moses, Reggie Robinson, Jim Bevel and James Forman were some of the SNCC workers who ran that meeting. When they asked for those to raise their hands who'd go down to the courthouse the next day, I raised mine. Had it up as high as I could get it. I guess if I'd had any sense I'd a-been a little scared, but what was the point of being scared? The only thing they could do to me was kill me and it seemed like they'd been trying to do that a little bit at a time ever since I could remember.

When she went to the courthouse and attempted to register to vote, Hamer was arrested. That evening she was told she was going to be evicted from her white-owned home. As she would tell the Credentials Committee of the 1964 Democratic National Convention:

> My husband came and said the plantation owner was raising cain because I had tried to register, and before he quit talking the plantation owner came, and said, "Fannie Lou, do you know—did Pap tell you what I said?"
>
> I said, "Yes, sir."
>
> He said, "I mean that," he said. "If you don't go down and withdraw your registration, you will have to leave."
>
> And I addressed him and told him and said, "I didn't try to register for you. I tried to register for myself." I had to leave that same night.[84]

In June 1963 she was almost beaten to death while under arrest in a jail in Winona, Mississippi. In 1964 she was part of an effort that registered 63,000 blacks in Mississippi and that created the Mississippi Freedom Democratic Party, and in August of that year she testified before the Credentials Committee of the national Democratic party demanding the right to be seated as a delegate to the convention.

When Senator Hubert Humphrey, who was about to be nominated to be Johnson's vice president, tried desperately to convince Hamer to accept a compromise in which the MFDP would be awarded two seats at the convention, she told him, "Senator Humphrey, I been praying about you, and I been thinking about you, and you're a good man. The trouble is, you're afraid to do what you know is right." The MFDP delegates did not share that fear, and though they failed in the political arena at the time, they were a powerful force in the convention and in the country. It was quite an extraordinary two years for Hamer and many other delegates who were, as Bob Moses said, "sharecroppers, domestic workers, and farmers" who were asking the national Democratic party to truly be the party of such people.[85]

Bob Moses has summed up what really changed in Mississippi between 1960 and 1964. The change had to do with much more than democracy defined as the right to vote. It had to do with the most fundamental meaning of democracy, the right of and the necessity for people to take control of all aspects of their lives and their communities.

> Today's commentary and analysis of the movement often miss the crucial point that, in addition to challenging the white power structure, the movement also demanded that Black people challenge themselves. . . . In these meetings, they were taking the first step toward gaining control over their lives, and the decision making that affected their lives, by making demands on themselves. This important dimension of the movement has been almost completely lost in the imagery of hand-clapping, song-filled rallies for protest demonstrations that have come to define portrayals of the 1960s civil rights meetings: dynamic individual leaders using their powerful voices to inspire listening crowds. Our meetings were conducted so that sharecroppers, farmers, and ordinary working people could participate, so that Mrs. Hamer, Mrs. Devine, Hartman Turnbow, all of them were empowered. They weren't just sitting there.[86]

The message of truly self-empowered poor people scared the convention, scared President Johnson, and scared many of the established civil rights leaders as well as most of white America. But though the MFDP did not get to vote at the convention, they would never return to the passivity and hopelessness of the past. They weren't just sitting there any longer.

The North and Malcolm

While the hopes of African Americans in the South generally focused on ending the brutal legalized segregation of buses and schools and on the right to vote and participate in the democratic electoral process, the hopes of northern blacks focused more on ending the region's extra-legal segregated housing patterns and the economic marginalization they experienced in low paying jobs for themselves and low quality schools for their children. And while there were many widely different currents within the northern civil rights movement, one of the most prominent symbols for the hopes of many of the North's poorest and most disenfranchised African Americans was Malcolm X. As Marcus Garvey had a generation earlier, Malcolm spoke of pride, self-sufficiency, and self-determination in a way that touched a very deep core for many people.

Malcolm was born Malcolm Little in Omaha, Nebraska, in 1925. While his mother was pregnant with him, the Ku Klux Klan terrorized their home because of his father's involvement in the Garvey movement. It was an ironic link between Garvey and the unborn child who would grow up to play a very similar role in the nation a few decades later. Soon after Malcolm's birth the family moved, settling in Lansing, Michigan. They continued to experience the worst of pre–World War II northern racism. In 1929 their house was burned by arsonists and in 1931, just as he was starting elementary school, his father was killed, most likely by a local affiliate of the Klan.[87] Malcolm well remembered the grinding poverty of Depression-era America, the racism, and after his father's death the efforts of the white welfare officers to break up their family.

Malcolm was expelled from school and found himself in a reform school where he experienced the quasi friendship of people who treated him as a mascot or an exception while talking about "the niggers" to his face. In the eighth grade he experienced one of those defining moments in the nature of American racism. A well-meaning white teacher said, "Malcolm, you ought to be thinking about a career. Have you been giving it thought?" While he hadn't actually given his future much thought, Malcolm responded, "Well, yes, sir, I've been thinking I'd like to be a lawyer." "Mr. Ostrowski looked surprised," Malcolm remembered. "He kind of half-smiled and said, 'Malcolm, one of life's first needs is for us to be realistic. . . . A lawyer—that's no realistic goal for a nigger. . . . Why don't you plan on carpentry?'" As he thought about it, something changed for Malcolm. He understood racism in a new way and pulled away from whites and from any aspirations to the black bourgeoisie as well. As soon as he could, he left Lansing to live with his half-sister Ella in Boston. It was the first of many dramatic turning points for him. As he said,

"All praise is due to Allah that I went to Boston when I did. If I hadn't, I'd probably still be a brainwashed black Christian."[88]

In Boston and later in New York's Harlem, the young Malcolm found freedom, a chance to make money, to hustle, and to escape the oppression he had known by pursuing a wild life of crime that eventually landed him in Charlestown State Prison. In February 1946, just before his twenty-first birthday, Malcolm received a ten-year sentence for a string of burglaries. And again, his life was changed. In his *Autobiography* he said, "I had sunk to the very bottom of the American white man's society when—soon now, in prison—I found Allah and the religion of Islam and it completely transformed my life."[89]

While he was in prison in Charlestown, Malcolm was converted to a growing movement within the African American community, the Nation of Islam or the Black Muslims as they were known in the white media. It was a conversion that turned his life around. He said, "For evil to bend its knees, admitting its guilt, to implore the forgiveness of God, is the hardest thing in the world." But he did it. When he was released from prison in 1952, Malcolm moved to Detroit to be with family and to further his education as a Muslim. A year later he was named assistant minister at Detroit Temple Number One and began his meteoric rise within the Nation of Islam until he was the most recognized preacher and leader after Elijah Muhammad, the founder of the Nation. The message he preached was very basic, "We didn't land on Plymouth Rock, my brothers and sisters—Plymouth Rock landed on *us!* . . . Give all you can to help Messenger Elijah Muhammad's independence program for the black man! . . . This white man always has controlled us black people, keeping us running to him begging." It was a mix of pride, of separation and disdain for the "white devils," and total allegiance to Allah and Allah's Messenger Elijah Muhammad.[90]

Malcolm the preacher disdained the focus on integration in the civil rights movement. In time, however, he also came to distrust Elijah Muhammad. Even while he was gaining increased fame as "the fiery Black Muslim," Malcolm was starting to have his doubts about Elijah Muhammad because of his total disengagement with black protest and because of the rumors that his mentor was, in fact, jealous of his success. Then, in 1963, Elijah Muhammad was accused of fathering children with two young secretaries. "I had discovered Muslims had been betrayed by Elijah Muhammad himself." It began a second major turning point.[91]

Early in 1964, having completed his break with the Nation of Islam and knowing he was under a death threat from them, Malcolm set off for a pilgrimage to Mecca, required of every good Muslim, though not a part of the Nation of Islam's practices. Suddenly Malcolm found himself among Muslims from all over the world. And he was transformed by the experience. When a fellow pilgrim asked him what about the Hajj had impressed him the most, Malcolm answered, "The *brotherhood!* The people of all races, colors, from all over the world coming together as *one!* It has proved to me the power of the One God." He reflected later on the way the trip changed him, "The color-blindness of the Muslim world's religious society and the color-blindness of the Muslim world's human society: these two influences had each day been making a greater impact, and an increasing persuasion against my previous way of thinking." No longer would he preach separation for its own sake. He was not one bit less militant, but Malcolm returned from Mecca as El-Hajj Malik El-Shabazz, a man totally committed to unified action in the cause of racial justice in America.[92]

In an impromptu press conference when he returned to New York in May 1964, Malcolm explained his new-found faith. He began by speaking of his growing conviction that American blacks should focus less on civil rights and more on taking their case directly to the United Nations for a censure of the United States for its "denial of human rights." He moved on to his experience in Mecca and how it changed him. "In the past, yes, I have made sweeping in-dictments of *all* white people. I never will be guilty of that again—as I know now that some white people *are* truly sincere, that some truly are capable of being brotherly toward a black man. The true Islam has shown me that a blan-ket indictment of all white people is as wrong as when whites make blanket in-dictments against blacks."

But his changing attitude toward some whites did not mean that he had lost any of his passionate hatred of racism, wherever it was found. He contin-ued to tell the press: "Why, here in America, the seeds of racism are so deeply rooted in the white people collectively, their belief that they are 'superior' in some way is so deeply rooted, that these things are in the national white sub-consciousness. Many whites are even actually unaware of their own racism, until they face some test, and then their racism emerges in one form or an-other."[93] As a result of his experience in Mecca, Malcolm had moved the fight against racism to a much deeper level.

Malcolm was also not willing to adopt the nonviolence of Martin Luther King and many other civil rights leaders. Late in 1964, just before Christmas, Malcolm met Fannie Lou Hamer for the first time at a small church rally in New York City. Four months earlier Hamer had testified at the Democratic convention and earlier in the same year Malcolm had been in Mecca. On that December day Malcolm heard Hamer describe the beating she had received in the Winona, Mississippi jail. When it was his turn to speak, Malcolm said, "When I listened to Mrs. Hamer, a black woman—could be my mother, my sister, my daughter—describe what they had done to her in Mississippi, I asked myself how in the world can we ever expect to be respected as *men* when we know that we will allow something like that to be done to our women and we do nothing about it?" In spite of the sexism, Malcolm was challenging the dominant nonviolence of the movement. He continued:

> I know I'm in church, I probably shouldn't be talking like this, but Jesus himself was ready to turn the synagogue inside out and upside down when things weren't going right . . . [but] Your own Patrick Henry said "liberty or death," and George Washington got the cannons out, and all the rest of them that you taught me to worship as my heroes, they were fighters. . . . But now, when the time comes for *our* freedom you want . . . somebody who's nonviolent and forgiving and peaceful and long-suffering. I don't go for that. I say a black man's freedom is as valuable as a white man's freedom.[94]

Malcolm's continued refusal to embrace nonviolence made headlines. But he was voicing the belief of a great many who were beginning to doubt the effectiveness of nonviolence or had never embraced it. The tendency of some later commentators to tame the post-Mecca Malcolm clearly can only go so far.

Malcolm never became much of an integrationist either. He had rejected his earlier dislike of all whites but not his distrust. Like many in Mississippi, he worried that when "whites join a black organization . . . pretty soon the blacks will be leaning on the whites to support it, and before you know it a black may be up front with a title, but the whites, because of their money, are the real controllers. I tell sincere white people, 'Work in conjunction with us—each of us working among our own kind.' . . . Let sincere whites go and teach nonviolence to white people!"[95] He was very willing to accept and respect white co-workers in the struggle against racism and injustice, but not to be led or controlled ever.

Malcolm was very clear about his goals and his dream:

> In our mutual sincerity we might be able to show a road to the salvation of America's very soul. It can only be salvaged if human rights and dignity, in full, are extended to black men. Only such real, meaningful actions as those which are sincerely motivated from a deep sense of humanism and moral responsibility can get at the basic causes that produce the racial explosions in America today. Otherwise, the racial explosions are only going to grow worse. . . . Sometimes, I have dared to dream to myself that one day, history may even say that my voice—which disturbed the white man's smugness, and his arrogance, and his complacency—that my voice helped to save America from a grave, possibly even a fatal catastrophe.[96]

In the end, this was his hope, that the catastrophe could be averted and that the vision of community he had seen in Mecca could be made real in the America of the 1960s. It took extraordinary courage to speak so critically and to dare to demand such dignity, but courage was one thing Malcolm never lacked. In February, 1965, Malcolm was assassinated, probably by Nation of Islam soldiers. But his dream would continue to inspire great hopes among generations not yet born.

Three years later, King too was dead, assassinated while assisting striking garbage workers in Memphis, Tennessee. The dream dimmed considerably after Malcolm and King and so many others died. It would be a long time before the hopes they represented would be as bright again, but their legacy of hope remained powerful for future generations. King himself had warned everyone that the march to justice would not be easy or quick or painless. In a speech to the Southern Christian Leadership Conference in 1967 he had said:

> I must confess, my friends, the road ahead will not always be smooth. . . . There will be those moments when the buoyancy of hope will be transformed into the fatigue of despair. Our dreams will sometimes be shattered and our ethereal hopes blasted. We may again with tear-drenched eyes have to stand before the bier of some courageous civil rights worker whose life will be snuffed out by the dastardly acts of bloodthirsty mobs. Difficult and painful as it is, we must walk on in the days ahead with an audacious faith in the future.[97]

That audacious faith in the future is a part of King's legacy, a part of the movement's legacy, a hope that still exists in the hearts of many.

THE MOVEMENT CONTINUES

THE DECADES AFTER THE HEIGHT of the civil rights movement have been times of great hope and great despair in the United States. The extraordinary pain, difficulty, and complexity of overcoming racism in its many forms can be deeply discouraging. Yet the legacy of the civil rights movement itself continues to be felt in the ongoing efforts by many different people and groups within and beyond the African American community to secure their rights. Speaking in 1981, Bernice Johnson Reagon, a cultural historian and a lead singer in the black women's ensemble Sweet Honey in the Rock, voiced both the pain and the optimism of the previous decade. She described the many powerful movements to end oppression that were flowering:

> I'm going to start with the Civil Rights movement because of course I think that was the first one in the era we're in. Black folks started it, Black folks did it, so everything you've done politically rests on the efforts of my people—that's my arrogance! . . . So once we did what we did, then you've got women, you've got Chicanos, you've got the Native Americans, and you've got homosexuals, and you got all of these people who also got sick of somebody being on their neck. And maybe if they come together, they can do something about it.[1]

Reagon's list of the emerging movements of the 1970s and 1980s is, if anything, too short, but her sense of the way in which the campaign for civil rights for African Americans inspired many others is right on target. Campaigns for civil rights—fueled by the hopes of many diverse groups that they can get somebody off of their neck and build a better future—have flourished.

What follows is far too short to give any of these movements their due. This epilogue is meant, however, as a reminder that neither the civil rights movement nor the long history of hope-filled movements in the United States are at an end. Hope is alive and well and flowering in dozens of different places. The few developments recorded here are but the tip of a wonderful and complex iceberg. Many new chapters are yet to be written about the history of hope in the United States.

ALCATRAZ

Paul Chaat Smith and Robert Allen Warrior in *Like a Hurricane* relate the daring move by a ragtag assortment of young people who decided to take their own civil rights protests to a new level of militance.

> Running without lights to avoid detection, the trawler all but disappeared into the night as it left the docks of Sausalito behind and moved into the spectacular, foreboding waters of San Francisco Bay. The passengers—there were about a dozen—tried not to think about the possibility of being crushed by an oil tanker that didn't see them, or intercepted by a Coast Guard cutter that did. . . . During the early morning hours of November 20, 1969, the trawler, along with several other boats carrying dozens more young people, headed due southeast, bound for the abandoned prison island of Alcatraz.[2]

The new occupiers decided to call themselves, appropriately, the Indians of All Tribes. They celebrated as "drums and singing from a victory powwow filled the air."[3] One of the group, Luwana Quitiquit, a Pomo, thought the name was just right. She said, "That's exactly what it was. We all had things to offer each other. Brotherhood. Sisterhood."[4] Thus began the year-and-a-half siege of the abandoned federal prison at Alcatraz island that brought the demands for respect and for a share of the nation's stolen resources by a new generation of American Indians, representatives of many different tribes, to national consciousness.

Richard Oakes, a Mohawk from the St. Regis Reserve in New York and a student at San Francisco State College, had been elected the first spokesperson for the occupation. Early on he told the press, "We're only young people concerned about our future. . . . These are the future leaders of most of these tribes . . . [and] we might—might just wake up the conscience of America."[5] Another young occupier wrote home to his parents. He described his days and continued, "Don't get paid for it, but I am getting something a whole lot better than money out of it. It has given me a goal in life. I will be able to look back and say I did something worthwhile."[6] Here was the language of the civil rights movement in a new and different place. Those whose ancestors had suffered on this continent even longer than the African Americans were saying "I did something worthwhile," and were making an appeal to "wake up the conscience of America" and seeming to have some success in the effort.

The occupation of Alcatraz was not the first or the most important stirring of Indian activism in the 1960s. In 1964 a young Vine Deloria, a thirty-year-old Standing Rock Sioux, had ousted the old leadership of the National Congress of American Indians. A new and far less accommodationist direction had begun for the nation's largest Indian organization. The American Indian Movement began quietly in Minneapolis among urban Indians but would, in the 1970s, become a major militant force on the reservations, making the names of some of its leaders like Russell Means and Dennis Banks well known. In 1973, American Indian Movement militants along with traditionalists among the local Sioux staged a dramatic takeover of the central village of the Pine Ridge reservation, site of the great Wounded Knee massacre of 1890, and dared the federal government to repeat the attack. The Wounded Knee standoff was both the high point of twentieth-century Indian militance and a powerful moment in the history of civil rights activity. Without question Wounded Knee put the civil rights of Native Americans back at the center of national consciousness, though at a high cost. The standoff also raised the sense of pride on the part of many. Gladys Bissonette, remembered, "Well, for myself, I think this was one of the greatest things that ever happened in my life. . . . We didn't have anything here, we didn't have nothing to eat. But we had one thing—that was unity and friendship amongst sixty-four different tribes and that's more than I could say that the Pine Ridge Reservation has ever had in my life." That such unity and friendship and pride could be duplicated was also a hope that would not die.[7]

FEMINISM REBORN

Alice Rossi, a sociologist, wrote, "There is no overt anti-feminism in our society in 1964, not because sex equality has been achieved, but because there is practically no feminist spark left among American women."[8] Whether two years or two decades later, no one could justifiably say such a thing. Feminism reemerged in the United States in the 1960s and came to stay. In fact, Rossi's comment was an overstatement even in the relative quiet of 1964. American women had resisted sexism in every generation just as people of color had resisted racism.

The League of Women Voters, the successor to the earlier suffrage organizations, continued to lobby for women's political rights through the Great Depression and World War II. The radical United Electrical, Radio, and Machine Workers of America union demanded equality for women working in the General Electric and Westinghouse plants where it was the bargaining unit. They also demanded child care and what Ruth Milkman called "a strong ideological commitment to gender equality."[9] The more mainstream International Ladies' Garment Workers Union nevertheless took a lead, along with others in organized labor, in organizing women workers throughout the middle of the century in spite of the stay at home ideology of the 1950s.

The struggle for women's reproductive rights never stopped. It was, after all, during the 1950s that Gregory Pincus and John Rock conducted their research—supported by the aging Margaret Sanger, Planned Parenthood, and individual donors—that led to the creation of the birth control pill in 1960; a development that significantly shaped feminism in the following decades.[10] In 1955 a lesbian couple founded the Daughters of Bilitis in San Francisco to create "a home for the Lesbian."

Modern women's history, which began to flourish in the mid-1960s, and continues to expand, owes much to Eleanor Flexner's path-breaking book, *Century of Struggle*, published in 1959. Flexner traced her interest in women's history to a course she taught in 1953–1954 that "marked the beginning of my real involvement in the issues of women's rights, my realization that leftist organizations—parties, unions—were also riddled with male supremacist prejudice and discrimination." In preparing for the course her text had been a 1952 United Electrical Workers pamphlet, *UE Fights for Women Workers*, by Betty Goldstein, later known as Betty Friedan.[11] And to the surprise of many, fifty thousand women participated in a one-day Women's Strike for Peace on November 1, 1961 to protest the Cold War.

By 1960 Ella Baker and Septima Clark had been arguing tirelessly with Martin Luther King and the other ministers and lawyers for some time about what they saw as the sexism of the civil rights leadership.[12] Clark's status as the founder of the freedom schools and the conscience of the Southern Christian Leadership Conference allowed her to challenge King, Ralph Abernathy, and other preachers in a way that few women or men would dare.[13] Baker, who had resigned from her staff position in the NAACP in 1946 because of her frustration with its hierarchical and male-dominated ways, joined the Southern Christian Leadership Conference in 1958 and quickly emerged as one of its most effective organizers; the one who turned the preacher's words into concrete actions. She admired King and saw him as unusually willing to listen. Still she resented the preacher fraternity's tendency to undermine the development of more widespread leadership. In 1960, when she took the lead in organizing the Student Nonviolent Coordinating Committee, she made sure that, at least in its early years, it maintained a very different style of communal decision making, though the organization would later disappoint her on that score.[14]

Pauli Murray, an African American lawyer who had won court cases against segregated law schools in the 1930s, urged President John F. Kennedy's Commission on the Status of Women not only to demand equal pay for equal work and an end to discriminatory treatment in the legal system and on the job, but to assert their rights under the clause of the Fourteenth Amendment to the Constitution that says that no state "shall deny to any person within its jurisdiction the equal protection of the laws." The commission did not accept Murray's challenge, but it was there.[15]

In 1963 Betty Friedan published *The Feminine Mystique*. The book changed the nation's consciousness, or at least the consciousness of a great many of the nation's citizens, both women and men. In retrospect, *The Feminine Mystique* was a narrowly focused book. When *The Feminine Mystique* was published, Gerda Lerner, who had been active in trade unions and was just then emerging as one of the nation's leading historians, wrote to Friedan praising her "splendid book" and continuing, "You have done for women what Rachael Carson [seen by many as the founder of the environmental movement] did for birds and trees [but] I have one reservation about your treatment of your subject: you address yourself solely to the problems of middle class, college-educated women."[16] It is a critique that would be repeated more than once in the future.

At its core *The Feminine Mystique* addressed "the problem that has no name," the quiet desperation of mostly middle-class white women, who saw themselves well provided for in "comfortable concentration camps" where their lives had no meaning other than living out prescribed service roles for husbands and children. Friedan traced the well-orchestrated campaign, "a propaganda campaign, as unanimous in this democratic nation as in the most efficient of dictatorships," that had driven women out of their World War II–era jobs and into a life of mind-dulling homemaking. To describe this reality in 1963, experienced by so many middle-class post–World War II women, was an extraordinarily radical journalistic effort. It challenged a generation of prosperous but generally quiet women to consider a wide range of options that had simply been beyond the bounds for the length of their lives. Once the challenge was made, moving beyond the bounds went far further than Friedan might have dreamed.[17]

Friedan's own radical background has often been obscured. In 1941, while still a student journalist at Smith College, Friedan, then Betty Goldstein, attended a writer's workshop at Highlander Folk School, then and later such an important gathering point for union and civil rights leaders. In 1946 she began a six year tenure as a reporter for the United Electrical Workers paper, the *UE News*, an experience that brought her into close proximity with many aspects of the American left in a union that was more effectively committed to equality for women and people of color than any other. Her life prior to the publication of the book that made her famous was not nearly as tame as she later portrayed it.[18]

Friedan herself joined with Pauli Murray and others to found the National Organization of Women (NOW) in 1966. Designed as a women's counterpart to the NAACP, NOW began immediately to demand implementation of some of the recommendations of the Kennedy-era Commission on the Status of Women using the opportunity offered by the 1964 Civil Rights Act. In an effort to make the whole bill seem silly, a reactionary Southern Democrat had added sex to race in order to assure the bill's defeat. In one of the great backfires of history, the bill became law and discrimination on the basis of gender, as well as race, was made illegal in the United States. While the federal government initially ignored that part of the legislation, Friedan, Murray, and their colleagues in NOW meant to take full advantage of the law. They made constant demands on government regulatory agencies, especially the Equal Employment Opportunities Commission, for action. And they quickly began to demand more. They adopted as a goal an Equal Rights Amendment to the U.S. Constitution that would, once and for all, assure the full political rights of women. In some ways NOW was the logical successor to the National Women's Party of the 1920s, which had also called for an Equal Rights Amendment to the Constitution, but in other ways it was something totally new on the American scene.[19]

In the years that followed, the movement for women's liberation developed in many different directions, embracing many different women, and focusing on many different issues. The aptly named 1982 book *All the Women are White, All Blacks are Men, But Some of Us Are Brave: Black Women's Studies*[20] served as an important reminder that the women's movement was never an all-white movement in spite of some stereotypes to that effect, though like all aspects of American society it was sometimes segregated by race and class. A group of African American feminists calling themselves the Combahee River Collective—in honor of a Civil War battle led by Harriet Tubman—issued a statement in 1977 that corrected the historical record: "A Black feminist presence has evolved most obviously in connection with the second wave of the American women's movement beginning in the late 1960s. Black, other Third World, and working women have been involved in the feminist movement from its start, but both outside reactionary forces and racism and elitism within the movement have served to obscure our participation."[21]

The Combahee River women also made clear the links between feminism and the civil rights movement, writing, "Black feminist politics also have an obvious connection to movements for Black liberation, particularly those of the 1960s and 1970s. Many of us were active in those movements (Civil

Rights, Black nationalism, the Black Panthers), and all of our lives were greatly affected and changed by their ideologies, their goals, and the tactics used to achieve their goals."[22] Mary King, a white woman active in the civil rights movement in the South with SNCC also reflected, "If you are spending your time [doing] community organizing ... it inevitably strengthens your own conceptions, your own ability."[23] The civil rights movement, union organizing, and the anti-war movement all had strengthened women's sense of their abilities while at the same time often subjecting them to glaring examples of male chauvinism in the very movements for liberation. All were fertile seedbeds for what would follow.

Within a few short years following the mid-1960s virtually no aspect of women's lives, women's relationships, or the place of women in the nation's culture would remain unexamined. Feminism was linked to the civil rights movement, the cultural changes of the 1960s, the anti-war movement, the renewed confidence of gay men and lesbians, and the student movement. And it was also more than and separate from all of these.

Federal legislation was passed in response to the feminist pressure and the changes in the culture. Congress approved Title IX of the 1972 Educational Amendments Act requiring any college or university that received federal funding—which meant virtually every institution of higher education in the land—to ensure equal facilities for women and men. That same year the Equal Rights Amendment passed both houses of Congress and was sent to the states for ratification. A reactionary opposition quickly emerged and the required two-thirds of the states never ratified it. In 1973 the United States Supreme Court in *Roe v. Wade* guaranteed a woman's right to choose by ensuring abortion rights across the country.[24] Freedom to control one's body, one's sexuality, was every bit as central to the feminist movement as economic and social rights. Progress, though slow, seemed to be taking place on all fronts.

Women did not turn only to state and federal legislation. Susan Brownmiller in *Against Our Will*, a careful and condemning analysis and description of the role of rape in women's lives throughout history, called for women to act: "Fighting back. On a multiplicity of levels, that is the activity we must engage in, together, if we—women—are to redress the imbalance and rid ourselves and men of the ideology of rape." Legislation was important, but it was far from enough for people such as Brownmiller. The culture and the image of women also needed to change and "the approach must be long-range and cooperative." Congresswoman Shirley Chisholm, while she strongly backed the ERA, also warned that even if it passed it would not be enough. "The law cannot do it for us," Chisholm said. "We must do it for ourselves. Women in this country must become revolutionaries. We must refuse to accept the old, the traditional roles and stereotypes.... We must replace the old, negative thoughts about our femininity with positive thoughts and positive actions."[25] Here was a call to a radical culture change, a change from which no aspect of the culture could be exempt.

VIETNAM AND THE HOPE FOR PEACE

In April 1971 the Vietnam Veterans Against the War (VVAW) spearheaded a massive rally in Washington, D.C. The VVAW members lobbied Congress, honored their dead comrades, and sought to rally the nation's conscience. At one march from Arlington National Cemetery—where they were denied admission—to the Lincoln Memorial, the veterans passed the headquarters of the Daughters of the American Revolution. A woman there said, "Son, I don't think what you are doing is good for the troops," and the vet replied, "Lady, we are the troops." They marched on from there, chanting "bring 'em home—bring our brothers home." Their demand was not granted nearly as quickly as they wished. If it had been, many fewer, both Americans and Vietnamese, would have died. But the VVAW was an essential element in the American antiwar movement that played a crucial role in ending the War in Vietnam in 1975.[26]

One strand of opposition to the Vietnam War came from older pacifist traditions. Pacifists had opposed every war conducted by the United States from the Quaker opposition to fighting in the American Revolution onward. The Fellowship of Reconciliation had been born out of opposition to World War I in 1915 while Quakers organized as the American Friends Service Committee in 1917. The War Resisters League was organized in 1923, also in response to the horrors of World War I. All three opposed U.S. involvement in Vietnam as they had opposed previous twentieth-century wars. But at the same time, Vietnam, with its length, its brutality, and its sheer insanity changed all of these organizations. As the war dragged on, it was impossible to merely oppose the war and not oppose a great deal more in the American government and, ultimately, in the American culture. Pacifists found themselves making common cause with nonpacifists who agreed that, whatever else, the U.S. should be out of Vietnam. Aging Quakers marched side by side with Communists, with Vietnam veterans, and with pot-smoking hippies. They defended "selective conscientious objectors" to the draft, young men who did not oppose all war but did oppose this war, and they held sit-ins and burned draft cards. It was a very different day for many pacifists.[27]

The grand old man of American pacifism, A. J. Muste, had become the executive secretary of the Fellowship of Reconciliation in 1936. At that time he had uttered his famous phrase, "There is no way to peace, peace is the way."

During and after World War II he had voiced a more tough-minded pacifism than some, arguing that one did not have to accept evil to be a pacifist. "To love a fellow man does not require that we cooperate with him in lying or exploiting others or some other evil thing. It requires the opposite, that we do not let him live, if he is so living, under the delusion that these things are good. It means that we love him even while he does evil, believe that he is capable of redemption, try to call to 'that God in him.' To love, to be truly human, is always to deal with others on the basis of reality."[28]

With such a hope in humanity, Muste had played a major role in the civil rights movement, helping to launch the Congress of Racial Equality (CORE) in 1942 and supporting its leaders, James Farmer and Bayard Rustin, in the most difficult years before the movement blossomed. Late in his long life, Muste became a militant opponent of the war in Vietnam. He was a key leader in helping other pacifists find common cause with many quite radical groups, with those who did not share their pacifism but did share their opposition to this particular war. In 1966 and 1967 he traveled to Vietnam, the second time meeting with Ho Chi Minh, in a continuing effort to end the war.[29]

Barbara Deming was a pacifist and member of the Committee for Nonviolent Action who linked her pacifism with radical feminism. She was confident that pacifism was the hope of the future and, in the middle of the war in Vietnam, insisted that "There is leverage for change here that has scarcely begun to be applied." In 1976 she wrote, "I now put my hopes for real social change above all else in the feminist movement and also my hopes for the further invention of nonviolence. I think the root of violence in our society is the attempt by men to claim women and children as their property."[30] Thus she, like many others of many different political and religious views, moved through the furnace of Vietnam and emerged far more radical in their social critique than when they had entered the antiwar movement.

Martin Luther King Jr. became a major critic of the American war in Vietnam. It was a hard issue for him. Many of his greatest supporters were part of the Johnson administration that was pursuing the war and the president himself had done more for civil rights than any of his predecessors since Abraham Lincoln. Nevertheless, in an April 1967 speech at Riverside Church in New York City, King directly challenged the Johnson administration's war policy and connected his opposition to the core of his civil rights beliefs. He told his audience that evening, "A time comes when silence is betrayal. That time has come for us in relation to Vietnam." He acknowledged that there were those who said, "Peace and civil rights don't mix," and those who asked, "Aren't you hurting the cause of your people?" But the reasons for opposing the war had become overwhelming to King.

The war was draining the money and the hope out of Johnson's nascent poverty programs while for African Americans it was "sending their sons and their brothers and their husbands to fight and die in extraordinarily high proportion relative to the rest of the population."[31] And it was causing terrible suffering among the people of Vietnam while building undying hatred of everything American in that land and in many parts of the world. Most of all the war was just plain wrong, and it violated the commandment to love that was at the heart of everything King stood for.

Action could no longer be postponed. "We still have a choice today; nonviolent coexistence or violent co-annihilation." It was time to decide: "We must move past indecision to action. . . . If we do not act we shall surely be dragged down the long dark and shameful corridors of time reserved for those who possess power without compassion, might without morality, and strength without sight." This was King's plea and his hope.[32]

Many others, of many differing perspectives, became part of the antiwar movement. And all were changed by it. In his actions during the last year of his life, Martin Luther King Jr. clearly linked the civil rights and antiwar movements. The Students for a Democratic Society moved from academic critique to a range of actions—nonviolent and violent—against the war and American imperialism. Young men resisted the draft and soldiers deserted to Canada and Sweden. The Women's Strike for Peace moved from a one-day demonstration to a long-term feminist opposition to the war. Moderate liberals became radicals, and radicals traveled illegally to Vietnam or fled from the U.S. government. And in the middle of the antiwar movement, as in the civil rights movement, many Americans found their voice, found their souls, and found a new and different hope for the future. William F. Crandell summarized the experience of many in his description of the Vietnam Veterans Against the War:

> When we went into the service, we had taken an oath to defend the Constitution against all enemies, foreign and domestic. In VVAW we served a second hitch. We made it possible for a nation that hated the Vietnam War to honor its veterans. Our truth helped make America free again. In the face of a great national tragedy, ours remained a prophetic voice, summoning America to be true to its deepest beliefs. What we learned is that a prophet is never without honor, whether the state bestows it or not.[33]

The wounds of Vietnam have yet to heal. Nevertheless, the courage of the wonderfully diverse coalitions that eventually played a major role in ending the war remains a part of the nation's legacy.

FARM WORKERS
AND THE GRAPE BOYCOTT

The list of hopeful movements continued to grow through the 1960s, 1970s, and 1980s. In 1965 the mostly Filipino Agricultural Workers Organizing Committee of the AFL-CIO and the mostly Mexican American National Farm Workers Association, led by Cesar Chavez, joined forces in the first successful strike by farm workers for union recognition. During the decade that followed Chavez became a national figure, many Americans boycotted table grapes for years, and farm workers won rights of which they had previously only dreamed.[34]

The development of the United Farm Workers as a union was very fast, due to a number of fortuitous circumstances. Union and community organizing efforts among California farm workers, however, had been going on since long before the dust bowl era of the 1930s. Ronald Takaki reminds modern readers that "the Chinese built the agricultural industry of California," at the time of the Civil War.[35] Almost from the beginning they were organizing to protect what they built from the absent owners of the land. As early as the 1920s, California growers had also been exploiting racial divisions, pitting Japanese, Filipino, Mexican, and Anglo-American workers against each other while workers tried to overcome these divisions and demand their rights, as they did in the Filipino-Mexican-Anglo-Agricultural Workers Industrial League in 1930.[36]

Nevertheless, something new and radically different began in the 1960s. Caesar Chavez began his organizing efforts in the grape-growing town of Delano, California in 1961. Initially the Farm Workers Association (FWA) that he proposed drew on both the community organizing model developed by Saul Alinsky in Chicago and on the older tradition of a mutual benefits association within the Catholic church. Chavez himself also had deep roots within the civil rights movement as well as Mexico's long revolutionary tradition and a total commitment to nonviolence.[37] While Chavez's goal was a union, the FWA first focused, as mutual benefit associations had for generations, on a credit union and funeral benefits organized around a tight community bound by solidarity and friendship. Initial support for the FWA's emergence into a nationally recognized union came from the Catholic church, especially from the work of some dedicated priests and nuns. In 1964, the California Migrant Ministry, organized by the Protestant National Council of Churches, joined forces and offered substantial financial and administrative support. In the early 1960s, critical support was also available from a number of other movements that were sweeping the country. Walter Reuther, the leader of the United Auto Workers, provided important financial support and national union connections; the federal government's war on poverty was at its height, and the

Office of Economic Opportunity provided direct grants (something the federal government would not have done a few years earlier or later); and student radicals from campuses such as Berkeley and Stanford, many fresh from campus-based protests and civil rights activity, joined in the effort. It was a powerful coalition, stretching far beyond the small towns of California's little noticed agricultural regions. Just as nineteenth century abolitionists, feminists, and union organizers had shared closer ties than have sometimes been recognized so the farm workers experience was an important twentieth century illustration of the links between religious and labor radicals and civil rights and later antiwar groups.[38]

In the spring of 1965, though Chavez did not think that the organization was ready, there were some small strikes called directly by groups of workers without asking advice from the leadership. These first strikes were easily undermined by pitting workers of different ethnicity—Mexican, Puerto Rican, and Filipino—against each other. In September 1965, Caesar Chavez and Larry Itliong, a leader of the Filipino farm workers, discussed a coordinated effort by Filipino and Mexican organizers. The Filipino workers were the first to call a major strike for the fall harvest in Delano. A meeting of 1,200 Mexican American workers on September 16, 1965, celebrated their revolutionary heritage with posters of Emiliano Zapata and the chant "Viva la Huelga! Viva la Causa!" The strike was a forgone conclusion when Chavez called for the vote late in the meeting. Initially the strike was not very successful, but the momentum and support grew, and the idea of a national boycott in support of the workers took hold among the strikers and their far-flung supporters. The great Delano strike and subsequent grape boycott were on.[39]

The United Farm Workers Union that emerged from the Delano strike, the boycott, and the formal merger of the initially separate ethnically based unions had its own checkered history. There were battles between an alternative Teamster-sponsored union, battles with the growers, and more difficult battles with discouragement. Nevertheless, on July 29, 1970, the Delano grape growers signed a contract recognizing the farm workers' union as their bargaining agent. Chavez declared, "From now on, all grapes will be sweet."[40] The battle for justice for agricultural workers was far from over, but hopes that had seemed impossible in 1961 had been realized.

STONEWALL AND
GAY AND LESBIAN RIGHTS

The *New York Times* for June 29, 1969, carried an article that reported a surprising shift in the culture of the city. It said:

Hundreds of young men went on a rampage in Greenwich Village shortly after 3 A.M. yesterday after a force of plainclothes men raided a bar that the police said was well known for its homosexual clientele. Thirteen persons were arrested and four policemen injured. The young men threw bricks, bottles, garbage, pennies and a parking meter at the policemen who had a search warrant authorizing them to investigate reports that liquor was sold illegally at the bar, the Stonewall Inn, 53 Christopher Street, just off Sheridan Square.[41]

A group of gay men, whom the police assumed would follow past practices and submit quietly to arrest, suddenly refused to do so any longer.[42] As with similar events for other groups, something shifted in the world of gay men and lesbians that early morning of June 28. Many who had long kept hidden and embarrassed suddenly stood up proudly. They were quite literally out of the closet and on to the streets. Many would never return to their former closeted lives. A year later, on the first anniversary of the Stonewall Riot, there was a major and very public demonstration in celebration of the new solidarity. And throughout the 1970s gay liberation became a major part of the hope and the celebration of liberation of the times.[43]

In November, 1974, Elaine Nobel was elected to the Massachusetts state legislature as the first openly lesbian or gay state representative in the United States. The following January, a Minnesota state senator, Allan Spear, announced that he too was gay and, inspired by Nobel, would no longer keep his sexual orientation a secret. And in 1977, Harvey Milk was elected to the San Francisco Board of Supervisors as the first openly gay board member, symbolizing the radical change that was taking place in the politics of that city and, indeed, the country.[44]

But gay men and lesbians in the United States before, and during, the ongoing battles for lesbian and gay rights continue to be in danger of far more than job loss, social ostracism, or an embarrassing arrest and exposure at what used to be the routine police raids on places like the Stonewall Inn. In November 1978, in San Francisco, long known as the city most friendly to gay citizens, Mayor George Moscone, a strong supporter of gay people, and Harvey Milk were both shot in their offices by a conservative former supervisor, Dan White. In 1973, the Up Stairs bar in New Orleans was burned in a probable arson attack and 32 gay men were killed. In October, 1998, a young student at the University of Wyoming, Matthew Shepard, was left to die tied to a fence on an isolated country road.[45] And throughout the 1980s and 1990s an epidemic of unimaginable proportions, Acquired Immune Deficiency Syndrome (AIDS), swept the country. Clearly the struggle for the rights of homosexuals was a battle for life itself. But after Stonewall, there was a new and wide-ranging consensus—things had to get better and lesbians and gay men would make it happen. It was a battle that took place on many fronts.

In October 1968, the fall before Stonewall, the Rev. Troy Perry founded a new denomination, the Metropolitan Community Church (MCC), specifically organized around creating congregations of lesbians and gay men who could worship and celebrate together. Perry was clear on what set the MCC apart from other denominations. The church accepted homosexuals, "as well as anyone else who feels the need of God's love," and the church, "believes in and advocates the legalization of homosexual marriages." These two points set it far apart from nearly all other religious bodies, but made the MCC an important source of spiritual nurturing as well as a public rallying point for the gay community.[46]

While the American Psychological Association had traditionally defined homosexuality as "a form of mental illness," as Charles Socarides of Albert Einstein College of Medicine did in 1970, pressure from outside and within its own ranks led to a 1973 change when the APA board voted to remove homosexuality from its list of psychiatric disorders. The APA leaders were clear that their reasons for the change were political as well as clinical. "We will be removing one of the justifications for the denial of civil rights to individuals whose only crime is that their sexual orientation is to members of the same sex," one of the leaders in making the change said.[47] It was an important step, though only the beginning of needed changes. In 1979, in "Reflections on Black Feminist Therapy," Eleanor Johnson talked about her work as a therapist bearing the brunt of racism and sexism, and the many ambivalent feelings among her clients about sexual orientation. She talked about the fear of claiming one's own identity, "You mean, it's not crazy, or anti-nationalistic for me, a Black woman, to admit that I do in fact love Black women?" This was, Johnson understood, "Clarity . . . maybe. Perhaps it's too painful, or too joyful."[48]

As the AIDS epidemic decimated the gay community around the world, the community reacted in many different ways, supporting the sick, consoling grieving lovers and their families, and organizing politically to demand research and health care. In October 1987, at a massive demonstration in Washington, lesbians, gay men, and supporters demanded both money for AIDS research and an end to homophobic discrimination. Harvey Fierstein, an actor and playwright, said, "This is indeed our day. . . . We have marched out of the closets. . . . We are gay and lesbian, and we did this." Like the civil rights march on Washington of 1963, and many similar civil rights and antiwar marches, the October 1987 event was a powerful symbolic moment, a reminder, as one activist, Tom McClain said, that "we have the power to do things and to change things."[49] As for so many other movements, a sense of power—potential and immediate—and the belief that change is possible created extraordinary hopefulness within the lesbian and gay communities.

A RAINBOW COALITION

The many hopes of the last decades of the twentieth century must not be seen as separate developments. Many people crossed many lines and participated in different movements in different ways. The historian Nancy A. Hewitt described her own political awakenings in which she was "Converted, and I do mean converted, to anti-war politics and radical feminism as a first-year student at Smith College in the late 1960s."[50] Barbara Smith described her emergence as a writer:

> I was around during the sixties and I had been involved in Civil Rights organizing focusing on school desegregation while I was still in high school in Cleveland, Ohio. Then I went to college in 1965 and I was involved in anti-war organizing. Because it was a virtually all-white college I was also involved in the wave of Black student organizing that was happening on campuses all over the country. . . . I was lucky enough to be in an all-Black women's group, which was our Afro-American Society. . . . The other thing that I wanted to mention was my involvement in the Combahee River Collective, which was a group of Black feminists, primarily Lesbians, that began in Boston in 1974."[51]

Many movements combined in the lives of many people such as Hewitt and Smith.

Bernice Johnson Reagon recalled that many experiences of different people and the links between different movements was what gave them their power to bring about change. She warned, "Watch these mono-issue people. They ain't gonna do you no good. I don't care who they are. . . . Watch these groups that can only deal with one thing at a time."[52] As difficult as coalition politics could be, Reagon insisted, it was the emergence of surprising and diverse coalitions that represented the greatest hope for change in the emerging new century.

In 1984 the Reverend Jesse Jackson ran for president of the United States. He emphasized the diversity of the movements of the day and asked to be seen as the leader of a Rainbow Coalition in a speech to the Democratic National Convention:

> We must heal and expand. The Rainbow Coalition is making room for Arab Americans. They, too, know the pain and hurt of racial and religious rejection. They must not continue to be made pariahs. The Rainbow Coalition is

making room for Hispanic Americans who this very night are living under the threat of the Simpson-Mazzoli bill [anti-immigrant legislation then pending in Congress]. And [for] farm workers from Ohio who are fighting the Campbell Soup Company with a boycott to achieve legitimate workers' rights.

The Rainbow is making room for the Native American, the most exploited people of all, a people with the greatest moral claim amongst us. . . .

The Rainbow Coalition includes Asian Americans, now being killed in our streets, scapegoats for the failure of corporate, industrial and economic policies.

The Rainbow is making room for young Americans. . . .

The Rainbow includes disabled veterans. . . . Don't leave anybody out. I would rather have Roosevelt in a wheelchair then Reagan on a horse.

The Rainbow is making room for small farmers. . . .

The Rainbow includes lesbians and gays. No American citizen ought to be denied equal protection under the law.

Jackson reiterated his plea to expand the Rainbow until all Americans were included, until truly none were excluded from the nation's family. And, finally, he directed his plea to all Americans. He called on the young, the coming generation, and especially the poorest and most marginalized of the young to "do me one favor"—

Exercise the right to dream. You must face reality—that which is; but then dream of the reality that ought to be—that must be. Live beyond the pain of reality with the dream of a bright tomorrow. Use hope and imagination as weapons of survival and progress. Use love to motivate you and obligate you to serve the human family. . . . Our time has come. Our faith, hopes and dreams will prevail. Our time has come.[53]

The speech was the highpoint of the convention. Jackson lost the nomination to former vice president Walter Mondale, and Mondale in turn was swamped by Ronald Reagan who was elected to his second term that fall. But while the votes and the power were pointing in one direction, the hopes of many citizens, the hopes for a future that had been part of the American dream for centuries were focused most clearly that night in San Francisco. The dream was alive and well. The time may not quite have come as soon as Jackson hoped, but another generation was confident that they could not only face reality, they could also "dream of the reality that ought to be" and then commit themselves to making that dream the actual reality. In the Rainbow Coalition the dream of the civil rights movement continued to be alive and well.

GLOBALIZATION

When the leaders of the world's major economic powers gathered for their regular meeting of the World Trade Organization (WTO) in Seattle, Washington, in December 1999, they were confronted by a strong new social movement that had been emerging in the United States and around the world. Protesters rallied, marched, and effectively disrupted the WTO meeting so that the official delegates departed without completing their agenda. In was an extraordinary victory for a coalition that had received only marginal notice up to that point. The story in the *New York Times* noted this: "The surprisingly large protests in Seattle by critics of the World Trade Organization point to the emergence of a new and vocal coalition . . . [that included] not just steelworkers and auto workers, but anti-sweatshop protesters from colleges across the nation and members of church groups, consumer groups, the Sierra Club, Friends of the Earth and the Humane Society."[54] And in reality these groups had been coming together for some time. As a column in the *Washington Post* noted, "The WTO meeting was merely the place where these people burst onto the American public's radar. Social movements around the world had already linked into grass-roots networks."[55]

The protesters in Seattle had diverse agendas but they were united by deep worries about the current form of globalization including the way in which organizations like the WTO were escalating the growth of poverty around the world and undermining social legislation in country after country as well as gutting environmental protection and threatening the environment in fundamental ways. The Seattle coalition, whose size and diversity surprised many, also bridged many gulfs. They were united not only in their opposition but by a vision of an interdependent and democratic world vastly different to that planned by the economic leaders of the WTO.[56] Some of those who were engaged in the Seattle protests and the continuing movements want the WTO and similar organizations to be run by different rules and standards, while others distrust all forms of international quasi-government and want to turn to national or much more local governments. On the other hand, nearly all are united in demanding the protection and expansion of worker's rights to organize and bargain collectively and to expand their share of the world's economic resources. They want to end the tendency of multinational corporations to move from country to country to undermine pay and living standards and the concomitant impoverishment of millions that has been one of the primary results of globalization in the last decade. They also want to expand the protection of the environment through national and local regulations and ensure that international treaties do not undermine national environmental protection efforts or other international efforts aimed at enhancing the world's natural environment.[57]

In a review of what they called the Battle of Seattle, writers for *The Economist* noted the deeper roots of the movement that came together in 1999.

> The watershed was the Earth Summit in Rio de Janeiro in 1992, when the NGOs [non-governmental organizations] roused enough public pressure to push through agreements on controlling greenhouse gases. In 1994, protesters dominated the World Bank's anniversary meeting with a "Fifty Years Is Enough" campaign, and forced a rethink of the Bank's goals and methods. . . . In the past couple of years another global coalition of NGOs, Jubilee 2000, has pushed successfully for a dramatic reduction in the debts of the poorest countries. . . . [and] One of the biggest successes of the 1990s was the campaign to outlaw landmines, where hundreds of NGOs, in concert with the Canadian government, pushed through a ban in a year.

In a decade that had been described by many as quiescent and lacking activism, a deeper look by reporters such as these found considerable activity, and indeed success and reason for hope. They concluded, "In short, citizens' groups are increasingly powerful at the corporate, national and international level."[58] And while the antiglobalization campaign is still very new, there was reason to believe that power would expand in the new century.

HOPE ON SEPTEMBER 11

The optimism with which many Americans greeted the new millennium collapsed along with the twin towers of the World Trade Center on September 11, 2001. A sense of safety and confidence, along with the sense that since the end of the cold war the nation was on the right course in the world, all crashed with the terrible tragedy of fear and death that day. It was a time, appropriately, for grief and loss more than hope. And yet, in the midst of tragedy, there was hope.

In New York City, the courage of firefighters and police officers was an inspiration to people trying to make sense of the day. Public School teachers showed extraordinary courage in ensuring the evacuation of all of the students in the several elementary and high schools that were in the immediate vicinity of the World Trade Center. Two paraprofessionals—teaching assistants Julia Martinez and Margaret Espinoza—symbolized the actions of many. Martinez and Espinoza were responsible for two wheelchair-bound students, 11th graders Becky and Stephanie at the High School of Leadership and Public Service, located within a block of the World Trade Center.

As the evacuation of the 750-student high school began soon after the first plane hit the first tower that Monday morning, wheelchairs were not easy to move. Eventually Martinez and Espinoza were blocked by debris and they simply picked up the girls and carried them. Trapped by a brick wall, they found a student and a stranger who helped them get the girls over the wall and the four-foot drop. Eventually the girls and their adult companions all made it to safety. Martinez remembered, "I didn't even have time to think about what to do that day. I didn't even think about my family. I just did it. I had to get my Stephanie out to safety." And one of the students, Becky, said, "I'm just very grateful. Without Margaret, I would have been more scared and would have had a lot more nightmare experiences. She comforted me every second."[59] The reality was that students like Becky probably would have perished with the airline passengers and office workers if it had not been for the heroic efforts of her companion. Such stories were repeated across the city that day. New Yorkers felt a pride, a sense of community, and a hope that was in direct contrast to the terror that surrounded them. As so many times before, working Americans—average everyday people who normally do not receive recognition—gave hope to each other and to the nation.

In the aftermath of September 11, fear seemed ready to overcome hope on many occasions. There were ugly signs of racism and ethnocentrism in attacks on Muslims in communities across the United States and around the world. Hard won civil liberties and civil rights seemed easy to surrender in return for an illusive homeland security. Yet again, there were surprising and encouraging voices of resistance to the fears that seemed at times to dominate the national discourse.

When in the immediate aftermath of the tragedy, President George W. Bush submitted a new Anti-Terrorism Bill to the Congress, many applauded, but some were deeply troubled. Wisconsin Senator Russell Feingold summed up the feelings of many when he warned of the danger of undermining the constitutional protection of civil liberties and the risks of indiscriminate attacks on Arab Americans and Muslim Americans. He told the Senate:

> Some have said rather cavalierly that in these difficult times we must accept some reduction in our civil liberties in order to be secure. Of course, there is no doubt that if we lived in a police state, it would be easier to catch terrorists. If we lived in a country that allowed the police to search your home at any time for any reason . . . that allowed the government to hold people in jail indefinitely based on what they write or think, or based on mere suspicion that they are up to no good, then the government would no doubt discover and arrest more terrorists. But that would probably not be a country in which we would want to live. . . . In short it would not be America. Preserving our freedom is one of the main reasons that we are now engaged in this new war on terrorism. We will lose that war without firing a shot if we sacrifice the liberties of the American people.

In those remarks in the immediate aftermath of September 11, Feingold was standing against a very popular tide of opinion. He was also was asking his colleagues to remember their duty to envision something better than a fearful and vengeful nation, to protect "both the American people and the freedoms at the foundation of American society."[60]

A CONTINUING SONG OF HOPE

From John Adams and Thomas Jefferson, Mother Jones and Rosa Parks, to Jesse Jackson and Russell Feingold; from the Pueblo Indians of Taos, to unnamed resistance fighters in rural New Mexico or urban Detroit, the protesters in Seattle and the paraprofessionals in the New York City Schools on September 11, Americans have kept hope alive and allowed that hope to fuel courageous efforts to build a better future in every generation. Hope is the alternative, not only to despair but to passive acquiescence in an oppressive reality. Hope has been the fuel that led people of every generation to heed the plea expressed in Maya Angelou's words, "Do not be wedded forever to fear, yoked eternally to brutishness."[61]

In his conclusion to *The Souls of Black Folk*, W. E. B. DuBois wrote "of the Sorrow Songs," the songs of his slave and free but impoverished ancestors, who recreated the culture of their African homeland and also created a new African American culture in the land where they found themselves. They created a music that "still remains as the singular spiritual heritage of the nation and the greatest gift of the Negro people." "They that walked in darkness sang songs in the olden days—Sorrow Songs—for they were weary at heart," he wrote. And yet, DuBois also saw much more than weariness in the songs. "Through all the sorrow of the Sorrow Songs there breathes a hope—a faith in the ultimate justice of things. The minor cadences of despair change often to triumph and calm confidence."[62] This faith in "the ultimate justice of things" runs through the long history of the United States. It gave hope to those escaping slavery and those surviving it. And in its own different melodies, it also gave hope to Native Americans and Mexicans resisting conquest, union organizers and immigrants resisting power elites, and modern civil rights workers of many stripes who hoped for a better justice and who were determined to create it. Far from being a diversion, songs have been one of the great carriers of some of the best and most hopeful in the history of the American nation.[63]

Hope runs through the songs of African Americans risking all to escape slavery and singing coded words such as:

Steal away, steal away, steal away to Jesus!
Steal away, steal away home, I don't have long to stay here![64]

This song could be interpreted, by slave and master alike, as a look for a heavenly home after death, but could also be a signal that a slave, or slave family, should be on the lookout for a conductor on the underground railroad, that they did not, indeed, have long to stay here.

Hope is what gave union men and women the courage to conceive of a different world, to reject the passivity that was urged on them by industrialists who said the world could not change, and to work together for a different future. In Lawrence in 1912 they walked the picket line and sang:

> As we come marching, marching,
> We bring the greater days
> The rising of the women
> Means the rising of the race.
> No more the drudge and idler—
> Ten that toil where one reposes,
> But a sharing of life's glories:
> Bread and Roses, Bread and Roses.[65]

While during the great Depression of the 1930s, in Detroit and across the nation, they sang:

> They have taken untold millions
> That they never toiled to earn
> But without our brain and muscle
> Not a single wheel can turn.
> We can break their haughty power,
> Gain our freedom when we learn
> That the union makes us strong.[66]

Hope is what farm workers in the hot sun of California's Central Valley held on to as they organized a union and sang:

> Long live the farm strike!
> Long live our historic cause!
> Our people crowned with glory!
> Will achieve the victory![67]

Few battles were as difficult as the organization of the Mexican American, Filipino, and Latino Farm Workers into a union powerful enough to win major concessions from California's powerful agribusiness. Without a hope that was larger than themselves, without a belief that they were part of a historic cause, they could not have done it.

Hope is what inspired civil rights workers—facing assassination and lynchings, facing the daily assault on their right to live as citizens—to sing one of America's anthems:

> We shall overcome,
> We shall overcome,
> We shall overcome some day;
> Oh, deep in my heart,
> I do believe,
> We shall overcome some day.[68]

This legacy of hope is the greatest gift of the singers, poets, organizers, and activists of the past to those who are and will be the citizens of the emerging new century. It is a story to be remembered.

NOTES

FOREWORD

1. Peter Gabel, "The Political Meaning of Bush v. Gore, " *Tikkun* (July/August 2001): 33–43.
2. The Dalai Lama, *How to Practice: The Way to a Meaningful Life* (New York: Pocket Books, 2002), p. 39.
3. William J. Bennett, *The Book of Virtues: A Treasury of Great Moral Stories* (New York: Simon & Schuster, 1993).
4. E. P. Thompson, *The Making of the English Working Class* (New York: Random House, 1963), pp. 12–13.
5. Robert B. Reich, *The Work of Nations: Preparing Ourselves for 21st-Century Capitalism* (New York: Vintage Books, 1992), p. 208.
6. Theodore Sizer, *Horace's Compromise* (Boston: Houghton Mifflin Co., 1985).
7. Maxine Greene, "In Search of Critical Pedagogy," *Harvard Educational Review* 56:4 (November, 1986): 427–441.
8. Langston Hughes, "Freedom's Plow," in *Selected Poems of Langston Hughes* (New York: Random House, 1974), pp. 291–297.
9. Maya Angelou, *On the Pulse of Morning* (New York: Random House, 1993), n.p.
10. James Green, *Taking History to Heart: The Power of the Past in Building Social Movements* (Amherst: University of Massachusetts Press, 2000), p. 6.
11. Arthur M. Schlesinger Jr., *The Disuniting of America* (Knoxville, Tenn.: Whittle Direct Books, 1991; republished New York: Norton, 1992).

PROLOGUE

1. I have made the most use of Robert Silverberg's *The Pueblo Revolt* (1970; reprint, Lincoln: the University of Nebraska Press, 1994): and Franklin Folsom, *Indian Uprising on the Rio Grande: The Pueblo Revolt of 1680* (Albuquerque: University of New Mexico Press, 1973, 2000). The most thorough documentary record of this history remains Charles Wilson Hackett, *Revolt of the Pueblo Indians of New Mexico* (Albuquerque: University of New Mexico Press, 1942).
2. Folsom, pp.92–100.
3. Silverberg, pp. 118–119. What makes Oraibi unique is the fact that an account of the day's events has been passed down within the Pueblo community. For a historical event the telling of which is almost totally dependent on the accounts of the losers, this is a valuable exception.
4. Silverberg, p. 120. This account and the quotation are taken from Otermín's account of the events after his return to Mexico.
5. Silverberg, p. 123.
6. Silverberg, pp. 118–130.
7. Alfonso Ortiz, introduction to Folsom, *Indian Uprising on the Rio Grande*, p. 17.
8. Silverberg, p. 125.
9. Ortiz, pp. 14–15.
10. Folsom, pp. 59–70.

11. Silverberg, p. 95.
12. Silverberg, pp. 96–97.
13. Silverberg, pp. 97–100, 113–118.
14. Silverberg, pp. 136–150.
15. Silverberg, p. 143.
16. Ortiz, pp. 14, 17–18.
17. Silverberg, pp. 151–177.
18. Folsom, p. 129.
19. Marc Simmons, introduction to Silverberg, *The Pueblo Revolt*, p. viii.

CHAPTER 1

1. David McCullough, *John Adams* (New York: Simon & Schuster, 2001), pp. 117–118.
2. Joseph J. Ellis, *American Sphinx: The Character of Thomas Jefferson* (New York: Alfred A. Knopf, 1997), pp. 57–59; McCullough, pp. 118–119, 126–129.
3. McCullough, p. 117.
4. Ellis, pp. 57–58.
5. Ellis, pp. 57–63; McCullough, pp. 117–136.
6. Julian P. Boyd, editor, *The Papers of Thomas Jefferson* (Princeton: Princeton University Press, 1950), Volume I, pp. 429–432; see also format in Alan Brinkley, *The Unfinished Nation* (New York: McGraw-Hill, 1997), p. A-5. (I have followed modern convention regarding the use of capital letters here and elsewhere throughout the chapter.)
7. Boyd, editor, *The Papers of Thomas Jefferson*, Volume I, pp. 429–432.
8. McCullough, pp. 136–142.
9. Adams as quoted in McCullough, p. 15. This much-cited quotation is from a letter John Adams wrote to Hezekiah Niles, February 13, 1818. The original is at the Maryland Historical Society. The letter was printed in Charles Francis Adams, editor, *The Works of John Adams, Second President of the United States: With a Life of the Author* (Boston, 1850–1856), ten volumes, Volume 10, pp. 282–289. I am grateful to Anne Decker Cecere of the Massachusetts Historical Society for tracking this quotation for me.
10. McCullough, pp. 15; 96–97.
11. McCullough, p. 97.
12. McCullough, pp. 96–97.
13. *Common Sense* is worth reading carefully. I have been guided in analysis here by my own reading of the pamphlet and by Gregory Tietjen's introduction to the 1995 edition, Thomas Paine, *Common Sense* (New York: Barnes & Noble, 1995), pp. vii-xxiv; and by Eric Foner, *The Story of American Freedom* (New York: W.W. Norton, 1998), pp. 15–28. See also Eric Foner, *Tom Paine and Revolutionary America* (New York: Oxford University Press, 1976) and Philip S. Foner, ed., *The Complete Writings of Thomas Paine*, 2 volumes. (New York: The Citadel Press, 1945).
14. Paine, p. 5.
15. Paine, pp. 11–13; Paine is citing the Old Testament Book of Judges, chapter 8 and the Book of I Samuel, chapter 8.
16. Paine, p. 16.
17. Paine, p. 27.
18. Paine, p. 28; see also pp. 32–37.
19. Paine, p. 43.
20. Paine, p. 44.
21. Paine, pp. 64, 66.
22. Paine, p. 59.
23. Paine, p. 67.
24. McCullough, p. 97.
25. Howard Zinn, *A People's History of the United States* (New York: HarperCollins, 1980, 1999), p. 77.
26. Brinkley, *The Unfinished Nation*, pp. 115–125; "the horrors of battle" quote is from Joseph P. Martin cited in Brinkley, p. 123.; see also, John Shy, *A People Numerous and*

Armed: Reflections on the Military Struggle for American Independence (New York: Oxford University Press, 1976); Charles Royster, *A Revolutionary People at War: The Continental Army and American Character* (Chapel Hill: University of North Carolina Press, 1979).

27. McCullough, pp. 73, 75–76.
28. McCullough, p. 99.
29. McCullough, p. 187; Brinkley, pp. 125–126.
30. Paine, pp. 26, 24.
31. William G. McLoughlin, ed., *The Diary of Isaac Backus*, 3 volumes (Providence: Brown University Press, 1977), II, 774; cited in Foner, *The Story of American Freedom*, p. 26.
32. Thomas Jefferson to Messrs. Nehemiah Dodge, Ephraim Robbins, and Stephen S. Nelson, A Committee of the Danbury Baptist Association, the State of Connecticut, Washington, January 1, 1802, reprinted in Gordon C. Lee, *Crusade Against Ignorance: Thomas Jefferson on Education* (New York: Teachers College Press, 1961), p. 69.
33. My own perspective on Jefferson's role in establishing the separation of church and state in the United States and on the development of religious freedom in this country has been developed in more detail in my book *Between Church and State: Religion and Public Education in a Multicultural America* (New York: St. Martin's Press, 1999). I have borrowed from that work in this section.
34. Thomas Jefferson, "A Bill for Establishing Religious Freedom," in Julian P. Boyd, editor, *The Papers of Thomas Jefferson* (Princeton, NJ: 1950), 2 volume, pp. 545–547.
35. Jefferson to Messrs. Dodge, Robbins, and Nelson, A Committee of the Danbury Baptist Association, January 1, 1802, cited in Lee, *Crusade Against Ignorance*, p. 69.
36. For a far more detailed version of this story, see chapters 1 and 2 in Sydney E. Mead, *The Lively Experiment: The Shaping of Christianity in America* (Toronto: HarperCollins Canada, 1963), and chapter 1 in Fraser, *Between Church and State*.
37. Mead, p. 4.
38. See Mead and Fraser cited above.
39. Phillis Wheatley, "To the Right Honourable William, Earl of Dartmouth, His Majesty's Principal Secretary of State for North America," *The Poems of Phillis Wheatley*, reprinted in Herb Boyd, Autobiography of a People (New York: Doubleday, 2000), pp. 29–30.
40. Lemuel Haynes, "Lexington, Massachusetts, 1775," in Boyd, 31–33.
41. Ruth Bogin, "'Liberty Further Extended': A 1776 Antislavery Manuscript by Lemuel Haynes," *William and Mary Quarterly*, 3 ser., 40 (January, 1983), 85–105; cited in Foner, *The Story of American Freedom*, p. 34.
42. Cited in Foner, *The Story of American Freedom*, p. 33.
43. McCullough, pp. 103–104.
44. Allen and Jefferson cited in Foner, *The Story of American Freedom*, p. 33.
45. McCullough, p. 116.
46. See Ellis, *American Sphinx*, pp. 363–367 for the conclusive results of DNA testing in proving Jefferson's paternity of the children of Sally Hemings.
47. Foner, *The Story of American Freedom*, p. 33.
48. Cited in Foner, *The Story of American Freedom*, p. 36.
49. Henry Mayer, *All on Fire: William Lloyd Garrison and the Abolition of Slavery* (New York: St. Martin's Press, 1998), p. 445.
50. Max Farrand, ed., *The Records of the Federal Convention of 1787*, 4 volumes (New Haven, 1911–1937) I, 135; Merrill Jensen, ed., *The Documentary History of the Ratification of the Constitution* (Madison: 1976), XIV, 707–708; both cited in Foner, *The Story of American Freedom*, p. 36.
51. McCullough's *John Adams* is on the top of the bestseller charts as this is being written, followed not far behind by Joseph J. Ellis, *Founding Brothers* (New York: Alfred A. Knopf, 2000). Also very helpful in understanding the "founding fathers" is Ellis, *American Sphinx*.
52. Foner, *The Story of American Freedom*, p. 16.
53. Philip S. Foner, ed., *Complete Writings of Thomas Paine*, II, pp. 243, 286–287, cited in Eric Foner, *The Story of American Freedom*, p. 16.
54. Foner, *The Story of American Freedom*, p. 17.

CHAPTER 2

1. There have been several excellent accounts of America's nineteenth-century communitarian movements including Dolores Hayden, *Seven American Utopias: The Architecture of Communitarian Socialism, 1790–1975* (Cambridge: MIT Press, 1976); John Humphrey Noyes, *History of American Socialisms* (Philadelphia: J. B. Lippincott & Co., 1870), Charles Nordhoff, *The Communistic Societies of the United States* (New York: Hopper & Brothers, 1875), and Alice Felt Tyler, *Freedom's Ferment* (Minneapolis: University of Minnesota Press, 1944). I have not included a discussion of the Mormons in this chapter although they certainly have similar origins in the fertile soil of nineteenth-century American religious movements and they remain certainly the most successful of the movements. See Tyler, pp. 86–107.

2. Stephen J. Stein, *The Shaker Experience in America* (New Haven: Yale University Press, 1992), pp. xiii. Stein's is certainly the best and most thorough account of the Shaker movement currently available. This chapter is also informed by the author's visits to Sabbath Day Lake, Maine, and a brief conversation with Mildred Barker.

3. Stein, p. 3–5.

4. Stein, pp. 4–5.

5. Nordhoff, pp. 119–125; Stein, p. 5.

6. See Stein, pp. 10–15, 32 for a much fuller description of Lee's life, journeys, and teachings. Stein also does an excellent job of describing the difficulty the modern historian faces in examining the earliest years of the Shaker movement, which is somewhat similar to the problems faced by historians of Christianity or other major religious movements whose leaders wrote little themselves yet established a community of followers that would seek to interpret their lives in light of future developments.

7. Stein, pp. 15–17.

8. Stein, pp. 34, 41–44.

9. Stein, p. 93.

10. Stein, p. 72.

11. "A Declaration of Junior Membership," cited in Julia Neal, *The Kentucky Shakers* (Lexington: University of Kentucky Press, 1982), pp. 52–53.

12. Cited in Neal, p. 51.

13. Stein tells the story of the split between Canterbury and Sabbath Day Lake and the continued life of the Shaker community in much more detail. For by far the best review of the recent past of the Shakers, see his study, especially Part V, pp. 355–442; see especially pp. 355–358, 370–371, 388.

14. Stein, p. xiii.

15. Stein, p. 191.

16. The biographical material on Noyes and other general information on the Oneida Community is taken from Spencer Klaw, *Without Sin: The Life and Death of the Oneida Community* (New York: Penguin Press, 1993).

17. For much more on Methodism see Emery S. Bucke, *History of American Methodism*, 3 volumes (1964).

18. Klaw, pp. 25–26, also citing John Humphrey Noyes, *Confession of Religious Experience*.

19. Klaw, p. 29.

20. Klaw, pp. 41, 60–64.

21. Klaw, pp. 65–75.

22. Klaw, pp. 154–158.

23. Klaw, pp. 73–74.

24. Jane Kinsley Rich, editor, *A Lasting Spring: Jessie Catherine Kinsley, Daughter of the Oneida Community* (Syracuse: Syracuse University Press, 1983), pp. 38–40.

25. Klaw, pp. 130–133.

26. Klaw, p. 85.

27. Klaw, pp. 81–84.

28. Rich, pp. 50–51.

29. Klaw, pp. 283–294.

30. Noyes, *History of American Socialisms*, 1870.
31. Robert Owen, *The Life of Robert Owen by Himself* (New York: A. M. Kelly, 1967), p. 22.
32. See Tyler, *Freedom's Ferment*, pp. 196–206.
33. Robert Owen, *Discourses on a New System of Society*, First Discourse, p. 11, cited in Tyler, p. 198.
34. Robert Dale Owen, *Threading My Way: Twenty-seven Years of Autobiography* (London: Trubner, 1874), p. 286.
35. See Paul Brown, "Twelve Months in New Harmony," in Tyler, *Freedom's Ferment*, p. 205.

CHAPTER 3

1. John Quincy Adams cited in Nash Candelaria, *Not By The Sword* (Tempe, AZ: Bilingual Press, 1982), p. 1.
2. Ronald Takaki, *A Different Mirror: A History of Multicultural America* (Boston: Little, Brown & Co., 1993), pp. 173–175. See also Alan Rosenus, *General Vallejo and the Advent of the Americans* (Berkeley, CA: Heyday Books, 1999) p. 35.
3. Cited in Takaki, p. 175.
4. See Takaki, p. 168–171.
5. James K. Polk, quoted in Norman Graebner, *Empire on the Pacific: A Study of American Continental Expansion* (New York, 1955), pp. 48–50, cited in Takaki, p. 172.
6. Takaki, pp. 166–167, 172; Rosenus, pp. 105–119.
7. Kearny's easy conquest of Santa Fe in 1846 has been misinterpreted as a lack of resistance to the American takeover. A year later a major uprising, centered in Taos and led by Pueblo Indians with support from conquered Mexicans led to an all-out battle and the killing of the first American governor of New Mexico, Charles Bent, before it was put down by the superior American fire power. See the prologue to this book and also Candelaria, *Not By the Sword*, Ivan B. Blum, *River of Souls* (Santa Fe, NM: Sunstone Press, 2000), and Den Galbraith, *Turbulent Taos* (Santa Fe, NM: Sunstone Press, 1983).
8. The history of the U.S. war with Mexico has been told by a number of historians. Here I have especially followed the careful work of Ronald Takaki, *A Different Mirror*, pp. 166–180, see especially pp. 176, 178–180.
9. Robert J. Rosenbaum, *Mexicano Resistance in the Southwest* (Dallas: Southern Methodist University Press, 1998), p. 15.
10. Roy P. Basler, editor, *Abraham Lincoln: His Speeches and Writings* (Cleveland: World Publishing, 1946), p. 202.
11. Henry David Thoreau, *Walden or, Life in the Woods* (1854; republished New York: Macmillan, 1962), p. 228–229; see also the introduction to the Macmillan edition by Charles R. Anderson, pp. 7–12.
12. Henry David Thoreau, *On the Duty of Civil Disobedience* (1848; republished New York: Macmillan, 1962, p. 236.
13. Thoreau, *Civil Disobedience*, p. 236.
14. Thoreau, *Civil Disobedience*, p. 237.
15. Thoreau, *Civil Disobedience*, p. 244.
16. Thoreau, *Civil Disobedience*, p. 240.
17. Thoreau, *Civil Disobedience*, p. 245.
18. Rosenus, p. 187.
19. Rosenus, pp. 152–153
20. M. G. Vallejo, "Historical and Personal memoirs," volume 3, pp. 109–117, cited in Rosenus, p. 239–240; see also pp. 3–16 and Rosenbaum, pp. 7–14, 28–33.
21. Rosenus, p. 14.
22. Rosenbaum, pp. 30–31.
23. Rosenbaum, pp. 29–31.
24. Rosenus, pp. 7–12; see also Charles A. Hale, *Mexican Liberalism in the Age of Mora, 1821–1853* (New Haven: Yale University Press, 1968).
25. M. G. Vallejo, "Historical and Personal Memoirs," volume 3, p. 384, cited in Rosenus, p. 41.

26. Rosenus, pp. 89–91.

27. Joseph Warren Revere, *A Tour of Duty in California* (New York and Boston: C. S. Francis, 1849), pp. 28–30.

28. Antonio Maria Osio, *The History of Alta California: A Memoir of Mexican California*, translated and edited by Rose Marie Beebe and Robert M. Senkewicz (Madison: University of Wisconsin Press, 1996), pp. 236, 232. Beebe and Senkewicz's translation and publication of Osio's manuscript, which was previously available only in Spanish and unpublished form in the Bancroft Library at the University of California, Berkeley, is a major addition to our understanding of the world view of the Californios.

29. "Epilogue," Osio, p. 247.

30. See Takaki, pp. 166–172; Osio, p. 226.

31. Larkin, Larkin Papers, volume 5, pp. 236–237, in Rosenus, p. 169.

32. Osio, p. 243.

33. Osio, pp. 243–246; Rosenus, pp. 177–182,

34. Rosenus, pp. 201–205.

35. Mariano G. Vallejo, "What the Gold Rush Brought to California," in Valeska Bari, *The Course of Empire, First Hand Accounts of California in the Days of the Gold Rush of '49* (New York: Coward-McCann, 1931), pp. 55–56, cited in Rosenus, p. 200.

36. See also Leonard Pitt, *The Decline of the Californios: A Social History of the Spanish-Speaking Californians, 1846–1890* (Berkeley: University of California Press, 1966, 1998)

37. Rosenus, pp. 218–220; It is worth noting that as early as 1849 another group, immigrants from China, also began arriving in California, drawn by high hopes of improving their lives from the wretched poverty of rural China, and quickly discovering marginalization and second-class citizenship in the new land. See Takaki, pp. 192–204.

38. For much more on the experience of Mexican people in California see Pitt, *The Decline of the Californios*, especially Ramon A. Gutierrez's excellent foreword to the 1998 edition. See also Genaro M. Padilla, *My History, Not Yours: The Formation of Mexican American Autobiography* (Madison: University of Wisconsin Press, 1993); Douglas Monroy, *Thrown Among Strangers: the Making of Mexican Culture in Frontier California* (Berkeley: University of California Press, 1990); Lisbeth Haas, *Conquests and Historical Identities in California, 1769–1936* (Berkeley: University of California Press, 1995); and Ramon A. Gutierrez and Richard J. Orsi, editors, *Contested Eden: California Before the Gold Rush* (Berkeley: University of California Press, 1998). For an excellent study of the contemporary situation, see Rodolfo F. Acuna, *Anything But Mexican: Chicanos in Contemporary Los Angeles* (London: Verso Press, 1996).

39. Rosenus, p. 110; see also Takaki, pp. 167–168.

40. Lester Raines, interview with Mary A. Fulgenzi, "Los Gorras Blancas," May 13, 1936, WPA File # 89, New Mexico State Records Center and Archives, Santa Fe, New Mexico. I am especially indebted to Melissa T. Salazar, senior archivist at the New Mexico State Records Center and Archives, who helped me locate this and many other documents used in this essay. Robert J. Rosenbaum's first-rate *Mexicano Resistance in the Southwest* first introduced me to the story of Las Gorras Blancas and the materials at the New Mexico Archives.

41. See Lewis Atherton, *The Cattle Kings* (Bloomington: Indiana University Press, 1961); E. E. Dale, *The Range Cattle Industry*, 2nd. ed. (Norman: University of Oklahoma Press, 1960).

42. Raines, interview with Mary A. Fulgenzi.

43. Rosenbaum offers an overview of many of these movements, not only Los Gorras Blancas. For more on the Taos Revolt of 1847 see my prologue, "The First Revolution."

44. Rosenbaum, p. 99.

45. See Rosenbaum, *Mexicano Resistance in the Southwest*, p. 101–103; and Andrew Bancroft Schlesinger, "Las Gorras Blancas, 1889–1891," *The Journal of Mexican American History* I:2 (Spring 1971), 94–97. The 1887 civil land suit, *Phillip Millhiser et al. v. Jose Leon Padilla et al.*, brought these two views into conflict in the San Miguel County Courthouse. The details are reported in Rosenbaum and Schlesinger.

46. Rosenbaum, pp. 101–103

47. J. Y. Lujan to L. Bradford Prince, July 25, 1890, Governor L. Bradford Prince Papers, Governors' Papers, Territorial Archives of New Mexico, New Mexico State Records Center and Archives, Santa Fe, New Mexico. (Hereafter cited as Prince Papers).

48. July 19, 1890, Prince Papers.

49. Rosenbaum, p. 118.

50. Miguel Salazar to L. Bradford Prince, July 23, 1890, Prince Papers.

51. Rosenbaum, pp. 120–124; Schlesinger, p. 107; Robert W. Larson, "The White Caps of New Mexico: A Study of Ethnic Militancy in the Southwest," *Pacific Historical Review* XLIV: 2 (May 1975), p. 175. Larson sees Herrera as the key figure: "The organization of the White Caps was due to the initiative of one man, Juan Jose Herrera." Schlesinger and Rosenbaum are more cautious, seeing him as more of a catalyst and less of a cause of the turmoil. My own interpretation is closer to Schlesinger and Rosenbaum.

52. *Las Vegas Daily Optic*, May 20, 1890.

53. Ironically, in addition to his exposure to labor radicalism Herrera may well have come into contact with another far less hopeful aspect of nineteenth-century populism. Larson, whose research is based on interviews with some of Herrera's descendants, insists that he was also influenced by the Ku Klux Klan. Certainly their method of disguise would support this odd and sad association. See Larson, pp. 172–173.

54. Larson, pp. 180–181.

55. Schlesinger, p. 135.

56. Ogden et al. to Powderly, August 8, 1890 in Rosenbaum, p. 121. See Rosenbaum, pp. 120–124, 209; and Schlesinger, p. 105.

57. Salazar to Prince, July 23, 1890, Prince papers.

58. Rosenbaum, p. 122.

59. *Las Vegas Daily Optic*, November 25, 1889, cited in Rosenbaum, p. 106.

60. Rosenbaum, pp. 106–107.

61. Rosenbaum, pp. 106–107; Schlesinger, pp. 98–99; *Las Vegas Daily Optic*, December 17, 1889.

62. John A. Garraty, *The American Nation*, volume II (New York: HarperCollins, 1995), 582–584.

63. For a good description of El Partido del Pueblo Unido, see Rosenbaum, chapter 9, pp. 125–139, and Schlesinger, pp. 115–122.

64. Copies of Nuestra Platforma can be found in the Prince Papers and in *Las Vegas Daily Optic*, March 12, 1890, and Rosenbaum, p. 166.

CHAPTER 4

1. The Taper story is told in John Hope Franklin and Loren Schweninger, *Runaway Slaves: Rebels on the Plantation* (New York: Oxford University Press, 1999), pp. 293–294, 324–325.

2. Joseph Taper, St. Catherines, Canada West, to Joseph Long, New Town, Virginia 11 November 1840, Joseph Long Papers, Special Collections Library, Duke University, Durham, North Carolina, cited in Franklin and Schweninger, pp. 324–325.

3. Harriet Jacobs, "Incidents in the Life of a Slave Girl," in Herb Boyd, editor, *Autobiography of a People* (New York: Doubleday, 2000) cited in pp. 90–92.

4. Franklin and Schweninger, p. 293.

5. See Franklin and Schweninger, chapters one and eleven.

6. Franklin and Schweninger, pp. 303–305,

7. Records of the General Assembly, Petition of Inhabitants of Clarendon, Clarmont, St. James, St. Stephen's, and Richland districts to Senate of South Carolina, ca. 1824, ND #1874, South Carolina Department of Archives and History, Columbia, South Carolina, cited in Franklin and Schweiniger, pp. 303–304.

8. Franklin and Schweninger, p.295.

9. Franklin and Schweninger, pp. 282–283.

10. David E. Swift, *Black Prophets of Justice: Activist Clergy Before the Civil War* (Baton Rouge: Louisiana State University Press, 1989), p. 115.

11. Frederick Douglass, *Narrative of the Life of Frederick Douglass: An American Slave* (1845; reprint, Cambridge: Harvard University Press, 1967), pp. 24–25.

12. Douglass, pp. 116–118.

13. Douglass, p. 120.

14. Douglass, pp. 142–145.

15. Biographical information on Tubman is taken primarily from Nancy A. Davidson, "Harriet Tubman," in *Notable Black American Women*, edited by Jessie Carney Smith (Detroit: Gale Research, 1992), pp. 11151–1155 and Judith Nies, *Seven Women: Portraits from the American Radical Tradition* (New York: Viking, 1977), pp. 34–59.

16. Sarah Bradford, *Harriet Tubman: the Moses of Her People* (1886; reprint, New York: Corinth, 1961), p. 23–24.

17. Bradford, pp. 31–32; Davidson, pp. 1151–1152.

18. See Nies, pp. 45–46.

19. Davidson, pp. 1153–1154.

20. Davidson, pp. 1151–1155; Nies, pp. 34–59.

21. Franklin and Schweninger, pp. 274–294.

22. Herbert Aptheker, *American Negro Slave Revolts* (New York, 1943); see also John Hope Franklin and Alfred A. Moss Jr., *From Slavery to Freedom: A History of African Americans*, seventh edition (New York: Alfred A. Knopf, 1994), pp. 143–147.

23. Franklin and Moss, p. 145.

24. For an excellent overview of the story of the Denmark Veysey revolt from which the material in this paragraph is taken, see David Robertson, *Denmark Veysey: The Buried Stories of America's Largest Slave Rebellion and the Man Who Led It* (New York: Alfred A. Knopf, 1999).

25. See Manning Marable and Leith Mullings, *Let Nobody Turn Us Around: Voices of Resistance, Reform, and Renewal: An African American Anthology* (Lanham, MD: Rowman & Littlefield, 2000), pp. 35–36.

26. "The Statement of Nat Turner, 1831," in Marable and Mullings, *Let Nobody Turn Us Around*, p. 37.

27. Franklin and Moss, pp. 146–147; see also Robertson, *Denmark Vesey*.

28. David Walker, *David Walker's Appeal in Four Articles; Together with a Preamble, to the Coloured Citizens of the World, but in Particular and Very Expressly, to those of the United States of America* (Boston: Revised and published by David Walker, 3rd ed., 1830), reprinted in Marable and Mullings, *Let Nobody Turn Us Around*, pp. 23–35.

29. Henry Highland Garnet, "An Address to the Slaves of the United States of America" (1843; reprinted in Marable and Mullings, Let Nobody Turn Us Around), pp. 58–63.

30. William Lloyd Garrison, *The Liberator*, October 21, 1859, cited in Henry Mayer, *All on Fire: William Lloyd Garrison and the Abolition of Slavery* (New York: St. Martin's Press, 1998), p. 494.

31. See Henry Mayer, *All on Fire: William Lloyd Garrison and the Abolition of Slavery*, pp. 494–505; Franklin and Moss, pp. 195–196.

32. Osborne Anderson, "A Voice from Harper's Ferry," in Herb Boyd, editor, *Autobiography of a People* (New York: Doubleday, 2000), pp. 103–108.

33. See Mayer, pp. 499–500 and the Child-Wise correspondence that was published by *The Liberator*, now available online from the Library of Congress.

34. Mayer, pp. 496–498. Citations from Thoreau and Garrison are from these pages in Mayer.

35. Mayer, p. 499.

36. Franklin and Moss, p. 196.

37. The best current study of Garrison's life and work is Mayer, *All on Fire*.

38. Mayer, p. 112.

39. Mayer, p. 112.

40. Mayer, p. 117.

41. Mayer, pp. 124–125.

42. Mayer, p. 302.

43. Mayer, pp. 118–125.

44. Mayer, p. 444–445.

45. Mayer, pp. 120–122, 237–238, xiii.
46. Charles G. Finney, *Memoirs of Rev. Charles G. Finney (An Autobiography)* (New York: Fleming H. Revell, 1876), p. 24.
47. "Introduction," in Gilbert H. Barnes and Dwight L. Dumond, eds., *Letters of Theodore Dwight Weld, Angelina Grimké Weld, and Sarah Grimké, 1822–1844*, 2 volumes (1934, reprint, Gloucester, MA: Peter Smith, 1965), hereafter cited as *Weld-Grimké*, volume I, p. xxi. For a fuller discussion of the importance of Angelina and Sarah see chapter six of this book.
48. *Weld-Grimké*, volume I, pp. xx–xxii.
49. In this analysis and subsequent parts of this chapter, I have drawn heavily on my earlier works, *Pedagogue for God's Kingdom: Lyman Beecher and the Second Great Awakening* (Lanham, MD: University Press of America, 1985), and especially *Schooling the Preachers: The Development of Protestant Theological Education in the United States, 1740–1875* (Lanham, MD: University Press of America, 1988). See also Lawrence Thomas Lesick, *The Lane Rebels: Evangelicalism and Antislavery in Antebellum America* (Metuchen, NJ: Scarecrow Press, 1980) is an exhaustive study of the topic, focusing especially on the relationship of evangelical theology and antislavery. For excellent earlier studies see also, Robert Samuel Fletcher, *A History of Oberlin College From Its Foundation through the Civil War*, 2 volumes. (Oberlin, OH: Oberlin College, 1943), especially volume I, pp. 150–166; Gilbert H. Barnes, *The Antislavery Impulse, 1830–1844: The Story of the First American Revolution for Negro Rights* (New York: Harcourt, Brace & World, Inc., 1933, 1964), pp. 64–73; Vincent Harding, "Lyman Beecher and the Transformation of American Protestantism, 1775–1863," Ph.D. dissertation, University of Chicago, 1965, pp. 460–505; and Malcolm Warford, "The Lane Student Rebellion," paper presented at Teachers College, Columbia University, New York, Spring 1971.
50. Weld to Arthur Tappan, Joshua Leavitt, and Elizur Wright Jr., Lane Seminary, Walnut Hills, Ohio, November 22, 1833," in *Weld-Grimké*, volume I, p. 120; for a biased but useful account of Weld's importance to the antislavery movement in America, see Barnes, *The Antislavery Impulse.*
51. Bertram Wyatt-Brown, *Lewis Tappan and the Evangelical War Against Slavery* (Baton Rouge: Louisiana State University Press, 1997), pp. 121–122.
52. See for example J. Earl Thompson Jr., "Lyman Beecher's Long Road to Conservative Abolitionism," *Church History*, Volume 42 (March, 1973), p. 98.
53. There are many descriptions of the "Lane Debates." See, for example, Fletcher, Volume I, pp. 150–166; Barnes, pp. 64–73; and Harding, pp. 460–505. While interpretation and details differ, the general outline is clear.
54. Weld to Lewis Tappan, Lane Seminary (Cincinnati, Ohio), March 18, 1834, in *Weld-Grimké*, volume I, p. 133.
55. See, for example, "Weld to James Hall," Editor of the *Western Monthly Magazine*, May 1834," in *Weld-Grimké*, volume I, pp. 136–146.
56. Lyman Beecher, *Autobiography*, 2 volumes (1864; edited by Barbara Cross; Cambridge: The Belknap Press at Harvard University Press, 1961), volume II, p. 246.
57. Beecher, *Autobiography*, volume II, p. 245.
58. Beecher, *Autobiography*, volume II, pp. 247–248; Fletcher, pp. 161–162.
59. "A Statement of the Reasons Which Induced the Students of Lane Seminary to Dissolve Their Connection with that Institution," December 15, 1834 (Cincinnati, OH: 1834).
60. There are several accounts of the "Lane Rebels" course after leaving Lane. Among the more useful are Wyatt-Brown, pp. 126ff.; Barnes, pp. 74ff.; and Finney, *Memoirs*, pp. 332–335.
61. By far the best history of Oberlin is Fletcher's, also useful is James H. Fairchild, *Oberlin: The Colony and the College, 1833–1883* (Oberlin, OH: E. J. Goodrich, 1883).
62. Wyatt-Brown, pp. 128–129; see also Fletcher.
63. Fletcher, volume II, p. 726.
64. "An Appeal to the Philanthropists of Great Britain on Behalf of Oberlin College—by Theodore and Angelina Weld," in *Weld-Grimké*, pp. 741–744.
65. Finney, *Memoirs*, pp. 332–333; Barnes, pp. 75–77. For a useful description of the role of an earlier institution, Noyes Academy, to both the intellectual and institutional origins

of Oberlin, see, Russell W. Irvine and Donna Zani Dunkerton, "The Noyes Academy, 1834–35: The Road to Oberlin Collegiate Institute and the Higher Education of African-Americans in the Nineteenth Century," *The Wisconsin Journal of Black Studies*, volume 22, no. 4, 1998, pp. 260–273.

66. Barnes, p. 76.
67. Barnes, p. 76.
68. Barnes, p. 76.
69. Barnes, p. 104.
70. Barnes, p. 77.
71. Barnes, p. 78.
72. Franklin and Moss, p. 199.
73. Cited in Franklin and Moss, p. 203.
74. Franklin and Moss, pp. 198–199, 203, 214–219, Roy P. Basler, *Abraham Lincoln: His Speeches and Writings* (Cleveland: World Publishing Company, 1946), p. 690.
75. Susie King Taylor, *Reminiscences of My Life in Camp* (Boston, 1902), pp.7–8, cited in Franklin and Moss, p. 204.
76. Elizabeth Cady Stanton, *Eighty Years & More: Reminiscences 1815–1897* (T. Fisher Unwin, 1898; reprint, Boston: Northeastern University Press, 1993), p. 238.
77. Stanton, *Eighty Years & More*, p. 236–238; Lynn Sherr, editor, *Failure Is Impossible: Susan B. Anthony in her own Words* (New York: Times Books, 1995).
78. Speech cited in Sherr, editor, *Failure Is Impossible: Susan B. Anthony in Her Own Words*, pp. 34–35
79. Letter, April 19, 1864, cited in Sherr, p. 37.
80. Mayer, pp. 586–587.
81. Basler, *Abraham Lincoln*, p. 427.
82. Basler, p. 793.

CHAPTER 5

1. It is worth noting that the Republic of Mexico had ended slavery in 1830—a major precipitating event in Texas's succession from Mexico—and slavery had been ended in all parts of the British Empire, including Canada, in 1838. The last vestiges of slavery in the Americas continued until emancipation in Cuba in the 1870s and Brazil in the 1880s. See Henry Mayer, *All on Fire: William Lloyd Garrison and the Abolition of Slavery* (New York: St. Martin's Press, 1998), pp. 151–165.
2. www.juneteenth.com
3. Eric Foner, *Reconstruction: America's Unfinished Revolution, 1863–1877* (New York: Harper & Row, 1988), p. 10.
4. Foner, *Reconstruction*, p. 72; the final quotation is from the S. Willard Saxton Journal, April 15, 1865, Rufus and S. Willard Saxton Papers, Yale University, cited in Foner.
5. Foner, *Reconstruction*, p. 73.
6. Foner, *Reconstruction*, p. 59.
7. Foner, *Reconstruction*, p. 10.
8. Foner, *Reconstruction*, p. 77.
9. For the most careful overview of the complexities of Reconstruction, see Foner's excellent volume cited above; also see chapters 12 and 13 of John Hope Franklin and Alfred A. Moss Jr., *From Slavery to Freedom: A History of African Americans*, seventh edition (New York: Alfred A. Knopf, 1994).
10. E. P. Thompson, *The Making of the English Working Class* (New York: Random House, 1963), p. 13.
11. Booker T. Washington cited in W. E. B. DuBois, *Black Reconstruction in America* (1903; reprint, Boston: Bedford Books, 1997), pp. 641–642; see also James D. Anderson, *The Education of Blacks in the South, 1860–1935* (Chapel Hill: University of North Carolina Press, 1988), pp. 4–32.
12. Foner, *Reconstruction*, pp. 96–97.
13. Anderson, p. 5.

14. Anderson, pp. 15–16.
15. Frederick Douglass, *Narrative of the Life of Frederick Douglass: An American Slave* (1845; Cambridge: Harvard University Press, 1967), p. 58.
16. Douglass, p. 59.
17. Douglass, pp. 63–71.
18. Foner, *Reconstruction*, p. 96.
19. D. Burt to J. R. Lewis, October, 1866, Tenn. Annual Reports to Asst. Comr., Ser. 32, Washington Headquarters Record Group 105: Records of the Bureau of Refugees, Freedmen, and Abandoned Lands, National Archives [FSSP A-6000], cited in Foner, p. 97.
20. Foner, *Reconstruction*, p. 97.
21. John W. Alvord, *Inspector's Report of Schools and Finances. U.S. Bureau of Refugees, Freedmen and Abandoned Lands* (Washington, D.C.: U.S. Government Printing Office, 1866), pp. 9–10, cited in Anderson, p. 7.
22. Anderson, p. 7.
23. W. E. B. DuBois, *The Souls of Black Folk* (1903; reprint, New York: Crest, 1961), p. 31.
24. Brenda Stevenson, editor, *The Journals of Charlotte Forten Grimké* (New York: Oxford University Press, 1988), pp. 380, 382.
25. Stevenson, pp. 382–383, 387, 390.
26. Stevenson, pp. 399, 392, 397–398.
27. Stevenson, p. 404.
28. Maria S. Waterbury, *Seven Years Among the Freedmen*, cited in Nancy Hoffman, *Woman's "True" Profession: Voices from the History of Teaching* (New York: Feminist Press, 1981), pp. 113–125.
29. Rupert Sargent Holland, editor, *Letters and Diary of Laura M. Towne* (1912; reprint, New York: Negro Universities Press, 1969), cited in Hoffman, pp. 181–183; see also Foner, pictures between pp. 194–195.
30. Anderson, p. 5.
31. Foner, *Reconstruction*, p. 99.
32. Philip S. Foner and George E. Walker, editors, *Proceedings of the Black State Conventions, 1840–1865* (Philadelphia, 1979) cited in Foner, *Reconstruction*, p. 113.
33. Alvord, "Inspector's Report," pp. 10, 20, cited in Anderson, p. 15.
34. See Foner, *Reconstruction*, pp. 144–145.
35. Anderson, p. 9.
36. Anderson, p. 11.
37. Franklin and Moss, pp. 225–227, 237–239.
38. Franklin and Moss, pp. 237–239.
39. W. E. B. DuBois, *Black Reconstruction in America*, pp. 641–649.
40. Foner, *Reconstruction*, p. 365.
41. Anderson, p. 285.
42. Anderson, p. 278.
43. Frederick Douglass, "What the Black Man Wants," in Marable and Mullings, *Let Nobody Turn Us Around*, pp. 125–131.
44. Douglass, "What the Black Man Wants."
45. Douglass, "What the Black Man Wants."
46. Speech on September 3, 1868, before the Georgia State Legislature, reprinted in Manning Marable and Leith Mullings, editors, *Let Nobody Turn Us Around: An African American Anthology* (Lanham, MD: Rowman & Littlefield, 2000), pp. 131–134.
47. Foner, *Reconstruction*, pp. 104–105, see also p. 159.
48. O. O. Howard, *Autobiography*, 2:239, cited in Foner, p. 160.
49. See Foner, *Reconstruction*, pp. 104–105.
50. Douglass, "What the Black Man Wants."
51. Sojourner Truth, 1867 speech in New York City, reprinted in Herb Boyd, editor, *Autobiography of a People* (New York: Anchor Books, 2000), pp. 144–145.
52. William L. Clay, *Just Permanent Interests: Black Americans in Congress, 1870–1992* (New York: Amistad Press, 1993), pp. 14–16.

53. "Death of Senator Hiram R. Revels," *Cleveland Gazette*, 18:39, May 4, 1901; Clay, pp. 14–19, 392–393.
54. Clay, p. 15.
55. Clay, pp. 16–17.
56. Clay, p. 18.
57. Clay, pp. 19–20; *Dictionary of American Biography*, volume II (New York: Charles Scribner's, 1958), p. 180.
58. *Congressional Globe*, 42nd Congress, second session, February 3, 1872, Appendix, p. 16, in Clay, p. 26.
59. Clay, pp. 13–43.
60. Franklin and Moss, pp. 237–246.
61. Franklin and Moss, pp. 247–251, Foner, *Reconstruction*, pp. 119–123.
62. Foner, *Reconstruction*, pp. 342–343.
63. Frederick Douglass, cited in John David Smith, *Black Voices from Reconstruction, 1865–1877* (Gainesville: University of Florida Press, 1997), p. 147.
64. Franklin and Moss, pp. 247–263; see especially U.S. Supreme Court, *United States v. Reese.*
65. Cleveland Gazette, 17:45, June 16, 1900.
66. Congressional Record, 46th Congress, second session, January 29, 1901, p. 1638 cited and described in Clay, p. 42.
67. See Clay, pp. 44–52; Franklin and Moss, chapter 13; and C. Vann Woodward, *The Strange Career of Jim Crow* (New York: Oxford University Press, 1966).
68. Nagueyalti Warren, "Frances E. W. Harper," in *Notable Black American Women*, edited by Jessie Carney Smith (Detroit: Gale Research, 1992), pp. 457–462.
69. Frances Smith Foster, "Introduction" to Frances E. W. Harper, *Iola Leroy* (1892; reprint, New York: Oxford University Press, 1988), pp. xxvii–xxxix.
70. Harper, p. 147.
71. Harper, p. 148.
72. Harper, p. 195.
73. Harper, p. 170.
74. Harper, pp. 206–207; 227.
75. Harper, pp. 231–232.
76. Frances E. W. Harper, *Iola Leroy*, edited by Deborah E. McDowell (Boston: Beacon Press, 1987), p. 282.

CHAPTER 6

1. Elizabeth Cady Stanton, Susan B. Anthony, and Matilda Joslyn Gage, editors, *A History of Woman Suffrage*, volume I (Rochester, NY, 1881), pp.
2. Elizabeth Cady Stanton, *Eighty Years & More: Reminiscences 1815–1897* (T. Fisher Unwin, 1898; reprint, Boston: Northeastern University Press, 1993), p. 145.
3. Stanton, Eighty Years & More, pp. 148–149.
4. Stanton, Eighty Years & More, p. 149.
5. Stanton, Eighty Years & More, p. 149.
6. I am grateful to Diane L. Moore for calling my attention to the importance of Matilda Gage. See her paper, "Savages, Sambos and Scabs: the Legacy of 19th Century White Feminist Radicals Matilda Joslyn Gage, Elizabeth Cady Stanton, and Susan B. Anthony" (1993); see also Matilda Joslyn Gage, *Woman, Church and State: The Original Exposé of Male Collaboration Against the Female Sex* (1893; reprint, with an introduction by Sally Roesch Wagner and forward by Mary Daly, Watertown, MA: Persephone Press, 1980); and Ida Harper, *Life and Work of Susan B. Anthony Including Public Addresses, Her Own Letters and Many from Her Contemporaries* (Indianapolis: Hollenbeck Press, 1898).
7. Stanton, *Eighty Years & More*, pp. 145–155.
8. Howard Zinn, *A People's History of the United States* (New York: HarperCollins, 1999), p. 110.
9. *The Anti-Slavery Bugle*, June 21, 1851, cited in Manning Marable and Leith Mullings, editors, *Let Nobody Turn Us Around* (Lanham, MD: Rowman & Littlefield, 2000), pp. 67–68.

10. See Marable and Mullings, pp. 67–68. I think there is reason to doubt some later versions of the speech that were rendered in the dialect of southern blacks because Truth spoke all of her life with the Dutch accent of her native Hudson Valley.

11. Lynn Sherr, *Failure is Impossible: Susan B. Anthony in her Own Words* (New York: Times Books, 1995), pp. 31–32. Sherr's is a popular and easily accessible collection of many of Anthony's most important papers, speeches, and publications.

12. For an excellent recent overview of the work of both sisters see the preface to Gerda Lerner, *The Feminist Thought of Sarah Grimké* (New York: Oxford University Press, 1998), pp. 3–46. For the classic study of the Grimké-Weld work, see Gilbert H. Barnes and Dwight L. Dumond, editors, *Letters of Theodore Dwight Weld, Angelina Grimké Weld and Sarah Grimké: 1822–1844*, 2 volumes (1934, reprint, Gloucester, MA: Peter Smith, 1965).

13. Elizabeth Ann Bartlett, editor, *Sarah Grimké, Letters on the Equality of the Sexes and Other Essays* (New Haven: Yale University Press, 1988), p. 4; see also Gerda Lerner, *The Feminist Thought of Sarah Grimké*, p. 19–27. My interpretation of the Grimkés rests primarily on Lerner's important biographical work on their lives. See also Gerda Lerner's *The Grimké Sisters from South Carolina: Rebels against Slavery and for Woman's Rights* (Boston: Houghton Mifflin, 1967).

14. Sarah Grimké, *Letters*, p. 11.

15. Sarah Grimké, *Letters*, p. 60.

16. Lerner, *The Feminist Thought of Sarah Grimké*, p. 25.

17. Sarah Grimké, *Letters*, pp. 122–123.

18. See Zinn, p. 119.

19. Stanton, *Eighty Years & More*, pp. 200–201.

20. Zinn, p. 119.

21. Michael Goldberg, "Breaking New Ground, 1800–1848," in Nancy Cott, editor, *No Small Courage: A History of Women in the United States* (New York: Oxford University Press, 2000), pp. 198–203.

22. My discussion of Anthony is based on several sources including Elizabeth Cady Stanton, Susan B. Anthony, and Matilda Joslyn Gage, *History of Woman Suffrage*, four volumes (Rochester, NY: Susan B. Anthony, 1881–1902); Ida Husted Harper, *Life and Work of Susan B. Anthony* (Indianapolis: Hollenbeck Press, 1898); Lynn Sherr, *Failure is Impossible*.

23. Harriet Sigerman, "Laborers for Liberty: 1865–1890," in Nancy F. Cott, *No Small Courage*, pp.306–307.

24. Sigerman, p. 307.

25. Sherr, pp. 107–109.

26. Stanton et al., *History of Woman Suffrage*, volume 2, pp. 630–689, cited in Sherr, 110–117, specifically pp. 110–111.

27. Stanton et al., *History of Woman Suffrage*, volume 2, pp. 630–689, cited in Sherr, 110–117, specifically, p. 112.

28. Stanton et al., *History of Woman Suffrage*, volume 2, pp. 630–689, cited in Sherr, 110–117, specifically, p. 115.

29. "Bread, Not the Ballot," in Harper, *Life and Work of Susan B. Anthony* (1898), (Salem, NH: Ayer, 1983) volume 2, pp. 996–1003, cited in Sherr, pp. 137–140.

30. Sherr, pp. 137–140.

31. Sigerman, p. 309.

32. *Woman's Journal*, June 9, 1888, reporting a May 30 speech to the New England woman Suffrage Festival in Boston, cited in Sherr, pp. 64–65; Hearing Before the U.S. Senate Committee on Woman Suffrage, U.S. Senate, February 13, 1900, cited in Sherr, p. 68.

33. Harper, *Life and Work of Susan B. Anthony*, three volumes, volume 3, p. 1375–1378, cited in Sherr, p. 273.

34. Sherr, p. 324.

35. See Sherr, pp. 319–330.

36. Stanton, "Woman's Pet Virtue" in *The Revolution* IV, n. 11 (September 16, 1869): 168–169, cited in Diane Lynn Moore, *"Ain't I A Woman?" Gender Essentialism and the Debate Over Reproductive Control in Liberal Protestantism*, Ph.D. dissertation (New York: Union Theological Seminary, 1996), p. 168.

37. Stanton, *Eighty Years & More*, pp. 24–25.

38. Stanton, *Eighty Years & More*, pp. 25–26.

39. SBA to ECS, July 24, 1895, Henry E. Huntington Library, San Marino, California, Anthony Family Collection, AF 24(2), cited in Sherr, p. 255.

40. SBA to ECS, probably April, 1896, Harper, *The Life and Work of Susan B. Anthony*, volume 2, p. 857, in Sherr, p. 257.

41. Stanton et al., *History of Woman's Suffrage*, volume 4, pp. 263–264, in Sherr, p. 255–256.

42. Stanton, *Eighty Years & More*, pp. 467–468.

43. See Ann D. Gordon, afterword, in Stanton, *Eighty Years & More*, pp. 469–483.

44. Alan Brinkley, *The Unfinished Nation: A Concise History of the American People* (New York: McGraw-Hill, 1997), p. A-25.

45. Nancy Woloch, *Women and the American Experience* (Boston: McGraw-Hill, 2000, pp. 359–361; Karen Manners Smith, "New Paths to Power, 1890–1920," in Cott, editor, *No Small Courage*, pp. 411–412.

46. Woloch, pp. 356–357; Smith, pp. 406–412.

47. Woloch, pp. 357–358; Smith, p. 411.

48. Woloch, pp. 357–360, Smith, pp. 406–412.

49. Sarah Jane Deutsch, "From Ballots to Breadlines, 1920–1940," in Cott, pp. 418–419.

50. Deutsch, in Cott, p. 422.

51. Deutsch, in Cott, pp. 422–423.

52. Emma Goldman, *Living My Life* (New York: Alfred A. Knopf, 1931), two volumes, volume I, p. 56.

53. Leslie Howe, *On Goldman* (Belmont, CA: Wadsworth, 2000), p. 55. The interpretation of Goldman that follows is indebted to Howe's work.

54. Howe, pp. 3–4.

55. Goldman, *Living My Life*, volume I, p. 9.

56. Goldman, *Living My Life*, volume I, p. 3.

57. Goldman, *Living My Life*, volume I, p. 31.

58. Goldman, *Living My Life*, volume I, pp. 46–47.

59. Goldman, *Living My Life*, volume I,. p. 173.

60. Emma Goldman, *Anarchism and Other Essays* (reprint, New York: Dover Publications, 1969), p. 176.

61. Goldman, *Living My Life*, volume II, p. 570.

62. Goldman, *Living My Life*, volume II, pp. 590–591.

63. Goldman, *Anarchism and Other Essays*, p. 50.

64. Goldman, *Anarchism and Other Essays*, p. 213.

65. Goldman, *Living My Life*, volume I, p. 87. See also Zinn, pp. 276–277.

66. Goldman, *Living My Life*, volume I, p. 91.

67. Goldman, *Living My Life*, volume II, p. 597.

68. Howe, pp. 18–21.

69. Emma Goldman, *My Further Disillusionment in Russia* (New York: Doubleday, Page & Company, 1924), p.168, cited in Howe, pp. 27–28.

70. Margaret Sanger, *An Autobiography* (New York: W. W. Norton Company, 1938, reprint, New York: Cooper Square Press, 1999), pp. 86–87. For the best overview of Sanger's life and work, see Ellen Chesler, *Woman of Valor: Margaret Sanger and the Birth Control Movement in America* (New York: Anchor Books, 1992). Also important are David Kennedy, *Birth Control in America: The Career of Margaret Sanger* (New Haven: Yale University Press, 1970); Linda Gordon, *Woman's Body, Woman's Right: A Social History of Birth Control in America* (New York: Penguin Books, 1977); and James Reed, *From Private Vice to Public Virtue: The Birth Control Movement and American Society Since 1930* (New York: Basic Books, 1978).

71. Sanger, *Autobiography*, pp. 89–92; Margaret Marsh raises a question as to whether Sadie Sachs ever existed or if she was a composite of many women whom Sanger had seen as a nurse. Those scholars most familiar with Sanger's writings know that she was certainly capable of embellishing history when it was convenient. In any case, Sanger's years as a nurse, plus her exposure to the radicalism of Emma Goldman and other socialists and

feminists in the New York of the early 1900s pointed in the same direction—the pressing need to change women's lives by giving them control of the births of their children. See Margaret Marsh, foreword, in Margaret Sanger, *Motherhood in Bondage* (1928; reprint, Columbus: Ohio State University Press, 2000), p. xvi.

72. Sanger, *Autobiography*, pp. 93–96.
73. Sanger, *Autobiography*, p. 104; see also Karen Manners Smith, "New Paths to Power: 1890–1920," in Cott, editor, *No Small Courage*, p. 403.
74. Kathryn Cullen-DuPont, introduction, in Sanger, *Autobiography*, p. ii, and M. E. Melody and Linda M. Peterson, *Teaching America About Sex* (New York: New York University Press, 2000), pp. 49–50.
75. Chesler, p. 68
76. See Moore, *"Ain't I a Woman,"* pp. 176–180.
77. Sanger, *Autobiography*, p. 108.
78. Sanger, *Autobiography*, pp. 106–120.
79. Cullen-DuPont, introduction, in Sanger, *Autobiography.*
80. Cullen-DuPont, introduction, in Sanger, *Autobiography*; see also Marsh, in Sanger, *Motherhood in Bondage*, pp. xxiv-xxxviii, and Melody and Peterson, pp. 49–71.
81. Marsh, in Sanger, *Motherhood in Bondage*, pp. xxxvii-xxxviii; Melody and Peterson, pp. 70–71.
82. Mimeographed letter to Voluntary Parenthood League members from President Myra P. Gallert, December 2, 1925., cited in Moore, p. 213.
83. Marsh's introduction to Sanger's *Motherhood in Bondage* is especially helpful on this point.
84. See for example, Marsh in Sanger, *Motherhood in Bondage*, pp. xiv-xvi.
85. Melody and Peterson, pp. 69–71; Sanger, *Autobiography*, p. 141.
86. Marsh, in Sanger, *Motherhood in Bondage*, p. xv.
87. Sanger, *Autobiography*, p. 107.
88. Marsh, in Sanger, *Motherhood in Bondage* p. xvi; Sanger, *Autobiography*, pp. 107–110.
89. Melody and Peterson, p 51.
90. Sanger, *Autobiography*, p. 377.
91. Melody and Peterson, p. 51.
92. Sanger, *Autobiography*, frontispiece.

CHAPTER 7

1. "Power Lies in the Hands of Labor to Retain American Liberty," May 1, 1930, in Philip S. Foner, editor, *Mother Jones Speaks: Collected Speeches & Writings* (New York: Monad Press, 1983), p. 366.
2. Elliott J. Gorn, *Mother Jones: the Most Dangerous Woman in America* (New York: Hill & Want, 2001), p. 9 and following.
3. For autobiographical data I have drawn primarily on Gorn's excellent, carefully researched biography *Mother Jones: the Most Dangerous Woman in America*, and on Fred Thompson's afterword in the 1990 edition of *The Autobiography of Mother Jones* (Chicago: Charles H. Kerr, 1925, 1990), as well as on stories from my own family in Trinidad, Colorado.
4. "Statement of Mrs. Mary Jones," Testimony Before Committee on Rules, June 14, 1910, in Foner, *Mother Jones Speaks*, p. 370.
5. Meridel LeSueur, foreword to the 1990 edition of *Autobiography of Mother Jones.*
6. Frontispiece, *The Autobiography of Mother Jones.*
7. Gorn, pp. 46–69.
8. Gorn, pp. 63–69.
9. John Brophy, *A Miner's Life* (Madison: University of Wisconsin Press, 1964), pp. 74–75, cited in Gorn, pp. 73–75.
10. See Gorn, p. 82.
11. The story of the Arnot strike is told in *The Autobiography of Mother Jones*, pp. 31–39.
12. See Foner, *Mother Jones Speaks*, pp. 226–230.

13. Mother Jones, from Proceedings, Special Convention of District Fifteen, United Mine Workers of America, Trinidad, Colorado, September 16, 1913, in Foner, *Mother Jones Speaks*, pp. 233–235.

14. *Seattle Post-Intelligencer*, May 31, June 1, 1914, in Foner, *Mother Jones Speaks*, p. 249.

15. See Foner's excellent account of the Colorado strike and the Ludlow massacre in Foner, *Mother Jones Speaks*, pp. 222–250. My account also benefited from an interview with my step-grandmother Mary Anselmo, who as a little girl marched with Mother Jones in Trinidad during the strike.

16. Mother Jones, reported in *New York Times*, July 4, 1923, and in Foner, editor, *Mother Jones Speaks*, p. 364.

17. *The Labor Leader*, Boston, August 27, 1887. See also Herbert G. Gutman, *Work, Culture & Society in Industrializing America* (New York: Alfred A. Knopf, 1976), p. 87. Gutman's essay, "Protestantism and the American Labor Movement: The Christian Spirit in the Gilded Age," in *Work, Culture & Society in Industrializing America*, pp. 79–117, offers a brilliant analysis of the power of grass-roots worker religious movements, especially those following in the perfectionist tradition of evangelical Protestantism, in giving energy to the early labor movement in the United States.

18. *Journal of United Labor*, Philadelphia, August 27, 1888, cited in Gutman, *Work, Culture & Society in Industrializing America*, p. 111.

19. *United Mine Workers' Journal*, March 29, 1894, cited in Gutman, *Work, Culture & Society in Industrializing America*, p. 92.

20. *National Labor Tribune*, Pittsburgh, February 3, 1877.

21. Albert Parsons, in *Tribune*, November 4, 1887, p. 2, and Letter to the Editor, *Knights of Labor*, December 11,1886, p. 11, cited in Bruce C. Nelson, *Beyond the Martyrs: A Social History of Chicago's Anarchists, 1870–1900* (New Brunswick: Rutgers University Press, 1988), pp.168–169.

22. Eugene V. Debs, Speech at Canton, Ohio, June 16, 1918, in William A. Pelz, editor, *The Eugene V. Debs Reader: Socialism and the Class Struggle* (Chicago: The Institute of Working Class History, 2000), p. 152.

23. In addition to Gutman's work noted above, see E. P. Thompson, *The Making of the English Working Class* (New York: Random House, 1963).

24. Philip S. Foner, editor, *The Factory Girls* (Urbana: University of Illinois Press, 1977), pp. xiii-xxv.

25. Foner, *Factory Girls*, pp. xxi-xxii.

26. Dover (NH) *Gazette*, reprinted in Foner, *Factory Girls*, pp. 11–12.

27. Dover *Gazette* in Foner, *Factory Girls*, pp. 11–12.

28. Harriet H. Robinson, *Loom and Spindle: Or Life Among the Early Mill Girls* (New York, 1898), pp. 86–88, cited in Foner, *Factory Girls*, pp. 12–13.

29. *Voice of Industry*, February 6, 1846, in Foner, *Factory Girls*, pp. 145–146.

30. William H. Sylvis, Address Delivered at Chicago, January 9, 1865, in James C. Sylvis, editor, *The Life, Speeches, Labors and Essays of William H. Sylvis* (Philadelphia: Claxton, Remsen & Haffelfinger, 1872), pp. 168–169, 171.

31. The best source of information on the life and work of William Sylvis is the biography collected by his son, James C. Sylvis, *The Life, Speeches, Labors and Essays of William H. Sylvis*. Like many nineteenth-century biographies, this is also a gold mine of original materials, articles, papers, and speeches by Sylvis. See also Richard O. Boyer and Herbert M. Morais, *Labor's Untold Story* (New York: United Electrical, Radio & Machine Workers of America, 1955, 1970), pp. 23–36.

32. Boyer and Morais, pp. 32–33.

33. Philip S. Foner, *Women and the American Labor Movement: From Colonial Times to the Eve of World War I* (New York: Free Press, 1979), p. 135.

34. Boyer and Morais, pp. 33–35.

35. Foner, *Women and the American Labor Movement*, pp. 132–134.

36. Terence V. Powderly, *Thirty Years of Labor, 1859–1889* (1890; reprint, New York: Augustus M. Kelley, 1968). This volume tells the story of Powderly's work with the National

Labor Union, the Industrial Brotherhood, and most of all, the Knights of Labor which Powderly led through most of its history.

37. Powderly, *Thirty Years of Labor.*

38. Eugene V. Debs, "Debs Writes Home," *The Labor Leader,* (Boston), October 12, 1895.

39. Election statistics from John A. Garraty, *The American Nation,* eighth edition, volume II (New York: Harper Collins, 1995), pp. A14-A15.

40. For a first-rate biography of Deb's life and work, see Nick Salvatore, *Eugene V. Debs: Citizen and Socialist* (Urbana: University of Illinois Press, 1984); for an earlier and somewhat idealized picture of Debs's life and especially his youth, see Ray Ginger, *The Bending Cross: A Biography of Eugene Victor Debs* (New Brunswick: Rutgers University Press, 1949), especially pp. 3–19.

41. Eugene V. Debs, "How I Became a Socialist," *New York Comrade,* April, 1902, in William A. Pelz, editor, *The Eugene V. Debs Reader: Socialism and the Class Struggle* (Chicago: Institute of Working Class History), p. 32.

42. Debs, "How I Became a Socialist," p. 34.

43. Debs, "How I Became a Socialist, " p. 35.

44. Debs, "How I Became a Socialist," p. 36.

45. Quotations and biographical information are from Arthur M. Schlesinger's introduction to *Writings and Speeches of Eugene V. Debs* (New York: Hermitage Press, 1948), pp. v-xiii. For a long time Schlesinger's 1948 book was the best source available of Debs's original writings and speeches. Pelz's new volume effectively replaces it as the definitive available work of Debs's words.

46. Debs, Opening speech delivered as candidate of the Socialist Party for President, Indianapolis, Indiana, September 1, 1904, in Pelz, pp.54–68; quotation from p. 68.

47. Address delivered Tuesday, October 30, 1923, Commonwealth Casino, 135th Street and Madison Avenue, New York City, under the Auspices of the 21st A. D. Socialist Party of New York, in Pelz, pp. 185–205; quotations from pp. 203 and 205.

48. Jacob Riis, *How the Other Half Lives* (New York: Charles Scribner, 1890).

49. Rose Schneiderman, in Irving Howe and Kenneth Libo, *How We Lived: a Documentary History of Immigrant Jews in America, 1880–1930* (New York: Richard Marek, 1979), pp. 140–143; cited, p. 141.

50. Howe and Libo, p. 142.

51. Howe and Libo, p. 142

52. Howe and Libo, pp. 142–143.

53. New York Times, May 12, 1911, cited in Irving Howe, *World of Our Fathers* (New York: Harcourt Brace Jovanovich, 1976), pp. 305–306.

54. Howe, *World of Our Fathers,* pp.387–388.

55. Patrick Renshaw, *The Wobblies: the Story of the IWW and Syndicalism in the United States* (Chicago: Ivan R. Dee, 1967, 1999), pp. 33–41. Renshaw's history of the IWW is an excellent piece of historical scholarship, sadly overlooked by too many even within the labor history arena. Anyone wanting to know more of the history of the IWW would be well served to start here.

56. Proceedings of the First IWW Convention, New York, 1905, Haywood, p. 1, and Debs, p. 114, cited in Renshaw, pp. 41–49.

57. Preamble, in Renshaw, front pages.

58. Eugene V. Debs, Speech at Chicago, November 25,1905, in Pelz, pp. 73–87; quotation from p. 87.

59. William D. Haywood, *Bill Haywood's Book* (New York: International Publishers, 1929), p. 239.

60. See Renshaw, pp. 195–238.

61. Joe Hill, the *IWW Songbook,* cited in Renshaw, pp. 75, 43.

62. Foner, *Women and the American Labor Movement,* pp. 426–429.

63. Foner, *Women and the American Labor Movement,* pp. 428–429.

64. Elizabeth Gurley Flynn, *The Rebel Girl: An Autobiography, My First Life, 1906–1926* (New York: International Publishers, 1955, 1994), pp. 127–128.

65. Michael Miller Topp, "The Lawrence Strike and the Defense Campaign for Ettor and Giovannitti: The Possibilities and Limitations of Italian American Syndicalism," unpublished paper presented at Massachusetts Historical Society, 2000, p. 1. See also Bruno Ramirez, "Italian Americans," in Mary Jo Buhle, Paul Buhle, and Dan Georgakas, editors, *Encyclopedia of the American Left* (New York: Oxford University Press, 1990, 1998), p. 389.

66. Flynn, p. 128.

67. Foner, *Women and the American Labor Movement*, p. 430.

68. Foner, *Women and the American Labor Movement*, p. 431; see also Flynn, p. 129.

69. Flynn, pp. 133–135.

70. Foner, *Women and the American Labor Movement*, p. 432.

71. Flynn, p. 137.

72. Flynn, p. 138.

73. Haywood, p. 253.

74. Flynn, p. 134.

75. Foner, *Women and the American Labor Movement*, pp. 430–431. A debate has emerged among historians as to whether the "bread and roses" phrase was actually used during the strike itself or only added after the fact. In either case, the phrase captures the hope and courage of those who made Lawrence a byword for successful labor militancy.

CHAPTER 8

1. The word progressive has come to mean so many different things that it is useful primarily as a descriptor of a very wide range of reform activities that took place in the United States in the late nineteenth and early twentieth centuries. For some of the debates about the nature of turn of the twentieth century progressivism see Samuel Hays, *The Response to Industrialism* (Chicago: University of Chicago Press, 1957), Robert Wiebe, *The Search for Order* (New York: Hill and Wang, 1967), Gabriel Kolko, *The Triumph of Conservatism* (New York: Free Press, 1963) Lawrence A. Cremin, *The Transformation of the School: Progressivism in American Education, 1876–1957* (New York: Vintage Books, 1961), and Richard Hofstadter, *The Age of Reform* (New York: Vintage Books, 1955). For my own interpretation on the impossibility of defining progressivism, see my "Who Were the Progressive Educators Anyway? A Case Study of the Progressive Education Movement in Boston, 1905–1925," *Educational Foundations* II:1 (Spring, 1988).

2. Jane Addams, *The Spirit of Youth and the City Streets* (New York: Macmillan, 1909; Champaign: University of Illinois Press, 1972), pp. 160–162.

3. Allen F. Davis, introduction to Addams, *The Spirit of Youth and City Streets*, p. xv. See also Allen F. Davis, *Spearheads for Reform: The Social Settlements and the Progressive Movement* (New York: Oxford University Press, 1967).

4. Jane Addams, *Twenty Years at Hull House* (New York: Macmillan, 1910; Signet Classics, 1961), p. 71. See also Davis, introduction to Addams, *The Spirit of Youth and the City Streets*, pp. vii-xxx.

5. Addams, *Twenty Years at Hull House*, p. 73.

6. Addams, *Twenty Years at Hull House*, p. 87.

7. Addams, *Twenty Years at Hull House*, p. 91.

8. Addams, *Twenty Years at Hull House*, pp. 263–269.

9. Nancy Woloch, *Women and the American Experience* (New York: McGraw-Hill, 2000), pp. 358–359.

10. Henry Steele Commager, foreword, *Twenty Years at Hull House*, pp. xvii-xix; and Woloch, pp. 358–359.

11. Addams, *Twenty Years at Hull House*, p. 205.

12. Addams, *The Spirit of Youth and the City Streets*, p. 16.

13. Addams, *The Spirit of Youth and City Streets*, pp. 120–122.

14. Addams, *The Spirit of Youth and City Streets*, pp. 122–123.

15. Addams, *The Spirit of Youth and City Streets*, pp. 124–125.

16. Addams, *The Spirit of Youth and City Streets*, pp. 143–146.

17. Addams, *Twenty Years at Hull House*, p. 295.

18. Jacob Riis, *How the Other Half Lives* (1890), p. 1.

19. Riis, p. 2.

20. Riis, pp. 4–5.

21. See Alan Brinkley, *The Unfinished Nation* (New York: McGraw-Hill, 1997), pp. 581–584 and 608–609.

22. Ernest Poole, "Waifs on the Street, *McClure's Magazine* xxi (May 1903).

23. Lincoln Steffens, *The Autobiography of Lincoln Steffens* (New York: The Literary Guild, 1931), pp. 615–618.

24. For a promising new study of journalism in the progressive era and beyond see William Serrin and Judith Serrin, editors, *Muckraking!: The Journalism That Changed America* (forthcoming 2002).

25. Charles M. Sheldon, *In His Steps: Or, What Would Jesus Do?* (1897; reprint, Chicago: John C. Winston, 1957), pp. 254–257.

26. Brinkley, p. 584.

27. George D. Herron, *Between Caesar and Jesus*, in H. Shelton Smith, Robert T. Handy, and Lefferts A. Loetscher, *American Christianity: An Historical Interpretation with Representative Documents*, volume two, 1820–1960 (New York: Charles Scribner's Sons, 1963), p. 392.

28. George D. Herron, *The Christian State: A Political Vision of Christ* (New York: Thomas Y. Cromwell, 1895, pp. 102–103, cited in cited in Edwin S. Gaustad, *A Documentary History of Religion in America Since 1865* (Grand Rapids: William B. Eerdmans, 1998), p. 131.

29. Walter Rauschenbusch, *The Righteousness of the Kingdom* (New York: Abingdon Press, 1968), pp. 70–72, cited in Gaustad, p. 125.

30. Walter Rauschenbusch, *A Theology for the Social Gospel* (New York: Macmillan, 1917; Louisville, KY: Westminster John Knox Press, 1997), pp. 5–6.

31. Reinhold Niebuhr, *Leaves from the Notebook of a Tamed Cynic* (1929; reprint, New York: Meridian Books, 1957), pp. 128–129.

32. Niebuhr, p. 62

33. Niebuhr, p. 194

34. James Gibbons, *A Retrospect of Fifty Years* (Baltimore: John Murphy, 1916), I, pp. 194–198, cited in Gaustad, p. 117.

35. Gaustad, pp. 117–122.

36. Edward McGlynn, cited in Gaustad, pp. 127–128.

37. Gaustad, p. 127.

38. John A. Ryan and Joseph Husslein, editors, *The Church and Labor* (New York: Macmillan, 1920), pp. 243–245.

39. Ryan and Husslein, pp. 243–245, see also Smith, Handy, and Loetscher, volume two, pp. 383–391.

40. Ryan and Husslein, pp. 243–245.

41. Irving Howe, *How We Lived: A Documentary History of Immigrant Jews in America, 1880–1930* (New York: Richard Marek Publishers, 1979), p. 161.

42. I. Benequit, memoirs translated from Yiddish and cited in Howe, pp. 158–159.

43. Central Conference of American Rabbis, Commission on Social Justice (1928), cited in Gaustad, pp. 123–124.

44. John Dewey, *The School and Society* (Chicago: University of Chicago Press, 1899), pp. 6–29, reprinted in James W. Fraser, *The School in the United States: A Documentary History* (New York: McGraw-Hill, 2001) p. 207.

45. Dewey, *The School and Society*, in Fraser, *The School in the United States*, p. 198–199.

46. Cremin, *The Transformation of the School*, p. viii.

47. See for example my discussion of progressive education in *The School in the United States: A Documentary History*, pp. 181–221.

48. Margaret A. Haley, "Why Teachers Should Organize," *National Educational Association, Addresses and Proceedings* (St. Louis: 1904), pp. 145–152, reprinted in part in Fraser, *The School in the United States*, pp. 188.

49. Haley, "Why Teachers Should Organize," in Fraser, pp. 189–190.

50. See for example David Tyack, *The One Best System: A History of American Urban Education* (Cambridge: Harvard University Press, 1974).

51. George S. Counts, *Dare the School Build a New Social Order?* (1932; reprint, Carbondale: Southern Illinois University Press, 1978), pp. 33–34.
52. Counts, pp. 4–5.
53. Counts, pp. 19–20.
54. John Dewey, "My Pedagogic Creed," *The School Journal* (January 16, 1897), pp. 77–80, cited in Martin S. Dworkin, editor, *Dewey on Education* (New York: Teachers College Press, 1959), p. 31.
55. Eugene V. Debs, "Speech Delivered at Nimisilla Park, Canton, Ohio, Sunday afternoon, June 16, 1918," in William A. Pelz, editor, *The Eugene V. Debs Reader* (Chicago: Institute of Working Class History, 2000), pp. 155–156.
56. Debs, Canton speech, pp. 156–157.
57. Debs, Canton speech, p. 151.
58. Debs, Canton speech, p. 165.
59. Debs, "Address to the Jury," September 12, 1918, in Pelz, p. 167.
60. Debs, "Statement to the Court," in Pelz, pp. 170–171.
61. Robert Cooney and Helen Michalowski, editors, from an original text by Marty Jezer, *The Power of the People: Active Nonviolence in the United States* (Philadelphia: New Society Publishers, 1987), p, 41.
62. Cooney and Michalowski, p.39.
63. Cooney and Michalowski, pp. 44–45.
64. Cooney and Michalowski, p.44.
65. Cooney and Michalowski, pp. 54–55.
66. Harry Emerson Fosdick, *The Challenge of the Present Crisis* (London: Student Christian Movement, 1917), pp. 59–62, cited in Gaustad, p. 146.
67. Cooney and Michalowski, p. 47.

CHAPTER 9

1. Nick Salvatore, *Eugene V. Debs: Citizen and Socialist* (Urbana: University of Chicago Press, 1984), p. 328.
2. My interpretation of the Sacco and Vanzetti case is drawn from many sources. I find Richard Polenberg's introduction to *The Letters of Sacco and Vanzetti*, edited by Marion Denman Frankfurter and Gardner Jackson (New York: Penguin Books, 1997) especially helpful. Also helpful is Roberta Strauss Feuerlicht, *Justice Crucified: The Story of Sacco and Vanzetti* (New York: McGraw-Hill, 1977. The extraordinary literature around the case includes a growing body focused on the continued discussion of their guilt or innocence. Whatever the conclusions regarding that issue, it seems clear to nearly all observers that they never received even the minimum protection of a fair trial and were tried much more for their anarchism—which they never denied—than for the specific murder of which they were accused. Finally, I am grateful to my neighbor and friend John DePietro, now in his eighties, for describing how he experienced the trial, execution, and funeral of Sacco and Vanzetti as a young boy in the then predominantly Italian neighborhood of East Boston, Massachusetts, where I now live.
3. Polenberg, pp. ix–xvi.
4. Polenberg, pp. x–xxiv. English was a second language for both men, and neither mastered it fully. Where appropriate I have silently corrected their spelling and grammar. Their meaning was clear enough.
5. Bartolomeo Vanzetti to Alice Stone Blackwell, Charlestown Prison, February 27, 1924, in *Letters of Sacco and Vanzetti*, pp. 117–122.
6. *Letters of Sacco and Vanzetti*, p. 117.
7. Preface to the 1928 edition of *Letters of Sacco and Vanzetti*, p. lx.
8. Polenberg, pp. xiii–xvi.
9. Feuerlicht, p. vii.
10. Frontispiece, original edition, *Letters of Sacco and Vanzetti* (1928); see Polenberg, p. xxxi.
11. Amy Jacques Garvey, editor, *The Philosophy and Opinions of Marcus Garvey* (Dover, MA: the Majority Press, 1986, originally published in two volumes 1923 and 1925), II: 38.

See also E. David Cronon, *Black Moses: The Story of Marcus Garvey* (Madison: University of Wisconsin Press, 1955, 1969), pp. 16–19.

12. See Cronon, pp. 21–36.

13. Cronon, pp. 41–47; see also John Hope Franklin and Alfred A. Moss, *From Slavery to Freedom: A History of African Americans* (New York: Alfred A. Knopf, 1994), pp. 356–359.

14. Marcus Garvey, "The Future As I See It," in Amy Jacques Garvey, I:73–74.

15. Amy Jacques Garvey, I: 75.

16. John Cartwright, lecture, Boston University.

17. Marcus Garvey, "Aims and Objects of Movement for Solution of Negro Problem," in Amy Jacques Garvey, I: 37–39.

18. Cronon, pp. 49–65.

19. Cronon offers a very detailed analysis of Garvey's economic downfall including the shaky financing of the Black Star Line and the subsequent trial. I have depended on his research for these paragraphs.

20. Marcus Garvey, *The Negro World*, June 6, 1925, reprinted many times as "African Fundamentalism" and included in Robert A. Hill and Barbara Blair, editors, *Marcus Garvey Life and Lessons* (Berkeley: University of California Press, 1987), pp. 3–6.

21. I first noticed this in a series of conversations with Mrs. Ruth Batson, heroic leader of the NAACP in Boston for many years, and have had it confirmed several times since. See also Franklin and Moss, p. 359–360.

22. See Henry Louis Gates Jr., and Cornel West, *The African American Century: How Black Americans Have Shaped Our Country* (New York: Free Press, 2000), p. 1–7.

23. See Gates and West; also Saunders Redding, introduction, 1961 edition, W. E. B. DuBois, *The Souls of Black Folk* (New York: 1903; Crest, 1961), pp. vii–xi.

24. DuBois, *The Souls of Black Folk*, "The Forethought."

25. DuBois, pp. 16–17.

26. DuBois, p. 17.

27. *Nashville Banner*, cited in Redding, p. x.

28. Cited in Franklin and Moss, p. 318.

29. Franklin and Moss, pp. 317–321; Gates and West, pp. 1–7.

30. DuBois, pp. 181–191.

31. There are, of course, many studies of the Great Depression. I still find John Kenneth Galbraith's *The Great Crash* (1954) most helpful. See also Michael Bernstein, *The Great Depression: Delayed Recovery and Economic Change in America, 1929–1939* (1987)

32. Franklin D. Roosevelt, Inaugural Address, March 4, 1933, in *The Public Papers and Addresses of Franklin D. Roosevelt* (New York: Random House, 1938), pp. 11.

33. Roosevelt, pp. 11–12.

34. Roosevelt, p. 16. Alan Brinkley, *The Unfinished Nation* (New York: McGraw-Hill, 1997), pp. 702–705

35. Brinkley, pp. 702–709.

36. Brinkley, pp. 718–179; see also Irving Bernstein, *A Caring Society: The New Deal, the Worker, and the Great Depression* (Boston: Houghton Mifflin, 1985).

37. Myles Horton with Judith Kohl and Herbert Kohl, *The Long Haul: An Autobiography of Myles Horton* (New York: Anchor Books, 1990), p. 43.

38. See especially William E. Leuchtenburg's *Franklin D. Roosevelt and the New Deal* (New York: Harper & Row, 1963) and his *The FDR Years: On Roosevelt and His Legacy* (New York: Columbia University Press, 1995).

39. See Eric Foner, *The Story of American Freedom* (New York: W. W. Norton, 1998), pp. 195–218, Sidney Fine, *Sit-Down: The General Motors Strike of 1936–1937* (Ann Arbor: University of Michigan Press, 1969), pp. 28–29.

40. Richard O. Boyer and Herbert M. Morais, *Labor's Untold Story* (New York: United Electrical, Radio & Machine Workers of America, 1970), pp. 290–293. See also Bruce Minton and John Stuart, *Men Who Lead Labor* (New York: Modern Age, 1937), pp. 85–86, Saul Alinsky, *John L. Lewis, An Unauthorized Biography* (New York: G. P. Putnam,

1949), Robert H. Zieger, *John L. Lewis: Labor Leader* (1988), and Melvyn Dubofsky and Warren Van Tine, *John L. Lewis* (1977).

41. John L. Lewis, July 6, 1936, cited in Boyer and Morais, p. 290.
42. Boyer and Morais, p. 293.
43. Ruth McKenney, *Industrial Valley* (New York: Harcourt, Brace, 1939), pp. 261–262 in Boyer and Morais, pp. 294–295.
44. Boyer and Morais, p. 295, song by UAW counsel, Maurice Sugar in Boyer and Morias.
45. Cited in Fine, p. 61.
46. See Foner, *The Story of American Freedom*, pp. 196–210.
47. Fine, pp. 56–57.
48. Fine, p. 1; Boyer and Morais, pp. 301–302.
49. Fine, pp. 1–13. Fine offers a colorful and detailed minute by minute account of the battle of January 11 as well as the rest of the Flint sit-down strike.
50. Fine, pp. 156–158.
51. Fine, pp. 157–172, see specifically p. 168.
52. Fine, pp. 112–113, 279.
53. Fine, p. 170.
54. Fine, p. 163.
55. Cited in Boyer and Morais, p. 308.
56. Fine, pp. 304–306.
57. Sarah Jane Deutsch, "From Ballots to Breadlines: 1920–1940," in Nancy F. Cott, editor, *No Small Courage: A History of Women in the United States* (New York: Oxford University Press, 2000), p. 457–460.
58. Deutsch, p. 458.
59. Mary McLeod Bethune, speech in the Mary McLeod Bethune Papers, Amistad Research Center, Tulane University, New Orleans, published in Manning Marable and Leith Mullings, editors, *Let Nobody Turn Us Around* (Lanham, MD: Rowman & Littlefield, 2000), pp. 320–323.
60. Mary McLeod Bethune, "Last Will and Testament," *Ebony*, August, 1955, in Franklin and Moss, p. 482.
61. Ronald Takaki, *Strangers from a Different Shore: A History of Asian Americans* (New York: Penguin Books, 1989), p. 221.
62. Franklin and Moss, pp. 436–437.
63. Franklin and Moss, pp. 436–437.
64. A. Philip Randolph, in Herb Boyd, *Autobiography of a People* (New York: Anchor Books, 2001), pp. 309–310.
65. Horton, p. 44.
66. Horton, p. 44.
67. Horton, pp. 1–7.
68. Horton, p.31.
69. Horton, pp. 33–55.
70. Horton, pp. 56–62.
71. Horton, pp. 63–84.
72. Horton, pp. 86–87.
73. Horton, p. 78.
74. Horton, p. 79.
75. Horton, p. 93.
76. Horton, pp. 96–97.
77. Horton, p. 87.
78. Horton, pp. 99–104; Cynthia Stokes Brown, *Ready From Within: Septima Clark and the Civil Rights Movement* (Trenton, NJ: Africa World Press, 1990), pp. 41–54.
79. Horton, p. 105. This approach sounds a great deal like what Jacqueline Jordan Irvine has come to call "culturally responsive pedagogy." See Jacqueline Jordan Irvine, editor, *Culturally Responsive Pedagogy* (New York: Palgrave, 2002).
80. Brown, pp. 62–64; Horton, pp. 96–108.
81. Horton, pp. 121, 186–187.
82. Horton, pp. 148–150.

83. Horton, pp.107–108.

CHAPTER 10

1. Martin Luther King Jr., "I Have a Dream," (1963) in James M. Washington, editor, A Testament of Hope: The Essential Writings and Speeches of Martin Luther King Jr. (San Francisco: Harper San Francisco, 1986), pp. 217–220, quotations from 219.
2. King, "I Have a Dream," p. 217.
3. Brown v. Board of Education 347 U.S. 483 (1954). For the best overall history of the Brown case and the twenty years of planning that led up to it, see Richard Kluger, *Simple Justice: A History of "Brown v. Board of Education" and Black America's Struggle for Equality* (New York: Alfred A. Knopf, 1975).
4. Thurgood Marshall, "Edwin Rogers Embree memorial Lectures," Dillard University, New Orleans, Louisiana, Spring, 1954, reprinted in Manning Marable and Leith Mullings, editors, *Let Nobody Turn Us Around: Voices of Resistance, Reform, and Renewal* (Lanham, MD: Rowman & Littlefield, 2000), p. 358. The many speeches and essays reprinted in Marable and Mullings make it one of the best places to begin for anyone wanting to get a flavor of the range of civil rights activity, not only in the era of the great civil rights movement but throughout the history of the United States.
5. Anne Moody, *Coming of Age in Mississippi* (New York: Laurel, 1968), pp. 126–128; Cynthia Stokes Brown, editor, *Ready from Within: Septima Clark and the Civil Rights Movement* (Trenton, NJ: Africa World Press, 1990), pp. 35–37.
6. John Hope Franklin and Alfred A. Moss Jr., *From Slavery to Freedom: A History of African Americans*, seventh edition (New York: Alfred A. Knopf, 1994), pp. 317–319, 354–355, 410–412; Henry Louis Gates Jr., and Cornel West, *The African American Century* (New York: Free Press, 2000).
7. Kluger, pp. 155–213; Franklin and Moss pp. 410–411; Lawrence A. Cremin, *American Education: The Metropolitan Experience, 1876–1980* (New York: Harper & Row, 1988), pp. 196–204.
8. Kluger, pp. 214–238, 748–778.
9. Kluger, pp; 215–216, 260–288; Cremin, pp. 198–199; Gates and West, pp. 261–264.
10. Taylor Branch, *Parting the Waters: America in the King Years, 1954–1963* (New York: Simon & Schuster, 1988), pp. 19–21.
11. Kluger, pp. 315–395; Cremin, pp. 199–201.
12. Marshall, in Marable and Mullings, p. 361.
13. Citations are all from Brown v. Board of Education (1954).
14. Kenneth B. Clark, interview in Studs Terkel, *Race: How Blacks and Whites Think and Feel About the American Obsession* (New York: New Press, 1992), p. 334.
15. Robert Moses and Charles E. Cobb Jr., *Radical Equations: Math Literacy and Civil Rights* (Boston: Beacon Press, 2001), p. 20.
16. Martin Luther King Jr., "Where Do We Go From Here?" (1967), in James M. Washington, editor, *I Have a Dream: Writings and Speeches that Changed the World* (San Francisco: Harper San Francisco, 1992), p. 179.
17. Douglas Brinkley, *Rosa Parks* (New York: Penguin Putnam, 2000), p. 107. Not surprisingly there are slightly different accounts of the exact words spoken, but complete agreement on the actions of the afternoon. See also Branch, *Parting the Waters*, pp. 128–129.
18. Branch, *Parting the Waters*, pp. 128–129. For anyone seeking a general overview of the American civil rights movement, especially from the perspective of the events related to Martin Luther King Jr., there is no better starting point than Branch's study, of which two of the projected three volumes are now available. As these notes indicate, Branch has been my primary source in this chapter. Also, Martin Luther King Jr., *Stride Toward Freedom* (1958) reprinted in James Melvin Washington, *A Testament of Hope: The Essential Writings and Speeches of Martin Luther King Jr.* (San Francisco: Harper San Francisco, 1986), pp. 423–424.
19. Eldridge Cleaver, cited in Brinkley, p. 2.
20. Branch, *Parting the Waters*, p. 121, Brinkley, pp. 52–53, 110–113.
21. Branch, *Parting the Waters*, p. 121.
22. Branch, *Parting the Waters*, pp. 129–130; Brinkley, p. 2.

23. Branch, *Parting the Waters*, pp. 121–123, 127, 130–131.
24. Branch, *Parting the Waters*, pp. 124–130.
25. Brinkley, pp. 11–29, see specifically pp. 12, 23, 25, and 28.
26. Brinkley, p. 38.
27. Brinkley, pp.38–43.
28. Brinkley, pp. 54–60.
29. Brinkley, pp. 57–59.
30. Brinkley, pp. 68–71, 86–97.
31. Brinkley, p. 59.
32. King, *Stride Toward Freedom* in Washington, p. 424.
33. Brinkley, p. 110.
34. Branch, *Parting the Waters*, p. 131, Brinkley, p. 114–118.
35. Branch, *Parting the Waters*, pp. 131–132, Brinkley, pp.121–123. See also Jo Ann Robinson's important *The Montgomery Bus Boycott and the Women Who Started It* (Knoxville: University of Tennessee Press, 1989). As Taylor Branch has noted, *Parting the Waters*, p. 132, a minor historical controversy has erupted over whether Robinson or Nixon first thought of the boycott. The reality is that Robinson took the first action and well before dawn both were in complete agreement on the one-day boycott.
36. Branch, *Parting the Waters*, 132–134, and King, *Stride Toward Freedom*, in Washington, pp. 424–425.
37. King, *Stride Toward Freedom*, in Washington, pp. 425–428.
38. King, *Stride Toward Freedom*, in Washington, p. 430.
39. King, *Stride Toward Freedom*, in Washington, p. 431.
40. Branch, *Parting the Waters*, p. 137.
41. King, *Stride Toward Freedom*, in Washington, p. 431–432.
42. King, *Stride Toward Freedom*, in Washington, p. 434.
43. King, *Stride Toward Freedom*, in Washington, p. 435.
44. King, *Stride Toward Freedom*, in Washington, p. 436.
45. King, *Stride Toward Freedom*, in Washington, p. 436.
46. King, *Stride Toward Freedom*, in Washington, p. 438.
47. King, *Stride Toward Freedom*, in Washington, pp. 438–439, 447.
48. King, *Stride Toward Freedom*, in Washington, p. 441.
49. Branch, *Parting the Waters*, pp. 149–158
50. Branch, *Parting the Waters*, pp. 159–160, 164–168, 192–193.
51. Branch, *Parting the Waters*, pp. 189–190.
52. Branch, *Parting the Waters*, p. 149.
53. Branch, *Parting the Waters*, pp.186–188, 190–194; King, *Stride Toward Freedom*, p. 456.
54. Branch, *Parting the Waters*, pp. 195–196.
55. Branch, *Parting the Waters*, pp. 196–204.
56. Anne Moody, *Coming of Age in Mississippi*, p. 135.
57. Moody, pp. 152–153.
58. Branch, *Parting the Waters*, p. 272; the original Woolworth counter from Greensboro is now on permanent display at the Smithsonian Institution in Washington, D.C.
59. See Branch, *Parting the Waters*, pp. 272–275.
60. Branch, *Parting the Waters*, pp. 274–275.
61. Branch, *Parting the Waters*, pp. 278–279.
62. Branch, *Parting the Waters*, pp. 275–276.
63. Martin Luther King Jr., "Love, Law, and Civil Disobedience," address to the annual meeting of the Fellowship of the Concerned of the Southern Regional Council, November 16, 1961, reprinted in Washington, pp. 43–53; see also Washington's introduction to the speech on p. 43.
64. "Love, Law, and Civil Disobedience," in Washington, pp. 50–52.
65. "Love, Law, and Civil Disobedience, in Washington, p. 53.
66. Moody, pp. 265–267.
67. See, for example, Robert P. Moses and Charles E. Cobb Jr., *Radical Equations: Math Literacy and Civil Rights*, pp. 38–39, 50–51; and Mary Stanton, *From Selma to Sorrow: The Life and Death of Viola Liuzzo* (Athens: University of Georgia Press, 1999).

68. Moody, p. 263.
69. Cited in Moses and Cobb, *Radical Equations*, pp. 69–70.
70. Taylor Branch, *Pillar of Fire: America in the King Years, 1963–1965* (New York: Simon & Schuster, 1998), pp. 267, 356–357.
71. See Moses and Cobb, *Radical Equations*, pp. 23–87; Moody, *Coming of Age in Mississippi*, pp. 261–384; Howard Zinn, *SNCC: The New Abolitionists* (Boston, Beacon Press, 1964); Branch, *Pillar of Fire*, 438–488.
72. Moses and Cobb, *Radical Equations*, p. 34.
73. Cited in Moses and Cobb, *Radical Equations*, p. 33.
74. Moses and Cobb, *Radical Equations*; p. 34, Zinn, pp. 33–34.
75. Cited in Zinn, p. 217.
76. Moses, and Cobb *Radical Equations*, p. 38.
77. Moses and Cobb, *Radical Equations*, pp. 41–42.
78. Moses and Cobb, *Radical Equations*, pp. 43–44; Branch, *Parting the Waters*, pp. 417–424.
79. Moses and Cobb. *Radical Equations*, pp. 50–51.
80. Moses and Cobb, *Radical Equations*, pp. 44–51; Moody, pp. 366–367.
81. Moses and Cobb, *Radical Equations*, p. 46.
82. Moses and Cobb *Radical Equations*, pp. 73–77.
83. Moses and Cobb, *Radical Equations*, pp. 78–79.
84. Branch, *Pillar of Fire*, p. 459.
85. Fannie Lou Hamer, "To Praise Our Bridges" from an oral autobiography reprinted in Clayborne Carson, et al., *The Eyes on the Prize Civil Rights Reader*; pp. 176–179; Moses and Cobb, *Radical Equations*, 78–81; Branch, *Pillar of Fire*, pp. 456–476.
86. Moses and Cobb, *Radical Equations*, p. 81.
87. Malcolm X, *The Autobiography of Malcolm X* (New York: Grove Press, 1965), pp. 1–17; Kofi Natambu, *The Life and Work of Malcolm X* (Indianapolis: Alpha Books, 2002), pp. 1–9.
88. *Autobiography of Malcolm X*, pp. 14, 26–28, 37–40.
89. *Autobiography of Malcolm X*, p. 153, see also pages 41–155.
90. *Autobiography of Malcolm X*, pp. 154–165, 173, 195, 205.
91. *Autobiography of Malcolm X*, pp. 276–286, 287, 295–297, 301.
92. *Autobiography of Malcolm X*, p. 345, see the chapter pp. 348.
93. *Autobiography of Malcolm X*, pp. 367–370.
94. Branch, *Pillar of Fire*, pp. 547–548.
95. *Autobiography of Malcolm X*, p. 384.
96. *Autobiography of Malcolm X*, p. 385.
97. Martin Luther King Jr., "Where Do We Go From Here?" (1967) in Washington, pp. 251–252.

EPILOGUE

1. Bernice Johnson Reagon, "Coalition Politics: Turning the Century," a presentation at the West Coast Women's Music Festival 1981, reprinted in Barbara Smith, editor, *Home Girls: A Black Feminist Anthology* (New York: Kitchen Table—Women of Color Press, 1983), p. 362.
2. Paul Chaat Smith and Robert Allen Warrior, *Like a Hurricane: The Indian Movement from Alcatraz to Wounded Knee* (New York: The New Press, 1996), pp. 1–2.
3. Smith and Warrior, p. 4.
4. Smith and Warrior, pp. 18–19.
5. Smith and Warrior, pp. 5, 24.
6. Smith and Warrior, p. 108.
7. Smith and Warrior, pp. 46, 99, 265.
8. Cited in Howard Zinn, *A People's History of the United States, 1492-Present*, Twentieth Anniversary Edition (New York: HarperCollins, 1999), p. 504.
9. Ruth Milkman, *Gender at Work: the Dynamics of Job Segregation by Sex during World War II* (Urbana: University of Illinois Press, 1987), pp. 77–78; and Daniel Horowitz, "Rethinking Betty Friedan and the Feminine Mystique: Labor Union Radicalism and Feminism in Cold War America," in Vicki L. Ruiz and Ellen Carol DuBois, editors, *Unequal Sisters: A Multicultural Reader in U.S. Women's History* (New York: Routledge, 2000), pp. 492–499.

10. Margaret Marsh, foreword, in Margaret Sanger, *Motherhood in Bondage* (1928, reprint, Columbus: Ohio State University Press, 2000), xxxvii-xxxviii; and M. E. Melody and Linda M. Peterson, *Teaching America About Sex* (New York: New York University Press, 2000), pp. 70–71.

11. Horowitz in Ruiz and DuBois, *Unequal Sisters*, p. 492.

12. See Nancy F. Cott, editor, *No Small Courage: A History of Women in the United States* (New York: Oxford University Press, 2000), pp. 464, 467, 525, 533.

13. Taylor Branch, *Parting the Waters: America in the King Years, 1954–1963* (New York: Simon and Schuster, 1988), p. 899.

14. Branch, *Parting the Waters*, pp. 231–233, 247.

15. William H. Chafe, "The Road to Equality, 1962-Today," in Nancy F. Cott, editor, *No Small Courage: A History of Women in the United States* (New York: Oxford University Press, 2000), pp. 545–549.

16. Cited in Horowitz, in Ruiz and DuBois, *Unequal Sisters*, p. 505.

17. Betty Friedan, *The Feminine Mystique* (New York: Norton, 1963); Chafe, p. 547.

18. Horowitz, in Ruiz and DuBois, *Unequal Sisters*, pp. 492–493, 497–499.

19. Cott, pp. 422, 548.

20. Barbara Smith, editor, *All the Women Are White, All the Blacks Are Men But Some of Us Are Brave: Black Women's Studies* (New York: The Feminist Press, 1982).

21. "The Combahee River Collective Statement," issues in 1977 and reprinted in Smith, *Home Girls*, p. 273.

22. "The Combahee River Collective Statement," in Smith, p. 273.

23. Mary King, cited in Cott, p. 548.

24. Cott, pp. 564–565.

25. Citations from both Brownmiller and Chisholm are from Zinn, pp. 510–511.

26. William F. Crandell, "They Moved the Town: Organizing Vietnam Veterans Against the War," in Melvin Small and William D. Hoover, editors, *Give Peace a Chance: Exploring the Vietnam Antiwar Movement* (Syracuse: Syracuse University Press, 1992), pp. 148–149.

27. David McReynolds, "Pacifists and the Vietnam Antiwar Movement," in Small and Hoover, pp. 53–70.

28. Robert Cooney and Helen Michalowski, *The Power of the People: Active Nonviolence in the United States* (Philadelphia: New Society Publishers), p. 139.

29. Cooney and Michalowski, p. 139.

30. Cooney and Michalowski, p. 204.

31. Martin Luther King Jr., "A Time to Break Silence," April 4, 1967, in James M. Washington, editor, *A Testament of Hope: The Essential Writings and Speeches of Martin Luther King Jr.* (San Francisco: Harper San Francisco, 1986), pp. 231–244.

32. King, "A Time to Break Silence," in Washington, pp. 231–244.

33. Crandell, p. 154.

34. See Ronald B. Taylor, *Chavez and the Farm Workers* (Boston: Beacon Press, 1975); and Mark Day, *Forty Acres: Cesar Chavez and the Farm Workers* (New York: Praeger, 1971).

35. Ronald Takaki, *A Different Mirror: A History of Multicultural America* (Boston: Little, Brown & Co., 1993), p. 199.

36. See Takaki, *A Different Mirror*, pp. 258–259, 266–276, and Ronald Takaki, *Strangers from a Different Shore: A History of Asian Americans* (New York: Penguin Books, 1989), p. 222.

37. See J. Craig Jenkins, *The Politics of Insurgency: The Farm Worker Movement in the 1960s* (New York: Columbia University Press, 1985) pp. 131–134. I have drawn primarily on Jenkins superb work in these paragraphs. See also Ronald B. Taylor, *Chavez and the Farm Workers* (Boston: Beacon Press, 1975), p. 127, 137–140.

38. Jenkins, pp. 137–144.

39. Jenkins, pp. 144–150; see also Ronald B. Taylor, pp. 122–129.

40. Jenkins, p. 172; see also Taylor, pp. 245–249.

41. *New York Times*, June 29, 1969 from the Columbia University "Stonewall and Beyond: Lesbian and Gay Culture" exhibition, http://www.columbia.edu/cul/libraries/events/sw25

42. The invisibility and passivity of the gay and lesbian communities prior to Stonewall can also be overstated. As Eric Foner reminds us, "Organized demands for gay rights lay far

in the future, but by the 1920s, with its tearooms, speakeasies, and dances, the gay community had become an important element of the [Greenwich] Village's reputation and lifestyle." *The Story of American Freedom* (New York: W. W. Norton, 1998), p. 167.

43. See Eric Marcus, *Making History: The Struggle for Gay and Lesbian Equal Rights, 1945–1990* (New York: HarperCollins, 1992); Donn Teal, *The Gay Militants* (New York: Stein and Day, 1971); Jill Johnston, *Lesbian Nation: The Feminist Solution* (New York: Simon and Schuster, 1973); J. R. Roberts, *Black Lesbians: An Annotated Bibliography* (Tallahassee: Naiad Press, 1981).

44. Chris Bull, editor, *Witness to Revolution: The Advocate Reports on Gay and Lesbian Politics, 1967–1999* (Los Angeles: Alyson Books, 1999), pp. 74, 77, 112.

45. Bull, pp. 53–62, 110–116, 414–429.

46. Bull, pp. 8–10.

47. Bull, pp. 26, 62–64.

48. Eleanor Johnson, "Reflections on Black Feminist Therapy," originally 1979, published in Smith, *Home Girls*, pp. 320–324.

49. Peter Freiberg, "The March on Washington: Hundreds of Thousands Take the Gay Cause to the Nation's Capital," in Bull, pp. 205–211.

50. Nancy A. Hewitt, "Beyond the Search for Sisterhood: American Women's History in the 1990s," in Ruiz and DuBois, editors, *Unequal Sisters*, p. 1.

51. Tania Abdulahad, Gwendolyn Rogers, Barbara Smith, and Jameelah Waheed, "Black Lesbian/Feminist Organizing: A Conversation," in Smith, *Home Girls*, pp. 295, 300.

52. Reagon in Smith, p. 363.

53. Jesse Jackson, "Address, Democratic National Convention, San Francisco, July 17, 1984, in Clayborne Carson, David J. Garrow, Gerald Gill, Vincent Harding, and Darlene Clark Hine, *The Eyes on the Prize Civil Rights Reader* (New York: Penguin Books, 1991), pp. 705–709.

54. Stephen Greenhouse, "After Seattle, Unions Point to Sustained Fight on Trade," *New York Times*, December 6, 1999, p. A28, in Jeremy Brecher, Tim Costello, Brendan Smith, *Globalization From Below: The Power of Solidarity* (Cambridge: South End Press, 2000), p. x.

55. Elaine Bernard, "The Battle in Seattle: What Was That All About?" *Washington Post*, December 5, 1999, p. B1, in Brecher, Costello, and Smith, p. x.

56. Brecher, Costello, and Smith, p. ix. This book has been very useful to me in the development of this section as have conversations with my research assistant, Gina Sartori.

57. Brecher, Costello, and Smith, pp. 38–42, 63–65.

58. "The Non-Governmental Order," *The Economist*, December 11–17, 1999, in Brecher, Costello, and Smith, p. 82.

59. *American Teacher*, published by the American Federation of Teachers, December 2001/January, 2002 (http://www.aft.org/publications/american_teacher/dec01_jan02).

60. Senator Russell Feingold, "Statement of U.S. Senator Russ Feingold on The Anti-Terrorism Bill," from the Senate Floor, October 25, 2001, web site, Senator Russell Feingold, D. Wisconsin.

61. Maya Angelou, "On the Pulse of Morning," The Inaugural Poem, January 20,1993 (New York: Random House, 1993).

62. W. E. B. DuBois, *Souls of Black Folk* (1903; reprint, New York: Fawcett, 1961), pp. 181–182, 189.

63. I am indebted to Russell W. Irvine of Georgia State University for helping me see the link between DuBois's description of the sorrow songs and the songs of other movements described in this volume.

64. See hymn and note in *The New Century Hymnal* (Cleveland, OH: The Pilgrim Press, 1995), p. 599.

65. Philip S. Foner, *Women and the American Labor Movement: From Colonial times to the Eve of World War I* (New York: Free Press, 1979), pp. 430–431.

66. Sidney Fine, *Sit-Down: The General Motors Strike of 1936–1937* (Ann Arbor: University of Michigan Press, 1969), pp. 156–158.

67. "Long Live the General Strike," in Jenkins, p. 131.

68. *New Century Hymnal*, p. 570.

BIBLIOGRAPHY

FOREWORD

Green, James. *Taking History to Heart: The Power of the Past in Building Social Movements.* Amherst: University of Massachusetts Press, 2000.

Reich, Robert B. *The Work of Nations: Preparing Ourselves for 21st Century Capitalism.* New York: Vintage Books, 1992.

Takaki, Ronald. *A Different Mirror: A History of Multicultural America.* Boston: Little, Brown & Co., 1993.

Thompson, E. P. *The Making of the English Working Class.* New York: Random House, 1963.

PROLOGUE

Folsom, Franklin. *Indian Uprising on the Rio Grande: The Pueblo Revolt of 1680.* Albuquerque: University of New Mexico Press, 2000.

Hackett, Charles Wilson. *Revolt of the Pueblo Indians of New Mexico.* Albuquerque: University of New Mexico Press, 1942.

Silverberg, Robert. *The Pueblo Revolt.* 1970; reprint, Lincoln: University of Nebraska Press, 1994.

CHAPTER 1

Ellis, Joseph J. *American Sphinx: The Character of Thomas Jefferson.* New York: Alfred A Knopf, 1997.

Ellis, Joseph J. *Founding Brothers.* New York: Alfred A. Knopf, 2000.

Foner, Eric. *The Story of American Freedom.* New York: W. W. Norton, 1998.

Foner, Eric. *Tom Paine and Revolutionary America.* New York: Oxford University Press, 1976.

Fraser, James W. *Between Church and State: Religion and Public Education in a Multicultural America.* New York: St. Martin's Press, 1999.

Lee, Gordon C. *Crusade Against Ignorance: Thomas Jefferson on Education.* New York: Teachers College Press, 1961.

McCullough, David. *John Adams.* New York: Simon & Schuster, 2001.

Paine, Thomas. *Common Sense.* New York: Barnes & Noble, 1995.

Shy, John. *A People Numerous and Armed: Reflections on the Military Struggle for American Independence.* New York: Oxford University Press, 1976.

Zinn, Howard. *A People's History of the United States.* New York: HarperCollins, 1999.

CHAPTER 2

Hayden, Dolores. *Seven American Utopias: The Architecture of Communitarian Socialism, 1790–1975.* Cambridge: MIT Press, 1976.

Klaw, Spencer. *Without Sin: The Life and Death of the Oneida Community.* New York: Penguin Press, 1993.

Nordhoff, Charles. *The Communistic Societies of the United States, from personal visit and observation.* New York: Dover Publications, 1966.

Noyes, John Humphrey. *History of American Socialisms.* New York: Dover Publications, 1966.

Owen, Robert. *The Life of Robert Owen by Himself.* New York: A. M. Kelly Publishers, 1967.

Stein, Stephen J. *The Shaker Experience in America.* New Haven: Yale University Press, 1992.
Tyler, Alice Felt. *Freedom's Ferment.* Minneapolis: University of Minnesota Press, 1944.

CHAPTER 3

Blum, Ivan B. *River of Souls.* Sante Fe: Sunstone Press, 2000.
Candelaria, Nash. *Not By the Sword.* Tempe, AZ: Bilingual Press, 1982.
Galbraith, Den. *Turbulent Taos.* Sante Fe: Sunstone Press, 1983.
Gutierrez, Ramon A., and Richard J. Orsi, eds. *Contested Eden: California Before the Gold Rush.* Berkeley: University of California Press, 1998.
Hale, Charles A. *Mexican Liberalism in the Age of Mora, 1821–1853.* New Haven: Yale University Press, 1968.
Rosenbaum, Robert J. *Mexicano Resistance in the Southwest.* Dallas: Southern Methodist University Press, 1998.
Rosenus, Alan. *General Vallejo and the Advent of the Americans.* Berkeley: Heyday Books, 1999.

CHAPTER 4

Barnes, Gilbert H. and Dwight L. Dumond, eds. *Letters of Theodore Dwight Weld, Angelina Grimké Weld and Sarah Grimké: 1822–1844.* 2 vols. Gloucester, MA: Peter Smith, 1965.
Bradford, Sarah. *Harriet Tubman: The Moses of Her People.* 1886; reprint, New York: Corinth, 1961.
Douglass, Frederick. *Narrative of the Life of Frederick Douglass: An American Slave.* 1845; reprint, Cambridge: Harvard University Press, 1967.
Franklin, John Hope, and Loren Schweninger. *Runaway Slaves: Rebels on the Plantation.* New York: Oxford University Press, 1999.
Fraser, James W. *Pedagogue For God's Kingdom: Lyman Beecher and the Second Great Awakening.* Lanham, MD: University Press of America, 1985.
Fraser, James W. *Schooling the Preachers: The Development of Protestant Theological Education in the United States 1740–1875.* Lanham, MD: University Press of America, 1988.
Lesick, Lawrence Thomas. *The Lane Rebels: Evangelism and Antislavery in Antebellum America.* Metuchen, NJ: Scarecrow Press, 1980.
Mayer, Henry. *All on Fire: William Lloyd Garrison and the Abolition of Slavery.* New York: St. Martin's Press, 1998.
Robertson, David. *Denmark Veysey: The Buried Stories of American's Largest Slave Revolt and the Man Who Led It.* New York: Alfred A. Knopf, 1999
Stanton, Elizabeth Cady. *Eighty Years and More: Reminiscences 1815–1897.* T. Fisher Unwin, 1898; reprint, Boston: Northeastern University Press, 1993.

CHAPTER 5

Anderson, James D. *The Education of Blacks in the South, 1860–1935.* Chapel Hill: University of North Carolina Press, 1988.
DuBois, W. E. B. *The Souls of Black Folk.* 1903; reprint, New York: Fawcett, 1961.
Foner, Eric. *Reconstruction: America's Unfinished Revolution, 1863–1877.* New York: Harper & Row, 1988.
Perry, Mark. *Lift Up Thy Voice: The Grimké Family's Journey from Slaveholders to Civil Rights Leaders.* New York: Viking, 2001.
Smith, John David. *Black Voices from Reconstruction, 1865–1877.* Gainesville: University of Florida Press, 1997.
Stevenson, Brenda, ed. *The Journals of Charlotte Forten Grimké.* New York: Oxford University Press, 1988.

CHAPTER 6

Chesler, Ellen. *Woman of Valor: Margaret Sanger and the Birth Control Movement in America.* New York: Anchor Books, 1992.

Cott, Nancy F. ed. *No Small Courage: A History of Women in the United States.* New York: Oxford University Press, 2000.

Goldman, Emma. *Living My Life.* 2 vols. New York: Alfred A. Knopf, 1931.

Goldman, Emma. *Anarchism, and Other Essays.* 1917; reprint, New York: Dover, 1969.

Harper, Ida Husted. *Life and Work of Susan B. Anthony.* 3 vols. Salem, NH: Ayer, 1983.

Lerner, Gerda. *The Grimké Sisters from South Carolina: Rebels Against Slavery and for Woman's Rights.* Boston: Houghton Mifflin, 1967.

Sherr, Lynn, ed. *Failure Is Impossible: Susan B. Anthony in Her Own Words.* New York: Times Books, 1995.

Stanton, Elizabeth Cady, Susan B. Anthony, and Matilda Joslyn Gage, eds. *A History of Woman's Suffrage.* 6 vols. Rochester, NY: 1881.

Stanton, Elizabeth Cady. *Eighty Years and More: Reminiscences 1815–1897.* 1898; republished Boston: Northeastern University Press, 1993.

CHAPTER 7

Boyer, Richard O., and Herbert M. Morais. *Labor's Untold Story.* New York: United Electrical, Radio & Machine Workers of America, 1955, 1970.

Buhle, Paul, Mary Jo Buhle, and Dan Georgakas, eds. *Encyclopedia of the American Left.* New York: Oxford University Press, 1990, 1998.

Flynn, Elizabeth Gurley. *The Rebel Girl: An Autobiography, My First Life, 1906–1926.* New York: International Publishers, 1955, 1994.

Foner, Philip S., ed. *Mother Jones Speaks: Collected Speeches and Writings.* New York: Monad Press, 1983.

Foner, Philip S. *The Factory Girls.* Urbana: University of Illinois Press, 1977.

Foner, Philip S. *Women and the American Labor Movement: From Colonial Times to the Eve of World War I.* New York: Free Press, 1979.

Gorn, Elliot J. *Mother Jones: The Most Dangerous Woman in America.* New York: Hill & Wang, 2001.

Gutman, Herbert G. *Work, Culture and Society in Industrializing America.* New York: Alfred A. Knopf, 1976.

Haywood, William D. *Big Bill Haywood's Book.* New York: International Publishers, 1929.

Howe, Irving. *World of Our Fathers.* New York: Harcourt Brace Jovanovich, 1976.

Howe, Irving, and Kenneth Libo. *How We Lived: A Documentary History of Immigrant Jews in America, 1880–1930.* New York: Richard Marek, 1979.

Jones, Mother. *The Autobiography of Mother Jones.* Chicago: C. H. Kerr for Illinois Labor History Society, 1976.

Nelson, Bruce C. *Beyond the Martyrs: A Social History of Chicago's Anarchists, 1870–1900.* New Brunswick: Rutgers University Press, 1988.

Pelz, William A., ed. *The Eugene V. Debs Reader: Socialism and the Class Struggle.* Chicago: Institute of Working Class History, 2000.

Renshaw, Patrick. *The Wobblies: The Story of the IWW and Syndicalism in the United States.* Chicago: Ivan R. Dee, 1999.

Salvatore, Nick. *Eugene V. Debs: Citizen and Socialist.* Urbana: University of Illinois Press, 1984.

Schlesinger, Arthur M. *Writings and Speeches of Eugene V. Debs.* New York: Hermitage Press, 1948.

CHAPTER 8

Addams, Jane. *The Spirit of Youth and the City Streets.* Champaign: University of Illinois Press, 1972.

Addams, Jane. *Twenty Years At Hull House.* New York: Macmillan, 1910; reprint, Signet Classics, 1961.

Cooney, Robert, Marty Jezer, and Helen Michalowski, eds. *The Power of the People: Active Nonviolence in the United States.* Philadelphia: New Society Publishers, 1987.

Counts, George S. *Dare the School Build a New Social Order?* Carbondale: Southern Illinois University Press, 1932, 1978.

Cremin, Lawrence A. *The Transformation of the School: Progressivism in American Education, 1876–1957.* New York: Random House, 1988.

Davis, Allen F. *Spearheads for Reform: The Social Settlements and the Progressive Movement, 1890–1914.* New York: Oxford University Press, 1967.

Dewey, John. *The School and Society.* Chicago: University of Chicago Press, 1899.

Haley, Margaret A. "Why Teachers Should Organize," *National Education Association, Addresses and Proceedings.* St. Louis: 1904.

Howe, Irving. *How We Lived: A Documentary History of Immigrant Jews In America, 1880–1930.* New York: Richard Marek Publishers, 1979.

Menand, Louis. *The Metaphysical Club: The Stories of Ideas in America.* New York: Farrar, Straus and Giroux, 2001.

Riss, Jacob. *How the Other Half Lives: Studies Among the Tenements of New York.* Cambridge: Belknap Press of Harvard University Press, 1970.

Ryan, John A., and Joseph Husslein, eds. *The Church and Labor.* New York: Macmillan Company, 1920.

Salvatore, Nick. *Eugene V. Debs: Citizen and Socialist.* Urbana: University of Chicago Press, 1984.

Tyack, David. *The One Best System: A History of American Urban Education.* Cambridge: Harvard University Press, 1974.

Woloch, Nancy. *Women and the American Experience.* New York: McGraw-Hill, 2000.

CHAPTER 9

Bernstein, Irving. *A Caring Society: The New Deal, the Worker, and the Great Depression.* Boston: Houghton Mifflin, 1985.

Boyer, Richard O., and Herbert M. Morais. *Labors Untold Story.* New York: United Electrical, Radio & Machine Workers of America, 1970.

Cronon, E. David. *Black Moses: The Story of Marcus Garvey.* Madison: University of Wisconsin Press, 1955, 1969.

Fine, Sidney. *Sit-Down: the General Motors Strike of 1936–1937.* Ann Arbor: University of Michigan Press, 1969.

Foner, Eric. *The Story of American Freedom.* New York: W. W. Norton, 1998.

Frankfurter, Marion Denman and Gardner Jackson, eds. *The Letters of Sacco and Vanzetti.* New York: Penguin, 1997.

Garvey, Amy Jacques, ed. *The Philosophy and Opinions of Marcus Garvey.* Dover, MA: Majority Press, 1986.

Gates Jr., Henry Louis and Cornel West. *The African American Century: How Black Americans Have Shaped Our Country.* New York: Free Press, 2000.

Takaki, Ronald. *Strangers from a Different Shore: A History of Asian Americans.* New York: Penguin Books, 1989.

CHAPTER 10

Branch, Taylor. *Parting the Waters: America in the King Years, 1954–1963.* New York: Simon & Schuster, 1988.

Brinkely, Douglas. *Rosa Parks.* New York: Penguin Putnam, 2000.

Brown, Cynthia Stokes. *Ready from Within: Septima Clark and the Civil Rights Movement.* Trenton, NJ: Africa World Press, 1990.

Carson, Clayborne, David J. Garrow, Gerald Gill, Vincent Harding, and Darelen Clark Hine. *The Eyes on the Prize Civil Rights Reader.* New York: Penguin Books, 1991.

Franklin, John Hope, and Alfred A. Moss Jr. *From Slavery to Freedom: A History of African Americans.* 7th ed. New York: Alfred A. Knopf, 1994.

Gates Jr., Henry Louis, and Cornel West. *The African American Century.* New York: Free Press, 2000.

Kluger, Richard. *Simple Justice: A History of Brown v. Board of Education and Black America's Struggle for Equality.* New York: Alfred A. Knopf, 1975.

Marable, Manning, and Leith Mullings, eds. *Let Nobody Turn Us Around: Voices of Resistance,*

Reform, and Renewal. Lanham, MD: Rowman & Littlefield, 2000)

Moody, Anne. *Coming of Age in Mississippi.* New York: Laurel, 1968.

Moses, Robert, and Charles E. Cobb Jr. *Radical Equations: Math Literacy and Civil Rights.* Boston: Beacon press, 2001.

Natambu, Kofi. *The Life and Work of Malcolm X.* Indianapolis: Alpha Books, 2002.

Robinson, Jo Ann. *The Montgomery Bus Boycott and the Women Who Started It.* Knoxville: University of Tennessee Press, 1989.

Stanton, Mary. *From Selma to Sorrow: The Life and Death of Viola Liuzzo.* Athens: University of Georgia Press, 1999.

Terkel, Studs. *How Blacks and Whites Think and Feel About the American Obsession.* New York: New Press, 1992.

Washington, James. *A Testament of Hope: The Essential Writings and Speeches of Martin Luther King Jr.* San Francisco: Harper San Francisco, 1986.

Williams, Juan. *Thurgood Marshall: American Revolutionary.* New York: Random House, 1998.

X, Malcolm. *The Autobiography of Malcolm X.* New York: Grove Press, 1965.

EPILOGUE

Brecher, Jeremy, Tim Costello, and Brendan Smith. *Globalization From Below: The Power of Solidarity.* Cambridge, MA: South End Press, 2000.

Bull, Chris, ed. *Witness to Revolution: The Advocate Reports on Gay and Lesbian Politics, 1945–1990.* Los Angeles: Alyson Books, 1999.

Cooney, Robert, and Helen Michalowski. *The Power of the People: Active Nonviolence in the United States.* Philadelphia: New Society Publishers, 1995.

Day, Mark. *Forty Acres: Cesar Chavez and the Farm Workers.* New York: Praeger, 1971.

DuBois, Ellen Carol, and Vicki L. Ruiz, eds. *Unequal Sisters: A Multicultural Reader in U.S. Women's History.* New York: Routledge, 2000.

Jenkins, J. Craig. *The Politics of Insurgency: The Farm Workers Movement in the 1960's.* New York: Columbia University Press, 1985.

Marcus, Eric. *Making History: The Struggle for Gay and Lesbian Equal Rights, 1945–1990.* New York: HarperCollins, 1992.

Roberts, J. R. *Black Lesbians: An Annotated Bibliography.* Tallahassee: Naiad Press, 1981.

Small, Melvin, and William D. Hoover, eds. *Give Peace a Chance: Exploring the Vietnam Antiwar Movement.* Syracuse: Syracuse University Press, 1992.

Smith, Barbara, ed. *All the Women Are White, All the Blacks Are Men But Some of Us Are Brave: Black Women's Studies.* New York: The Feminist Press, 1982.

Smith, Barbara, ed. *Home Girls: A Black Feminist Anthology.* New York: Kitchen Table—Women of Color Press, 1983.

Taylor, Ronald B. *Chavez and the Farm Workers.* Boston: Beacon Press, 1975.

Teal, Donn. *The Gay Militants.* New York: Stein and Day, 1973.

Smith, Paul Chaat, and Robert Allen Warrior. *Like a Hurricane: The Indian Movement from Alcatraz to Wounded Knee.* New York: New Press, 1996.

INDEX

ABOUT THE AUTHOR

James W. Fraser is Professor of History and Education and Dean of the School of Education at Northeastern University, Boston, Massachusetts. Prior to his appointment as founding Dean of the School of Education in 1999, Fraser was the Director of the Center for Innovation in Urban Education at Northeastern from 1993–1999. At Northeastern, Fraser also regularly teaches a graduate seminar in the History of American Education.

Before coming to Northeastern University, Fraser was Professor of Education and Dean of the Division of Educational Studies and Public Policy at Lesley College, Cambridge, MA. In 1987–1988 he served as Special Assistant to the Massachusetts Chancellor of Higher Education. His previous teaching includes the University of Massachusetts at Boston, Boston University, and Public School 76 Manhattan where he taught fourth grade.

Fraser has been active in education efforts in Boston for the past two decades. He is one of Mayor Thomas Menino's representatives on the Boston School Committee Nominating Panel. He is also a member of the Board of Directors of the Mission Hill School, and a Board Observer for the Boston Plan for Excellence—Boston's Public Education Foundation. He has been co-chair of the Boston School Committee's Task Force on Student Assignment, a member of the Board of Directors of the CityWide Educational Coalition, the Freedom House, and the Mayor's Blue Ribbon Commission for Community Learning Centers.

In addition to his efforts in education, Fraser is an ordained minister in the United Church of Christ and pastor of Grace Church in East Boston, a United Church of Christ and Episcopal federated congregation. He has been the pastor of this small church since 1986 and remains active in the East Boston neighborhood. He and his wife, Katherine Hanson, also live in East Boston. They have four daughters and two granddaughters. Since 1997, Fraser has also been a Visiting Lecturer in Education at the Divinity School at Harvard University.

Professor Fraser holds a Ph.D. degree from Columbia University (1975) and an M.Div. from Union Theological Seminary, New York (1970).

Fraser has published numerous books and articles in the history of education and related educational policy issues. His most recent publications include *The School in the United States: A Documentary History* (Boston: McGraw-Hill, 2000); *Between Church and State: Religion and Public Education in a Multicultural America* (New York: St. Martin's Press, 1999); *Reading, Writing, and Justice: School Reform As If Democracy Matters* (Albany, NY: State University of New York Press, 1997); *Mentoring the Mentor: A Critical Dialogue with Paulo Freire*, co-edited with Paulo Freire, Donaldo Macedo, Tanya McKinnon, and William T. Stokes (New York: Peter Lang, 1997), *Freedom's Plow: Teaching in the Multicultural Classroom*, co-edited with Theresa Perry (New York: Routledge, 1993). He has also written numerous articles and reviews for *Education Week*, *The Journal of American History*, *Teachers College Record*, and other publications.